W9-CEB-321

THE DHARMA OF JESUS

Montante Family Library
D'Youville College

THE DHARMA OF JESUS

GEORGE M. SOARES-PRABHU

Francis X. D'Sa, editor

ORBIS BOOKS

Maryknoll, New York 10545

Founded in 1970, Orbis Books endeavors to publish works that enlighten the mind, nourish the spirit, and challenge the conscience. The publishing arm of the Maryknoll Fathers & Brothers, Orbis seeks to explore the global dimensions of the Christian faith and mission, to invite dialogue with diverse cultures and religious traditions, and to serve the cause of reconciliation and peace. The books published reflect the views of their authors and do not represent the official position of the Maryknoll Society. To learn more about Maryknoll and Orbis Books, please visit our website at www.maryknoll.org.

Compilation and introduction copyright © 2003 by Francis X. D'Sa
Essays of George M. Soares-Prabhu copyright © 2001 by Jnana-Deepa Vidyapeeth, Pune, India

Published by Orbis Books, Maryknoll, New York 10545-0308.

All rights reserved.

No part of this publication may be reproduced or transmitted in any form or by any means, electronic or mechanical, including photocopying, recording or any information storage or retrieval system, without prior permission in writing from the publisher.

Queries regarding rights and permissions should be addressed to:
Orbis Books, P.O. Box 308, Maryknoll, NY 10545-0308.

Manufactured in the United States of America.

Library of Congress Cataloging-in-Publication Data

Soares-Prabhu, George.
    The dharma of Jesus / George M. Soares-Prabhu ; Francis X. D'Sa, editor.
      p. cm.
    Some chapters are reprinted from various books.
    ISBN 1-57075-459-4 (pbk.)
    1. Jesus Christ—Person and offices. 2. Jesus Christ—Teachings. I. D'Sa, Francis X. II. Title.
BT203 .S63 2003
232—dc21

2002014823

BT 203
.S 63
2003

CONTENTS

NOV 1 7 2003

Part IV
The Mission of Jesus

ACKNOWLEDGMENTS

We acknowledge with gratitude permission from the original publishers to reproduce the following articles in this volume.

Jeevadhara: Journal of Christian Interpretation, Alleppey, India.
1. "Jesus the Prophet," *Jeevadhara* 4 (1974): 206-17. (chapter 3)
2. "The Synoptic Love-Commandment: The Dimensions of Love in the Teaching of Jesus," *Jeevadhara* 13 (1983): 85-103. (chapter 13)
3. "Radical Beginnings: The Jesus Community as the Archetype of the Church," *Jeevadhara* 15 (1985): 307-25. (chapter 6)
4. "The Table Fellowship of Jesus: Its Significance for *Dalit* Christians in India Today," *Jeevadhara* 22 (1992): 140-59. (chapter 7)
5. "The Church as Mission. A Reflection on Mt 5:13-16," *Jeevadhara* 24 (1994): 280-92. (chapter 18)

St Pauls, Mumbai, India.
1. "Following Jesus in Mission: Reflections on Mission in the Gospel of Matthew," in *Bible and Mission in India Today*, ed. J. Kavunkal and F. Hrangkhuma, 64-92 (Bombay: St Pauls, 1993). (chapter 19)
2. "Expanding the Horizon of Christian Mission: A Biblical Perspective," in *Paths of Mission in India Today,* ed. A. Kanjamala, 33-48 (Bombay: St Pauls, 1997). (chapter 17)

Bible Bhashyam, Kottayam, India
1. "The Miracles of Jesus Today," *Bible Bhashyam* 5 (1975): 189-204. (chapter 8)
2. "Jesus and the Spirit in the Synoptic Gospels," *Bible Bhashyam* 2 (1976): 101-24. (chapter 1)
3. "'Good News to the Poor': The Social Implications of the Message of Jesus," *Bible Bhashyam* 4 (1978): 193-212. (chapter 16)
4. "'And There Was a Great Calm': A 'Dhvani' Reading of the Stilling of the Storm (Mk 4:35-41)," *Bible Bhashyam* 5 (1979): 295-308. (chapter 9)
5. "The Dharma of Jesus: An Interpretation of the Sermon on the Mount," *Bible Bhashyam* 6 (1980): 358-81. (chapter 12)

Concilium, Nijmegen, The Netherlands
1. "Speaking to Abba: Prayer as Petition and Thanksgiving in the Teaching of Jesus," *Concilium* 229 (1990): 31-43. (chapter 14)

2. "'As We Forgive': Inter-human Forgiveness in the Teaching of Jesus," *Concilium* 184 (1986): 57-66. (chapter 15)

Xavier Board of Education, Bangalore, India
1. "Jesus the Teacher: The Liberative Pedagogy of Jesus of Nazareth," in *Christian Perspectives in Education: The Mission of the Catholic College in India Today,* ed. H. Morissette, 85-101 (Bangalore: Xavier Board, 1985). (chapter 2)

The Way, London, U.K.
1. "Jesus and Conflict," *The Way* 26 (1986): 14-23. (chapter 11)
2. "The Unprejudiced Jesus and the Prejudiced Church," *The Way* 27 (1987): 4-14. (chapter 10)

Orbis Books, Maryknoll, New York
1. "The Jesus of Faith: A Christological Contribution to an Ecumenical Third World Spirituality," in *Spirituality of the Third World,* 139-64 (Maryknoll, N.Y.: Orbis Books, 1994). (chapter 5)

I am grateful to Cynthia Pinto from my staff who helped me in the preparation of the computer copy, to Claude Farias for assistance in computer matters, and most especially to my editor, Susan Perry, to work with whom has been an enriching experience, both personally and professionally.

GEORGE M. SOARES-PRABHU

A Theologian for Our Times

Francis X. D'Sa

In an age when globalization is proclaimed with religious-like fervor, it is probably a risky proposition to introduce a contemporary Indian theologian whose vision is critical of globalization because of its negative impact on developing countries. The purpose in stating this, however, is to highlight the fact that George Soares-Prabhu was one of those rare theologians who was aware of the global ramifications of economics and politics on theology. So it is not surprising that he was also acutely conscious of the economic and political power that often drives religious and theological enterprises.[1]

The theological approach of George Soares-Prabhu was always holistic. He maintained that it is as important to know *who* is teaching theology as it is to understand what kind of theology is being taught. He was convinced that the *Sitz im Leben* of a school of theology is as significant as the *Sitz im Leben* of the Gospel passage that it interprets. An authentic theology must identify the concerns that were operative in the emergence of a text (and not necessarily only the thematic or the religious concerns) and make them interact with the concerns of the reader. The world of the text and the world of the reader have to interact for a relevant reading to emerge. This is the general direction of the theological thought process of Soares-Prabhu.

George M. Soares-Prabhu was born in Igatpuri in 1929. He was greatly influenced by the British on his father's side (his father was the first Indian medical

I am grateful to my colleagues Kurien Kunnumpuram, S.J., and Anthony da Silva, S.J., for their incisive critique and helpful comments.

officer of the Indian Railways of the British Raj; one of his uncles was a well-known professor of English literature in Gujarat; another uncle was the principal of a renowned school in Goa) and by the Portuguese on his mother's side (but symptomatically this aspect was less thematized than the other). He went to school in Jabalpur and took a degree in science (B.Sc.) with the Jesuits at St. Xavier's College in Mumbai (formerly known as Bombay) before joining the Society of Jesus. Though he did not pursue further studies in science after becoming a member of the Jesuits, the influence of science on him was far-reaching, notwithstanding his lifelong love of English literature and poetry. A scientific bent of mind remained a constant feature of George's teaching, research, and writing.

In India promising Jesuit students are chosen in advance for specialized studies to prepare them for future assignments in the different faculties. Interestingly, albeit very accidentally, George's first assignment as a Jesuit was to lecture on "philosophical questions in science" in the Faculty of Philosophy at the Pontificium Athenaeum in Pune. The success of this course was immediate, and there was a groundswell of opinion that George should specialize in philosophy. But, as things turned out, George was sent for higher studies in theology. After postgraduate studies in Scripture (Pontifical Biblical Institute, Rome) and doctoral studies under Xavier Léon Dufour (Fourvière-Lyon, France),[2] he began his teaching career at Jnana-Deepa Vidyapeeth (Pontificium Athenaeum) in Pune in 1969. His goal was to work out a biblical theology that could respond to contemporary issues and challenges in India (and Asia).

By any standard George was a brilliant teacher—clear and convincing in his teaching, scientific and social in his approach, and above all, thorough and thought-provoking in content. The varied audiences that he addressed were won over instantly. He was an equally creative author with a natural flair for writing. Though known to express extreme views in discussions, when it came to writing he was meticulous in his research, cautious in his judgment, and precise in his formulations. Although he was open to different methods of interpretation, he was one of the few scholars who went to great lengths to take the text seriously and, at the same time, had enough hermeneutical sense not to fall prey to biblicism. Although his concerns were contextual, his vision was universal.

At the time George was writing, inclusive language had not yet arrived in India. His texts, written in the 1970s through the early 1990s, did not use inclusive language and may at times seem somewhat jarring to the contemporary reader. In the same way in which he was open to different methods of interpretation and aware of the importance of historical contexts, if George were writing today he would surely have recognized the importance of using language that was not exclusionary.

He was a confident scholar. He knew where he stood and could situate fairly accurately his own views vis-à-vis those of other scholars. He was always appreciative of the contributions of his colleagues to exegesis, although at times he was critical of their presuppositions.[3] In general, however, he was a stickler for method and was no friend of *laissez-faire* in exegesis. There were no two ways about it: one had to treat a text with respect if one expected the text to reveal itself to the reader.

Accordingly, George's work invariably emphasized exegesis of the biblical text. He was familiar with the latest research and critiqued it from his perspective. His own position was rarely extreme or one-sided, and he was always open to new methods of investigating a text.[4] He never failed to acknowledge his sources and to appreciate their insights, but he was unfailingly critical of hegemonic tendencies—whether in exegesis or in economics.

George believed that interpretation without a sound exegetical foundation was building on sand. Structurally, his writings begin with a discussion of the problematic, then engage in a thorough exegesis of the text *and* its historical context, and, finally—what is rare in the field of biblical exegesis[5]—proceed to work out its significance in the light of today's challenges.[6] Though highly critical of the historical-critical method and its pretensions,[7] he employed it sedulously when it came to a study of the text.

SPELLING OUT THE DHARMA OF JESUS

George was equally brilliant in his interpretation of the significance of the text. Here his originality came into its own. George was not just a first-rate exegete; he was a first-rate theologian and an original thinker. His search was for the Dharma of Jesus.[8] Dharma, like Karma, is a protean word in the greater part of the Asian world. In the Indian subcontinent it stands for the complex of relationships that one thing has with every other thing. The basic meaning of Dharma circles around "holding," "holding together," "bearing," and "supporting." These meanings include both cosmic and transcendental dimensions. Thus, Dharma holds a society together not merely physically but also on the level of "meaning," which makes possible a sense of identity.[9] Dharma, then, can be summarized as the principle of being and acting.[10] As the former it is related to every being in a specific manner, and as the latter it enjoins a specific kind of behavior towards every being.[11]

George's originality consisted in working out the Dharma of Jesus for today in an India that is pluralistic and poverty-stricken.[12] He had no quarrel with those who paraphrased the so-called doctrines of the Western Christian tradition, affixed the appropriate quotations from Scripture and tradition, and called it theology;[13] however, he did not see its bearing on the concerns of the developing countries. In a multireligious and multicultural Asia, it was imperative, he felt, that Jesus' Dharma be presented so that any person of good will would be able to understand and appropriate it.[14] The so-called traditional dogmatic approach did not appeal to him for the simple reason that it was ahistorical. It presented a Jesus who was of no significance, for example, to the chemical-gas victims of Bhopal or the Dalits (the *anawim* or outcastes) of India.[15]

While Western exegetes and theologians often distinguish between the Jesus of history and the Christ of faith, George did not go along with this distinction because he rejected the dichotomy between history and faith.[16] Faith without history is empty, and history without faith is blind. The Jesus that he uncovered through the tools of historical-critical exegesis was seen, gradually, through the eyes of faith as the "Jesus of faith." As one at home in the religiously pluralistic culture of India he preferred to speak of the Dharma of Jesus.[17] As such, the Dharma of Jesus refers to the comprehensive relationship between "God, World, and Man."[18] Such a Dharma, George believed, had much to offer the beleaguered and impoverished majority of Asia's inhabitants. The recurring theme of his writings was to respond "effectively to the Third World's cry for life."[19]

When George began lecturing in Pune, scriptural studies (too grandiloquent a phrase for what was done at the time!) followed the directions of dogmatic theology. It was he who introduced biblical courses that were critical but which at the same time deepened one's sense of faith. The result was an increasingly richer and more inspiring understanding of the Jesus movement. He familiarized the students with different methods of exegesis, using illustrations that brought out in bold relief the person and Dharma of a Jesus who faced challenges, took the side of the weak, healed the sick, and confronted those who lorded it over others.

George was a fearless but at the same time prudent man whose heart had been completely won over by the Divine Mystery he called "Abba!"—a heart that went out to the poor and oppressed. His study of the Synoptic Gospels convinced him that the "*Abba* experience" was central to Jesus' life—an experience that expressed itself in an almost exclusive commitment to the liberation of those who suffered one or another kind of discrimination. This theme became the leitmotif that runs through almost all his writings.

EISEGESIS OR EXEGESIS?

George's unique way of interpreting Scripture, especially his Dharma of Jesus, might occasion for us traditionalist Indians questions such as, Is a reading like this legitimate? Can we read Scripture as we like? Isn't Soares-Prabhu doing his own thing? Is he not guilty of reading into the text (*eisegesis*), instead of reading out of the text (*exegesis*)? Isn't his theological method an arbitrary, subjectivistic enterprise? Yet, far from being arbitrary, his writings are constructed on the basis of a scientific approach to the text *and* its varied commentators. In fact, George was a severe critic of theological work that was not based on sound exegesis.

The point of departure of his contextual theology was a biblical theology which he then interpreted—often very creatively—in the Indian context. His interpretation did not lean on dogmatic theology. Although throughout his exegetical work he operated as a believer, he was careful to follow the accepted canons of exegesis; however, sometimes he challenged even them, but from a scientific rather than a faith perspective.[20] He allowed his faith perspective to become operative in the last section of his work. What has a follower of Jesus to believe and do *today* in order to remain a faithful disciple?

THE IMPORTANCE OF THE FAITH PERSPECTIVE

George's primary concern was not with "doctrinal preoccupations" but with a faith that does good work and a truth that liberates! This does not imply that he was not concerned about doctrine: a cursory glance at his seminal article entitled "The Jesus of Faith"[21] should convince a reader of the opposite. He was not overly preoccupied with traditional doctrines, because the depth of his hermeneutical awareness had led him to the conviction that doctrines were answers to questions and problems of a particular age and culture that can be relevant neither universally nor for all times. Second, he was convinced that believers generally tend to understand beliefs and doctrines as synonyms while, indeed, they are two different things. Beliefs are immediate expressions of faith, and doctrines are intellectual paraphrases of beliefs that are specific to the culture wherein they are articulated. That is the reason why beliefs, as they come alive, mediate faith experiences. This is not true of doctrines.

It is precisely this last consideration that inspired George to struggle to make the belief world of the Bible come alive. All his exegetical efforts were directed toward this goal. His work aimed not at more detailed information of the biblical world but at a deeper experience of that mysterious person who spoke with authority proclaiming a new faith vision of "God, World, and Man."[22] The way the believing community has spoken of this mystery and Jesus' faith vision at different periods of history has depended on its interaction with a specific culture.

In earlier times the scholastic distinction of form and matter was often used to express this continuity, but today this creates more problems than answers. In our context the metaphor of two eyes might be more suitable. The two eyes, when synchronized, make depth of vision possible. The one eye sees the world of "real" but problematic relations (social, economic, political, religious, cultural, and so on) and the second eye sees the world of "ideal" but healthy and healing relationships. The contrast, to put it starkly, between the sick world and the healthy world—between the world of perception and the world of faith—makes us see how and in which direction our everyday relationships must move in order to be healed or, in George's language, liberated. The depth of vision of wholeness emerges from the synchronization of the two eyes; for it alone is the source of all healing.

THE JESUS OF SOARES-PRABHU

Understandably then, George's primary concern was to ensure that we truly encounter the world of God's Kingdom that Jesus proclaimed. His sensitive exegesis was a preparation for an encounter with the world of the Kingdom. George's Jesus was not the metaphysical Jesus of the ecumenical councils.[23] He found nothing wrong with such attempts, except that our cultures today are far removed from those of the first councils.[24] In the context of our questions the council formulations (built on the pillars of *ousia, physis, hypostasis, prosōpon, homoousios*) do not evoke any meaningful response. This is not surprising, since the conciliar attempts represent "a narrow, culturally conditioned, and even politically motivated development which exploits only a very small fraction of the christological potential that the New Testament offers."[25]

The intention of George's enterprise was precisely this: to present a Jesus to India (and Asia) who responds to the challenges of our cultures,[26] a prophetic and provocative Jesus[27] who helps in discerning the signs of the times and whose life and lifestyle make claims on our life and lifestyle;[28] a Jesus who taught in metaphors and parables,[29] not to win the favor of the crowds but to make the *anawim* aware that the Kingdom of God is theirs;[30] a Jesus whose table fellowship with sinners and tax collectors questioned the social[31] and religious divisions prevalent at the time;[32] a Jesus who, born of the Spirit,[33] worked miracles such as stilling the storm[34] not in the manner of a wonder-worker but as one witnessing to the presence and power of God's Kingdom;[35] a Jesus who, living with conflict,[36] preached love,[37] remained free of prejudice,[38] stressed forgiveness[39] and still survived because of his experience of and trust in his "Abba."[40]

George's Jesus, the "Jesus of Faith,"[41] commissioned the apostles to make disciples in the whole world but this meant "far more than merely obeying a command to go out and recruit members for the Christian community."[42] Following Jesus in mission "can never be a 'crusade,' an act of violence against religions and cultures (options which Jesus explicitly refused), but always an act of loving service, carried out as Matthew has told us, in poverty and powerlessness, in dependence on God, in persecution and conflict."[43] The true disciples of Jesus are like the salt of the earth and the light of the world;[44] for them mission consists in making God's love present in whatever way they can,[45] "for all true Christian mission is ultimately the continuation of the mission of Jesus, who did not come primarily to build a Church or even found a religion, but to bring total liberation to humankind."[46]

Sadly, hardly had George become professor emeritus in mid-November 1994 when he met with a fatal accident. On the afternoon of July 22, 1995, on his way to a meeting of a social development agency of which he was a founding member and which supported projects that worked in villages with the poor,[47] a truck ran him down in front of the National Gandhi Memorial in Pune as he was crossing the road on a bicycle. Mercifully, he died instantly. "It is symptomatic," says colleague K. J. Scaria, "that G. M. Soares-Prabhu's death did not occur within the confines of a religious institution/house comforted by relatives and friends nor in a well-known hospital attended by competent doctors and committed nurses but on a dusty road where so many poor and oppressed breathe their last."[48] George's sudden and tragic death left us all stunned. We had hoped, along with him, that as professor emeritus he would have more time and leisure to develop thematically fresh topics related to Indian Christian theology.

George's way of interpreting the Scriptures inevitably made the Emmaus narrative come alive. And when he, all of a sudden, disappeared from our midst, after our first days of shock and silence, we his colleagues and students began spontaneously echoing the words of the two disciples, "Weren't our hearts burning within us as he explained the Scriptures?"

NOTES

1. Soares-Prabhu, "Towards an Indian Interpretation of the Bible," *Bible Bhashyam* 6 (1980): 151-81; idem, *Biblical Themes for a Contextual Theology for Today,* Collected Writings of George M. Soares-Prabhu, vol. 1, ed. Isaac Padinjarekuttu (Pune: Jnana-Deepa Vidyapeeth, 1999), 212ff.

2. George submitted his doctoral thesis in May 1969 but revised most of it thoroughly before it was published as *The Formula Quotations in the Infancy Narrative of Matthew: An Enquiry into the Tradition History of Mt 1-2*, Analecta Biblica: Investigationes Scientificae in Res Biblicas 63 (Rome: Biblical Institute Press, 1976).

3. Soares-Prabhu, "Towards an Indian Interpretation of the Bible," 208ff.

4. See his "'And There Was a Great Calm': A 'Dhvani' Reading of the Stilling of the Storm (Mk 4:35-41)" (chapter 9 below).

5. Raymond Brown remarks that "many commentators choose to confine themselves to the task of explanation" but that "commentators cannot rest content with being archaeologists of meaning" ("Hermeneutics," in *The New Jerusalem Bible Commentary*, ed. Raymond E. Brown, S.S., Joseph A. Fitzmyer, S.J., and Roland E. Murphy, O.Carm. (Englewood Cliffs, N.J.: Prentice Hall, 1989), 1162.

6. For a concrete illustration, see his "The Kingdom of God: Jesus' Vision of a New Society" (chapter 4 below).

7. See his "The Historical Critical Method: Reflections on Its Relevance for the Study of the Gospels in India Today," in *A Biblical Theology for India*, Collected Writings of George M. Soares-Prabhu, S.J., vol. 2, ed. Scaria Kuthirakkattel (Pune: Jnana-Deepa Vidyapeeth, 1999), 3-48.

8. Soares-Prabhu, "The Dharma of Jesus: An Interpretation of the Sermon on the Mount" (chapter 12 below).

9. Following this, George states that [homologously] the *dharma* of Jesus is "that complex blend of worldview and values, of beliefs and prescriptions, which 'holds together' the followers of Jesus, and integrates them into a recognisable community" ("'As We Forgive': Interhuman Forgiveness in the Teaching of Jesus," chapter 15 below).

10. See John M. Koller, "'*Dharma*': An Expression of Universal Order," *Philosophy East & West* 22, no. 2 (1972): 131-44.

11. See Francis X. D'Sa, "Dharma as Delight in Cosmic Welfare: A Study of Dharma in the Gita," *Bible Bhashyam* 6, no. 4 (1980): 335-57.

12. Soares-Prabhu, "The Dharma of Jesus" (chapter 12 below).

13. In " The Miracles of Jesus Today" (chapter 8 below), Soares-Prabhu characterizes such theology as "the defensive, over-abstract, largely unbiblical theology of the 'siege years' from Trent to Vatican II."

14. See Soares-Prabhu, "The Dharma of Jesus" (chapter 12 below). [Editor's note: "The Dharma of Jesus" was composed (1980) much before inclusive language reached the shores of India. Compare this with "The Jesus of Faith" (chapter 5 below) written in 1992.]

15. See Soares-Prabhu, "The Miracles of Jesus Today" (chapter 8 below):

Apocalyptic expectation has long given way to social concern. It is in the idiom of this new mood that the word of God must now speak. And indeed, were Jesus to appear among us today, would he, one wonders, come as a healer and exorcist, competing with the doctors and psychiatrists who have adequately assumed these functions? Would he not come rather as one who gives vision and purpose to a dispirited and drifting people, who sparks hope in a people driven to despair? Would he not open their eyes to the grim realities of injustice and oppression among which they blissfully live in stubborn blindness, rouse them from their paralysed inaction and strengthen their sinews so that they may stand up for the poor to whom he proclaimed (how ironical it sometimes sounds!) the 'good news' of salvation? Would he not exorcise the demons of self-righteousness, of intolerance, of the lust for power, of divisiveness, casteism and unconcern, which sit contentedly in the swept and empty spaces of their lives? Would he not start fashioning communities in which the outcaste would be welcome and the oppressed find relief; communities in which men would learn the courage to love, find the strength for commitment, and be given the truly suprahuman ability to forgive?

16. See Soares-Prabhu, "The Historical Critical Method," 6f.

17. Soares-Prabhu, "The Dharma of Jesus" (chapter 12 below).

18. Soares-Prabhu, "The Dharma of Jesus" (chapter 12 below). I am following R. Panikkar's practice of employing "Man" for human beings only when they are taken as one of the three centers constituting reality, the other two being God and World.

19. Soares-Prabhu, "The Jesus of Faith: A Christological Contribution to an Ecumenical Third World Spirituality" (chapter 5 below).

20. Soares-Prabhu, "Commitment and Conversion: A Biblical Hermeneutic for India Today," in *Theology of Liberation: An Indian Biblical Perspective*, Collected Writings of George M. Soares-Prabhu, vol. 4, ed. Francis X. D'Sa (Pune: Jnana-Deepa Vidyapeeth, 2001), 24-52.

21. "The Jesus of Faith" (chapter 5 below).

22. See note 18 above.

23. H. Denzinger and A. Schönmetzer, *Enchiridion symbolorum, definitionum et declarationum de rebus fidei et morum* (Freiburg: Herder, 1976), 303.

24. Soares-Prabhu, "The Jesus of Faith." "For this Christology, however 'correct' it might be, represents a narrow, culturally conditioned, and even politically motivated development which exploits only a very small fraction of the christological potential that the New Testament offers. The dogmatic Christology of the post-apostolic Hellenistic church, to which we are all heirs, developed along a single line which took off from the Logos-Christology of John, itself a rare though not wholly unrepresentative growth in the complex jungle of New Testament theology. It eventually crystallized in the formulae of Nicaea (325 C.E.), Ephesus (431 C.E.), and Chalcedon (451 C.E.), which became the normative 'dogmas' for succeeding ages."

25. See note 24 above.

26. Soares-Prabhu, "Radical Beginnings: The Jesus Community as the Archetype of the Church" (chapter 6 below).

27. Soares-Prabhu, "Jesus the Prophet" (chapter 3 below).

28. Soares-Prabhu, "Anti-Greed and Anti-Pride," in *Biblical Themes for a Contextual Theology for Today*, ed. Isaac Padinjarekuttu, 241-59.

29. Soares-Prabhu, "Jesus the Teacher" (chapter 2 below).

30. Soares-Prabhu, "'Good News to the Poor': The Social Implications of the Message of Jesus" (chapter 16 below).

31. Ibid.

32. Soares-Prabhu, "The Table-Fellowship of Jesus" (chapter 7 below).

33. Soares-Prabhu, "Jesus and the Spirit in the Synoptic Gospels" (chapter 1 below).

34. Soares-Prabhu, "'And There Was a Great Calm'" (chapter 9 below).

35. Soares-Prabhu, "The Miracles of Jesus Today" (chapter 8 below).

36. Soares-Prabhu, "Jesus and Conflict" (chapter 11 below).

37. Soares-Prabhu, "The Synoptic Love Commandment: The Dimension of Love in the Teachings of Jesus" (chapter 13 below).

38. Soares-Prabhu, "The Unprejudiced Jesus and the Prejudiced Church" (chapter 10 below).

39. Soares-Prabhu, "'As We Forgive': Interhuman Forgiveness in the Teaching of Jesus" (chapter 15 below).

40. Soares-Prabhu, "Speaking to 'Abba': Prayer as Petition and Thanksgiving in the Teaching of Jesus" (chapter 14 below).

41. Soares-Prabhu, "The Jesus of Faith" (chapter 5 below).

42. Soares-Prabhu, "Following Jesus in Mission" (chapter 19 below).

43. Ibid.

44. Soares-Prabhu, "The Church as Mission" (chapter 18 below).

45. Soares-Prabhu, "Expanding the Horizon of Christian Mission" (chapter 17 below).

46. Soares-Prabhu, "Following Jesus in Mission" (chapter 19 below). One could briefly critique George's theology on two issues: (1) it is only in the last years of his life that he employed inclusive language because its awareness dawned rather late on the Indian horizon; (2) George's theology is anthropocentric to a great extent; it is rare to find in his writings a place for the salvific role of the cosmos.

47. In 1970 with the support of George and Kurien Kunnumpuram, S.J., I started a donor agency, Training for Development Scholarship Scheme, to train talented young women and men in various professions. Over the years the scheme has become a more professional registered society, Training for Development Scholarship Society, which helps prepare young Indians to work in villages as well as supporting active groups working in villages.

48. K. J. Scaria, "Christ, the Self-emptying High Priest," in *The Dharma of Jesus: Interdisciplinary Essays in Memory of George Soares-Prabhu, S.J.,* ed. F. X. D'Sa (Pune: Institute for the Study of Religion & Anand: Gujarat Sahitya Prakash, 1997), 177 n. 208.

Part I

PORTRAITS OF JESUS
AND HIS COMMUNITY

1

JESUS AND THE SPIRIT
IN THE SYNOPTIC GOSPELS

The Spirit plays a conspicuous part in the life of Jesus as this is described in
the first three Gospels. Its role is particularly prominent in the two-volume work
of Luke (Luke-Acts), where the Spirit controls the origins and directs the activi-
ties of both Jesus (Lk 1:35; 3:22; 4:1, 14, 18; 10:21) and the early Church (Acts
1:2, 3, 5, 8; 2:4, 38; 4:31; 15:28). But in both Matthew and Mark too Jesus and
the Spirit are associated often enough to suggest that the role of the Spirit in the
life and the ministry of Jesus is not just a theme of Lukan editing, but belongs to
the Synoptic tradition from which all three Gospels derive. Indeed this element
of the tradition almost certainly goes back to Jesus himself. For it was surely his
experience of the Spirit—his intense awareness that the Spirit of God, eagerly
awaited as the eschatological gift of the "last days" (Joel 3:1ff; Is 44:3; Ez
39:29), was in fact at work in and through him (Mt 12:28)—that was the source
of his confident proclamation of the arrival of the Kingdom (Mk 1:15) and of the
extraordinary authority of his teaching (Mt 7:29).[1] But it is not Jesus' own experience of the Spirit that is primarily our subject here. Rather we shall explore
what the Synoptic Gospels have to tell us about the role of the Spirit in the life
and ministry of Jesus. According to these Gospels, the Spirit plays a significant
part in the birth of Jesus, and in his call too and preparation for his ministry. It is
active too in the ministry itself, and is the object of stray sayings of Jesus which
throw light on this activity. Each of these elements of the Synoptic tradition must
be examined in turn.

This article first appeared in *Bible Bhashyam* 2 (1976): 101-24 and then in *A Biblical Theology
for India*, Collected Writings of George M. Soares-Prabhu, S.J., vol. 2, ed. Scaria Kuthirakkattel
(Pune: Jnana-Deepa Vidyapeeth, 1999), 126-40.

1. THE SPIRIT IN THE INFANCY OF JESUS

The Spirit plays an important part in the infancy narratives of Matthew and Luke. It is specially active in Luke's infancy narrative, where it appears in two characteristic Old Testament roles: as the *creative* Spirit, active in the beginnings of the new creation (cf. the conception of the Baptist in Lk 1:15; and the conception of Jesus in Lk 1:35), as it once was in the beginnings of the Old Testament (Gen 1:2); and as the *prophetic Spirit*, speaking through the Spirit-filled utterances of New Testament prophets (cf. Elizabeth in Lk 1:41; Zachary in Lk 1:67; Simeon in Lk 2:27ff), as it once spoke through the Spirit-inspired prophets of the Old Testament (Num 24:2; 1 Sam 10:10; 1 Kgs 22:24; Hos 13:15; Mic 3:8). It is the first of these roles that is the more important, and indeed the only one taken up by the infancy narrative of Matthew. For here the events of the infancy of Jesus are interpreted not through the Spirit-filled utterances of New Testament prophets, but through revelations made in dreams (cf. the dream narratives of Mt 1:18-25; 2:13-15; 2:19-21) and through explicit references to Scriptures (cf. the formula quotations of 1:23; 2:6; 2:15; 2:18 and 2:23).[2]

That Jesus is born of the Holy Spirit is affirmed by both Matthew and Luke, and so is a tradition that antedates both. In both Gospels the tradition is linked to that of the virginal conception of Jesus, the link being closer in Matthew than in Luke. Indeed in Matthew the birth of Jesus from the Spirit is mentioned precisely to explain the virginal conception—that is, to quieten Joseph's doubts and show how Mary could have conceived a child before she had come to live with her betrothed (Mt 1:18f). Yet even in Matthew the motif of birth from the Spirit (Mt 1:20) is not purely apologetical (an attempt to explain the "irregular" birth of Jesus and rebut the calumnies to which it could and did give rise),[3] but is theological as well. It grounds the divine sonship of Jesus—a motif not yet explicit in the infancy narrative but implied there in the introductory formulae of the first two formula quotations (Mt 1:22; 2:15), whose unusual *hypo kyriou* ("by the Lord") identifies the "son," mentioned in the texts quoted, as the Lord's (i.e. God's) Son—and so makes him truly "God with us," Emmanuel (Mt 1:23).

This theological motif is even clearer in the infancy narrative of Luke. That Jesus is to be born of the Spirit is part of the angel's annunciation to Mary in Lk 1:26-38. The angel promises Mary, in the stereotyped formulae of an Old Testament birth oracle,[4] the conception and birth of a son (Lk 1:31) and paints in glowing colors his future destiny. The destiny of the child is sketched out in two parallel predictions (Lk 1:32f; 1:35) separated from each other by Mary's puzzled question (Lk 1:34):[5]

He will be great
and will be called the Son of the Most High;
and the Lord God will give to him the throne of his father David,
and he will reign over the house of Jacob for ever,
and of his Kingdom there will be no end. . . .

The Holy Spirit will come upon you,
and the power of the Most High will overshadow you;
therefore the child to be born will be called holy,
the Son of God.

The two predictions stand in climactic parallelism to each other, with the second fulfilling as it were the first and realizing it on a higher plane. The messianic "Son of the Most High" (Lk 1:32) stands revealed as the Spirit-born "Son of God" (Lk 1:35).[6]

Each prediction is itself made up of synthetically parallel elements (*great || Son of the Most High; throne of his father David || reign over the house of Jacob* in 1:32f; *Holy Spirit || power of the Most High; holy || Son of God* in 1:35) of which the second element in each pair interprets the first. The first prediction (1:32f) thus describes the destiny of Jesus in terms of orthodox messianic expectation. The child is to be "great"; that is, he is to be "the Son of the Most High." This is a strictly messianic designation, for it is at once interpreted (in obvious allusion to the prophecy of Nathan in 2 Sam 7:12-16) as implying that he will be given "the throne of David," and will rule on it forever. But Davidic messianism gives way to a more exalted sonship. For in the second prediction (1:35) the messianic "Son of the Most High" is proclaimed "holy" and the "Son of God" because he is to be born of the "power of the Most High," that is, by the "overshadowing" of his mother (a possible allusion to the covering of the Tabernacle by the cloud of God's presence in Ex 40:34f)[7] by the Holy Spirit. So "the child will be indeed 'Son of God' not only in virtue of the kingly inheritance, which will entitle him to that designation (v. 32), but also because, in his very origin, he is sprung from God."[8]

In both Matthew and Luke, then, birth from the Spirit grounds the divine sonship of Jesus, a sonship that goes beyond that traditionally attributed to Israel (Ex 4:22; Hos 11:1), to Israel's king (2 Sam 7:14; Ps 2:7) or to the Messiah,[9] though it is probably not yet thought of in the metaphysical terms of later theology.[10] It is a sonship which in Matthew makes Jesus Emmanuel, "God with us" (Mt 1:23; 28:20), and in Luke makes God the Father of Jesus in an altogether unique way. For in the final episode of Luke's infancy narrative, the finding of the boy Jesus in the Temple (Lk 2:41-51), the unique sonship of Jesus is strikingly revealed, when Mary's reproachful question is countered by Jesus' own:

2:48	2:49
Son why have you treated us so?	Why is it that you were looking for me?
Behold your father and I have been looking for you anxiously.	Did you not know that I must be in my Father's house?

The carefully contrived opposition between the "your father" of Mary's reproach and the "my father" of Jesus' reply makes it clear that, for Luke, God is the Father of Jesus in a way that no human father is.

2. THE SPIRIT AND THE BEGINNINGS
OF JESUS' MINISTRY

The Spirit which is active at the beginnings of the human existence of Jesus is active too at the beginnings of his ministry. In the Synoptic Gospels the ministry of Jesus begins with his baptism by John, whose prophetic call to conversion (Mk 1:4) and whose promise of an imminent savior/judge who will baptize with the Holy Spirit (Mk 1:8), that is, communicate the eschatological gift of the "last days" (Joel 3:1ff), effectively prepare the way for the appearance of Jesus. As the one who is to baptize with the Holy Spirit, Jesus must receive the fullness of the Spirit. This he will do at his baptism by John.

A. *The Baptism of Jesus*
(Mk 1:9-11; Mt 3:13-17; Lk 3:21-22)

In the Synoptic tradition the baptism of Jesus is associated with a *theophany*—a vision in which Jesus sees the heavens opened and the Spirit descending upon him in the form of a dove (Mk 1:10), and hears a voice from heaven saying to him: "Thou art my beloved son; with thee I am well pleased" (Mk 1:11).[11] The symbolism of the theophany is extraordinarily rich and complex. The "heavens" (in Jewish cosmology a solid "firmament," conceived of as "a gigantic hemispherical and ponderous bell")[12] are "torn open" (*schizomenos*) to allow the Spirit to come down. The rending of the heavens thus answers the desperate longing of post-exilic Israel, deprived of prophecy (i.e., of the Spirit) and feeling hopelessly abandoned by God, a longing powerfully expressed in the communal lament of Is 63:7-64:12, to which the Synoptic narrative of the baptism of Jesus almost certainly refers.[13] Mindful of Yahweh's saving deeds in the past (Is 63:1-9) and so the more conscious of his present abandonment of his people (Is 63:11b-19), the prophet cries out with desperate urgency: "O that thou wouldst rend the heavens and come down" (Is 64:1). It is this cry that the baptism of Jesus answers. The heavens are indeed rent and the Spirit of God comes down. Communication with God (long interrupted) is reestablished; the quenched Spirit is active again; the age of salvation has dawned.

The opening of the heavens allows the Spirit to come down in the form of a dove—a symbol not normally used for the Spirit in the Judaism of New Testament times.[14] But an early rabbinic tradition does speak of the Spirit in Gen 1:2 as "brooding on the face of the waters like a dove,"[15] while in the Old Testament the dove is sometimes used as a poetic symbol for Israel (Song 2:14; 5:2; Hos 7:11). It is likely, then, that the dove in the Synoptic baptism narrative identifies the ministry of Jesus as the new creation, and points too to the outcome of this creative ministry, the new people of God.

The dove-like Spirit comes down upon Jesus to "anoint" him (Acts 10:38: "how God anointed Jesus of Nazareth with the Holy Spirit and with power") as the Servant Messiah. For the voice from heaven, the authentic interpretation of the Spirit's descent addresses Jesus in words taken from a royal enthronement and eventually *messianic Psalm* (Ps 2:7: "He said to me, 'you are my son, today I have begotten you'"), and from the first *Servant Song* of Deutero-Isaiah (Is 42:1: "Behold my servant, whom I uphold / my chosen beloved in whom I am pleased"). So the Spirit received by Jesus at his baptism is that promised in the Old Testament to the Davidic Messiah and the Isaianic Servant of God. It is "the spirit of wisdom and understanding, the spirit of counsel and might, the spirit of knowledge and the fear of the Lord that will rest upon the branch that grows out of the stump of Jesse" (Is 11:1f); it is the spirit "put upon" the Servant of God to enable him to "bring forth salvation (*mišpāṭ*) to the nations" (Is 42:1); and it is the spirit that "anoints" (i.e., commissions) the anonymous "evangelist" of Is 61:1 (Trito-Isaiah's re-edition of the "Servant")[16] to "bring good tidings to the poor."

The baptism of Jesus is thus seen by the Synoptic tradition as his messianic installation.[17] Jesus is proclaimed "Son" (here, Messiah), who is to exercise his sonship (messiahship) as the spirit-filled Servant. The opening of the heavens indicates the dawn of the messianic age, and suggests the radical change in man's relation to God that the messianic ministry of Jesus portends. The dove-like descent of the Spirit points to the ultimate outcome of this ministry, the creation of the eschatological community of salvation, the new people of God. It is for this task that Jesus at his baptism is anointed (commissioned and equipped) by the creative and prophetic power of the Spirit.

B. The Temptations of Jesus
(Mk 1:12f; Mt 4:1-11; Lk 4:1-13)

The divine sonship of Jesus revealed at his baptism in the Jordan is at once put to a test that further brings out its meaning. Jesus, who has received the Spirit and has been proclaimed "Son of God," is at once driven out by the Spirit into the wilderness, the classical locus of Israel's encounter with God and with demons,[18] to be tested as God's son ("if you are the son of God . . .") by the devil (Mk 1:12). Two versions of the temptation of Jesus have come down to us in the Synoptic tradition. The shorter Markan version (Mk 1:12f) merely reports that Jesus spent forty days in the wilderness tempted (presumably all the time) by Satan, and that (after the temptation?) he was with wild beasts, while angels served him. Matthew and Luke have slightly different versions of a much more elaborate temptation story (deriving probably from their common sayings source, Q), which describe in detail three temptations posed by the devil and Jesus' reaction to them (Mt 4:1-11; Lk 4:1-13). The temptation-encounter between Jesus and the devil is here presented as a scribal debate, in which quotations from Scripture form the basis of the argument—a form followed in similar rabbinic accounts of the temptations of Abraham and Moses.[19] The biblical texts quoted (Deut 8:3;

6:16; 6:13 by Jesus; Ps 91:11f by the devil) show that the Q temptation story intends to present Jesus as the true Israel, God's faithful Son, who relives the temptations of Israel, also God's son (Ex 4:22; Hos 11:1), in the wilderness (for the three texts quoted by Jesus all refer to these temptations of Israel), and overcomes where Israel had failed.[20] The three temptations may point too to three ways of fulfilling his mission (the use of spiritual power for personal profit, reliance on stunts [signs and wonders!] to win the allegiance of the people, success through political manoeuvre), or to three forms of current messianic expectation (the Messiah like Moses who would repeat the miracles of the Exodus; the priestly Aaronic Messiah who would appear with wonder-working power in the Temple; the political Son of David who would restore the kingdom to Israel), all of which Jesus rejects in favor of the way of the Servant shown to him at his baptism. Jesus thus proves himself to be the Son of God not through the exercise of miraculous power or political clout, but by his absolute obedience and his total refusal (against all three temptations—for this, ultimately, is what each of the three temptations is really urging him to do) to rely on anything other than the naked word of God.

The single text quoted by the tempter (Ps 91:11f) suggests that this obedience of Jesus leads to an utterly decisive victory over Satan. The point is made particularly by Mark, whose temptation story seems largely based on Ps 91. For in Mark, Jesus in the wilderness who is "with beasts" (as their conqueror) and is ministered to (i.e., protected) by angels is very like the protagonist of the Psalm, who, defended by angels ("he will give his angels charge over you, to guard you in all your ways"), is victorious over wild beasts, symbolizing the forces of evil that threaten the life of man ("you will tread on the lion and adder, the young lion and the serpent you will trample under foot"). Alternatively, Mark's temptation story may allude to the paradise story of Gen 2, and show Jesus in the wilderness (like Adam in paradise) at home with beasts and ministered to (i.e., fed) by angels, as Adam too, in the Jewish legends about him, was fed in paradise with angels' food.[21] Given the polyvalent character of symbols, both allusions (Jesus as the conquering warrior of Ps 91, or Jesus as the new Adam of Gen 2) might have been intended by Mark. But the conflict character of his Gospel, which presents the ministry largely in terms of a struggle against human enemies (controversies) and evil spirits (exorcisms), suggests that the first allusion is primary. Mark's temptation story thus describes Jesus' decisive victory over Satan, and possibly too the resultant restoration of the primal harmony of paradise that this victory brings. The strong man has been bound, and the "stronger man" Jesus can now, through his exorcisms, plunder his goods (Mk 3:27). The Spirit thus not only identifies Jesus as the Son, the authenticity of whose sonship is revealed through his fidelity in temptation; it also invests him with power to overcome evil, a power that he will exercise throughout his ministry, to free men from the bonds of Satan, sickness and sin.

3. THE SPIRIT IN THE MINISTRY OF JESUS

That the Spirit animates the whole ministry of Jesus is particularly evident in Luke, where Jesus after his temptation returns to Galilee "in the power (*dynamis*) of the Spirit" (Lk 4:14), and goes at once to Nazareth to proclaim himself, in a programmatic inaugural discourse which defines the scope of his mission, as the Spirit-filled "evangelizer" of Is 61:1 who has been "anointed" (commissioned and equipped) by the Spirit to "preach good news to the poor" (Lk 4:18).

A. *Jesus the Spirit-Filled Evangelizer*

This inaugural proclamation is of great importance to Luke. To provide it with an appropriate setting he has dislocated the story of Jesus' rejection at Nazareth from its original place in the Synoptic tradition, and put it at the very beginning of the Galilean ministry of Jesus (Lk 4:16-30) instead of much later, as Mark and Matthew have done (Mk 6:1-6; Mt 13:54-58). The proclamation thus becomes Jesus' manifesto, his policy declaration, setting out his own special understanding of his mission as a preaching of good news to the poor. The setting in which the proclamation occurs (the rejection of Jesus at Nazareth), with its two moments of approval (Lk 4:22: "all spoke well of him and wondered at his gracious words")[22] and rejection (Lk 4:28f: "all in the synagogue were filled with wrath, and they rose and put him out of the city"), so that "proclamation becomes a Passion narrative,"[23] is thus a preview of the life of Jesus; a gospel within the Gospel.[24] And the whole first section of Luke's account of the ministry of Jesus with its description of Jesus' unsuccessful day at Nazareth among his own (4:16-30) followed at once by a most successful day at Capernaum among strangers (4:31-41) foreshadows the rejection of Jesus by the Jews and his acceptance by the gentiles, which is the major theme of Luke's two-volume presentation of salvation history (Luke-Acts).

The inaugural proclamation of Lk 4:16-30 thus expresses characteristically Lukan theology. But its presentation of Jesus as the Spirit-filled evangelizer of Is 61:1 goes back to the Synoptic tradition, indeed ultimately to Jesus himself. For an allusion to Is 61:1f is clear in the undoubtedly authentic beatitudes of Lk 6:20f (echoed in a somewhat spiritualized form in Mt 5:3-6), as well as in the equally authentic Q saying of Mt 11:2-6 ‖ Lk 7:22f, in which Jesus, replying to the Baptist's question, refers (in the words of Is 35:5f; 61:1) to his healings and to his proclamation of the good news to the poor (explicitly in the beatitudes, implicitly in his table fellowship with tax collectors and sinners) as the credentials of his messianic ministry.

The Synoptic tradition thus presents Jesus as the Spirit-filled "evangelizer" of Is 61:1 filled with the Spirit and committed to a programme of liberation ("he has sent me to bind up the broken-hearted, to proclaim liberty to captives and the opening of the prison to those who are bound"). Jesus liberates the "poor"—that is, the outcast and the oppressed, all who in their deprivation and helplessness look to and have a special claim on the God who "executes justice for the orphan, the widow and the refugee" (Deut 10:18) and who "saves all the oppressed (*'ănāwîm*) of the earth" (Ps 76:9).[25] He liberates them by proclaiming forgiveness of sin in word (Mk 2:5; Lk 7:48) and in deed (i.e., by his table fellowship with sinners—Mk 2:15; Lk 15:1f), and by freeing men through his healings (cf. Lk 13:16) and his exorcisms (cf. Mk 5:1-20) from the dark demonic forces that threaten their lives. Both aspects of the liberating work of Jesus derive from the Spirit. For the forgiveness of sin is an eschatological gift, awaited in the "last days"[26] and associated with the eschatological gift of the Spirit (Jn 20:22f: "Receive the Holy Spirit! If you forgive the sins of anyone they are forgiven"), while the healings and exorcisms of Jesus are presented as *dynameis* (Mt 11:20f; Mk 6:2, 5, 14), "mighty works" wrought in the power (*dynamis*) of the Spirit (Lk 4:14f—cf. also 4:36; 5:17; 6:19).[27] This is particularly evident in the exorcisms of Jesus.

B. Jesus the Spirit-Empowered Exorcist

Jesus himself points to his exorcisms as a particularly clear manifestation of the power of God (the Spirit) at work: "If it is by the finger of God (Mt: the Spirit of God) that I cast out demons, then the kingdom of God has come upon you" (Lk 11:20 ‖ Mt 12:28).

This Q saying with "high claims to authenticity"[28] is pivotal for our understanding of Jesus' experience of the kingdom. It complements such futurist sayings as Mk 1:15 ("the kingdom of God is at hand" [*ēggiken*]) with the clear assertion that the kingdom has already come [*ephthasen*]. As evidence for the arrival of the Kingdom, Jesus points to his exorcisms, in which he sees the power of God at work. Luke's designation of this power as the "finger of God" (alluding to Ex 8:19) is probably original,[29] but Matthew's "Spirit of God" is a satisfactory equivalent, which catches the meaning of Luke's formula correctly. For in the Old Testament, "Spirit of God" is used in parallel to "hand of God" (Ez 3:14; 8:1-3; 37:1), and so is presumably synonymous too with "finger of God," a much less used expression with the same meaning. In his exorcisms, then, Jesus experiences the Spirit at work in him. And because the Spirit is the eschatological gift of salvation, these exorcisms are for Jesus an irrefutable sign that the eschatological kingdom has come.

That is why to attribute the exorcisms of Jesus to Satan is to blaspheme against the Spirit and commit the unforgivable sin:

Mk 3:28f	Mt 12:31f	Lk 12:10
Truly I tell you all sins will be forgiven the sons of men and whatever blasphemy they may utter;	Therefore I tell you every sin and blasphemy will be forgiven men,	

	But the blasphemy against	
but whoever blasphemes against the Holy Spirit never has forgiveness, but is guilty of an eternal sin.	the Spirit will not be forgiven. And whoever says a word against the Son of Man will be forgiven: but whoever speaks against the Holy Spirit will not be forgiven; either in this age or in the age to come.	And everyone who speaks a word against the Son of Man will be forgiven; but the one blaspheming against the Holy Spirit will not be forgiven.

This curious saying has come down to us in two forms: a Markan form (Mk 3:28f), which does not mention blasphemy against the Son of Man (but speaks rather of "sons of men" blaspheming), and a Q form (Lk 12:10), which does. Matthew appears to have conflated the two forms, so that he has the saying twice (Mt 12:31f). Both forms probably derive from an Aramaic original whose *bar nāšā* could have been understood either as a title ("Son of Man") or as a generic singular ("man" or "sons of men"), and either as the subject or the object of the verb "to blaspheme." The saying could then have been read either as "all that the sons of men blaspheme will be forgiven" (cf. Mk 3:28) or as "all who blaspheme against the Son of Man will be forgiven" (cf. Lk 12:10).[30] Mark probably gives us the original meaning and the authentic context of the saying. The saying, that is, was probably occasioned by a dispute about the origins of Jesus' power to exorcise. To blaspheme against the Holy Spirit would then mean to attribute the Spirit-empowered exorcisms of Jesus to Satan. This would be the one unforgivable sin—precisely because it consists in an obdurate refusal of forgiveness! For to dismiss the clearly perceptible signs of the Spirit's action as satanic is to deliberately and irremediably close oneself to the presence of the Spirit, which alone brings forgiveness and salvation. Indeed "the man who (is) capable of calling good Evil, of painting the Source of holiness in the colours of Hell, (is) beyond repentance and therefore beyond forgiveness; his sin must pass with him unremitted into the next aeon, to which the earthly mission of the Saviour (does) not extend."[31]

The Q form of the saying (Lk 12:10), with its distinction between blasphemy against the Son of Man, which is forgivable, and blasphemy against the Holy Spirit, which is not, is more difficult to understand. Possibly the saying has to be understood in terms of the post-Easter mission of the early Church. It might then be contrasting the forgivable rejection of Jesus during his earthly ministry as the hidden Son of Man with the unforgivable rejection of the risen Lord proclaimed by the post-Pentecost Church in the power of the Spirit,[32] or (less plausibly) the forgivable rejection of Jesus by those outside the Church, who thus sin only against the Son of Man, with the unforgivable apostasy of those within the Church, who, because they have received the Spirit, sin, by apostatizing, against the Spirit too.[33] Alternatively the Q saying too may have referred to the earthly

Jesus and taught that "while an attack on Jesus' own person, as son of Man and therefore 'hidden,' is pardonable, any speaking against the *power* by which he works (i.e. the divine endowment for the messianic ministry) will not be pardoned."[34] Indeed, as this form of the saying probably arose as a misunderstanding of its Aramaic original, it may never have made full sense even to the early Christian communities which transmitted it. But whatever its meaning, one thing is abundantly clear: the Spirit is so central to Jesus' mission of salvation that to reject it is to reject the mission itself.

4. THE SPIRIT IN THE TEACHING OF JESUS

Yet Jesus speaks of the Spirit rarely enough! Apart from the few sayings describing the role of the Spirit in his own ministry which we have discussed above, he scarcely seems to mention the Spirit at all. A text from the Psalms quoted in a theological dispute with his Jerusalem adversaries is attributed to the Spirit, speaking through David (Mk 12:36), so that for Jesus the Spirit is evidently the inspiring principle of Scripture. A saying on prayer in Luke (11:13) identifies the Spirit as the gift given by God to those who pray earnestly to him ("how much more will your heavenly Father give the Holy Spirit to those who ask him?"); but the "Holy Spirit" here is probably Luke's editorial interpretation of the "good things" (*agatha*) promised in the original Q saying (cf. Mt 7:11)— a legitimate interpretation, since "good things" here probably stand for the gifts of the messianic age, among which the Spirit is conspicuous.[35]

Again, Jesus urges his disciples to rely on the Spirit, who will help them to witness to their faith when they are persecuted and brought to trial (Mk 13:11: "And when they bring you to trial and deliver you up, do not be anxious beforehand what you are to say; but say whatever is given to you in that hour, for it is not you who speak but the Holy Spirit")—an exhortation and a promise which must have made a deep impression on his followers, because it has been preserved in three different forms (and in as many different settings) by the Synoptic tradition, and may also lie behind the Paraclete sayings of John (14:16, 26). In Mark (13:11) the saying, as part of Jesus' eschatological discourse, refers to the post-Easter mission of the disciples in the time of troubles immediately preceding the imminent parousia. A very similar Q form of the saying is put by Luke (12:11f) in a loose collection of sayings about confessing Jesus. Matthew (10:19f) conflates Mk and Q to fashion a saying for his mission discourse, where the Spirit's help is promised to the Twelve for crisis situations in their missionary tour of Israel (the prototype of the post-Easter mission of the Church) during the actual ministry of Jesus. And in a variant version, in which the Spirit is replaced by Jesus himself, promising his hard-pressed followers wise speech when occasion demands ("I will give you a mouth and a wisdom which none of your adversaries will be able to withstand or resist"), the saying occurs in Luke's great eschatological discourse (21:14f), as his parallel to Mk 13:11. The saying is thus very well attested. But if, as Barrett suggests, Lk 24:14f (with its strongly Semitic coloring and its obvious allusion to Ex 4:12) is its earliest form, the reference to the Spirit would not go back to Jesus, but would again be an interpretative formulation of the early Church.[36]

As an enduring presence, and not just for the time of crisis, the Spirit is promised by the risen Jesus to his disciples in Lk 24:49 ("And behold I send the promise of my Father upon you"). As in Acts 1:4 the "promise of the Father" refers to the Spirit to be given at Pentecost. The saying thus presupposes the salvation history scheme of Luke (compare Jn 20:2f, where the Spirit is given by the risen Lord on Easter evening) so that in its formulation at least the saying is a piece of Lukan redaction. Redactional too is the prescription in Mt 28:19 which imposes baptism in the name of the Father and of the Son and of the Holy Spirit on all those who are to be made disciples of the risen Lord. For whether we take it to be a liturgical formula or a theological statement on the meaning of baptism which "combines the disciples' inherited Jewish faith in God ('the name of the Father'), their new faith in the Son (i.e. the Son of Man) and their experience of the Holy Spirit, the earnest of the New Age,"[37] the trinitarian formula of Mt 28:19 is certainly secondary, even if the command to baptize may go back to Jesus himself.[38]

5. JESUS AND THE SPIRIT

The Synoptic Gospels are not effusive about the Spirit.[39] References to the Spirit are few, specially when compared to those in John and Paul, and of these a fair number can be traced back to the editorial hand of Luke (Lk 4:14; 4:18; 10:21; 11:13; 24:49). The references that do indeed go back to the Synoptic tradition are divided about equally between sayings of Jesus (Mk 3:28f; 13:11 par; Mt 12:28; 28:19) and narratives about him (Mt 1:18, 20; Mk 1:8 par; 1:10 par; 1:12 par). The most authentic of these sayings are those in which Jesus speaks about the role of the Spirit in his own life and mission (Mk 3:28f; Mt 12:28); for in Synoptic sayings about the Church, references to the Spirit tend to be early Christian interpretation (Mk 13:11 par; Lk 11:13; 24:49; Mt 28:19). The authentic sayings of Jesus thus link up with the references to the Spirit in the Synoptic narratives: both, that is, speak primarily about Jesus and the Spirit.

On the whole, the Synoptic tradition thinks of the Spirit that inspires the life and mission of Jesus along the lines of the Old Testament *rûaḥ yahweh*, that is, as a creative and inspiring power (Lk 1:35; Mt 12:28). This power fills up the whole existence of Jesus, indeed takes possession as it were of it (Mk 1:12: "the Spirit immediately drove him out [*ekballei*] into the wilderness"). Its effect on Jesus is not, however, depicted in terms of Pentecostal enthusiasm. There is no indication that Jesus ever spoke in tongues, only a single obscure saying to suggest that he saw visions or dreamed dreams (Lk 10:18: "I saw Satan fall like lightning from heaven"—a saying sometimes interpreted as the description of a visionary experience),[40] and little evidence that he enjoyed moments of ecstatic inspiration. In the one text that might suggest this (Lk 10:21: "In that hour he exulted [*ēgalliasato*] in the Holy Spirit and said"), the allusion to his exulting in the Spirit is probably Lukan editing, as the parallel in Matthew shows (Mt 11:25: "At that time Jesus answered and said")—though the saying that follows in each case ("I thank you Father . . . that you have hidden these things from the wise and understanding and revealed them to babes") does indeed suggest a revelatory experience of some kind.

So "this 'resting' of the Holy Spirit upon Jesus is sharply distinguished by the Evangelists from the 'enthusiasm' of an ecstatic prophet's inspiration."[41] It shows itself instead in the authority (*exousia*) of his teaching, and the power (*dynamis*) of his healings and exorcisms: in works that are wholly redemptive. Rather than the "temporary and partial Spirit-possession of a prophet" this demands "a continuous and enduring endowment of Jesus with the 'authority' and 'power' (greater than that of the scribes and prophets) which are manifested in his teaching and mighty works."[42]

The Spirit that rests on Jesus is thus creative rather than prophetic. It is the Spirit that brings the new creation into being. As such it stands at the origins of Jesus' ministry, anointing him as the Spirit-filled Messiah promised in the Old Testament; and it stands too at the origins of the human existence of Jesus, marking these origins as those of one who is uniquely Son of God. Ultimately, then, the Spirit resting on Jesus is seen by the Synoptic tradition as the Spirit of sonship. For whether it is speaking of the descent of the Spirit that makes Jesus the messianic "Son of God" (Mk 1:9-11) or the birth from the Spirit that makes him "Son of God" by origin in an altogether unique way (Lk 1:35), divine sonship is always the outcome of the presence and power of the Spirit. And here the tradition touches on the experience of Jesus himself. For as the Synoptic Gospels clearly show, *Sonship* (the experience of God as "*Abba*," Father) and *Spirit* (the experience of the eschatological power of God working in and through him) were in fact the twin poles of Jesus' experience of God.[43]

NOTES

1. See J. D. G. Dunn, *Jesus and the Spirit* (London: SCM Press, 1975), 47f.

2. On the form and significance of the dream narratives and on the role of the formula quotations in Matthew's infancy narrative, see G. M. Soares-Prabhu, *The Formula Quotations in the Infancy Narrative of Matthew* (Rome: Biblical Institute, 1976), 192-293.

3. Ibid., 16. It is likely that a pre-Matthean apologetical story has been taken up by Matthew and given a theological slant; see ibid., 231-53.

4. Cf. Gen 16:11f (Ishmael); Judg 13:3-5 (Samson); Is 7:14 (Emmanuel). The birth oracle (1) announces the conception and birth of a child ("Behold you have conceived and will bear a son"); (2) imposes a name ("you shall call his name Ishmael" [= *yišmāʾēl:* God hearkens]), often adding an explanation for it ("because the Lord has hearkened [*šāmaʿ*] to your affliction"); and (3) goes on to describe the future role of the child in the history

of salvation ("he shall be a wild ass of a man"). In the annunciation story of Lk 1:26-38 the birth oracle has been integrated into a call narrative, on which see Soares-Prabhu, "The Priesthood as a Call in the Old Testament," in *Vocation: God's Call to Man,* ed. T. Thyaparambil (Poona: National Vocation Service Centre, 1975), 53-70.

5. Mary's question in Lk 1:34 parallels that of Zachary in Lk 1:18, both corresponding to the "objection" which is an integral part of a call narrative (see n. 4 above). Yet as their very different sequels show, we are doubtless intended to understand Zachary's question as due to unbelief and Mary's as "called forth by the struggle to believe"; see H. B. Swete, *The Holy Spirit in the New Testament* (London: Macmillan, 1909), 25.

6. See H. Flender, *St. Luke: Theologian of Redemptive History* (London: SPCK, 1967), 43f.

7. See R. Laurentin, *Structure et théologie de Luc I-II* (Paris: Etudes Bibliques, 1957), 73-79.

8. J. M. Creed, *The Gospel According to St. Luke* (London: Macmillan, 1930), 19.

9. Whether "Son of God" was indeed a messianic title in pre-Christian Judaism is disputed. But the application of 2 Sam 7:12ff to the "shoot of David" in a Qumran anthology (4QFlor) does suggest that the idea of divine sonship, and possibly the title "Son of God" too, was in fact applied to the Messiah; see F. Hahn, *The Titles of Jesus in Christology* (London: Lutterworth, 1969), 281-83.

10. Ibid., 288-99.

11. The original form of the Synoptic baptism narrative has been identified as a *deute Vision* (an explanatory vision) by F. Lentzen-Deis, *Die Taufe Jesu nach den Synoptikern: Literarkritische und Gattungsgeschichtliche Untersuchungen* (Frankfurt/Main: Josef Knecht Verlag, 1970). The vision character is maintained in Mark, where only Jesus sees and hears the baptismal theophany. But Matthew's declaratory form of the words from heaven ("*This is* my son" for Mark's "*Thou art* my son") suggests a public proclamation, while in Luke the theophany is described as an objective occurrence, with the Spirit coming down "in bodily form as a dove."

12. G. von Rad, *Genesis,* 3rd ed. (London: SCM Press, 1972), 53.

13. See I. Buse, "The Markan Account of the Baptism of Jesus and Isaiah 63," *Journal of Theological Studies* 7 (1956): 74-75.

14. See C. K. Barrett, *The Holy Spirit and the Gospel Tradition,* 5th ed. (London: SPCK, 1970), 35-39, for a good discussion of the dove symbolism in the Synoptic baptism story.

15. Ibid., 38.

16. R. N. Whybray, *Isaiah 40-66* (London: New Century Bible, 1975), 39-40.

17. See J. D. G. Dunn, *Baptism in the Holy Spirit* (London: SCM Press, 1970), 26f; Barrett (n. 14 above), 44. As Dunn points out, the question of the messianic installation of Jesus is independent of the problem of his messianic consciousness. "The descent of the Spirit on Jesus effects not so much a change in Jesus, his person or his status, as the beginning of a new stage in salvation-history. The thought is not so much of Jesus becoming what he was not before, but of Jesus entering where he was not before—a new epoch in God's plan of redemption . . ." (p. 28).

18. See U. Mauser, *Christ in the Wilderness* (London: SCM Press, 1963), 15-52.

19. See H. A. Kelly, "The Devil in the Desert," *Catholic Biblical Quarterly* 26 (1964): 200-202, for illustrations from rabbinic literature.

20. See J. Dupont, "L'arrière-fond biblique du récit des tentations de Jésus," *New Testament Studies* 3 (1956-57): 287-304.

21. See A. Feuillet, "L'épisode de la Tentation de'après l'Evangile selon saint Marc," *Estudios Biblicos* 19 (1960): 49-73.

22. But cf. J. Jeremias, *Jesus' Promise to the Nations* (London: SCM Press, 1958), 44-46, where Lk 4:22 is interpreted negatively to read: "They witnessed against him (*emartyroun autō*) and were angrily astonished (*kai ethaumazon*) at his words of God's mercy" (*epi tois logois tēs charitos*)—because, that is, he had omitted the words about messianic vengeance contained in the text (Is 61:1) he had quoted. Jeremias' exegesis is ingenious, but too strained to be convincing.

23. A. Schlatter, *Das Evangelium des Lukas,* 2nd ed. (Stuttgart: Calwert, 1960), 221.

24. So H. Schürmann, *Das Lukasevangelium I* (Freiburg: Herder, 1969), 225.

25. See J. Dupont, *Les Béatitudes, II* (Paris: Etudes Bibliques, 1969), 65-90.

26. See J. Jeremias, *The Prayers of Jesus* (London: SCM Press, 1967).

27. Dunn, *Jesus and the Spirit,* 70f.

28. N. Perrin, *Rediscovering the Teaching of Jesus* (London: SCM Press, 1967), 64.

29. See T. W. Manson, *The Teaching of Jesus,* 2nd ed. (Cambridge: Camgbridge University Press, 1935), 82f. But Dunn (*Jesus and the Spirit,* 44-46) attempts to make a case for the priority of Matthew's "Spirit of God."

30. Dunn, *Jesus and the Spirit,* 49f.

31. Swete, *Holy Spirit,* 117.

32. See E. Schweizer, *The Good News According to Matthew* (London: SPCK, 1976), 287f.

33. See C. K. Barrett, *Holy Spirit,* 105-7, taking up a common patristic interpretation.

34. D. Hill, *The Gospel of Matthew* (London: New Century Bible, 1972), 218.

35. J. Jeremias, *The Parables of Jesus* (London: SCM Press, 1963), 144f.

36. Barrett, *Holy Spirit,* 131f.

37. G. R. Beasley-Murray, *Baptism in the New Testament* (Exeter: Paternoster Press, 1972), 83, presenting the position of F. C. Grant.

38. Ibid., 77-92.

39. Cf. the chapter "Why Do the Gospels Say So Little about the Spirit?" in Barrett, *Holy Spirit,* 140-62.

40. So W. G. Kümmel, *Promise and Fulfillment* (London: SCM Press, 1957), 113f.

41. G. W. H. Lampe, *The Seal of the Spirit,* 2nd ed. (London: SPCK, 1967), 35.

42. Ibid.

43. Dunn, *Jesus and the Spirit,* 67.

2

JESUS THE TEACHER

The Liberative Pedagogy of Jesus of Nazareth

Almost everything we know about the Jesus of history comes to us from the Gospels, and primarily from the first three Gospels (the so-called Synoptic Gospels). The Gospel of John, though containing historical traditions of great value, is much less reliable than the Synoptics as a historical source.[1] And all three Synoptics feature "teaching" as a prominent element in the ministry of Jesus. It is mentioned conspicuously by Matthew in his strategically placed summaries of the Galilean ministry of Jesus, which tell us how he "went around Galilee, *teaching* in their synagogue, *preaching* the good news of the Kingdom, and *healing* every disease and every infirmity" (Mt 4:23; 9:35; 11:1). Mark too likes to show Jesus teaching great crowds on the shores of the lake of Gennesaret (Mk 2:13; 4:1; 6:34), and Luke has frequent references to Jesus teaching in synagogues (Lk 4:15; 4:31; 6:6; 13:10) or in the Temple (Lk 19:47; 20:1; 21:37).

What was this "teaching" of Jesus like? What sort of educational model did he follow? Such questions are not easy to answer, since the Gospels (which alone give us access to the words and works of Jesus) are not "biographies" in any presently accepted sense of the term. They are not memoirs, reporting a remembered sequence of events, or handing down carefully memorized sayings of Jesus in exactly the circumstances in which they were originally uttered. Instead they are "mosaics," carefully edited compilations of stories about and sayings of Jesus, which circulated as isolated units in the oral tradition of the early Church and were then put together by the evangelists to give us theological profiles of Jesus.[2] The Gospels are thus "narrative Christologies," which spell out for us in

This article first appeared in *Christian Perspectives in Education: The Mission of the Catholic College in India Today*, ed. H. Morissette (Bangalore: Xavier Board, 1985), 85-101, and then in *A Biblical Theology for India*, Collected Writings of George M. Soares-Prabhu, S.J., vol. 2, ed. Scaria Kuthirakkattel (Pune: Jnana-Deepa Vidyapeeth, 1999), 141-55.

story and saying the significance that the Jesus experience in its totality had for the evangelists and their communities.

This imposes severe limitations on any attempt to get to know the pedagogy of Jesus. We cannot, for instance, hope to derive from the Gospels a systematic "theology of education." Jesus obviously never propounded any such theology. He was not like Plato a philosopher, elaborating a method for the education of philosopher-kings; he was the end-time prophet announcing God's definitive offer of salvation and urgently summoning people to conversion (Mk 1:14-15). No systematic "discourse" of Jesus on his educational theory has come down to us. And even the occasional sayings of his that might throw light on his pedagogy are available to us only in the loose collections of the sayings of Jesus that we find in the Gospels; and these have been strung together thematically with little reference to the original circumstances in which they were uttered. To discover the original, "author meaning" of such sayings is difficult enough; to reconstruct a "theology of education" from them would be impossible.

Neither do the Gospels give us a coherent picture of the pedagogical praxis of Jesus from which we might derive his educational theory. They do not allow us to follow consistently any major educational project of his—as, for instance, his formation of the Twelve. For the Gospels give us only occasional glimpses of Jesus with the Twelve, these too not always in chronological order (so that it is impossible to trace the development of Jesus' relationship to them) and usually in the form of short pronouncement stories or miracle stories which (like the story of the call of the first disciples in Mk 1:16-20, or of the stilling of the storm in Mk 4:35-41) have been considerably adapted to respond to the needs of the post-Easter community.

Yet, in spite of all these difficulties, the task of getting to know Jesus the teacher is not an altogether hopeless one. For while the Gospels do not supply us with much reliable biographical information about Jesus, they do allow us to encounter him. The accuracy of many of the details they report about Jesus is disputable, but the overall "impression" of Jesus that they communicate is certainly accurate enough.[3] And the Jesus they reveal is conspicuously a "teacher," whose educational perspective is, I believe, substantially indicated in the three comments which the Synoptic tradition makes about his teaching: that he "went about *among the villages* (of Galilee) teaching" (Mk 6:6); that he "taught them as one who had *authority* and not as the scribes" (Mk 1:22); and that he taught everything *in parables* (Mk 4:33). There is no reason to doubt the historical accuracy of these comments on the teaching of Jesus. If we study them carefully we shall come to know Jesus the Teacher and to learn a great deal about the pedagogy he used.

1. TEACHING IN THE VILLAGES

The "teaching" (*didaskein*) of Jesus is clearly distinguished in the Gospel tradition (explicitly in Matthew, implicitly elsewhere) from his "preaching" (*keryssein*). For while Jesus "preaches" the "good news of the Kingdom" (Mt 4:23), that is, announces God's definitive offer of salvation as already present; he "teaches" the "way of God" (Mt 22:16), that is, spells out what our proper response to the proclamation of the Kingdom must be. Preaching is thus proclamation, the announcing of the good news; teaching is ethical and religious instruction, an explanation of the form that the "repentance" or "conversion" (*metanoia*) brought about by our acceptance of the good news must take. Preaching and teaching are thus complementary aspects of the educational project of Jesus.

A Non-elitist Pedagogy

This educational project is, according to the Synoptic tradition, a public project. The teaching of Jesus is not academic teaching, restricted to the members of a scribal school trained in the Law (as was the teaching of the Jewish scribes of his time); nor is it a secret religious teaching given only to a select group of initiates who have been admitted into "the covenant of grace" (as with the Essene sectarians at Qumran).[4] Instead, the Gospel tradition shows us Jesus going around the towns and villages of Galilee (Mt 9:35; Mk 6:6; Lk 13:10), teaching all who were ready to listen to him—indeed especially "the uneducated, the poor, the sinners, and the social outcasts."[5] It is truly the "poor" who have the good news preached to them by Jesus (Mt 11:6; Lk 4:18).

Indeed the obscurity of Jesus' constituency is remarkable. Apart from Jerusalem, he appears to have taught in none of the major cities of Galilee or Judea. Neither Sepphoris nor Tiberias, capital cities of Galilee, is mentioned in the Gospels as a place visited by Jesus. Instead we find him moving around obscure hamlets like Nazareth, mentioned nowhere outside the New Testament (Mt 2:23; Mk 1:9); in remote fishing villages like Bethsaida (Mk 6:45; 8:22; Lk 9:10); and in small rural townships like Capernaum, which seems to have been his headquarters during his Galilean ministry (Mt 9:1; Mk 1:21; 2:1; 9:33; Lk 10:15). It has been said of his "mission field" that:

> whenever we have any specific information (as distinct from vague general statements) the terms used are such as to point unmistakably to the countryside . . . I would emphasize that in so far as we can trust the specific information given us by the gospels, there is no evidence that Jesus ever even entered the urban area of any Greek city. That should not surprise us: Jesus, as I indicated at the beginning, belonged wholly to the *chōra*, the Jewish countryside of Galilee and Judea.[6]

Jesus, that is, taught in the villages (*kōmai*) rather than in the cities (*poleis*) of Palestine. He was more at home in the rural countryside (*chōra, agroi merē, horia*) than in the hellenized (one might say "westernized") urban settlements (*poleis*).

The teaching of Jesus is thus far removed from the intellectual elitism of the Academy, or the spiritual elitism of the Indian theological schools, which demanded a high level of spiritual and emotional maturity ("discrimination of what is eternal and non-eternal; renunciation of all desire to enjoy the fruits of one's work here and hereafter; the acquirement of tranquillity, self-restraint and the other means; and desire for release") as "antecedent conditions" for the "enquiry into the Brahman."[7] Jesus makes no such demands. To understand him one needs no unusual intellectual ability, no particular moral probity, no special spiritual stature. His teaching is open to (indeed especially intended for) the "little ones," unlearned in the law; and the "tax collectors and sinners," who have no moral or religious standing whatever. All that is required is an open heart—for ultimately the teaching of Jesus is not the imparting of doctrine but the communication of love.[8]

A Praxis-oriented Pedagogy

This message of love is proclaimed by Jesus in word and in deed. Preaching and teaching are complemented by healing in Matthew's summaries of Jesus' Galilean ministry (Mt 4:23 = 9:35); and Mark, quite strikingly, proposes the first miracle of Jesus, his exorcism in the synagogue at Capernaum (Mk 1:21-27), as "teaching"—for the "chorus" or acclamation which the miracle provokes relates the exorcism to Jesus' authoritative teaching, mentioned immediately before (Mk 1:22): "What, then, is this?" the crowds cry out, "A new teaching? With authority he commands even the unclean spirits and they obey him" (Mk 1:27). The exorcism is thus presented by Mark as Jesus' authoritative teaching become deed.[9]

This in fact is how Jesus understands all his miracles. They are not for him "signs from heaven," proofs authenticating his person or his mission: for Jesus consistently refuses to offer such proofs (Mt 4:1-11; Mk 8:11-12; Lk 11:29; Jn 4:48).

But they are "signs of the Kingdom," indicating to those who have the eyes to see that the saving power of God is already at work among them. The healings of Jesus are signs that the Kingdom of God is dawning (Mt 11:2-6); his exorcisms, signs that Satan's oppressive rule is coming to an end (Mt 12:25-29).[10] And this too is how Jesus understands his table fellowship with "tax collectors and sinners" (Mk 2:15; Lk 15:1). For such "communion" with the untouchables of his society, so scandalous to his pious contemporaries, was a proclamation in action, powerfully announcing the wholly unconditioned character of the Father's love (cf. Mt 6:45).

Word and deed thus go hand in hand in the teaching of Jesus, and one would be quite unimaginable without the other. In the concrete, action-oriented biblical culture to which Jesus belonged, words without deeds to "fulfill" them, would have been as empty as deeds without words to expound their meaning. The sharp dichotomies between spirit and matter, soul and body, word and action, preaching and social concern—so characteristic of the post-Cartesian West, and indeed of post-Upanishadic India—would have made little sense to Jesus, whose own teaching avoided both the "verbalism" of the unauthentic word unable to transform reality and the "activism" of frenzied activity deprived of reflection.[11] Indeed his pedagogy is an authentic example of the fine blend of action and reflection which Paulo Freire calls *praxis,* reminding us:

> Within the word we find two dimensions, reflection and action, in such radical interaction that if one is sacrificed—even in part—the other immediately suffers. There is no true word that is not at the same time a praxis. Thus, to speak a true word is to transform the world.[12]

This is profoundly true of the word spoken by Jesus.

2. TEACHING WITH AUTHORITY

The effectiveness of the word spoken by Jesus—always a performative word or a language event which does not merely inform about, but which *transforms* reality—derives ultimately from the authority (*exousia*) with which it is spoken. "Authority" is a conspicuous feature of the teaching of Jesus as reported in the Gospels. The crowds who hear him (whether in the synagogue at Capernaum witnessing his first miracle, as in Mark; or on the "mountain" in Galilee, listening to his first sermon, as in Matthew) are "astonished at his teaching, for he taught them as one having authority, and not as the scribes" (Mk 1:22; Mt 7:29).

This is an astonishing comment; for the scribes at the time of Jesus were not without considerable authority of their own. They belonged to one of the three dominant classes of the Jewish society of the time, rivaling and eventually superseding both the priestly aristocracy (the "chief priests"), and the lay nobility (the "elders") in their claim to influence and power.[13] Their influence derived not from their birth (as did that of the priestly aristocracy, who belonged to one or other of the four high-priestly families), nor from the wealth they could command (as did that of the "elders," who were either large rural landowners or merchant princes from Jerusalem), but from their learning. "It was knowledge alone," reports Joachim Jeremias, "that gave power to the scribes."[14] For though some scribes, like the historian Josephus, may have belonged to the priestly aristocracy, or like Johanan ben Zakkai the restorer of Judaism after the debacle of 70 C.E., may have been prosperous merchants, most came "from the unprivileged part of the population." They were largely artisans, like Shammai, a carpenter, or Saul a tent-maker—that is, manual workers who owned the tools of their trade and so would belong to what we would call today the *petite bourgeoisie.* Occasionally they were even, like the great Rabbi Hillel, who, it is said, earned his keep as a day laborer, "proletarians," owning no means of production at all.[15]

Yet the scribes enjoyed great authority because of their learning—that is, because of their specialized and even esoteric knowledge of the Torah and of the oral traditions, both legal (*halakhah*) and religious (*haggadah*), which had grown up around it.[16] Such knowledge, acquired through long years of assiduous discipleship in the scribal schools, and institutionally recognized by an "ordination" (*sĕmîkâ*), which made them "ordained scholars" (*ḥăkāmîm*), equipped the scribes for "key positions in the administration of justice, in government and in education," in a society which was still strongly theocratic;[17] and set them up before the people as prestigious religious leaders with special competence in religious affairs.

How, then, could it be said that Jesus taught "with authority and not as the scribes"? Obviously the point being made is not that Jesus had authority (for the scribes had authority too), but that his authority was of a very different kind from that exhibited by the scribes.

A Revolutionary Authority

The scribes had authority as custodians of an authoritative tradition, which they had been trained to master, to hand down with meticulous fidelity, and to defend with well-honed arguments derived from the Torah through well-established traditional methods of interpretation. Their authority, to use Max Weber's convenient classification, was "legal." It rested "on a belief in the 'legality' of patterns of normative rules and the right of those elevated to authority under such rules to issue commands."[18] Scribal authority was thus strictly institutional.

The authority of Jesus was of a very different kind. For Jesus had no official standing in his society. He did not command the power of wealth (he was a "wandering charismatic" with "nowhere to lay his head" [Mt 8:20]);[19] he was academically unschooled (*mē memathēkōs*, untrained in the scribal schools as Jn 7:15 says of him);[20] he was cultically incompetent, since he was not born into a priestly family (Mt 1:1-17). Thoroughly "lay" (religiously and academically) by birth and by upbringing, Jesus accentuates his institutional powerlessness by opting out of the structures of his society and becoming a "wandering charismatic." He thus de-classes himself, leaving the ranks of the *petite bourgeoisie* into which he was born for those of the property-less proletariat. His authority, then, derives not from the traditional institutions of his society, but from his own personal charisma. It is an almost perfect example of what Max Weber calls "charismatic authority," which rests on "devotion to the specific and exceptional sanctity, heroism or exemplary character of an individual person, and of the normative patterns or order revealed or ordained by him."[21]

More precisely, the charismatic authority of Jesus is "prophetic," similar to that of the Old Testament prophets. His charisma, like theirs, is based not on personal magnetism but on the possession of the "spirit." It derives, that is, from a profound religious vocation experience, in which "a man is grasped by God, who authorizes him to be his messenger and preacher and speaks through him."[22] Jesus probably had such a call experience at his baptism by John (Mk

1:9-11). For when he is asked by "the chief priests and the scribes and the elders" (representatives, that is, of the Sanhedrin, the supreme religious authority of the Judaism of his time) to legitimate his teaching ("by what authority do you do these things or who gave you the authority to do them?"), Jesus replies by referring them to his baptism by John: "the baptism of John, was it from heaven or from men?" (Mk 11:27-33). This is not an attempt to evade the issue by posing an embarrassing question, which, by reducing his questioners to silence, will relieve Jesus of the need for replying. It is a genuine answer to a question legitimately posed by the religious authorities of his people. For by referring to the baptism of John, Jesus is really asking official Judaism whether it is prepared to recognize extra-institutional, prophetic authority, such as is claimed by John (Mk 11:32) and by himself; and he is probably pointing to his baptism by John as the moment of his prophetic calling.

Joachim Jeremias has argued, quite plausibly, that the baptism of Jesus by John was the occasion for his "*Abba* experience"—the overwhelming experience of God as unconditional love, which was to be the basis of Jesus' life and the ground of his mission.[23] For all Jesus' preaching, teaching, and healing was centered on the Kingdom of God; and the Kingdom (God's definitive saving action) comes precisely in this revelation of his unconditional love. The baptism of Jesus, his act of submission to the Baptist and of identification with sinful humanity,[24] thus becomes the occasion for a "foundational" experience, homologous to the "enlightenment" of the Buddha under the boddhi tree, or the call experience of the Old Testament prophets. Here Jesus becomes "conscious of being authorized to communicate God's revelation, because God had made himself known to him as Father."[25] The authority of Jesus is ultimately rooted in this experience of God as *Abba.*

Such charismatic authority is always innovative. "The genuine prophet," notes Max Weber, "like the genuine military leader and every true leader in this sense, preaches, creates, or demands *new* obligations."[26] Indeed the whole point of charismatic leadership (at least in the biblical tradition) is that it is summoned for tasks which the necessarily conservative institution cannot possibly undertake. Charismatic leaders are raised up ("called") to initiate new moments in salvation history (Abraham, Moses); to counter new threats (Gideon); to renew a people grown slack in their observance of the Covenant, or tepid in their single-minded devotion to the Covenant God (Amos, Isaiah, Jeremiah).[27] Charismatic authority is thus extra-institutional, and as such inevitably attracts the hostility of the institution. The prophet becomes an "authorized transgressor." His teaching (like the teaching of Jesus) is inevitably sensed as subversion. "Within the sphere of its claims," Max Weber reminds us, "charismatic authority repudiates the past, and is in this sense a specifically revolutionary force."[28] How true this is of the authority of Jesus, with his radical critique of law and cult (Mk 2:23-28; 7:1-23), his revolutionary image of God (Lk 15:1-32), his new and utterly radical demands on his followers (Mt 5:21-48; Lk 10:25-27), needs no elaboration.

A Liberative Authority

But if charismatic authority is revolutionary vis-à-vis the larger society in which the charismatic group exists, it tends to be paternalistic and authoritarian within the limits of the group. The charismatic leader, because of his strongly personal charisma, tends to exercise absolute personal control over his followers. This is strikingly evident in the *guruvada* of Hinduism, which identifies the *guru* with the deity itself, and calls for the total surrender of the disciple to the Master. "The *guru is* Brahman, the *guru is* Vishnu, the *guru is* the Lord Achutya; greater than the *guru* there is no one whatsoever in all the three worlds," intones the *Yogashikopanishad,* one of 108 Upanishads which are part of the official religious literature of Hinduism;[29] so that, as Bhagawan Shree Rajneesh reminds us, "struggle is not the key with the Master, surrender is the key."[30]

The implications of such a master-disciple relationship have been spelled out by Arun Shourie in his sharp critique of Hinduism:

> The basic propositions here are threefold: first, that I do not have the capacity to find my own way as my current capacities and attainments are limited; second, that it is, therefore, imperative that I should follow the prescriptions of another; and, third, that in order to be able to do so I must completely surrender myself to him, in particular, that I should completely delegate my thinking function to him.[31]

How similar these are to the presuppositions of what Paulo Freire has called the "banking system of education" is obvious. For here too:

> Education becomes an act of depositing, in which the students are the depositories and the teacher is the depositer. Instead of communicating the teacher issues communiques, and "makes deposits" which the students patiently receive, memorize, and repeat. . . . Knowledge is a gift bestowed by those who consider themselves knowledgeable upon those whom they consider to know nothing. . . . The teacher presents himself to his students as their necessary opposite; by considering their ignorance as absolute, he justified his own existence.[32]

Obviously teaching of this sort can scarcely be liberative. Instead it belongs, as Paulo Freire would say, to "the ideology of oppression"[33] and is, as Arun Shourie has convincingly demonstrated, an effective means of the "repressive socialization" which creates servile subjects for authoritarian rulers. For "an individual who has internalized these notions and has conditioned himself to such abject acceptance of authority in the spiritual realm shall be equally servile to authority in the temporal realm."[34]

Is the teaching of Jesus, which issues from his charismatic authority, of this kind? There is no doubt that we find in it apodictical statements of great power

(Mt 5:21-47; Lk 22:23-26), uttered with an authority ("but I say unto you"; "it shall not be so among you") that goes well beyond the authority of the Old Testament prophets speaking in the name of Yahweh ("thus says the Lord"). It is certain too that Jesus demanded from his followers an unswerving fidelity to his person, outweighing all other human values and ties, a demand quite unparalleled in the history of his people (Mt 10:37 = Lk 14:25-26). It is also regrettably true that the teachings of Jesus have been used extensively by the Christian community as a means of repressive socialization; for history shows clearly enough how frequently the Gospels have been invoked to legitimize feudal oppression, colonial exploitation, anti-Semitism, and religious persecution of every kind. Freedom has scarcely been a value greatly cherished by the Christian churches! But it *was* a value for Jesus—precisely because his teaching was not so much the imparting of "sound doctrine" as the communication of a message of love. But there can be no love without freedom—that is why there is always a dialogical element in the teaching of Jesus, a profound respect for the interlocutor, rare in the utterances of charismatic leaders. This appears strikingly in the characteristic form that Jesus chose for his teaching—his parables.

3. TEACHING IN PARABLES

The parables of Jesus are possibly the most authentic form of his teaching that we possess: so strikingly personal in their style that "we stand right before Jesus when reading his parables."[35] Not only do the parables bring us right back to the Jesus of history; they also reveal to us a basic dimension of all his teaching. For as Mark tells us in his concluding comment to the parable discourse, "with many such parables he spoke the word to them, as they were able to hear it; he did not speak to them without a parable, but privately to his own disciples he explained everything" (Mk 4:33-34). Now Mark obviously cannot mean that Jesus did not use other, non-parabolic forms of discourses in addressing the crowds. What he is saying is that there is a "parabolic" character to all Jesus' public teaching. By this Mark probably meant that the teaching of Jesus is always "mysterious revelation," a disclosure of "the secret" (Mt 4:11) that the Kingdom of God comes not in power but in lowliness and suffering.[36] But the parabolic character of the teaching of Jesus, rightly pointed out by Mark, can also be understood differently. It means, I suggest, that all the teachings of Jesus, his words as well as his deeds, are, like the parables, dialogical and critical: they involve the listener in creative response, and they put into question the accepted values of his "world."

A Dialogical Teaching

The parables of Jesus are dialogical. They do not convey information, offer prescriptions, or give lessons to a passive and receptive listener. Instead by telling a "shocking" story, they provoke and tease the listener into a radically new insight into his own situation, which the parable has put before him in story form. The way this happens is beautifully brought out in the parable which the prophet Nathan tells David in 2 Sam 12:1-7, an unusually clear example of the way in which parables work. Nathan's story of a rich man, who, though owning "very many flocks and herds," yet steals the "one little ewe-lamb" which his poor neighbor possesses in order to feed the unexpected guest who has arrived at his place, provokes David to violent anger. "As the Lord lives," cries the king, "the man who has done this deserves to die"—only to be told with shattering effect: "You are the man." By narrating David's "theft" of Uriah's wife figuratively, in parable form, Nathan is thus able to get David to "see" his situation for what it is. He is made aware of his sin—personally and not just notionally, at gut-level and not just in the head. A direct confrontation, say a moralizing sermon by Nathan, full of righteous indignation, would never have achieved this. It would only have made David more defensive. But Nathan's parable is able to bring David to a new understanding of his situation, and to induce him to pass a judgment on it. And it is this judgment that provides the "lesson" of the parable and completes it.

The parables of Jesus are like that. They too are not "moral stories" teaching lessons. Sayings of Jesus have indeed been added to the Gospel parables to serve as lessons (cf. the long list of such sayings added to the parable of the Dishonest Steward in Lk 16:9-13); but these are additions of the early Christian tradition and not part of the parables as spoken by Jesus. In its original form, every parable of Jesus is a story which "remains 'suspended' . . . so long as the listener has not decided for or against the new possibilities for living opened up in it."[37] It is the listener who must supply the "lesson" as he hears the parable and feels it strike home. His reaction is integral to the parable, for without it the parable would remain incomplete. It takes two to make a parable: for the parable is essentially an open-ended, dialogical form.

For all its authority, then, the teaching of Jesus is not authoritarian. His pedagogy is neither indoctrination nor propaganda. Jesus, in his parables, does not attempt to inform or persuade: he tries only to make his listeners aware. The parables of Jesus are in fact a form of what Paulo Freire has called "conscientization."[38]

Critical Teaching

The awareness to which the parables of Jesus provoke the listener is a critical awareness; for the parable, as John Dominic Crossan has brilliantly demonstrated, is essentially a subversive form. As such, the parable is the "binary opposite" of another kind of symbolic story, the myth. For where myth establishes and sustains a "world" (that is, a particular way of structuring and interpreting reality), parable subverts it.[39]

The parables of Jesus are, in fact, continually subverting the world of his listeners: inverting their expectations, upsetting their accepted attitudes and values. In them laborers are paid the same wage for unequal hours of work (Mt 20:1-15); respectable law-abiding people are said to be less acceptable to God than dishonest "tax collectors" and shameless "sinners" (Lk 18:9-14; Mt 21:31); priests dedicated to God's service callously ignore a wounded man lying on the road, while a half-pagan Samaritan cares for him (Lk 10:29-37); gentiles are invited to the messianic banquet from which the "children of the Kingdom" are excluded (Mt 8:11-12; 22:1-10). Truly the listener's "world" is turned upside-down. Such subversion, Crossan suggests, opens the listener to the action of God (the Kingdom) by upsetting the "certain certainties" on which he runs his self-sufficient and self-centered life. It confronts him with "transcendence."

> The parables of Jesus are *not* historical allegories telling us how God acts with mankind; neither are they moral example stories telling us how to act before God and towards one another. They are stories which shatter the deep structure of our accepted world and thereby render clear and evident to us the relativity of the story itself. They remove our defenses and make us vulnerable to God. It is only in such experiences that God can teach us, and only in such moments does the Kingdom of God arrive. My own term for this relationship is *transcendence*.[40]

But this, I suspect, is too narrow a way of understanding the parables of Jesus. There is more to them, namely, than merely the communication of an individual experience of transcendence.[41] For there is a positive side to the parables underlying their negative function of subversion. The parables of Jesus subvert our "world," only because they point (figuratively, metaphorically, in a glass, darkly) to another "world," where relationships are structured not by ambition, greed, and selfishness, but by love.

All education, it has been said, is either education for domestication or for freedom.[42] That the non-elitist, transforming, prophetic, dialogical, and critical pedagogy of Jesus was highly liberative is evident. Certainly his first followers experienced it as such. "Christ has set us free in order that we might remain free," exclaims Paul in his letter to the Galatians (5:1)—and we can still catch in this exultant cry the joyful rush of freedom that must have been experienced by those who were exposed to the liberative pedagogy of Jesus. This pedagogy was liberative in a double way. As a non-elitist, dialogical teaching, it liberated people by making them conscious of their worth as children of the one Father in heaven (Mt 6:9), whose value derived not from personal ability or social status but from the inalienable reality of the Father's love (Mt 6:26; 18:10-14). And as prophetic and critical teaching it freed them from the manipulative myths which legitimized their oppressive and alienating society. Any pedagogy that claims to be Christian, must be liberative in this double sense.

NOTES

1. Raymond E. Brown, *The Gospel According to John X-XII,* Anchor Bible 29A (New York: Doubleday, 1966), xlvii-li.

2. Soares-Prabhu, "Are the Gospels Historical," *Clergy Monthly* 38 (1974): 112-24; 163-72, and in *Biblical Theology for India,* 4:105-25.

3. See Günther Bornkamm, *Jesus of Nazareth* (London: Hodder & Stoughton, 1960), 25-26; Eduard Schweizer, *Jesus* (London: SCM Press, 1971), 11-12; C. H. Dodd, *The Founder of Christianity* (London: Collins/Fontana, 1973), 47-48.

4. Geza Vermes, *Jesus the Jew* (London: Collins/Fontana, 1976), 26-27.

5. Ibid.

6. Geoffrey de Ste Croix, "Early Christian Attitudes to Property and Slavery," in *Church Society and Politics,* ed. Derek Baker (Oxford: Blackwell, 1975), 3. See also Gerd Theissen, *The First Followers of Jesus: The Sociology of Early Palestinian Christianity* (London: SCM Press, 1978), 47-48.

7. So Shankaracharya commenting on the first of the Brahma Sūtras of Bādarāyana; see Klaus Klostermeier, *Kristvidya* (Bangalore: Christian Institute for the Study of Religion and Society, 1967), 11-16, for the prerequisite attitudes demanded by the various schools of Hinduism.

8. This has been well understood by Bhagawan Shree Rajneesh, who with much insight contrasts Jesus' way of love, open to "ordinary people," with the Buddha's way of awareness, accessible only to an intellectual elite. See his *I Say Unto You: Talks on the Sayings of Jesus,* vol. 1 (Poona: Rajneesh Foundation, 1980), 54-55.

9. Rudolf Pesch, *Das Markusevangelium I,* Herders theologischer Kommentar zum Neuen Testament (Freiburg: Herder, 1976), 124.

10. Soares-Prabhu, "The Miracles of Jesus Today," *Jeevadhara* 5 (1975): 189-204 (chapter 8 in this volume).

11. See Paulo Freire, *Pedagogy of the Oppressed* (Harmondsworth: Penguin Books, 1972), 60.

12. Ibid. Praxis is defined by Freire as "the action and reflection of men upon their world in order to transform it" (ibid., 52).

13. Joachim Jeremias, *Jerusalem in the Time of Jesus* (London: SCM Press, 1969), 233.

14. Ibid., 234.

15. Ibid., 233-34.

16. Ibid., 237.

17. Ibid., 235-36. See also Emil Schürer, *The History of the Jewish People in the Age of Jesus Christ.* Vols. 1 and 2 revised and edited by Geza Vermes et al. (Edinburgh: T & T Clark, 1979), 2:325-36.

18. Max Weber, *The Theory of Social and Economic Organization,* ed. Talcott Parsons (New York: Free Press, 1964), 328.

19. The expression is from Theissen (*First Followers of Jesus*), where it is used to describe the itinerant prophets of early Christianity, who together with their sympathizers in various local communities determined the shape of the "Jesus movement." Jesus' connection with charismatic Judaism is discussed by Vermes, *Jesus the Jew,* 78-82.

20. Jeremias, *Jerusalem in the Time of Jesus,* 236.

21. Weber, *Theory of Social and Economic Organization,* 328. Note also the comment of Howard Clark Kee in his *Community of the New Age: Studies in Mark's Gospel*

(London: SCM Press, 1977), 117: "Mark's favourite designation for Jesus is teacher. . . . Yet Jesus does not appear as a rabbinic interpreter of the scriptures, but as a charismatic, divinely authorized spokesman for God." Scribal features in the Gospel portrayal of Jesus come from the early Church, particularly from Matthew. For as Werner Kelber has pointed out: "Insofar as the gospels depict Jesus as a prophetic, eschatological teacher, moving from one place to another and surrounded by listeners and engaged in debate, they will have retained a genuine feature of the local performer. The specifically scribal, rabbinic model of Jesus as the authoritative interpreter of the Torah, on the other hand, was clearly shaped by the scribal interests of Matthew and the Matthean school tradition" (Werner H. Kelber, "Mark and Oral Tradition," *Semeia* 16 [1980]: 23).

22. Joachim Jeremias, *New Testament Theology,* vol. 1 (London: SCM Press, 1971), 52.

23. Ibid., 49-68. This is not to deny that Jesus may have been conscious of a special relationship to the Father even before his baptism. Without entering into the vexed question of his "messianic consciousness" (a question which, in any case, cannot be answered historically, through a critical study of the Gospel texts), I would suggest that the baptism of Jesus was the occasion of an extraordinary religious experience—one that was not so much "Christological" (i.e., a discovery of identity) as "prophetic" (i.e., a call to mission). See Soares-Prabhu, "Jesus and the Spirit in the Synoptic Gospels," *Bible Bhashyam* 2 (1976): 106-8, and in *A Biblical Theology for India,* Collected Writings of George M. Soares-Prabhu, S.J., vol. 2, ed. Scaria Kuthirakkattel, 126-40. See chapter one of this volume. James D. G. Dunn, *Baptism in the Holy Spirit* (London: SCM Press, 1970), 26-28.

24. On the significance of this gesture of Jesus for Asian Christianity, see the quite extraordinarily insightful article of Aloysius Pieris, "Monastic Poverty in the Asian Setting," *Dialogue* 7 (1980): 104-18, esp. 113-15.

25. Jeremias, *New Testament Theology,* 68.

26. Weber, *Theory of Social and Economic Organization,* 361.

27. Soares-Prabhu, "The Priesthood as a Call in the Old Testament," in *Vocation: God's Call to Man*, ed. Thomas Thyparambil (Poona: National Vocation Service Centre, 1975), 53-70.

28. Weber, *Theory of Social and Economic Organization,* 361-62.

29. Quoted in Arun Shourie, *Hinduism: Essence and Consequence* (Ghaziabad: Vikas, 1979), 356-57.

30. Bhagawan Shree Rajneesh, *The Mustard Seed: Discourses on the Sayings of Jesus Taken from the Gospel According to Thomas* (Poona: Rajneesh Foundation, 1975), 8.

31. Shourie, *Hinduism,* 372.

32. Freire, *Pedagogy of the Oppressed,* 46.

33. Ibid.

34. Shourie, *Hinduism,* 372.

35. Joachim Jeremias, *The Parables of Jesus* (London: SCM Press, 1972), 12.

36. Madeleine Boucher, *The Mysterious Parable, Catholic Biblical Quarterly* Monograph Series 6 (Washington, D.C.: Catholic Biblical Association, 1977), 80-84.

37. Edward Schillebeeckx, *Jesus: An Experiment in Christology* (London: Collins, 1979), 158.

38. For a systematic examination of the term "conscientization," see Paulo Freire, *Cultural Action for Freedom* (Harmondsworth: Penguin Books, 1972), 51-83; and for an earlier and simpler presentation, see his *Education for Critical Consciousness* (New York: Seabury Press, 1973), 3-58. Obviously the parables of Jesus are not "conscientization" in

the precise and technical sense defined by Freire, but in the more general and popular meaning of the word, as used for any form of "awareness raising." There are striking similarities between the teaching of Jesus and the pedagogy of the oppressed proposed by Freire, and these merit further study. Freire's *Pedagogy of the Oppressed* strikes me as being, in its presuppositions, one of the most "Christian" books I have read.

39. John Dominic Crossan, *The Dark Interval* (Niles, Ill.: Argus Communications, 1975), 54-62. A truly beautiful little book!

40. Ibid., 121-22.

41. Boucher (*Mysterious Parable,* 14-25) rightly warns against Crossan's overnarrow understanding of the parable as a literary form. To this one might add a warning against Crossan's existentialist reductionism (common in Western exegesis since Bultmann), which tends to reduce the content of Jesus' proclamation (the "Kingdom") to individual decision alone.

42. João da Veiga Coutinho, in his Preface to Freire, *Cultural Action,* 9, which correctly proposes this as the basic thesis of Paulo Freire.

3

JESUS THE PROPHET

No one formula can comprehend adequately the mystery of Jesus, for his words and deeds refuse to be reduced to the stereotype of any conventional category. Still, the term "prophet" describes adequately enough the Jesus of history, Jesus as he must have appeared to his contemporaries. True, Jesus in the Gospels receives the courtesy title of "Rabbi" (Mk 9:5; 11:21; 14:45), uses rabbinic forms of teaching (cf. the parables of Mt 13), engages in rabbinic discussions (cf. the controversies of Mk 2:1-3:6; 12:13-37), interprets the Law as a rabbi (cf. the antitheses of Mt 5:21-47), and gathers disciples to instruct them as the rabbis were wont to do (Mk 1:16-20; 6:7-11).[1] But his power-filled words and deeds are far more reminiscent of the great prophets of ancient Israel than of the hair-splitting "canon lawyers" of the scribal schools of his day.

For when Jesus taught, he taught "as one having authority and not as their scribes" (Mt 7:28). Indeed, the absolute assurance of his "amen, amen I say to you" goes well beyond not only the "it is written" of the scribes, but even the "thus says the Lord" of the Old Testament prophets. It is not canonical Scripture, nor even the consciousness of being the spirit-filled mouthpiece of the Lord, that is the source of Jesus' authoritative utterance, but his own innate sense of authority and mission. The burden of this authoritative teaching, too, is not the casuistic interpretation of the Law, but the prophetic proclamation of imminent salvation ("The Kingdom of God is at hand"), with its call to urgent and radical decision ("Be converted and believe in the good news"). And Jesus proclaims this coming of the Kingdom not in words alone, but in "mighty deeds," in exorcisms which signal the end of Satan's domination (Mt 12:27) and in healings which announce the dawning of God's Reign (Mt 11:2-6), deeds that are not unlike those wrought by the great "men of God" (Elijah and Elisha) who stand at the beginnings of Israel's prophecy.[2] Jesus resorts too, like the classical book-prophets of Israel (Isaiah, Jeremiah, Ezekiel) to symbolic actions, acted parables

---

This article first appeared in *Jeevadhara* 4 (1974): 206-17.

(such as the triumphal entry into Jerusalem in Mk 11:1-10, or the cursing of the fig tree in Mk 11:12-14, 20-23), which powerfully drive home his message.[3] Neither a priest (for, unlike John the Baptist, he was not born into a priestly family), nor a scribe (for, unlike Paul, he was not brought up in a scribal school), Jesus is most emphatically a prophet, a spirit-filled man (Mk 1:9-11), "mighty in deed and word" (Lk 24:19), called out of the anonymity of a wholly unpretentious "lay" existence (Mk 6:3) to speak (in an utterly unique and authoritative way) *for* God and to announce his salvation.

It is not surprising, then, that the "crowds" recognize Jesus as a prophet (Mk 6:15; Mt 21:11; Lk 7:16)—indeed as *the* prophet, that is, as the eschatological *avatār* of Moses promised in Deut 18:15 (Jn 6:14). His disciples too acknowledge him as one (Lk 24:19); and Jesus himself twice at least compares his destiny to that of a prophet, for like a prophet he is "not without honor except in his own country" (Mk 6:4); and he too must die in Jerusalem like a prophet (Lk 13:33).

THE PROPHET IN ISRAEL

Old Testament prophecy offers thus a convenient and illuminating model for understanding the ministry of Jesus. What then are the characteristic elements of this model? In complementary contrast to the institutional offices of priest and king (both of which are not original to Israel but were introduced more or less ready-made from outside),[4] the Old Testament prophet is a *charismatic* figure. For while priesthood and kingship are stable structures into which persons are inducted by "ordination" or birth, prophetism is a dynamic function specific (in its Old Testament form) to Israel, to which an individual is summoned by a special call.[5] This special call is an essential part of the prophet's role—necessarily so, because the prophet is an extra-institutional figure, summoned to special tasks unforeseen by and beyond the competence of the traditional institutional structures of his community. He must communicate a new understanding of God, spell out the new demands posed by the changed circumstances of history, "renew" a people grown slack in their observance of the covenant stipulations, or lukewarm in their trust in the covenant God. The prophet is thus God's instrument for the renewal of the institution. He is the goad which prods the people of God, to keep it moving in dynamic response to the changing situations of history and to bring it back to the right path in case it has strayed. He is God's answer to the bureaucratic routinization that is the occupational disease of every institution. He is God's agent of permanent revolution. He is the assertion of the absolute sovereignty of God who sits in judgment over every institution, even his own, and will allow no structure, no matter how sacred, to usurp the place which belongs to him alone.[6]

Because of this his extra- (and so inevitably anti-) institutional role, the prophet is always a figure of conflict. Unlike the false prophets of peace who, belonging to the coteries of the court and the Temple, are the professional supporters of the status quo, complacently proclaiming (in obstinate blindness to the crises brewing) "'peace, peace,' when there is no peace" (Jer 6:14; cf. also 1 Kgs 22:11; Jer 14:13; 23:16; Ezek 13:16; Mic 3:5), the true prophets of Yahweh are predominantly prophets of judgment.[7] They disturb, threaten, denounce, challenge, condemn. Indeed a characteristic, if not *the* characteristic, form of prophetic utterance is the *rîb*, the courtroom arraignment in which the prophet as God's advocate addresses a charge sheet against his sin-laden people (cf. Is 1:2-3; Jer 2:4-13; Mic 6:1-8).[8]

Seared by his experience of the unutterable holiness of God, and obsessed by the need for radical conversion that this holiness demands from everyone who encounters it (Is 6:1-6), the prophet becomes the tireless champion of God's absolute sovereignty, summoning his community to an unconditional (almost foolhardy!) trust in and an absolute commitment to its God. Such trust and commitment must show themselves in an inner uprightness and a social concern that go well beyond the formal pieties of ritual and law. So the prophets reject a cult in which ritual has become a substitute for uprightness of life (Is 1:10-17; Amos 5:21-24). They demand a real conversion of heart (Jer 31:31f; Ezek 36:27; Hos 2:14). They will have nothing to do with a political prudence that refuses to risk all on the covenant fidelity of God alone (Is 8:5-8; 30:1-7). They denounce every form of exploitation (Amos 4:1-3; 8:4-9) and demand a radical concern for the defenseless and the needy (Is 58:6-12), because the God they encountered and in whose name they speak is a God who "executes justice" for the widow, the orphan, and the refugee (Deut 10:17; Ps 68:5), and "saves all the oppressed of the earth" (Ps 76:9; 103:6; 146:7-10).

THE PROPHETIC ROLE OF JESUS

Jesus stands well within this prophetic tradition. Indeed he brings this tradition to its apogee, embodying the values of Old Testament prophetism in an altogether unique way. Like the prophets of Israel, he too is overwhelmed by the reality of God and the demands that this makes upon the man who encounters it. Indeed he proclaims this with a special urgency, because he is aware that in him the "Kingdom," God's definitive offer of salvation, has come, precipitating a crisis in the lives of men and summoning them to a most radical decision. "The time is fulfilled, and the Kingdom of God is at hand; repent and believe in the Gospel," says Mark (1:15), summarizing accurately, though in the language of the early Church, the burden of Jesus' preaching.[9] The time has come for the decisive intervention through which God will free the world from the forces of sin and death which hold it in their grip, and men must respond to this dramatic and urgent challenge by "repentance" (*metanoia*)—a word to be understood not in the Hellenistic sense of a feeling of remorse for one or other action, but in the Old Testament prophetic sense of a total turning (*sûb*) of the whole person towards God.

Such a total turning (conversion) demands the unreserved acknowledgment of God as God, and therefore as the one in whom alone we place our security and trust. It demands, too, a radical concern for our fellow men, because God is the creator who "claims his creation and therefore requires our unconditional love of our neighbour and our unqualified readiness to serve and forgive, because anything less means the ruin of every creature."[10] Obedience and love are thus the two coordinates of the eschatological existence lived and proclaimed by Jesus. On the first two commandments "depend all the law and the prophets" (Mt 22:40); and these commandments are "much more than all burnt-offerings and sacrifices" (Mk 12:33).

Both law and cult are thus overshadowed by love in the prophetic proclamation of Jesus. For not only does Jesus continue the prophetic protest against a cult that has become a mechanical ritual (Mt 9:13 = Hos 6:6), and a law that has degenerated into casuistic legalism (Mk 7:9-13), but he comes as the "eschatological alternative" which takes the place of law and cult. Salvation is now no longer the automatic outcome of the performance of prescribed rites, nor a merited reward for the faithful observance of the detailed prescription of the Law. It is a free gift from God to be accepted by faith in Jesus and shown forth in a life of love. It is in this sense that Jesus both fulfills (Mt 5:17-21) and at the same time abrogates (Rom 10:4; Heb 10:12) law and cult. That is to say, he relativizes them, subsuming them into a higher economy where law and cult have no independent value of their own, but are significant only as expressions of that inner attitude of obedience and concern in which man's true renewal consists.

JESUS AND THE CULT

Such relativizing is particularly evident in Jesus' attitude toward cult. "Within the holy Temple area, even within sight of the reeking altars themselves," writes E. Lohmeyer, commenting on Mk 12:33, "the complete overthrow of sacrifice and Temple is proclaimed. . . . Man does not require any particular holy sacrifice or mediation of priests, or Jewish nationalism; his relationship to God is determined not by what he gives to God at a holy place but by whether or not he loves God in his neighbour."[11]

God is therefore to be worshiped neither in Jerusalem nor on Gerizim, for the time has come "when true worshipers will worship the Father in spirit and truth" (Jn 4:23). The coming of Jesus has sacralized the cosmos, eliminating the distinction between the sacred and the profane. There are now no "holy" places (whether Jerusalem or Rome!) to which the presence of God is confined; no intrinsically "holy" things (whether trees, rivers, stones, medals, images) endowed with an innate sanctifying power. There are only saving *events* (the death and resurrection of Jesus), of which things and places can, when associated with the appropriate interpreting word, become the sacramental sign. Every place can now be the locus of a man's encounter with God; for it is the risen Christ, present everywhere, who is now "the 'place' where men of any time or place can at last be free of 'place' in their worship of God."[12]

And just as there are no "holy" places, there are now no "unclean" things. "Nothing that goes into a man from the outside [what he eats, drinks or touches] can defile him; it is the things that come out of him (his thoughts, words, and feelings) that defile him," says Jesus (Mk 7:15), abrogating all the rules of ritual purity at a stroke. He thus challenges not only "the letter of the Torah and the authority of Moses himself," but, beyond that, "the presuppositions of the whole cultic ritual of antiquity with its sacrifice and atonement."[13]

The Sabbath too is "made for man, not man for the Sabbath" (Mk 2:27)—a dramatic reversal which, once and for all, puts every institution in its place, subordinating it to man's welfare and demanding that it be a means of service and not an instrument of power. And because "the Son of Man has authority on earth to forgive sins" (Mk 2:6-10), reconciliation with God is now effected not through expiatory rites, but only through a personal faith encounter with the eschatological Lord.

Cult, then, is radically disempowered. "No prescribed ritual can any longer promise purity. No sacrifice can blot out sins, no holy Sabbath laws are any longer valid. . . ."[14] And so religious outcasts (the tax collectors and the prostitutes) enter the kingdom before the learned scribes and the pious Pharisees (Mt 21:31); and the disparaged gentiles come from the East and the West to enjoy the messianic banquet from which the "chosen people" are excluded (Mt 8:11-15). Truly, traditional thinking about cult is turned topsy-turvy by the prophetic preaching of Jesus. For with him "a silent step, tremendous in its silence, is taken from cultic constraint into the freedom of moral action."[15]

JESUS AND THE LAW

Jesus, who liberates us from the restraints of cult, sets us free from the burden of the Law as well. For though Jesus does not reject the Law outright, he does propose a new and liberating understanding of the Law which rids it of its oppressiveness. This new understanding is very different from that of rabbinic Judaism. For the Jewish contemporaries of Jesus, the Law was treasured as law (that is, as something decreed) and it was to be observed in a strictly formal way, that is, by the faithful execution of everything prescribed, *because it was prescribed.* The obligation of the Law and the merit that accrued from obeying it thus depended "no longer on content but on formal authority; not *what* was commanded determined the will of the person, but the fact *that* it was commanded."[16] And so innumerable scribes studied the Law night and day, hoping to find, through ingenious and often quite fanciful interpretation, rules of conduct for every possible situation in life; so that in everything he had to do, a man might have a prescribed alternative, by performing which he could practice obedience and earn merit.

Against this legalistic understanding of the Law Jesus reacts sharply. Not only does he reject the "tradition of the Elders," where this has distorted the spirit of the Law (Mk 7:9-13), but he even corrects the Torah itself, when he finds it an inadequate expression of what man really is (Mk 10:2-9). Because, for Jesus, the Law is not just positive law, a collection of unrelated and arbitrary precepts, which bind merely because they have been commanded; it is "natural" law, whose prescriptions grow organically out of the basic needs of human existence, and are binding because they encode the "natural" conduct of man as creature and child of God.

As such the Law is interpreted far more radically by Jesus than it is by the scribes. Its demands now reach down to the innermost intentions of the heart and do not stop short at the external performance of an action (Mt 5:21-47). They embrace a man's life in its entirety (all of it and everything in it), and not only those areas which can be brought under formulated law. And they require not just the avoidance of evil ("thou shalt not"), but a positive, never ending endeavor to do good, which reaches out to the perfection of God himself (Mt 5:48). Yet these demands are liberating demands. For they are not arbitrary norms imposed on man from outside, but merely spell out for him the implications of the obedience and the love which are his spontaneous response to the acceptance of the Gospel. The Law as radicalized by Jesus (as in the Sermon on the Mount) is therefore not meant to be a collection of decrees telling us to do this or that; it is meant, rather, to be a picture of what we potentially are, what we should be, what we shall become, if only we surrender to the transforming spirit of Jesus. The law of Jesus, then, does not constrain our spirit, but invites us to grow in love. For love is ultimately the essence of the Law, as it is of our being. And all the demands of Jesus come down eventually to this one demand: that a man give himself away wholly in love, so that by losing his life he may truly find it (Mt 10:39).

So we are not to worry anxiously about the future, piling up treasures on earth (Mt 6:19) or merit in heaven; and striving desperately to keep our record clean, so that, like the one-talent servant in the parable (Mt 25:14-30) we might be "safe" before an exacting God. That way leads to the scrupulosity and self-righteousness that are the inevitable pathologies of legalism. Rather, the law of Jesus invites us to confront the future with the simplicity and confidence of a child (Mt 18:2-4), fully conscious of our sinfulness and need, but with the joyous assurance that we have indeed been forgiven. For the God of Jesus is not the law-giving Judge who remorselessly metes out reward and punishment, according to the merits and demerits we have acquired by our observance or infringement of each tiny precept of the Law. He is *Abba*, our dear Father, who invites (and enables) us to love him and to live according to that love (Lk 15:11-32). Love wholly casts out fear, in Jesus' understanding of the Law.

JESUS AND HIS COMMUNITY

The prophetic preaching of Jesus leads to the formation of a community of disciples, who gather around him in "concentric circles" by responding to his proclamation of the kingdom through conversion and faith.[17] Jesus calls this community (the germ of the post-Easter Church) his "little flock" (Lk 12:32), and so sees it as the "faithful remnant" spoken of by the prophets as those who in the "last days" are to receive the salvation promised to Israel (Is 10:20f; Jer 31:7; Mic 5:7-15).

Because it grows up around Jesus, who comes as the "eschatological alternative" to Law and cult, this new community of the last days is not distinguished primarily by a new law or a new cult. Indeed Jesus and his disciples, and even the post-Easter Palestinian church until its expulsion from the Synagogue toward the end of the first century C.E., continue to live as practicing Jews. What distinguishes them is not a new institution but a new spirit: their faith in Jesus and the spirit of openness, love, and hope which grows out of this faith.

For the Jesus community, unlike other Jewish groups of its time (like the Pharisees or the sectarians of Qumran), is an open community. It is not a closed group restricted to the pious and the respectable, but it reaches out to the needy (the poor, the weeping, the hungry of Lk 6:20f), to the socially outcast (the tax collectors and sinners of Mk 2:15), and to the religiously ignorant (the "little ones" of Mt 11:25). So the community places its trust not in money, power, or prestige, but solely in God, out of whose love and truth it lives. It is therefore, necessarily, a community of truth, love, and service. Its language is not that of devious diplomacy of political compromise, but the plain "yes" and "no" which need no oath to guarantee their truth (Mt 5:33-37). Its heart is not set on money and the power that money brings, but on "the Kingdom of God and his saving love," for it knows that God is able and ready to care for its needs (Mt 6:33). It avoids all ostentation in its piety, knowing that it is not the applause of men but the approval of God that ultimately counts (Mt 6:1-18).

The community of Jesus is profoundly concerned about the total welfare of all men, for it knows that it is not the will of the Father that even one of his little ones should perish (Mt 18:14), and that help given to anyone in need is given to Jesus himself (Mt 25:31-46). It steadfastly refuses titles of honor (always subtly corrupting), conscious of itself as a brotherhood that has only one Father in heaven, and only one Master, the Christ (Mt 23:9-10). It looks on office as an occasion for service, not as a symbol of status or an instrument of power; for it always has before its eyes the overwhelming example of Jesus who came "not to be served but to serve, and to give his life as a ransom for many" (Mk 10:45).

The community of Jesus is not afraid to proclaim its scandalous Gospel that salvation is offered to the undeserving poor (Lk 6:20-21; Mt 11:5-6), in spite of the opposition that the revolutionary thrust of this message invariably arouses among the powerful and the unjust. For it is content to suffer persecution in imitation of its crucified and calumniated Lord (Mt 10:24-25). The community of

Jesus lives in the serene and unruffled hope of a final vindication, because it has the firm assurance that its risen Lord who has overcome death will be with it till the end of time (Mt 28:20).

This, then, is Jesus' vision of the community he came to found; this is Jesus' dream. And a strangely irrelevant dream it must appear to us! For with the stifling ritualism of our worship and the unbridled legalism of our canon law, with all our ecclesiastical careerism, our petty tyrannies, our delight in tinsel titles, and our unceasing clamor for our "minority" rights, with our large neglect of the poor, our shoddy compromises with the powerful, our connivance at injustice, and our worship of wealth, we are, surely, far indeed from the dream that Jesus dreamed. But this should not discourage us. Poised between the "already" of the resurrection and the "not yet" of the parousia, the Church of Jesus is a pilgrim church: a community not of the perfect but of those who are walking toward perfection. The important thing is that we do not stop walking, that we continue to be pulled by Jesus' dream.

And when our complacency and self-righteousness, our cynicism and our sloth, tempt us to put away the dream of Jesus, gently urging us to come to terms with hard reality, to lower our sights to a more realistic goal, then the voice of Jesus the prophet rings out, breaking into our apathy and summoning us to creative action. Jesus will not be satisfied with less than his dream and his urgent demands challenge us still. For Gospels are not dead stories of things long past, but the word of God addressing us here and now. And in them Jesus speaks not to Pharisees long since dead but to the Pharisee who lurks in each of our hearts. So the Gospels become the abiding conscience of the Church, and in them the voice of Jesus the prophet is raised to challenge us to a permanent revolution and to call us to renewal without end.

NOTES

1. See C. H. Dodd, "Jesus as Teacher and Prophet," in *Mysterium Christi: Christological Studies by British and German Theologians*, ed. G. K. Bell and A. Deissmann (London: Longmans, 1930), 53-66, esp. 53-55. But note that the Gospel conception of discipleship follows the prophetic rather than the rabbinic tradition. For, while the disciples of the rabbis choose the master they are to study under, and are his disciples only until they become rabbis themselves, the disciples of Jesus are called by him (Mk 1:16-20; 2:14) to a permanent relation of discipleship (Mt 28:19). The Synoptic stories of the calling of the first disciples (Mk 1:16-20 par) are, in fact, modeled closely on the Old Testament narrative of the calling of Elisha to his prophetic function (1 Kgs 19:19-21).

2. Compare, for instance, the resuscitation of the widow's son by Jesus in Lk 7:11-17 with the resuscitation of the son of the Shunammite woman by Elisha in 2 Kgs 4:32-37; and the feeding of the Five Thousand in Mk 6:34-43 with the feeding miracle worked by Elisha in 2 Kgs 4:42-44.

3. Cf. 2 Kgs 13:14-19; Isa 8:1-4; 20:1-5; Jer 27:1-7; Ezek 4:1-17; 5:1-12; Hos 1:2-8.

4. See W. Eichrodt, *Theology of the Old Testament*, vol. 1 (London: SCM Press, 1961), 392.

5. See Max Weber, *The Sociology of Religion* (London: Methuen, 1966), 46: ". . . the personal call is the decisive element distinguishing the prophet from the priest. The latter lays claim to authority by virtue of his service in a sacred tradition, while the prophet's claim is based on personal revelation and charisma."

6. On Old Testament prophetism, see especially Eichrodt, *Theology of the Old Testament,* 1:338-91; G. von Rad, *Old Testament Theology*, vol. 2 (Edinburgh: Oliver & Boyd, 1965), 50-125; L. Ramlot, "Prophétisme: La prophétie biblique," *Dictionnaire de la Bible, Supplement,* 14 vols. (Paris: Letouzey et Ané, 1971), 7:909-1222.

7. Ramlot, "Prophétisme," 1049-50.

8. See R. North, "Angel-Prophet or Satan-Prophet," *Zeitschrift für die alttestamentliche Wissenschaft* 82 (1970): 31-67; H. B. Huffmon, "The Covenant Lawsuit in the Prophets," *Journal of Biblical Literature* 78 (1959): 285-95.

9. See L. Legrand, *Good News and Witness* (Bangalore: Theological Publications in India, 1973), 13-25.

10. E. Käsemann, *Jesus Means Freedom* (London: SCM Press, 1969), 25.

11. E. Lohmeyer, *The Lord of the Temple* (Edinburgh: Oliver & Boyd, 1961), 47.

12. J. Marsh, *The Gospel of St. John* (London: SCM Press, 1968), 218.

13. E. Käsemann, quoted in G. Bornkamm, *Jesus of Nazareth* (London: Hodder & Stoughton, 1960), 98.

14. Lohmeyer, *Lord of the Temple,* 68.

15. Ibid., 72.

16. R. Bultmann, *Jesus and the Word* (London: Nicholson & Watson, 1935), 54.

17. J. Jeremias, *New Testament Theology*, vol. 1 (London: SCM Press, 1971), 167.

4

THE KINGDOM OF GOD

Jesus' Vision of a New Society

1. THE VISION OF A NEW SOCIETY
AND THE KINGDOM OF GOD

Did Jesus have a vision of a new society? Did his eschatological consciousness, dominated by the expectation of an imminent irruption of God's reign, allow him to envisage a new society at all? And if it did can we come to know this vision? Are not the Gospel records not of the experience of Jesus himself but of the faith of the early Church, expressing not his vision but their concerns? These difficulties have been formulated pointedly by Lucien Legrand in his contribution to the seminar. They reflect the skepticism that colors much of Western exegesis today about the possibility of deriving a relevant social ethic or of constructing an authentic "theology of liberation" from the teachings of Jesus.[1]

Ideological commitment is, after all, a moment in every hermeneutical circle; for there really is no value-free exegesis.[2] And how, except in terms of an ideologically colored interpretation, can one explain the emergence of a Christian theology, based ostensibly on the Bible, which encouraged colonial brigandage, tolerated for centuries the gruesome cruelties of slave trade, still functions (in some circles) to legitimize racial and sexist oppression, and lives everywhere in happy collaboration with the cultural imperialism and the neo-colonial exploitation of the Christian West?[3]

Research Seminar entitled "The Indian Church in the Struggle for a New Society" organized by and held at National Biblical, Catechetical, Liturgical Centre, Bangalore. The papers of this seminar were published in a book of the same title and edited by D.S. Amalorpavadass (Bangalore: National Biblical, Catechetical, Liturgical Centre, 1981), 579-608 and in *Theology of Liberation: An Indian Biblical Perspective*, Collected Writings of George M. Soares-Prabhu, S.J., vol. 4, ed. Francis X. D'Sa (Pune: Jnana-Deepa Vidyapeeth, 2001), 223-51.

It is significant too that theologians who find it so difficult to derive a new vision of society from the teachings of Jesus seem to have little trouble finding in them a ready-made model of the Church, finished down to its last little detail—where pope, bishop, male priest, deacon, primacy, infallibility, and seven sacraments are all seen as "immediately and directly" instituted by Christ. Yet the difficulties urged against Jesus' vision of a new society might with equal cogency be brought against Jesus' institution of the church! Of course theologians today, aware of the problems posed by the critical exegesis of the New Testament, interpret such "direct" institution broadly, understanding the hierarchical and sacramentally equipped church which emerged in the postapostolic age as continuous with the intention of Jesus, rather than formally founded by him.[4] Jesus, that is, had a *vision* of the church—at least implicitly, in that such a structured community was implied in the logic of the movement he began. But he gave no *blueprint* for the church. It was left to the spirit-filled post-Easter community to elaborate an appropriate structure (or structures, for several types of church order seem to have existed in New Testament times)[5] consonant with this vision. Just so, I suggest, Jesus had a vision, explicit or implicit, of a new society, though he offered no blueprint for it. It is for his followers to elaborate in the light of their particular historical experience the particular sociopolitical model or models in which this vision will be best realized.[6]

That the Gospels do not give us immediate access to the Jesus of history, or that this Jesus was a religious prophet rather than a social reformer, need not rule out the reality of this vision nor preclude the possibility of our discovering what it is. Few today would side with Bultmann in dismissing the sayings of Jesus that have come down to us as largely community creations.[7] A substantial number of them can be shown to be authentic,[8] and these allow us to reconstruct with some confidence—as even Bultmann admits[9]—the central message of Jesus (the "Kingdom of God"), the core experience from which this message derives (the "*Abba* experience"), the values that it announces (freedom, fellowship, and justice), and so, ultimately, the vision of a new human society that is implicit in it. For every religious experience does in fact include a vision of man and society— particularly when the experience occurs (as Jesus' did) in a tradition in which God is experienced as revealing himself in history, in which religious belonging is expressed in terms of a political category (the "covenant"), and in which salvation is expected not as an escape from material reality ("saving souls") but as the renewal of man in his totality ("the resurrection") and of the world he lives in ("a new heaven and a new earth").[10]

In the biblical world (indeed in all traditional societies), the nice distinctions between the religious and the sociopolitical that obtain in our neatly compartmentalized secular society have little relevance. The religious realm overflows into the sociopolitical. The king is also the priest. The people are both an ethnic and a religious group. The prophet is a social reformer. A religious movement, like the one started by Jesus, will be heavy with political consequences. Indeed one of the most certain facts about Jesus is that he was "crucified under Pontius

Pilate" (Mk 15:26). It would be naïve to dismiss this as due merely to the mis-understanding of a stupid and cowardly governor (the Pilate we know from Jose-phus was neither),[11] duped and pressurized by the religious opponents of Jesus. This no doubt is the line taken by the Passion tradition of the New Testament. But the obvious pro-Roman and anti-Jewish bias of this tradition[12] should caution us against taking it at its face value. Apologetical motifs have obviously been at work here. And without going as far as Eisler or Brandon in making Jesus a Zealot or a Zealot sympathizer,[13] we must surely reckon (as his opponents obvi-ously did) with the political dimensions of the movement he set afoot. The "reli-gious" movement started by Jesus had very definite sociopolitical overtones.[14] His "religious" proclamation included a vision of society.

The eschatological consciousness of Jesus would have sharpened this vision, rather than have eliminated it. For the eschatology of Jesus was certainly colored by apocalyptic—even if Jesus rejected the more esoteric fantasies of this then widely current mind-set, and complemented its almost exclusive interest in the future (for salvation in apocalyptic belongs not to this evil age but to the age to come!) with a healthy insistence on the presence of salvation here and now.[15] But a prime concern of apocalyptic has always been "the new heavens and the new earth," the liberated community of the age to come, when every tear will be wiped away and the "sea" (home of the great "beasts" which symbolize the demonic powers, cosmic and political, that oppress mankind) will be no more (Rev 21:1-4).

Perrin has pointed out that a distinctive feature of the language of Jesus is that he uses "Kingdom of God" not only to describe God's eschatological act of salvation (as the rabbis do), but also to indicate in a comprehensive and global way the eschatological blessings that follow from this act, and for which rabbinic theology never uses the rubric "Kingdom of God," but employs instead the famil-iar apocalyptic designation (rarely used by Jesus) of "the age to come" (*hā'ôlām hābā'*).[16] Understood in this way the Kingdom of God would, for Jesus, stand for the "New Israel," that is, for the eschatological realization of the community which he inaugurated when he appointed twelve of his followers to represent the traditional twelve tribes of the covenant people (Mk 3:13f; Mt 19:28).[17] Not just God's eschatological intervention into human history, but also the liberated com-munity that results from this intervention, are thus the objects of Jesus' concern. Both are taken up into the expression "Kingdom of God," which defines the "central theme of the public proclamation of Jesus."[18] It is by exploring Jesus' understanding of this theme, then, that we shall discover his vision of the new society.

2. JESUS' PROCLAMATION
OF THE KINGDOM (MK 1:14-15)

The proclamation of the Kingdom of God is certainly the central concern of the words and works of Jesus.[19] Not only is the Kingdom of God the central theme of his preaching (Mk 1:14f), the referent of most of his parables (Mt 13:1-52), and the subject of a large number of his sayings (Mt 8:11f; Mk 9:1; Lk 16:16); it is also the content of the symbolic actions which form so large a part of his ministry: his table fellowship with tax collectors and sinners and his healings and exorcisms. For in his "communion" with outcasts Jesus lives out, as it were, the Kingdom, demonstrating in action God's unconditional love for undeserving sinners (Mk 2:17).[20] And he understands his miracles as signs of the Kingdom, for his healings show the dawning of God's reign (Mt 11:2-6), and his exorcisms the end of Satan's rule (Mk 3:27).[21]

Indeed the frequency with which Jesus uses the expression is quite unique. For "Kingdom of God," or its equivalent "Kingdom of the Heavens" (in secondary, more rabbinic formulation preferred by Matthew),[22] is found rarely in the Old Testament or in intertestamental literature, occurs only occasionally in the targums (translations of the Old Testament into Aramaic, the vernacular of Palestine at the time of Jesus), is "comparatively infrequent" in rabbinic literature, and is found only thrice in Qumram (1QM 6:6; 12:7; 1QSb 4:25f).[23] In the New Testament, too, the expression occurs overwhelmingly in the Synoptic Gospels (some 90 times as against twice in John, about six times each in Acts and Paul, and once in the Apocalypse), and here too almost always in sayings of Jesus.

"Kingdom of God," then, is an expression characteristic of Jesus, expressing his own particular consciousness of mission and his own personal experience of God. As such, this expression occurs in a great variety of his sayings. These have been conveniently classified in terms of their function into three easily recognizable categories: sayings that announce the Kingdom (proclamation), those that teach about it (catechesis), and those that defend this teaching (controversy).[24] If (as is plausible) the New Testament can be described as "an explanatory 'superstructure' [catechesis and controversy] built upon an evangelical 'foundation' [proclamation]"[25] then the proclamatory sayings which announce the Kingdom will probably reflect more immediately and directly Jesus' own understanding of it than the catechetical sayings which spell out its implications or the controversial sayings which defend these. Among such proclamatory sayings Mk 1:14-15 is of particular importance. It occurs in what is arguably the earliest of the Gospels,[26] and functions there as a key text, which "summarizes the message of the entire work."[27] It offers us a convenient starting point for inquiring into Jesus' understanding of the Kingdom, and the vision of the new society implied in it.[28]

> Now after John was arrested, Jesus came into Galilee,
> preaching the Gospel of God, and saying, . . .
> "The time is fulfilled, the Kingdom of God is at hand;
> repent, and believe in the good news" (Mark 1:14-15).

A. The Context of Mk 1:14-15

It serves the Gospel both as a transitional link joining Mark's introduction to the ministry of Jesus (1:1-13) with his narrative account of the ministry itself

(1:16-13:37) and as a *programmatic summary* spelling out for us the meaning of his ministry. What precedes it (Mk 1:1-5) is not part of Mark's account of Jesus, but is a sort of theological prologue to the Gospel (homologous to the prologue in Jn 1:1-18), in which we are told who Jesus really is.[29] In three closely linked episodes (the preaching of John the Baptist, the baptism of Jesus, and his "testing" in the wilderness) Jesus is presented as the one who has come to fulfill the preaching of the Baptist, indeed that of the whole line of Old Testament prophets in whose tradition the Baptist stands (1:1-8); who is anointed by the Spirit as the Servant Messiah at his baptism in the Jordan, ushering in the eschatological age of the Spirit (1:9-11); and who as the New Adam overcomes Satan through his testing in the wilderness, setting free the world from the oppressive power of this "strong man" (1:12-13). But all this is not yet part of the ministry of Jesus: it is merely the prelude to it. The ministry of Jesus begins in Mk 1:16-20 with the calling of the first disciples. It is from the first an ecclesial ministry, exercised by Jesus in the company of his followers. Mark prefaces his narrative of this ministry with a summary statement of the programme of Jesus (Mk 1:14-15). This functions as a sort of introductory abstract, a manifesto almost (compare the "manifesto" in Lk 4:16-21), which tells us what the ministry of Jesus to be about. Mk 1:14-15 has thus a crucial role in the structure of the Gospel. Its place there can be diagrammed as follows:

1:1-13	1:14-15	1:16-13:37	14:1-16:8
Theological	Programmatic	Ministry	Passion in
Prologue	Summary	in Galilee	Jerusalem

B. An Analysis of Mark 1:14-15

The text of this programmatic summary falls into two clearly distinct parts. The setting of Jesus' ministry of proclamation (v. 14) is followed by a description of the proclamation itself (v. 15).

1. THE SETTING (V. 14)

The setting is spelled out for us in terms of the three circumstances of time, place, and action.

a) Jesus begins his ministry "after John had been delivered up (*paradothēnai*)"—an expression which indicates how closely the mission of Jesus is related in God's plan of salvation to that of John, and how similar to John's is his destiny. Jesus begins his mission only after the ministry of John has been brought to an end, and his destiny is foreshadowed in that of John. For like John Jesus too will be "delivered up (*paradidotai*) into the hands of men," to be put to death by them (Mk 9:31).

b) Jesus exercises his ministry by coming "into Galilee"—that is, into the despised (Jn 1:46), barbarous (Mt 26:73), religiously backward (Jn 7:41), gentile-ridden (Mt 4:15) upcountry of the north, rather than into the "holy city" (Mt 4:5; 27:53; Rev 11:2) of Jerusalem. Indeed Jerusalem in Mark's Gospel is always the place of conflict (cf. 7:1, where scribes from Jerusalem come to harass Jesus in Galilee); of sharp controversy (Mk 12:15-40); of judgment pronounced by Jesus on Israel and its Temple (12:1-11; 13:1-2); of a relentless conspiracy against him (12:12; 14:1-2); and of his suffering and death (14:3-15:47). It is despised Galilee that is the place for salvation. For it is in Galilee that the earthly Jesus announces the coming of the Kingdom (Mk 1:14f), explains it in parables (4:1-34), makes it visible in his exorcisms (Mk 1:29-34; cf. Mt 11:2-60), and lives it out in his table fellowship with tax collectors and sinners (Mk 2:15-17; cf. Lk 15:1-32). And it is also in Galilee that the risen Christ is expected to appear either in a post-Easter apparition or in his glorious *parousia* (Mk 14:28; 16:7).[30] From the very beginning, then, the Markan Jesus adopts an anti-elitist stance. He makes the unexpected, indeed scandalous (Mt 11:6), choice of opting for the religious outcast (Galilee) rather than for the religiously respectable (Jerusalem).

c) Jesus exercises his ministry through proclamation. For as Mark tells it, Jesus "came proclaiming (*ēlthen kēryssōn*) the good news of God." Proclamation thus defines the very essence of his coming. The Jesus of Mark is the "runner" who rushes through Galilee, announcing everywhere with passionate urgency the "good news (*to euaggelion*) of God."[31] Just what this "good news" is appears in Mark's summary description of the content of Jesus' proclamation which immediately follows.

This description of the setting of Jesus' proclamation (v. 14) is generally acknowledged to be an editorial composition by Mark, expressing therefore his own particular theology.[32] But it uses traditional terminology and themes (*kēryssein, paradothēnai*), and in its depiction of Jesus proclaiming the good news in Galilee it faithfully represents the Jesus of history. For from the evidence available to us it is clear that Jesus' activity was located largely in Galilee, and indeed in the more obscure quarters of this "up country" province. Neither Sepphoris nor Tiberias, capital cities of Galilee, is mentioned in the Gospels as places where Jesus preached.[33] Instead he seems to have lived out his life in hamlets like Nazareth, mentioned only in the New Testament (Mt 2:23; Mk 1:9); in fishing villages like Bethsaida (Mt 11:21; Mk 6:45; 8:22; Lk 9:10), and in small townships like Capernaum, which seems to have been the center of his missionary operations in Galilee (Mt 4:13; 8:5; 9:1; 17:24; Mk 1:21; 2:1; 9:33; Lk 10:15). However one understands the mission of Jesus, the obscurity of its location is surely striking. And given Jesus' well-attested and explicitly affirmed option for the poor (Mt 10:6; 11:5; Mk 2:15-17; Lk 4:16-21; 6:20-26), it is likely that this was not just an accident of history, but a willed expression of this option. Salvation was to be proclaimed and realized not among the rich, the powerful, the cultivated population of the urbanized cities, but among the "poorest, the lowliest, and the lost." The seed that was to grow into a mighty, world-overshadowing tree was tiny indeed.

2. Proclamation (v. 15)

The programmatic proclamation of Jesus is presented to us in two pairs of parallel expressions, formulated according to the synonymous parallelism of Semitic verses.

It reads:

a. The time is fulfilled,
b. And the Kingdom of God is at hand,
c. Repent,
d. And believe in the good news.

A pair of indicatives (*a* & *b*) is thus followed by a pair of imperatives (*c* & *d*), and in each pair the second member, in typical Semitic fashion, takes up and explicates the first. So *b* explains *a:* the time is fulfilled because the Kingdom of God is at hand; and *d* explains *c:* to repent means to believe in the good news.

Opinions about the origin of this carefully formulated proclamation range all the way from those who, like Chilton and Pesch, would identify the whole verse (or almost all of it) as an authentic saying of Jesus,[34] through those who, like Trilling and Mussner, would attribute it partially at least to the pre-Markan tradition of the early Church,[35] to those who, like Marxsen, Ambrozic, and Kelber, ascribe it almost entirely to the editorial activity of Mark.[36] In spite of the many differences of opinion there is, however, an emerging consensus that no matter how the proclamation may have been shaped by Mark or his tradition, it does echo the authentic voice of Jesus himself.[37] Themes like Kingdom of God and repentance in particular, as even more extreme partisans of Markan redaction will concede, can be "traced back to the preaching practice of Jesus."[38]

It seems reasonable, then, to suppose that the core of the passage (*b* & *c*) is an accurate transcription of what Jesus himself would have preached—for "Kingdom of God" was surely a characteristic theme of his preaching, and the call to "repent" fits in well with the image he projected of a charismatic prophet (cf. Mt 21:11; Lk 7:16). But the framework (*a* & *d*) is almost certainly an explanatory addition by Mark or his tradition—for "the time is fulfilled" is typical of early Christian fulfillment apologetic (cf. Gal 4:4; Mt 26:56); and "believe in the good news" distinctly echoes the language of the early Christian mission (cf. Acts 11:17f; 20:21).[39] Mk 1:14-15 would then have originated as follows:

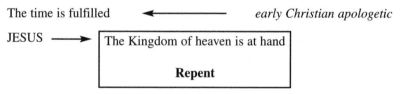

The time is fulfilled ⟵ *early Christian apologetic*

JESUS ⟶ The Kingdom of heaven is at hand

Repent

Believe in the good news ⟶ *early Christian mission preaching*

C. The Meaning of Mark 1:14-15

The proclamation of the Kingdom of God and the call to repentance thus belong to the core of the preaching of Jesus. If then we are to understand this preaching and disclose the vision of the new society it contains, we must ask ourselves what exactly Jesus meant when he spoke of the "Kingdom of God," and what exactly he meant by "repentance."

1. THE KINGDOM OF GOD

Although Jesus steadfastly proclaimed the coming of the Kingdom and frequently attempted to describe it obliquely in the allusive language of the parables, he nowhere tells us clearly just what the Kingdom really is. This is because the Kingdom of God is in fact a symbol, and as such impervious to conceptual definition,[40] and also because it is a symbol that was familiar enough to his contemporaries to need no further elaboration.

For our "Kingdom of God" translates the Greek *basileia tou theou* of the Gospels, and this in turn stands for the Aramaic *malkût di ᵓelāhāᵓ* or *malkût di yy,* which Jesus would have used. To his listeners the Aramaic formula would have indicated not so much a place ruled over by God (which is what the English world "Kingdom" suggests), as the activity through which God reveals himself as a king. For "Kingdom of God" (*malkût di yy*) is used in Jewish literature, and notably in targums (Aramaic translations of the Hebrew Old Testament), as a circumlocution for Old Testament expressions like "God reigns" (*mālak yhwh*) or "God is King" (*melek yhwh*), which are judged too "concrete" to be used of God. Awed by the immense majesty of Yahweh "the great, the mighty, the terrible God" (Deut 10:17), the Judaism of Jesus' time tended to avoid verbal statements about him (God *does* this or that), replacing them with abstract noun forms. So the targums speak of the "divine presence" (*shekināh*) or the "word of God" (*mēᵓmar di yy*), where the Hebrew Old Testament would simply say that "God dwells" (*shākēn yhwh*) or that "God speaks" (*ᵓāmar yhwh*). In the same way *malkût di yy* (Kingdom of God) appears in rabbinic writings and in the targums as a substitute for verbal expressions like *yimlôk* or *mālak yhwh* (God reigns) in the Hebrew Bible.[41] "Kingdom of God" is thus synonymous with "God reigns." Although nominal in form, the expression is verbal in meaning. It stands not for the territory ruled over by God (kingdom), nor even for his royal power ("kingship"), but for the concrete exercise of this power ("rule") in actions through which he shows himself to be king. The Kingdom of God is God's *kingly activity.*

The theology of the times pictures this kingly activity of God in two different ways. God shows himself to be king by creating the universe and by liberating his people through his mighty deeds in history.[42] Both these types of action are acts of kingship, because they are both acts of salvation. As such they characterize God as king, because the function of a king according to the Near Eastern ideal of kingship is precisely to save.[43] The code of Manu comes very close to this Near Eastern ideal when it says: "if the king did not untiringly afflict punishment on those to be punished, the strong would roast the weak like a fish on a spit."[44] The role of the king, then, is to defend the weak against the strong. This is what God does when he creates the universe and when he sets his people free.

(a) The Kingdom as Creation

God shows himself as Creator-King inasmuch as he created and sustains the universe. For creation is understood in the Bible in mythical rather than in metaphysical terms. It is depicted as a sort of gigantic rescue operation in which God rescues the world from the turbulent waters of the primaeval chaos (much as the boar *avatāra* of Vishnu rescues the earth goddess Laxmi from the waters of the primordial ocean) and maintains it in its precarious state of existence, by staving off the destructive forces of chaos that are always threatening to engulf it (Gen 1:1-3; Ps 74:12-17; 89:8-14). Creation thus becomes a saving event, so closely parallel to the great saving event of the Exodus that it figures as the first of the series of saving deeds for which God is acclaimed in Ps 136:1-26. At the same time creation imagery (the primordial waters personified as the primordial monster Rahab) is used to describe the Exodus event in Ex 15:5 ("the primal waters [*tĕhōmōt*] cover them"); in Is 30:7 ("for Egypt's help is worthless and empty, therefore I have called her 'Rahab who sits still'"), and specially in Is 51:9f ("Was it not thou that didst cut Rahab in pieces . . . was it not thou that didst dry up the sea?"). God is therefore acclaimed as Creator and King in the so-called enthronement Psalms (Pss 47; 93; 96; 97; 99) of the Old Testament in which the refrain "Yahweh reigns" (*yhwh mālak*) introduces references to creation. Thus his role of Creator-King is a firm part of the Jewish consciousness of God at the time of Jesus, for the rabbis speak of God's eternal or hidden kingship (acknowledged by Israel, yet to be manifested to the gentiles), which he exercises by his providential care for all created things (cf. Mt 5:15; 6:26-30).

Yet this way of conceiving the kingship of God is not of primary importance to the Old Testament, nor original to it. It is a late and secondary motif which Israel has borrowed, probably at the time of the monarchy, from her neighbors in Babylon and Canaan.[45] It is rather in her awareness of God as the Liberator King who sets his people free that the specific note of Israel's theology is struck.

(b) The Kingdom as Liberation

God is Liberator King, exercising an (ultimately) eschatological kingship, inasmuch as he intervenes in history to save his people from the situations of desperate peril they encounter. He rescues them from slavery in Egypt (Exodus), from starvation in the wilderness (Numbers), from annihilation by powerful enemies during the wars of the conquest (Joshua, Judges) and from exile in Babylon (Deutero-Isaiah). It is in these mighty saving acts that Israel has its specific encounter with its God, experiencing him as the Covenant God deeply concerned about the concrete historical welfare of his people. Israel is his *segullah*, his prized possession (Ex 19:5; Deut 7:6; Ps 135:4); he is her "redeemer," her *gōʾēl* (Is 41:14; Jer 50:34; Ps 78:35).

Indeed the very name *Yahweh* by which Israel addresses her God indicates this, as the Priestly narrative of the call of Moses in Ex 6:2-8 shows, "I appeared to Abraham, to Isaac, and to Jacob, as God Almighty (*ʾēl shaddāy*), but by my name the Lord (*yhwh*) I did not make myself known to them" (v. 2), says Yahweh to Moses in this theologically dense narrative, which presents us with Israel's mature reflection on the significance of her long experience of God. As *ʾēl shaddāy* God had "established a covenant" with the patriarchs "to give them the land of Canaan" (v. 4). He had revealed himself to them, that is, as the God of promise. Now he reveals himself to Moses by a new name: "I am Yahweh" (vv. 2, 6, 7). And since a name in the Old Testament is not just a casual label but an indication of the nature and function of the person named, the significance of the new name is spelled out in a striking passage framed by a double affirmation of the name (vv. 6-7):[46]

> I am Yahweh
>> and I will bring you out from under the burden of the Egyptians
>> and I will deliver you from their bondage,
>> and I will redeem you with an outstretched arm
>> and with great acts of judgement,
>> and I will take you for my people
>> and you shall know that
> I am Yahweh, your God
>> who has brought you out from under the burden of the Egyptians.

Much later on God will make himself known by yet another name, revealing himself as "*Abba*" the "dear Father" who loves all men with a universal and wholly unconditional love. But his name before this new revelation through Jesus remains *Yhwh*: and *Yhwh* means the God who redeems. Israel experiences God primarily as the liberator God.

Yet it is precisely this core experience of Israel which leads to the great creative tension which dominates the whole of her history. For while Israel trusts implicitly in the promises made to her by her liberator God, she does not experience the realization of these promises. What has been promised is the "land"—a comprehensive symbol for salvation, conceived of in a very material way, as freedom, peace, long life, prosperity (Ex 3:17; Deut 28:1-14).[47] What is experienced is poverty, conflict, oppression, colonization, exile. Promise clashes with fulfillment, resulting in a tension that can be resolved only by projecting the fulfillment of the promise into the future. The promises of the liberator God will *one day* be fulfilled. God will *one day* fully liberate his people. God's Kingdom (his definitive saving act) will one day come. The kingship of the Liberator King becomes an eschatological kingdom.

So the core experience of Israel (God experienced as the concerned and caring Lord of history) leads inevitably to the basic attitude of the Old Testament, an attitude of steadfast hope. From beginning to end the Old Testament is a book of hope, just as the New Testament is from beginning to end a book of love. But this hope takes various forms in the course of Israel's history. Two forms are especially important, because they have largely determined the thought patterns of the New Testament, and indeed Jesus' own understanding of his mission. They are messianic expectation and apocalyptic hope.

(1) *Davidic messianism* is conspicuous among the writings of the great eighth-century prophets like Amos, Isaiah, Micah, and Hosea. It looks forward to the realization of God's promise of liberation through a descendant of David (a "Son of David"), who will be raised up by God as the "Messiah," that is, the "anointed one" or the king *par excellence*. The Messiah is to establish a worldwide kingdom of justice, peace, and prosperity in which all the promises symbolized by the "land" will finally be realized.[48]

Such messianism takes off from the prophecy of Nathan in 2 Sam 7:12-16, where David is promised an eternal dynasty, and reaches its finest flowering in prophetic oracles like that of Is 11:1-9, which tells of a "shoot from the stump of Jesse" (v. 1) who will be so abundantly endowed with the gifts of the Spirit (vv. 2-3) that he will be the ideal king, deeply concerned about the poor (vv. 4-5), and will reign with compassion and firmness over a kingdom that will enjoy the peace and the total harmony of paradise itself (vv. 6-9).

Mythological imagery of this sort frequently colors the language of Davidic messianism. The Messiah is pictured as the ideal King, sharing the traits of the mythical primal man (*Urmensch*) who once reigned over paradise (Mic 5:2-3; Is 11:6-9); and his kingdom is seen as the restoration of a lost golden age of perfect freedom, peace, and prosperity. In it swords will be turned into plowshares and spears into pruning hooks (Is 2:4), and the heavy boots and blood-stained uniforms of marauding soldiers will be burnt up as fuel (Is 9:5). The poor will be looked after with compassion and justice (Is 11:4f), and the land will be so abundantly fertile that a man—heedless of the damage the animal may cause—will cheerfully tie up his ass to a vine (Gen 49:10-12). The wolf will live amicably with the lamb, and children play safely with poisonous snakes (Is 11:6-9)! Everywhere the perfect peace of paradise will reign, so that man will be reconciled with man, and live in perfect harmony with nature too. But such mythological language notwithstanding, the hope expressed in Davidic messianism (at least in its earlier forms) is a thoroughly this-worldly one. God's promises are to be realized in a this-worldly kingdom to be established on earth and within *our* history.

Davidic messianism received a severe setback with the fall of Jerusalem and the Babylonian exile of 587 B.C.E. The dynasty of David, which had ruled over the Southern Kingdom in unbroken continuity from the time of David right up to the exile, now disappears from the pages of history. The exiles who return are no longer led by Davidic kings, though Sheshbazzar and Zerubbabel, possibly members of the royal family (cf. Ezra 1:8 and Neh 2:2), seem to have played some undefined role in the refounding of Jerusalem,[49] but by the priestly scribes Ezra and Nehemiah. Not unnaturally Davidic messianism finds itself giving way to a new type of expectation strongly colored by influences from the Persian and Babylonian religions which Israel had encountered during her exile. This is apocalyptic hope.

(2) *Apocalyptic* looks forward to an imminent, catastrophic intervention of God, in which he will destroy "this evil age" and usher in "the age to come" by creating "a new heaven and a new earth" (Is 65:25; Rev 21:1), as the home of the risen just (Dan 12:1-3).[50] God will destroy this world because it is unredeemably evil. It is a world given over to Satan, the "ruler of this world" (Jn 12:31), who controls it through demons that cause sickness and suffering, and through demonic men (the rulers of the great world empires) who oppress the people of God (Dan 8:17-27). In its place God will create a new material universe ("a new heaven and a new earth")—for apocalyptic affirms not a vertical opposition between "this world" (earth) and "the other world" (heaven) but a temporal opposition between "this age" (the unjust, oppressive, physically and socially distorted structures of our world) and "the age to come" (the eschatological order of total peace and harmony to be given in the renewed cosmos). Apocalyptic hope, unlike messianism, is thus strictly eschatological. It foresees salvation not as the fulfillment of our history but as its end. History will come to an end and give way to eschatology—to a last, definitive, enduring state of harmony and bliss in a new "world" (cf. 1 Enoch 91:14-17).

(c) Jesus and the Kingdom

Davidic messianism and apocalyptic are only two of the many other forms that the hope of Israel assumed at the time of Jesus.[51] As we have described them above, these two kinds of hope are to be taken not as a concrete description of the actual expectations of people but as paradigms, schematic outlines of theoretical types, which were rarely, if ever, realized in their pure form. Various other kinds of hope existed, and the concrete expectations of most people would have been a confused mixture of messianic, apocalyptic, and other elements. Texts from Qumran, for instance (e.g., CD 14:19; 19:10; 20:1; 1QSa 2:12) speak of a messianic priest, "the anointed Aaron" (*měšîaḥ ʾahărôn*) and a messianic king, "the anointed of Israel" (*měšîaḥ yiśrāʾēl*), to which the *Community Rule* (1QS 9:11) adds a third messianic figure, "the prophet" (*nābîʾ*). And the *Book of Enoch*, one of the more important of the apocryphal writings of the intertestamental period, which had considerable influence on early Christian thinking, combines messianic expectation and apocalyptic hope. It promises the setting up of a messianic kingdom where the righteous will be rewarded and the wicked punished here on earth, to be followed by "the great eternal judgement," in which the old heaven will pass away and the new heaven appear (*1 Enoch* 92-105).

All these varied forms of hope are taken up into the expression "Kingdom of God." For "Kingdom of God" is not, as we have seen, a concept that can be precisely defined, but a polyvalent symbol standing for all Israel's hopes of liberation.[52] Each of the listeners of Jesus would have understood the "Kingdom" in his own particular way. For the symbol would have evoked different responses in different individuals, always bringing to expression the particular form of hope nourished by each. When, therefore, Jesus announces the coming of the Kingdom, what he is saying is that Israel's long-sustained hope of liberation (no matter what form this takes) is about to be, indeed is being, *fulfilled.* That is, it is being realized, but in a new, more perfect, and therefore wholly unexpected way.

What, then, is this new and more perfect way in which Israel's hopes for liberation are being realized in Jesus' proclamation of the Kingdom? All Israel's expectations, no matter what their form, looked for liberation through an outpouring of power. Davidic messianism relied on the political power of the ideal king. The zealot nationalists of Jesus' time opted for the power of arms, wielded in a "holy war" waged for and under God. The Pharisees trusted in the moral power generated by their perfect observance of the Law. The apocalyptists hoped for a mighty display of cosmic power by God. All such ways are rejected by Jesus (Mt 4:1-11). For him power is not the key. There can be no genuine liberation through an exercise of power, for power does not really free; it merely creates new structures of unfreedom. The only truly liberating force in the world is love, and it is just this that Jesus offers when he proclaims the coming of the Kingdom.

For when Jesus announces that the Kingdom of God has come (that is, that God is revealing himself as the Liberator King by definitively fulfilling the hopes of his people), he is drawing on his own experience of God as *Abba,* the dear Father who has declared his unconditional love for men.[53] It is this revelation of God's love (God as *Abba*) that is the true content of Jesus' proclamation of the Kingdom. For it is only when we encounter this love and respond to it appropriately in trusting surrender that we experience genuine freedom as individuals and in community. The Kingdom of God proclaimed by Jesus, then, is ultimately his *revelation of God's unconditional love.*

When the Kingdom of God is understood in this way, many of the paradoxes with which Jesus invests it are resolved. One begins to see why the kingdom does not come the way the apocalyptists thought it would, as a catastrophic event overwhelming us once and for all. Instead it floods in imperceptibly (as love usually does) in a slow and silent process. The Kingdom grows (Mk 4:30-32). That is why Jesus can speak of it as both present (Lk 17:20f) and future (Mk 9:1); for like any unfinished process the Kingdom is both "already" and "not yet"; it has already begun and is not yet over.

So too the Kingdom of God cannot possibly be what the zealots and Pharisees thought it was, the result of or the reward for human achievement. For love cannot be merited or earned. The Kingdom therefore is, as Jesus repeatedly insists, a wholly free gift (Mk 4:26-29; Lk 17:7-10). Yet this gift is not "cheap grace," making up for an absence of human initiative and endeavor. Rather, like any offer of love, it puts us on the spot, breaking into our lives as a challenge that summons us to decision (Lk 16:1-10). The Kingdom of God is thus both gift and challenge. The offer of God's love that the Kingdom symbolizes demands from us a response. This response has been defined by Jesus as "repentance."

2. REPENTANCE

Although the Greek word for "repent" used in the Gospels (*metanoein*) means literally "to change one's mind," "to have after-thoughts," and therefore "to have remorse for some one action or the other," this is not what Jesus intends by his call to repentance. For underlying the Greek *metanoein* of the New Testament is the prophetic ideal of repentance, expressed in the well-known Hebrew word *šûb* ("to be converted," "to turn"), which in the Old Testament always signifies the turning of the whole man to God (Is 31:6; Jer 3:12-14; Hos 14:1).[54] In line with this, the repentance demanded by Jesus involves the whole man and not some one compartment of his life; and it involves him in a dramatic positive movement of turning to God, and not primarily in the negative movement of turning away from sin.

As our response to the proclamation of the Kingdom, which as we have seen is the revelation of God's unconditional love for us, repentance or the turning of ourselves to God can only mean our wholehearted and trusting acceptance of this love. That is why Mark correctly interprets Jesus' call to repentance as a call to "believe in the good news" (Mk 1:15d). The "good news of God" that Jesus announces is the coming of the Kingdom, that is, the declaration of God's unconditional love for man. To believe in the good news (to repent) is therefore to accept the fact (personally and not merely notionally) that God loves us, and to allow our lives to be transformed by this love (1 Jn 4:7-12).

Briefly, then, the core message of Jesus contains an *indicative*, which epitomizes all Christian theology, and an *imperative*, which sums up all Christian ethics. Its indicative is the proclamation of the Kingdom, that is, the revelation of God's unconditional love. Its imperative is a call to repentance, that is, the demand that we open our hearts to this love and respond to it by loving God in neighbor. Behind the high and tangled hedge of abstract speculation that the theology has built around it, this is really what the message of Jesus is all about. We can therefore formulate the basic message of Jesus as follows:

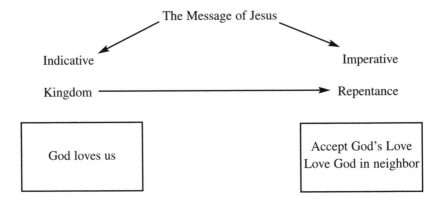

3. THE SIGNIFICANCE OF THE KINGDOM:
THE NEW SOCIETY

When the revelation of God's love (the Kingdom) meets its appropriate response in man's trusting acceptance of this love (repentance), there begins a mighty movement of personal and societal liberation which sweeps through human history. The movement brings *freedom* inasmuch it liberates each individual from the inadequacies and obsessions that shackle him. It fosters *fellowship*, because it empowers free individuals to exercise their concern for each other in genuine community. And it leads on to *justice*, because it impels every true community to adopt the just societal structures which alone make freedom and fellowship possible. Freedom, fellowship, and justice are thus the parameters of the Kingdom's thrust toward the total liberation of man. Together they spell out the significance of the Kingdom, and tell us what the Kingdom in practice, means today.

A. Freedom: The Kingdom and the Human Person

The Kingdom brings freedom inasmuch as it liberates a man from the internal compulsions and the external pressures that inhibit him. These compulsions and pressures spring from his deep needs and fears, both of which, psychologists assure us, are ultimately caused by an absence of love. It is the unloved person who is driven by his emptiness ("we are made for thee, O Lord," Augustine tells us, "and our hearts are restless until they rest in thee") to fill the gaping void in his life by grasping compulsively at possessions, position, or power. It is the unloved person too who is so deeply insecure that the fear of rejection and a desperate need for the approval of others make him incapable of truly independent action. The experience of unconditional love (the Kingdom) cures this. Love so fills his heart with joy that he no longer needs the transient satisfaction that "things" may give; and it gives him so great a sense of his own self-worth that he no longer has to depend on the approval of others. He is truly "free."

Jesus himself is of course the supreme example of such freedom. He moves through the pages of the Gospel as the supremely free man. He is driven by no demons of greed or ambition—for the Son of Man "has nowhere to lay his head" (Lk 9:58) and has come "not to be served but to serve" (Mk 10:45). He is daunted neither by the pressures of heteronomous Law (Jn 8:1-10) nor by the violence of established authority (Lk 13:31-33). With supreme freedom he challenges the most sacred institutions of his people when his concern for his fellow men impels him to do so. He breaks the Sabbath (Mk 7:1-15), touches lepers (Mk 1:42), dines with the socially outcast and with sinners (Mk 2:15-17).[55]

In freedom Jesus makes us free. He has left us an enormous legacy of freedom, for his entire ministry was spent in bringing freedom of every kind to man. So Jesus frees us from sin and guilt (Mk 2:1-12). He frees us from the dread of demons (Mk 1:21-28), from the deadening routine of ritualism (Mt 6:7), and from the oppressive burden of the Law (Mt 11:28-30 + 23:4). He frees us too from the terrible isolation to which we can be condemned by social ostracism (Lk 19:1-10), ritual uncleanness (Mk 1:40-45), or mental ill-health (Mk 5:1-21). He summons his followers to freedom from the hampering weight of possessions (Mk 1:16-18; 10:21), or from the clinging hindrance of overdeveloped family ties (Lk 9:61). He empowers them with the freedom to love (Lk 7:36-50). The total liberation of man, that ringing freedom that comes from a trust in God so absolute that one needs no other security in life (Mt 6:25-34), is thus a conspicuous value of the Kingdom that Jesus proclaims.

B. Fellowship: The Kingdom and Community

The freedom of the Kingdom leads inevitably to a fellowship of mutual concern. Born of an experience of unconditional love, the freedom of the Kingdom empowers and impels the free man to surrender his freedom in love. Paul has expressed this well in his dialectic of freedom and slavery. "Christ has set us free in order that we might remain free," he tells the Galatians (Gal 5:1); but then adds: "you were called to freedom, brothers, only do not use your freedom as an occasion for indulging the natural man, but through love be slaves (*douleuete*) of one another" (5:13). And of himself too he can say to the Corinthians: "though I am free of all men, I have made myself a slave (*edoulosa*) to all in order that I might win many" (1 Cor 9:19).

The freedom of the Kingdom finds its fulfilment not in selfish wilfulness but in commitment. It is a freedom that moves from love to love. Born of an experience of God's unconditional love for us, the freedom of the Kingdom finds its fulfilment in our unconditional love for others. For man becomes truly man only by relating to his fellows in love—that is, only through that free surrender of his freedom that every such relation entails. Only by losing one's freedom does one find it (Mk 8:35)! For the fulfilment of freedom is fellowship.[56]

The fellowship of the Kingdom is strongly urged by Jesus, who both practices and preaches a radical and absolutely universal concern for every one in need (Lk 6:27-36; 10:25-37). The great commandment of Judaism, the *šĕmac yiśrā'ēl* ("hear, O Israel") of Dt 6:4-6, which urges us to love God with all our hearts, is modified by Jesus into his "love-commandment" (Mk 12:28-34 par) by the addition of an obscure and rarely quoted text from Lev 19:18 which commands us to love our neighbor as ourselves. Not only does this addition bring God and neighbor together at the same time; but it profoundly modifies our understanding of the *šĕmac*. For by adding Lev 19:18 to Dt 6:4-5 Jesus is probably proposing a new interpretation of the great commandment of Judaism. To love God with all one's heart now means to love one's neighbor as oneself. The love commandment of Jesus is, then, that we love God by loving neighbor.[57]

This at least is how the New Testament seems to have understood Jesus' love commandment. Except for Mk 12:28-34 par (the "love-commandment") and Lk 11:42 (an obscure woe which condemns the Pharisees for having neglected "justice and the love of God") the New Testament scarcely ever speaks about our loving God. Instead it urges on us the "royal law" of loving one's neighbor as oneself (Jas 2:8; Gal 5:14; Rom 13:8; 1 Pet 4:8; Heb 3:11), or the "new commandment" of Jesus that we love one another as he has loved us (Jn 13:34; 15:12; 1 Jn 3:23; 4:7-12; 2 Jn 5). Our appropriate response to God's love for us, is not that we love God in return (for God cannot be the object of our concern: "no one has ever seen God," as 1 Jn 4:12 says), but that we love our neighbor (Jn 3:19-21)—in whom we encounter God (Mt 25:31-46). Fellowship, that is, radical concern for the neighbor (*agapē*) thus becomes the great value of the Kingdom.

C. Justice: The Kingdom and Human Society

Where there is genuine fellowship there will be justice. The radical concern of the Kingdom will not tolerate passivity in the face of social, economic and political structures which oppress man and dehumanize him. In a post-Marxian age which has begun to realize just how oppressive and dehumanizing such structures can be, and how deeply they influence the personal and communitarian life of man, the follower of Jesus cannot be content with merely rescuing the victims of these structures, or attempting (with dubious success) to convert the exploiters who maintain them. It is the dehumanizing structures themselves, of which both the oppressors and the oppressed are the victims, that must be challenged and changed.

Jesus himself gives us an example of this. True, he refuses an explicitly political option (Mt 4:1-11; Jn 6:15; Mk 12:13-17), and is certainly not aware of the operation of socio-economic structures, as we are today. Yet his opposition to the burdensome legalism of the scribes (cf. the Sabbath controversies of Mk 2:23-3:6), his slashing condemnation of a casuistry which leaves no room for compassion (cf. his rejection of "Qorban" in Mk 7:9-13), his consistent violation of the rules of caste separation (cf. his table-fellowship with tax-collectors and sinners in Mk 2:15-17), and his violent protest against the exploitation of the priestly aristocracy (cf. his cleansing of the Temple in Mk 17:15-19)—are all a sustained attack on an "establishment," which, like the mediaeval papacy, was not just a religious authority but packed much economic and political clout as well. Implicitly at least, then, Jesus did not merely convert individuals, but attacked structures also.

He does this in his miracles too. For Jesus understands his miracles not just as works of compassion which bring relief to the handful of the sick and disturbed who reach him, but as skirmishes in a great battle of liberation in which he destroys the demonic power-structure which is the cause of all human ills. He has come to take away sickness, not just to heal some sick. "No one can enter a strong man's house and plunder his goods," says Jesus referring to his healings and exorcisms, "unless he first bind the strong man; then indeed he may plunder his goods" (Mk 3:27). So Jesus sees his healings and exorcisms as the binding of the "strong man." They signify the decisive defeat of Satan and the definitive end of his rule. The whole of the demonic power-structure through which Satan, according to the apocalyptic worldview of the times, dominated the world, is being steadily eroded, Jesus tells us, through his healings and exorcisms. The fact that the apocalyptic worldview of Jesus' time, in which a multitude of spirits determine cosmic processes and historical events is not one which we post-Einsteinians will readily accept today, must not blind us to the fact that Jesus did in fact see himself as opposing a power structure. He may have thought of the structure in mythological terms, but he thought of it as a structure none the less. And in opposing this structure Jesus shows us again that the concern of the Kingdom cannot be content with the individual rescue, but must challenge the "demonic" power structures of the day, however and wherever such oppressive structures are perceived.[58]

The Kingdom proclaimed by Jesus thus leads to freedom, fellowship and justice. It leads, that is, to *new liberating relationships* with God and with men (God is experienced as *Abba*, the Father who loves us unconditionally, and men and women are experienced as brothers and sisters accepting each other in a fellowship of mutual concern), and to *new liberating structures* in society (the end of economic exploitation and political domination of one class by another). The Kingdom thus calls for a change of hearts and change of structures. Both are necessary. A change of hearts without a change of structures, besides being suspect (for love must show itself in deeds—1 Jn 3:17), will leave present oppression unchanged. A change of structures without a change of hearts will lead to new oppressions, as the "liberated" oppressed are driven by the as yet unexorcised demons of selfishness and greed that possess them to become oppressors in their turn. Only the two together can shape a world in which there will be neither oppressor nor oppressed, because men have learnt to live together in fellowship and freedom without exploiting one another.

It is to such a community of free people living in a non-exploitative society that the Kingdom of God summons us, and to which it leads by its own inherent dynamism of love. This is what the love of God revealed to us in Jesus will achieve—if only we allow it to work in our lives, and make the hard options that love demands. A new society is implicit in the dynamics of the Kingdom.[59]

Like the Kingdom itself, this new society is never clearly defined in the sayings of Jesus. It remains a "vision," shimmering in the distance, a summons rather than a plan, an inspiration more than a programme of action. Yet there are moments of more precise articulation in the Gospels, when sayings of Jesus, read perceptively, reveal the shape of the new society more correctly. The antitheses of the Sermon on the Mount (Mt 5:21-48) are one such moment. For in their extreme radicalization of traditional ethics they call for a radically new society in which violence is eradicated at its roots (vv. 21-26), where women are no longer treated as sex objects and discriminated against by men (vv. 27-32), where simplicity of speech and the transparency of inter-human relationships makes external guarantees unnecessary (vv. 33-37), where order is maintained not through the fear of retaliation but through the concern of love (vv. 38-42), and where men and women accept each other, across all barriers of class, caste, race and culture, as the children of the one Father in heaven (vv. 43-48).

Several other sayings of Jesus too point the same way. For Jesus' consistent defence of man against a religious legislation insensitive to human need (Mk 2:23-28; 3:1-6; 7:1-15); his vigorous polemic against consumerism and money (Mk 10:23-27; Mt 6:24; Lk 12:13-21);[60] his revolutionary interpretation of authority and service (Mk 9:33-35; 10:35-45); and his radical condemnation of titles of honor (Mt 23:8-10)—these are all demands for a non-consumer, non-competitive, fully egalitarian society (so very different from our own!), which will be geared to the satisfaction of the fundamental needs of the many rather than to the artificially created demands of a few, in which domination will be replaced by service, and in which man will be more important than money.[61]

Yet even a social reading of the Gospels, which spells out the significance of all such sayings of Jesus, will not reduce Jesus' vision of a new society to a blue-print. For the vision of Jesus is theological, not sociological. It spells out the values of the new society (freedom, fellowship, and justice), not the concrete social structures through which these values are realized and protected. To elaborate these is our never-to-be-ended task—for no "perfect" society is possible in history. One cannot fully actualize the vision of Jesus: one can merely approach it asymptotically! Ultimately, then, the vision of Jesus indicates not the goal but the way. It does not present us with a static pre-fabricated model to be imitated, but invites us to a continual refashioning of societal structures in an attempt to realize as completely as possible in our times the values of the Kingdom. The vision of Jesus summons us, then, to a ceaseless struggle against the demonic structures of unfreedom (psychological and sociological) erected by mammon; and to a ceaseless creativity that will produce in every age new blueprints for a society ever more consonant with the Gospel vision of man. Lying on the horizons of human history and yet part of it, offered to us as a gift yet confronting us as a challenge, Jesus' vision of a new society stands before us as an unfinished task, summoning us to permanent revolution.

NOTES

1. See A. Rauscher, "Befreiung: Christliche und marxistische Interpretation," in *Kirche und Befreiung,* ed. F. Hengsbach et al. (Aschaffenburg: Pattloch, 1975), 29-46; and in more general terms, Robert Kress, "Theological Method, Praxis and Liberation," *Communio* (1979): 113-34.

2. See Juan Luis Segundo, *The Liberation of Theology* (Maryknoll, N.Y.: Orbis, 1976), 10-13.

3. The involvement of the Christian churches with colonialism is too well known to need elaboration. See K. M. Pannikar, *Asia and Western Dominance* (London: Allen & Unwin, 1953), 375-460. This, if anything, underrates the role of Christian mission in legitimizing the European colonial enterprise; is insufficiently aware of the context to which the "chosen people" complex of Christians contributed to their racial attitudes towards the "lesser breeds without a law"; and fails to mention the considerable part that the mission-

ary writings played in creating the "white man's burden" image of Asia and Africa. See Milton Singer, *When a Great Tradition Modernizes* (Delhi: Vikas, 1972), 16-21. The evidence is all there, even in Western studies with their fairly obvious apologetic bent. See Karl Hammer, *Weltmission und Kolonialismus* (Munich: Deutscher Taschenbuch Verlag, 1980), and the more defensive and querulous work of Stephen Neill, *Colonialism and Christian Missions* (London: Lutterworth, 1966). The extent to which the anti-communism of the Christian churches and their heavy investments in the market economy of the West has resulted in their long tolerance of capitalist exploitation is discussed by Joseph Comblin in his *The Church and the National Security State* (Marknoll, N.Y.: Orbis, 1980). Whether and how far the official theologies, and even more the official liturgies, of the Christian churches in the Third World are a form of "cultural imperialism"—neatly defined by Johan Galtung in his *The True Worlds: A Transactional Perspective* (New York: Free Press, 1980), 108, as the attempt of a society "to reproduce its own social configuration elsewhere, thereby creating the type of homology between states so useful for any type of domination"—needs to be studied.

4. See Aeldred Cody, "The Foundation of the Church: Biblical Criticism for Ecumenical Discussion," *Theological Studies* 34 (1973): 3-18: with its conclusion that "the question whether or not Jesus before his death and exaltation founded the Church as we know it—as an institution with a given structure and a given sacramental system and so on—cannot be given an affirmative answer based on historically certain evidence. . . . The Church does have Jesus as its founder, though not in the strictly juridical sense" (p. 15); and Karl Rahner, *The Church and the Sacraments* (London: Burns & Oates, 1963), 41-74, with its thesis that "the institution of a sacrament can (it is not necessarily implied that it must always) follow simply from the fact that Christ founded the Church with its sacramental nature" (p. 41).

5. See Hans Küng, *The Church* (New York: Sheed & Ward, 1967), 15-20; see also the discussion on "The Unity and Diversity of New Testament Ecclesiology" between Ernst Käsemann and Raymond E. Brown in *Novum Testamentum* 6 (1963): 290-308.

6. Note the comment of Carl E. Braaten in his *The Flaming Center: A Theology of Christian Mission* (Philadelphia: Fortress Press, 1977), 134: "The Kingdom of God does not give the Church a blueprint for the perfect society, but it does inspire the vision of a more meaningful society than the one we have."

7. Rudolf Bultmann, *The History of the Synoptic Tradition*, trans. John Marsh (Oxford: Blackwell, 1963), 69-205: especially 81-108 (on wisdom sayings), 125-30 (on prophetic and apocalyptic sayings), and 145-50 (on legal sayings).

8. Joachim Jeremias, *New Testament Theology,* vol. 1 (London: SCM Press, 1971), 3-37.

9. Rudolf Bultmann, "The Study of the Synoptic Gospels," in Rudolf Bultmann and Karl Kundsin, *Form Criticism: Two Essays on New Testament Research*, trans. F. C. Grant (New York: Harper Torchbooks, 1962), 61: "Though one may admit the fact that for no single word of Jesus is it possible to produce positive evidence of its authenticity, still one may point to a whole series of words found in the oldest stratum of tradition which do give us a consistent representation of the historical message of Jesus."

10. See, for instance, Cristoph Barth, *Diesseits und Jenseits im Glauben des späten Israel* (Stuttgart: Katholisches Bibelwerk, 1974).

11. Josephus in his occasional references to Pilate (*Bellum* 2.9.2-4; *Ant.* 18.4.2) shows him to have been cruel, violent, ruthless, and likely to have been an anti-Jewish person (more Reagan than Carter!) who would not have been squeamish about spilling inno-

cent blood (particularly if Jewish), nor likely to have been intimidated or cajoled by the persuasion of the Jewish leaders or the pressures of a Jewish mob. See the discussion in S. G. F. Brandon, *Jesus and the Zealots* (New York: Scribner's, 1967), 68-80.

12. Xavier Léon-Dufour, "Passion," in *Dictionnaire de la Bible, Supplément* (Paris: Letouzey et Ané, 1960), vol. 6, col. 1434.

13. See Robert Eisler, *The Messiah and John the Baptist*, trans. and ed. A. H. Krappe (London: Methuen, 1931), an abridged English edition of his massive two volume German work *Iesous Basileus ou Basileusas* (Heidelberg, 1929-30); and Brandon, *Jesus and the Zealots*.

14. See the discussion in Alfredo Fierro, *The Militant Gospel: A Critical Introduction to Political Theologies*, trans. John Drury (Maryknoll, N.Y.: Orbis, 1977), 152-65.

15. Paul Hoffmann, "'Eschatologie' und 'Friedenshandeln' in der Jesusüberlieferung," in *Eschatologie und Frieden, Band II,* ed. Gerhard Liedke (Heidelberg: FEST, 1978), 179-223. Hoffmann describes the particular perspective of Jesus as a synthesis of apocalyptic and wisdom worldviews, in which future hope was linked to creation faith (p. 190).

16. Norman Perrin, *Rediscovering the Teaching of Jesus* (London: SCM Press, 1967), 59f.

17. See Rudolf Pesch, *Das Markusevangelium, Band I* (Freiburg: Herder, 1976), 206, for a cogent defense of the historicity of the "Twelve" and of the symbolic role assigned to them by Jesus.

18. Jeremias, *New Testament Theology,* 1:96.

19. On Jesus' proclamation of the Kingdom, see Norman Perrin, *The Kingdom of God in the Teaching of Jesus* (London: SCM Press, 1963), and Gösta Lundström, *The Kingdom of God in the Teaching of Jesus* (Edinburgh: Oliver & Boyd, 1963), for comprehensive surveys of recent discussion on the subject. Perrin has continued his explorations into Jesus' idea of the Kingdom in his *Rediscovering the Teaching of Jesus* (London: SCM Press, 1967), 54-108; and his *Jesus and the Language of the Kingdom* (London: SCM Press, 1976), 15-88. Together the three works constitute the best introduction available to recent discussion of the Kingdom. Yet, in spite of its exegetical acumen, clarity of exposition, and balance of judgment, Perrin's work is already dated, because it does not take into account recent political and liberation theology, which calls into question the strongly existentialist interpretation he gives to the teaching of Jesus. The same could be said too of the otherwise excellent work of Rudolf Schnackenburg, *God's Rule and Kingdom* (New York: Herder & Herder, 1963), and even more so of the solidly competent but avowedly conservative study of George Eldon Ladd, *Jesus and the Kingdom* (London: SPCK, 1966). For a more recent discussion within the perspectives opened up by political and liberation theology, see W. Schmithals, "Jesus und die Weltlichkeit des Reiches Gottes," *EvKom* 1 (1968): 313-20; G. Klein, "'Reich Gottes' als biblischer Zentralbegrift," *Evangelische Theologie* 30 (1970): 642-70; E. Grässer, "Zum Verständnis der Gottesherrschaft," *Zeitschrift für die neutestamentliche Wissenschaft* 65 (1974): 1-26; and A. Feuillet, "Le caractère purement religieux et universel du Règne de Dieu d'après les Évangiles synoptiques," *Divinitas* 22 (1978): 153-75.

20. E. Fuchs, "The Quest of the Historical Jesus," in his *Studies of the Historical Jesus* (London: SCM Press, 1964), 11-31, especially 21-24, where it is argued that "Jesus' conduct was itself the real framework of his proclamation."

21. R. H. Fuller, *Interpreting the Miracles* (London: SCM Press, 1963), 39-45; Jeremias, *New Testament Theology*, 1:85-96.

22. Jeremias, *New Testament Theology*, 1:97, against G. Dalman, *Die Worte Jesu,*

Band I (Leipzig: Hinrichs, 1930), 70. Dalman holds that Matthew's "Kingdom of the Heavens" is more original, because more Jewish. Against this Jeremias argues: "the complete silence of the Jewish inter-testamental literature makes it highly improbable, if not completely inconceivable, that the expression 'kingdom of heaven' was already current language at the time of Jesus and was taken up by him" (p. 97).

23. K. G. Kuhn, "*malkût shamayim* in Rabbinic Literature," in *Theological Dictionary of the New Testament,* ed. G. Kittel (Grand Rapids: Eerdmans, 1964), 1:572; Jeremias, *New Testament Theology,* 1:32.

24. See Bruce D. Chilton, *God in Strength: Jesus' Announcement of the Kingdom* (Freistadt: Plochl, 1979), 14.

25. Ibid., 13, citing C. F. D. Moule, *The Birth of the New Testament* (London: Black, 1962), 3.

26. In spite of the spirited attack by the Griesbachians (who hold that Mk is an abridgment of Mt and Lk), there is still a lot to be said for the priority of Mk, even though the Two Source theory (Mt and Lk depend on Mk and "Q") is no longer the unquestioned dogma of critical orthodoxy it once tended to be. For a good discussion of the pros and cons of the question, see *Jesus and Man's Hope* (Pittsburgh: Pittsburgh Theological Seminary, 1970), 1:51-98 and 131-70; and J. J. Griesbach, *Synoptic and Text Critical Studies,* ed. B. Orchard and T. R. Longstaff (Cambridge: Cambridge University Press, 1978), 50-67 and 154-69.

27. Aloysius M. Ambrozic, *The Hidden Kingdom: A Redaction Critical Study of the Reference to the Kingdom of God in Mark's Gospel,* Catholic Biblical Quarterly Monograph Series (Washington, D.C.: Catholic Biblical Association, 1972), 1.

28. What follows is the revision of an article entitled "The Central Message of Jesus: A Contemporary Interpretation of Mt 1:14-15," published in *Nirjhari*, the Annual of the Adhyatama Vidya Pitha, Bangalore (1978/79): 58-72. An abridged version appeared as "The Mission of Jesus," *Vaidikamitram* 12 (1979): 281-96. A first unpublished draft of this was used by Bishop Patrick D'Souza in preparing his talk on "Church and Mission in Relation to the Kingdom of God, Especially in Third World Countries," subsequently published in Federations of Asian Bishops Conferences Papers no. 22. This explains points of resemblance between his presentation and mine.

29. See Leander E. Keck, "The Introduction to Mark's Gospel," *New Testament Studies* 12 (1965): 352–70; Wolfgang Trilling, "Die Botschaft vom Reiche Gottes," in his *Christus Verkündigung in den synoptischen Evangelien* (Munich: Kösel, 1969), 257-75; Franz Mussner, "Gottesherrschaft und Sendung Jesu nach Mk 1:14f," in his *Praesentia Salutis* (Düsseldorf: Patmos, 1967), 81-98. There is some discussion about the exact limits of Mark's prologue. Does it reach only up to v. 13, with 1:14 marking the beginning of the ministry of Jesus (so Trilling with most commentators)? Or does it extend to v. 15 with the Galilean ministry beginning only at 1:16 (so Keck with Wellhausen and Zahn)? The problem, I believe, is solved if one takes Mk 1:14-15 as a programmatic summary which belongs neither to the prologue (with Trilling) nor to the narrative of the ministry (with Keck) , but which serves as a transitional passage linking one with the other.

30. Mark as we have it now ends at 16:8. The remaining verses of ch. 16 (vv. 9-20) are clearly a later addition, not found in the earliest manuscripts of the Gospel. Whether, then, the promise of Jesus in 14:28 and 16:17 ("I will go before you into Galilee") refers to an Easter apparition reported in a now lost ending of the Gospel, or to the parousia which Mark expected as imminent when he wrote his book, is debatable. See J. Alsup, *The Post Resurrection Appearance Stories of the Gospel Tradition* (Stuttgart: Calwer, 1975), 88 n. 266; and Willi Marxsen, *Mark the Evangelist* (Nashville: Abingdon, 1965), 75-116.

31. See Lucien Legrand, *Good News Witness* (Bangalore: Theological Publications in India, 1973), 3.

32. See Ambrozic, *Hidden Kingdom:* "we can assert with practical certainty that vs. 14 is redactional." Most authors would agree with this while allowing for Mark's use of early Christian mission terminology; so Marxsen, *Mark,* 127; Trilling, "Die Botschaft vom Reiche Gottes," 46; Mussner, "Gottesherrschaft," 82; or of traditional themes like "after the arrest of the Baptist" and "preaching the Gospel" (Chilton, *God in Strength*, 29-53).

33. Sepphoris is not mentioned in the Gospels at all; Tiberias only in Jn 6:23, which speaks of "boats from Tiberias" coming to the place of the multiplication of the bread. The "sea of Tiberias" is mentioned in Jn 6:1 and 21:1.

34. Chilton, *God in Strength*, 49-53; Pesch, *Das Markusevangelium,* 1:100-104.

35. Trilling, "Die Botschaft vom Reiche Gottes," 49-53; Mussner, "Gottesherrschaft," 82.

36. Ambrozic, *Hidden Kingdom,* 4-6; Werner Kelber, *The Kingdom in Mark: A New Place and a New Time* (Philadelphia: Fortress Press, 1974), 3-4; Marxsen, *Mark,* 126-38.

37. So Vincent Taylor, *The Gospel According to St. Mark* (London: Macmillan, 1952), 165; Eduard Schweizer, *The Good News According to Mark* (London: SPCK, 1971), 44; Walter Grundmann, *Das Evangelium nach Markus* (Berlin: Evangelische Verlagsanstalt, 1973), 36; Hugh Andersen, *The Gospel of Mark* (London: Oliphants, 1976), 83; Pesch, *Das Markusevangelium,* 100; Trilling, "Die Botschaft vom Reiche Gottes," 54-56; Mussner, "Gottesherrschaft," 83-84.

38. Ambrozic, *Hidden Kingdom,* 6.

39. So Trilling, "Die Botschaft vom Reiche Gottes," 52; Mussner, "Gottesherrschaft," 82; Schweizer, *Mark,* 44; against Pesch, *Das Markusevangelium,* 1:103, who feels that the whole summary reflects the language of Jesus.

40. Perrin, *Language,* 33-34.

41. Kuhn, "*malkût*," 571; see also B. D. Chilton, "Regnum Dei, Deus est," *Scottish Journal of Theology* 31 (1978): 261-70, who, examining the eight occurrences of the expression in the Targum to the Prophets, finds it a "contemporary catchword" referring to God's activity.

42. Perrin, *Language*, 16-32.

43. J. Dupont, *Les Béatitudes* (Paris: Gabalda, 1969), 2:53-90.

44. A. C. Burnell (trans.), *Hindu Polity: The Ordinances of Manu* (Ludhiana: Kalyani Publishers, 1972), 150.

45. Sigmund Mowinckel, *The Psalms in Israel's Worship,* vol. 1 (Oxford: Blackwell, 1962), 114-15.

46. For an excellent analysis of Ex 6:2-8, see K. J. Scaria, "Social Justice in the Old Testament," *Bible Bhashyam* 4 (1978): 174-76.

47. Walter Brueggemann, *The Land* (Philadelphia: Fortress Press, 1977), 2. The book is well worth reading as an exciting new attempt at doing biblical theology with "the land" as a basic category.

48. On Jewish messianism, see E. Jenni, "Messiah, Jewish," in *The Interpreter's Dictionary of the Bible* (Nashville: Abingdon, 1962), 3:360-64. Sigmund Mowinckel, *He That Cometh* (Oxford: Blackwell, 1956), 155-86; and especially Joachim Becker, *Messianic Expectation in the Old Testament* (Philadelphia: Fortress Press, 1980).

49. John Bright, *A History of Israel* (London: SCM Press, 1960), 344-49. S. Talmon, "Ezra and Nehemiah," in *Interpreter's Dictionary of the Bible: Supplementary Volume* (Nashville: Abingdon, 1976), 317-21.

50. On Jewish apocalyptic, see D. S. Russell, *The Method and Message of Jewish Apocalyptic* (London: SCM Press, 1964) or more briefly his *Between the Two Testaments* (London: SCM Press, 1960).

51. Paul Volz (*Die Eschatologie der jüdischen Gemeinde in neutestamentlichem Zeitalter* [Tübingen: Mohr, 1934]) gives a thorough and extensive survey of Jewish eschatological expectations at the time of Jesus, to be complemented for Qumram documents by A. S. van der Woude, *Die messianischen Vorstellungen der Gemeinde von Qumran* (Assen: Van Gorcum, 1957).

52. Perrin, *Language,* 33.

53. On Jesus' experience of God, see James D. G. Dunn, *Jesus and the Spirit* (London: SCM Press, 1975), 12-40.

54. E. Würthwein, "Repentance and Conversion in the Old Testament," in *Theological Dictionary of the New Testament,* ed. G. Kittel (Grand Rapids: Eerdmanns, 1967), 4:980-89.

55. Sebastian Kappen, *Jesus and Freedom* (Maryknoll, N.Y.: Orbis, 1977), 119-32; Soares-Prabhu, "Jesus the Prophet," *Jeevadhara* 21 (1974): 206-17 (see chapter 3 of this volume); Rudolf Pesch, "Jesus—ein freier Mann: Eine Auslegung der neutestamentlichen Überlieferung," *Bibel und Kirche* 32 (1977): 103-9.

56. See Rudolf Bultmann, "New Testament and Mythology," in *Kerygma and Myth,* ed. Hans Bartsch (New York: Harper Torchbooks, 1961), 32f. "The event of Jesus Christ is therefore the revelation of the love of God. It makes a man free from himself and free to be himself, free to live a life of self commitment in faith and love."

57. I have developed the point in detail in an issue of *Anawim,* a series of "tracts introducing Jesus to the contemporary man," published for private circulation by S. Kappen, from the Centre for Social Reconstruction, H-129/5: 34th Cross Street, Basant Nagar, Madras 600 009. The relevant issue, *Anawim* 21, is entitled "The Love Commandment: The Jesus Way as a Way of Revolutionary Concern," and appeared in August 1979.

58. See Soares-Prabhu, "The Miracles of Jesus: Subversion of a Power Structure?" *Anawim* 14 (April 1978). A similar attempt to spell out in contemporary language the significance of the Kingdom as a struggle against demonic powers (interpreted as "all that which destroys human life and fellowship") has been worked out in depth by T. Lorenzmeier, "Zum Logion Mt 12:28; Lk 11:20," in *Neues Testament und christliche Existenz* [Festschrift für H. Braun] (Tübingen: Mohr, 1973), 289-304.

59. Some relation between the "new society" and the Kingdom is envisioned by Vatican II in *Gaudium et Spes* § 39:

> Therefore, while we are warned that it profits a man nothing if he gain the whole world and lose himself, the expectations of a new earth must not weaken but rather stimulate our concern for cultivating this one. For here grows the body of a new human family, a body which even now is able to give some kind of foreshadowing of the new age.
>
> Earthly progress must be carefully distinguished from the growth of Christ's kingdom. Nevertheless, to the extent that the former can contribute to the better ordering of a human society, it is of vital concern to the Kingdom of God.

The new society, then, is vitally related to the Kingdom of God, though just what this relation is has yet to be determined. Vatican II is studiedly vague. The new humanity, it tells us, "foreshadows" the new age, but we are not told how; and human progress is said to be of "vital concern" to the Kingdom of God, but we are not told why. The precise relation between the new society to be built in history and the eschatological Kingdom of God which (presumably) is to bring history to an end is as yet an unresolved problem of Christian theology.

60. See Soares-Prabhu, "Good News to the Poor: The Social Implications of the Message of Jesus," *Bible Bhashyam* 4 (1978): 195-201; see chapter 16 of this volume.

61. Compare these to the nine goals which together with a tenth (ecological balance) are proposed by Johan Galtung as those to be aimed at in the construction of a "preferred world." See his *True Worlds*, 62. Looking at the society in terms of "actors" and "structures," defining its goals in terms of both "being" and "having," and arranging these goals in terms of "level" (= concentration on a person, a structure), "dispersion" (= distribution between persons and structures), or "relation" (= connection between persons or structures), Galtung offers the following classification of these goals and (in brackets) their antonyms:

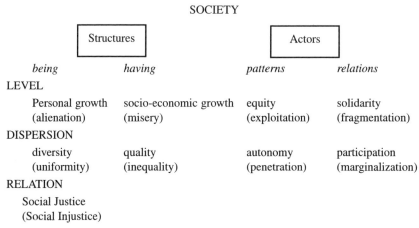

SOCIETY

	Structures		Actors	
	being	*having*	*patterns*	*relations*
LEVEL				
	Personal growth (alienation)	socio-economic growth (misery)	equity (exploitation)	solidarity (fragmentation)
DISPERSION				
	diversity (uniformity)	quality (inequality)	autonomy (penetration)	participation (marginalization)
RELATION				
	Social Justice (Social Injustice)			

These goals have been formulated by Galtung in view of the five "fundamental needs" (three physical and two social) which must be satisfied if man is to form an economically, biologically, and culturally self-sufficient society (pp. 20-21). These fundamental needs are: *food* (to maintain the input-output balance of the individual); *clothing and shelter* (to preserve his climatic balance with nature); *health* (to make up for malfunctioning of his organism); *community* (to satisfy his need for togetherness and procreation); and *education* (to provide him with the means of socialization and symbolic interchange). Such "fundamental needs" stand in sharp contrast to the often artificially stimulated "demands" of the rich, comprising 30 percent of the world population. Demands can be curtailed; fundamental needs cannot. Unfortunately "the present world is structured in such a way that it is very often more responsive to demands articulated in the very effective language of money than to needs, ineffectively articulated in the mute protests of the empty stomach, the body exposed to diseases and other hazards of nature, the mind left unfertilized by community and communication" (p. 17). If capitalism (particularly of the Reaganomics brand) is a social system catering by definition to the "demands" of a market economy in which production is for profit not for people, and if socialism, ideally at least, can be described as "a political and economic system that gives top priority to the satisfaction of fundamental needs, starting with those at the bottom" (p. 19), then the option for the Christian, moved by the vision of Jesus, is clear.

5

THE JESUS OF FAITH

A Christological Contribution to an Ecumenical Third World Spirituality

This paper attempts to spell out some of the problems which arise when one attempts to determine the role of Jesus in an ecumenical Christian spirituality that will respond effectively to the Third World's cry for life. It does this in two parts. The first part provides a historical and hermeneutical survey of the christological discussion in the early Church and the New Testament to make us aware of some of the problems implicit in an attempt to construct an ecumenical Christian theology for the Third World; the second offers a meditation on the "Jesus of faith" as a basis for christological reflection. The whole paper is not meant to offer a finished Christology but to stimulate christological reflection. Like so much in Third World theology today, it poses more questions than it answers.

I. A HERMENEUTICAL PROLOGUE

How does one engage in "Christ-talk" in a way that will both be responsive to the cry for life which emerges in many different voices and in many different tones throughout the Third World today, and be acceptable to Christians as Christians (perhaps even as "anonymous" Christians) and not merely to some particular churches or sects among them? To do this, one cannot simply take over the considerable volume of christological writing (some of it quite excellent) current in theological circles today, however much it may derive inspiration and insight

This article was published in *Spirituality of the Third World: A Cry for Life*, ed. K. C. Abraham and B. Mbuy-Beya (Maryknoll, N.Y.: Orbis, 1995), 139-64 and *in Theology of Liberation: An Indian Biblical Perspective*, Collected Writings of George M. Soares-Prabhu, S.J., vol. 4, ed. Francis X. D'Sa (Pune: Jnana-Deepa Vidyapeeth, 2001), 223-51.

from it.[1] Jesus, the giver of life, in our Third World situation of anguish and of death, must be sought afresh by confronting Christian tradition with contemporary Third World experience.

1. Early Christian Tradition

The Christian tradition with which contemporary Third World experience must interact cannot be the classical christological tradition of the early church, from which most modern Christologies derive, and which finds its normative expression in conciliar formulae, notably that of Chalcedon. For this Christology, however "correct" it might be, represents a narrow, culturally conditioned, and even politically motivated development which exploits only a very small fraction of the christological potential that the New Testament offers. The dogmatic Christology of the post-apostolic Hellenistic church, to which we are all heirs, developed along a single line which took off from the Logos Christology of John, itself a rare though not wholly unrepresentative growth in the complex jungle of New Testament theology.[2] It eventually crystallized in the formulae of Nicaea (325 C.E.), Ephesus (431 C.E.), and Chalcedon (451 C.E.), which became the normative "dogmas" for succeeding ages.

Many factors prompted this unilinear and, I believe, ultimately impoverishing development, which has led to the progressive alienation of Jesus from the world, by robbing him of his individuality as a human being: "he became," as the church historian W. H. C. Frend has said, "man but not a man."[3] The Logos theology of John obviously offered an easy entry into Hellenistic philosophical thinking, so that it was natural that it should be taken up by the Church Fathers theologizing in a Hellenistic world,[4] and developed in terms of the then current neo-Platonic philosophical categories of "nature" (*physis*), "substance" (*ousia*), "subsistence" (*hypostasis*), and "person" (*prosōpon*), however imprecisely and ambiguously these were then understood. Christ-talk in the early Church adopted one particular philosophical idiom, but within it proceeded to develop an endless series of aggressively competing models, each more intricate than the one before.[5]

But when, with the conversion of Constantine in 312 C.E., the prophetic religion of Jesus became (paradoxically) the legitimizing ideology of the Roman Empire,[6] then the imperial unity required an end to theological dissension and some kind of uniformity of belief. It was, partly at least, because of such concerns for "imperial integration" that the Council of Nicaea, the first ecumenical council,[7] was convoked by Constantine in 325, and largely managed by him. Indeed the fateful *homoousios* (consubstantial), the crucial expression of the Nicene Creed, which became the "most disputed word of the fourth century,"[8] was probably inserted into the baptismal credo of Syro-Palestinian provenance which the council had adopted as its consensus formula, at the behest of the emperor.[9]

This imperial venture in theology did not, of course, bring an end to the christological controversies of the early Church. These continued with unabated vigor all through the fourth century, pitting the Antiochenes and their *dya hypostaseis* (two subsistences), which gave full importance to the humanity of Jesus, since this alone could offer "a perfect pattern of virtue and redemption to humankind" against the Alexandrians and their *mia physis* (one nature), which stressed his divinity, so that eucharistic participation in the body of the true Word of God would provide "an antidote to the corruption of death."[10] A brilliant if somewhat patchwork synthesis was eventually reached at Chalcedon in 451. This affirmed faith in "one and the same Christ, Son, Lord, Only Begotten, made known in two natures [which exist] without confusion, without change, without division, without separation . . . concurring into one person (*prosōpon*) and one subsistence (*hypostasis*) not parted into two persons but one and the same Son, and Only begotten, the divine Logos, the Lord Jesus Christ."[11] But this did not put an end to the controversy. The formula became, indeed, the norm for all christological development in the Latin West, much of the Greek and some of the Syriac East; but it provoked fresh controversies, even more violent than before in Egypt and Syria, creating new divisions which have yet to be healed.[12] "It settled very little in the East," Jaroslav Pelikan suggests, providing the terms for subsequent controversies, "rather than the solution for past ones."[13]

I suggest three conclusions be drawn from this rapid survey of the christological controversies of the early Church from which the traditional Christology of our Christian churches has emerged:

(1) Any attempt to encapsulate the mystery of Jesus into a formula, however intricate, subtle, and complex, is bound to be inadequate, theologically and pastorally. The mystery of Jesus cannot be conceptualized, delimited, defined, or packaged into neat philosophical categories, and attempts to do this lead only to the alienation of Jesus from life. A different kind of analysis (one which will focus on the life-giving "mystery" of Jesus and not on the conceptual "mechanism" which pretends to explain him), and a different mode of expression (metaphorical not ontological) are needed if we are to understand the significance of Jesus for Third World *spirituality* of liberation and dialogue today.

(2) No christological formula has in fact been accepted as normative by Christians as a whole. Nicaea was rejected by the Arians, Ephesus by the Nestorians, Chalcedon by the Monophysites, not to speak of innumerable other barely remembered sects with unpronounceable names, squabbling with quite extraordinary ferocity over obscure points of doctrine. It would be easy, of course, to discount all these as "heretics" living in a state of stubborn error and unworthy of serious attention, except to be taken out and burnt at the stake. But distinctions of "orthodoxy" and "heresy" depend on one's point of view;[14] and accusations of heresy (usually mutual) do not negate the fact that all who profess faith in Jesus, no matter how they articulate this faith (whether as Arians, or as Nestorians or as Monophysites, or as Roman Catholics, or Anglicans or Protestants) are authentic Christians, whose understanding of Jesus is an integral and indispensable part of the ecumenical Christian tradition. A theology which pretends to be ecumenical

cannot limit itself to the christological conceptions of one or the other church, or group of churches, no matter how important they might be for the moment.

(3) This christological development, in which religious passion was so strongly contaminated by ecclesiastical rivalry and political ambition, and where theological argument was so frequently supplemented by mob violence and court intrigue,[15] took place within the compass of a single cultural tradition, what Raimundo Panikkar has called "the Mediterranean world and its cultural colonies,"[16] or as Karl Rahner more accurately describes it, the Hellenistic church.[17] Even the so-called oriental churches were Hellenistic in their theology even if Semitic in their language. The Christologies of the Copts or the Syrians were different and opposite variants of Roman or Byzantine Christology. For even in these oriental churches (which are not East but West, looked at from India or China or Japan!) theological discussion was pursued in the Greek categories, because these areas had already been absorbed into the Hellenistic world. Possibly the common people would have maintained links with their traditional culture and religions (as in India today, where the veneer of westernization of the so-called educated classes is paper thin), but the theologians (as also in India) were brought up to theologize in the dominant Hellenistic idiom. Christian theology is much less catholic than it imagines itself to be.

It is only with the end of the Vasco da Gama age that non-Hellenistic theologies begin hesitatingly to appear. EATWOT (Ecumenical Association of Third World Theologians) has been a powerful midwife for these in the harsh Egypt of our north-dominated theological culture, where barrenness and infant mortality among non-establishment theologies is high, because the Christian churches, by and large, are still far too dominated by the northern ecclesiastical policies and academic forms. Third World theologies (except for Latin American liberation theology, which has taken off and become, I believe, the most significant theology in the Christian world today) have yet to acquire a life and configuration of their own. Any useful christological contribution to a *Third World* spirituality will obviously have to break out of such northern domination. If it is to do this, it will not be able to draw on the christological tradition of the early Church, which is Hellenistic, sectarian, and flawed by unacknowledged political biases, but will have to reach behind it to the New Testament, from which all Christian theology ultimately derives.

2. The New Testament

The New Testament too is, of course, culturally conditioned. It is largely a Hellenistic text with a Semitic (Aramaic) substratum. But, unlike the christological formulae of the early Christian tradition, the New Testament is a privileged text, accepted as sacred and normative by all Christian denominations. The New Testament is this because it expresses (it is believed) the faith experience of the "apostolic church," that is, of the Christian community at the privileged moment of its beginnings. It is, as it were, the constitution of the church, embodying (as the constitution of a nation state does) the salient features of the specific identity it assumed at the moment of its birth. A Christian community will remain true to itself (that is, will be Christian) only as long as it remains true to the foundational experience of Jesus (understood both as object and subject) which brought it into being. But this originary experience (the faith experience of the apostolic community) is precisely what the New Testament embodies. For the New Testament is, by definition, made up of just those writings in which the community sees its originary faith experience authentically expressed.[18] The New Testament is thus the unique textual source for a genuinely ecumenical Christian theology.

The foundational experience of Jesus which is the basis of the whole Christian tradition is expressed in the New Testament in a variety of ways. For each New Testament writing has a Christology (one might even say is a Christology) which interprets and articulates Jesus' experience in response to the specific needs of its community. Since community settings differ and evolve, Christologies are strikingly varied. They use a variety of *titles* drawn from various cultural backgrounds (Hebrew and Greek) to express the significance of Jesus (Son of God, Son of Man, the eschatological Prophet); they compare Jesus to various Old Testament types to indicate his saving function (Jesus is the new Moses, the new Israel, the new Elisha, the new Solomon); and, rarely, they use concepts derived from Hellenistic Judaism or Hellenism to attempt a description of his being (the wisdom Christology of Matthew and of Paul, the Logos Christology of John). By and large these Christologies are largely functional, not (like the Christologies of the post-apostolic tradition) ontological. They are concerned more with describing the significance of Jesus (his role in saving history) rather than with explaining the structure of his being.[19]

Attempts have been made to organize the various New Testament Christologies into a linear sequence, showing the development in christological thinking as Christianity grows out of its Palestinian homeland and enters the Hellenistic Jewish Diaspora (Paul) and eventually the gentile Hellenistic world (John). Raymond Brown has spelled out this development in terms of the progressive retrojection of the "Christological moment," that is the moment when Jesus was believed to have become the Christ.[20] Christological speculation was sparked off by the Easter experience, however this is conceived. It was this that first awakened the followers of Jesus to his true significance. But then their understanding of Jesus as the Christ developed, it is suggested, gradually, and several stages can be noted in this development:

(1) The first followers of Jesus were Palestinian Jews; they shared the standard messianic expectations of their people.[21] They believed that the risen Jesus would return shortly as the victorious political Messiah of the kind expected by their people. Jesus was not yet the Christ even after his resurrection (he had not yet fulfilled Jewish messianic expectations), but he would return as the Christ in the near future. In Acts 3:19-21 Peter urges his Jewish listeners to repent so that "times of refreshing may come from the Lord and that he may send the Christ who has been appointed for you, Jesus who must remain in heaven until the time

comes for God to restore everything he promised long ago." If the people repent, Peter claims, the risen Jesus will soon return as the triumphant Messiah. The Christology implied in this curious and very ancient text (a fragment of an early Jewish Christian credal formula which Luke has incorporated into his description of Peter's speech) is thus a *future Christology* whose christological moment is the parousia.[22]

(2) This future Christology soon becomes a *present Christology*. In the earliest formulae used in Christian preaching, as these have been preserved for us in the Letters of Paul (Rom 1:3-4) or in the speeches of Peter and Paul reported in the Acts (Acts 2:32-36; 5:31; 13:32-33) Jesus becomes the Christ (the Son of God invested by the Spirit) at the resurrection. Obviously he is a Christ very different from the one awaited in popular messianic expectation. He is now, in the Hellenistic Jewish Christianity of Paul, the heavenly Lord enthroned in heaven, ruling over his people through the power of his spirit, experienced by them in the cult. The political Messiah of Judaism has been spiritualized. The Kingdom of Jesus is not of this world; he liberates not from earthly oppression but from sin; his peace is "heavenly peace," tranquillity of soul. The spiritualism of Greek thinking with its dichotomy of matter and spirit has begun to infect the holistic earthy spirituality of the Palestinian Christianity.

(3) In subsequent moments of the tradition the christological moment is pushed further and further back into the pre-Easter life of Jesus. In the Gospel of Mark, Jesus is already the Christ in his pre-Easter earthly existence, because he is anointed by the Spirit as "Son of God" or Messiah at his baptism (Mk 1:9-11). In the infancy narratives of Matthew (1:18) and Luke (1:35) he is the "Son of God" invested with the Spirit from the moment of his conception. A present Christology thus becomes an increasingly past Christology, as the christological moment is pushed back from Jesus' resurrection, to the beginning of his public ministry, and, last of all, to his conception. From the first moment of his existence (but not before, there is no suggestion of preexistence in the Synoptic Gospels) Jesus is the Christ. New understandings of messiahship are demanded by this retrojection of the christological moment. Jesus is the suffering Messiah who realizes his sonship in his death on the cross in Mark (15:39); he is incarnate Wisdom who exercises his messianic office by teaching the will of God in Matthew (11:28-30; 23:34). The title can be applied to Jesus only by doing violence to its original content!

(4) The content is again radically transformed in John (for the Messiah in Jewish thinking is never divine) when, in the largely gentile church for which he is writing, he presents Jesus as the preexistent, divine Messiah, the incarnation of the Logos, the word made flesh: "the word became flesh and made his dwelling among us" (Jn 1:14). Past Christology has become the *preexistence Christology* we are familiar with. Such preexistence Christology is, I believe, first found in John, though there may have been intimations of it earlier.[23] It is possible of course that there are references to preexistence in the hymns quoted by Paul in

Philippians 2:6-11 and Colossians 1:15-20. But this is not at all certain. For neither the Adam Christology of Philippians, nor the cosmic (or wisdom) Christology of Colossians necessarily implies preexistence. The hymn in Philippians interprets Jesus as the new Adam, like him in the image of God, but who unlike Adam does not grasp at divinity. The hymn in Colossians portrays Jesus in terms of Wisdom, the attribute of God associated with creation and salvation, which Hellenistic Judaism personifies, without making it a person distinct from God (Prov 8:27-30; Wis. 8:4-6; Sir. 51:23-27). The exalted Christ is seen as the supreme manifestation of divine wisdom, the crown of creation and of saving history. "Jesus," as J. D. G. Dunn says, "is to be seen as the wise activity of God, as the expression and embodiment of God's wisdom more fully than any previous manifestation of the same wisdom whether in creation or in covenant."[24]

This rather simplified overview of the development of New Testament Christology gives us a feel for the richness and complexity and relativity of the christological thinking in the New Testament and suggests a number of lessons:

(1) We realize how strongly *contextual* the Christology of the New Testament is. New Testament Christology "evolves" under the influence of its environment. As long as the first Christians remained predominantly Jewish (whether in Palestine or in the Diaspora) they subscribed to its radical monotheism, and could not possibly have conceived of theology which would have made Jesus in any way divine. Palestinian Judaism looked for a future political Messiah (Acts 3:19-20) or saw Jesus as the eschatological prophet (Q). The most that Hellenistic Judaism (also radically monotheistic) would concede was the spirit Christology of Matthew and Luke, according to which Jesus is conceived by the Spirit of a virgin, analogously to the conception of great figures in the Hebrew Bible from barren women; or the Wisdom (or cosmic) Christology of Paul (1 Cor 8:6; Col 1:15-20) and possibly Matthew (Mt 11:2-19; 11:28-30; 23:34), which sees Jesus as the supreme manifestation of God's wisdom. A divine, incarnate Jesus first appears in the Hellenistic and sectarian community of John. New Testament Christology shows, to quote the provocative title of a recent work on the subject, a movement "from Jewish Prophet to Gentile God."[25]

(2) This scheme of an evolving Christology, while it is useful for pointing out how New Testament Christologies have changed with the changing context of the early church, must not be taken too literally. We must not suppose that New Testament Christology evolved in the sense that it underwent a simple progression from the simple to the complex, or the imperfect to the perfect, so that its earlier forms were rendered obsolete by later ones. The earlier Christologies of the New Testament were not provisional Christologies waiting to be superseded by others. The appearance of the Logos Christology of John does not make Mark's interpretation of Jesus as the suffering servant, or Q's interpretation of him as the eschatological prophet, irrelevant. These earlier Christologies have been complemented by Johannine Christology, not surpassed or "fulfilled" by it as non-Christian religions are sometimes said to be "fulfilled" (and therefore surpassed) by

the coming of Christianity. The New Testament shows a *pluralism of Christologies* (corresponding to the pluralism of theologies in a multireligious world), in which each adds a new dimension to the christological whole, a new insight into the mystery of Christ, a new configuring of the gestalt of Jesus. The many Christologies of the New Testament offer glimpses from various angles into the ineffable mystery of Christ, just as the various religious traditions of humankind offer glimpses from different standpoints into the inexhaustible and incomprehensible mystery of God.

(3) Unlike traditional dogmatic Christology, which is exclusive and works for the imposition of a single, "orthodox" christological model, New Testament Christology is inclusive and pluriform. Every community evolves its own understanding of Jesus responding to its own cry for life. And because life changes, Christologies change too. The New Testament preserves all these different Christologies, without opting exclusively for any one among them, because it does not wish to offer us (as dogmatic theology pretends to do) a finished product, to be accepted unquestionably by all. Rather its pluralism indicates a *christological open-endedness*, inviting us to discover our own particular Christology, that is, the specific significance of Jesus for our situation in the Third World today. The New Testament, then, does not offer us a specific model for our Christology, for its christological models are, historically and culturally, quite as conditioned as the christological formulae of early Christian tradition. It makes no more sense today (outside academic circles) to talk of Jesus as "Son of Man" or even "Son of God" or "the Word made flesh" than it would to talk of him (especially in advaitic India) as consubstantial with the Father, or (especially in the postmodern north) as having no human "personhood." Instead the New Testament gives us a model for our christologizing by mediating an encounter with Jesus and inviting us to articulate his significance for us today in our own local language, just as the New Testament writings did in theirs. To follow Jesus one need not (to answer Panikkar's anguished question) become spiritually a Semite any more than one need become intellectually a Greek.[26]

(4) At the heart of all the New Testament Christologies lies an *experience of Jesus,* the impact he made on the first followers through his life and teaching, his death and his resurrection.[27] It is this total experience of Jesus, mediated to the New Testament authors through the communities to which they belonged, which was the starting point of their Christology, as it has to be of ours. The language of the New Testament is metaphorical, and is made up not of sharply defined concepts (like "nature" or "person") which are tied to a particular philosophical system and unintelligible outside it but of rich symbols (like "Son of God," "bread," "light," "life") which, while emerging from a particular culture, are rooted in a common human experience and so can be transposed from one worldview to another. That is why the New Testament is able to communicate the experience of Jesus which underlies its many Christologies to us. It is this transcultural *experience of Jesus* received (and inevitably interpreted by us in and for our situation) that must be the starting point of our Christology, as it was of theirs.[28]

3. Christology in the Third World Today

Our christological task, then, is not to repeat or elaborate the formulae of traditional Christology (whose metaphysical categories make little sense for us in the Third World today), nor to adopt and adapt one or other christological model from the New Testament (whose Christologies are expressly tied to particular communities living in concrete historical situations). Our task is to create new Christologies, by confronting the cry for life which resounds in our Third World with our own experience of Jesus. The starting point of our Christology, then, is the dialectic confrontation of our Jesus experience with our Third World situation. A word must be said about each.

3.1. THE THIRD WORLD SITUATION: THE CRY FOR LIFE

The Third World situation in which our Christology is to be elaborated has been correctly presented as a cry for life. This cry for life has, I suggest, three elements, related to the three basic dimensions that shape human life: the economic dimension which grounds our physical existence, the affective dimension which grounds our psychic life, and the symbolic or meaning-giving dimension which finds expression in our religious quest. A human being does not live by "bread alone"; he or she also needs the "word" that will affirm his or her dignity as a free human person and will disclose what life is all about. Both bread and the word are urgently needed in a Third World marked by its massive economic poverty; its racist, sexist, and caste discrimination (which cannot be reduced to merely economic factors, however much Marxists have tried to do this); and its pluriform religiosity, which throws up competing worlds of meaning. Its cry for life is a cry for survival, for recognition, and for meaning. It is a cry for liberation (economic and cultural) and for dialogue. It is within these parameters that Jesus must be interpreted for the Third World.

3.2. THE CHRISTIAN EXPERIENCE OF JESUS: THE JESUS OF FAITH

The Jesus we try to interpret as a response to the Third World cry for life is not the "historical Jesus" unearthed for us by historical criticism, whose methods are much less effective, and whose results are much less assured than is generally realized.[29] Nor is it the "Christ of faith" presented to us in the dogmatic or liturgical formulae of the churches, which are tied to worldviews and ontologies that are not necessarily those shared by Third World Christians today. Instead, it will be what I venture to call "the Jesus of faith," that is, the Jesus presented to us in the confessional history of the New Testament, which is not necessarily identical with its critical history.[30] This Jesus is the real Jesus who lived in Palestine, but he is Jesus not simply as he "actually lived" (the *wie es eigentlich gewesen* of positivistic historiography), but as he was encountered and experienced by his first followers. That is why we speak of "Jesus" (not of "Christ"), but the Jesus of "faith" (not of "history"). The Jesus of faith is the Jesus of history as experienced by his faithful followers (and not, for example, as experienced by the religious and political leaders who opposed him). It is a category that lies between the Jesus of history and the Christ of faith, taking off from the Jesus of history and moving toward the interpretative explicitness of the Christ of faith.

Such a starting point avoids the danger of constructing our interpretations of Jesus on the continually shifting results of a supposedly neutral historical-critical method, which, in fact, operates with its own unacknowledged biases;[31] and it allows us to build on the whole Jesus experience and not only on those aspects of it which are amenable to historical investigation (like his ministry and his death, but not his incarnation and his resurrection!). Obviously the Jesus of faith has to be continually adjusted to the faith of the community, on the one hand, and the critical study of the Gospels, on the other. It emerges, in fact, in *the dialectic interaction of the critic's Jesus of history and the community's Christ of faith.*

Unlike the Jesus of history, which is the result of critical search for information (and so belongs to the noetic level of speculation), the Jesus of faith is the object of an experience (and belongs to the level of personal encounter). If our Christology is not to be an academic exercise which leaves us and our world untouched (as the immensely greater part of northern theology does) it must start off not from information but from experience. The Jesus we interpret must be a Jesus we "know," not just a Jesus we know about. As Raimundo Panikkar has put it:

> The identity (read "the experience") of Christ we are looking for is not that which comes from accurate historical information, nor even what a philosophical scrutiny of his words and doctrines may yield concerning who he is, but the identity which is found in the encounter with a person, that knowledge which springs up when we really know and love somebody, which is more than, and different from, the results of all examination of the objective data.[32]

But Panikkar's formulation tends to be over-individualistic. The experience of the Jesus of faith is not to be confused with the subjective experience of the individual. It is—and in this it differs from that personal experience of enlightenment which is a primary religious category in Asian religions—a *community experience.* The Jesus of faith is the community's Jesus, who is encountered in the living faith of the local Christian community, of which Scripture and tradition are constitutive parts, and where faith meets scholarship in a mutually corrective tension. The theologian reads the New Testament not as a neutral scholar, but as a critical believer steeped in a tradition, who has encountered Jesus in the Christian life of his or her community, confronts this experience with the biblical text read critically, and reflects on the implications of this critically corrected Jesus experience for the world in which he lives. All this is done as part of a holistic, organic, doubly dialectical process, in which (1) the Jesus of faith emerges through the dialectic interaction of our lived experience of Jesus and the study of the Gospel text about him, and (2) a meaningful Christology develops through the dialectical encounter between the Jesus of faith and the world in which he is experienced and proclaimed.

The place in which the Jesus of faith is encountered and a Third World Christology elaborated is, therefore, not primarily the academy and its search for the Jesus of history, nor merely the church in its worship of the Christ of faith, but the *community* which is shaped by and gives expression to the experience of Jesus in the totality of its life, its worship, its study, and its action. Christological theory presupposes (and is presupposed by) christological faith and *praxis*. That is why Third World Christologies cannot be produced in classrooms, nor in theological conferences like ours, but only in Christian communities, where Jesus Christ is encountered, experienced and "lived."

These communities in which Jesus is actively experienced and understood are, I would suggest, not merely communities of professing Christians, like the basic Christian communities of the Christian Third World (in Latin America, the Philippines, and parts of Africa); but also (in the massive non-Christian Third World, elsewhere in Asia and Africa) communities of those who profess basic human values (freedom, love, and justice), which ultimately are what Jesus proclaimed, lived by, and died for. For is not Christianity after all ultimately a "true humanism," in which Jesus tells us what the human person in the nexus of its relationships with God, fellow humans and the cosmos should aspire to be? Such basic human communities will, I believe, carry the christological quest a great step forward. For Jesus, as Mahatma Gandhi has said, "belongs not only to Christianity, but to the entire world."[33] Incomparable christological insights into his significance for the suffering world have been given, not least by Mahatma Gandhi himself;[34] by non-Christian social activitists like Baba Amte, winner of the Magsaysay award, whose impressive work for the rehabilitation of lepers was inspired, he confesses, by his reading of the Gospel;[35] or even by a notorious pop-guru like the Osho Rajneesh, whose eight books on Jesus, though they always trumpet the Osho's own tantric-advaita, abound in extraordinary creative insights (unavailable elsewhere) into what Jesus means today.[36] A great wealth of christological material lies untapped in the christological insight and the christological praxis of such "outsiders" who, like the centurion in Mt 8:5-13, have come to know Jesus, even though they are not numbered among his followers; or in the "precursors" of Jesus (like Nachiketas of the *Katha-Upanishad!*) which a discerning Christian can find in extra-biblical religious texts. It is here that dialogue enters into the christological process.

Such dialogue, and the Third World Christology it nourishes, will focus on the "mystery" of Jesus, not on the "mechanisms" that have been put forward to explain this mystery. By "mystery" is meant the person of Jesus, or the events in his confessional history (like his incarnation, the cross, the resurrection) inasmuch as these are enduring sources of significance for the person who seeks to "understand" them. "Mechanisms" are the models that have been proposed to explain the mystery, like the two natures in one person of Chalcedon or the popular understanding of the resurrection as the reunion of the soul of Jesus with his resuscitated body. Mysteries mediate significance; mechanisms offer explanations. Mysteries are therefore articulated in metaphors (like "Son of God," "the Word made Flesh"); mechanisms are articulated in precisely defined concepts that depend on specific ontologies. Mysteries unite, for all Christians assent to and find life in Jesus as savior, and believe in his incarnation, cross, resurrection, however differently they may understand them; mechanisms (as the history of theology amply shows) divide, because they are tied to specific culturally conditioned worldviews. The incarnation would be understood very differently in the non-dualistic Indian world from the way it has been understood in the dualistic Greek one, or is understood in the post-Enlightenment secular world. The resurrection was understood as the emergence of a shade from the world of the dead (*sheol*) into the world of the living (the new heavens and the new earth) in the Palestinian world of Jesus; it was reconceptualized as the reunion of an "immortal soul" surviving in "heaven" after the dissolution of the body, with a recreated earthly body in the Hellenistic world of the post-apostolic church. Mysteries endure but mechanisms change. Mysteries belong to what Schillebeeckx has called "theologies of Jesus," which focus on the significance of Jesus of Nazareth; mechanisms belong to what he calls "Christologies," which propose models to explain the divinity of Christ.[37] A Christology which hopes to contribute to a spirituality that is both Third World and ecumenical, relevant to Third World concerns and acceptable across denominational groups, cannot afford to get lost in the "network of metaphysical clouds"[38] that invest mechanisms, but must focus on the mystery of Jesus. It is after all the mystery that counts. For while mechanisms as provisional models may satisfy the human craving for intellectual clarity, it is the mystery that gives life and endures.

Traditional Christology has moved from mystery to mechanism. In a post-modern situation which is suspicious of mechanisms, and in a Third World which has learned at its expense how quickly preoccupation with "explanation" blunts the prophetic edge of the "Word," Third World theology would usefully adopt an alternative process, a "hermeneutical circle," which moves from experience/praxis to mystery and back to experience. It is in terms of such a hermeneutics of the mystery of Jesus presented in the Gospels that the following christological meditation on the Jesus of faith has been attempted, as a possible way toward a Third World Christology, but here (as in so much of Third World theologizing), there really is no way. The way, as the poet has said, is made by going.

II. A MEDITATION ON THE JESUS OF FAITH

Every religious tradition begins with an originary experience of the Absolute Mystery that we name God. The Christian tradition too begins with Jesus' experience of God. What we call an experience of God is not an insight into the "being" of God or into the ontological structure of reality. For God is not to be thought of as a "being" out there, standing over and against us, to whom we relate as we might relate to other human beings. God is not someone we can "objectify," measure, gather information about, study. God is the absolute mystery in whom we have our being.

The Experience of God

God is, therefore, as all religious traditions tell us, absolutely transcendent, irreducible to any created category, always beyond name and form. To see God, says the Bible, is to die. The Tao that can be known is not the real Tao. Kiteme, the Luo diviner tells the missionary, "is totally different and apart from humankind and apart from all creation." The Buddha when questioned about the existence of God answers with a smile.

We cannot therefore properly speak of God, but may only invoke him. His name, it has been said, is justified only in the vocative. For God is not a "he" or a "she" or an "it" but an I, indeed *the "I."* God is the I-am, the I-am-who-am, the *aham.* God is therefore not the one spoken about; rather the one who speaks. God is the I who speaks, and each of us is a spoken thou of God. Every one of us is the "thou art" uttered by the "I am."

As such, God is not only utterly transcendent but wholly immanent as well. God is the origin and the goal of the cosmos and of history (*Īśā Upanishad* 1:1). God must not be thought of as distinct from the universe as the crypto dualism (the standing temptation) of our Christian myth invites us to do. Neither is he wholly identical with it, as the monism, which is the standing temptation of oriental religion, supposes. God and the universe are not one, nor are they two. For whatever metaphor we adopt (creator–creature, whole–part, soul–body), God cannot be enumerated side by side with the world.

When we speak about "God" we are not therefore speaking of a being distinct from, other than the world. We are speaking of "the ground of our being," the infinite horizon of our self-transcending existence, the ultimate meaning of life, the absolute value. Any statement about God is always a statement about the world.

An experience of God is therefore not so much an insight into the ontological structure of reality; it is an insight into the meaning of life; telling us what life is all about, offering us a guide for living, showing us the way (*hodos, tao, mārga*). Theologians of course will offer us mechanisms to explain the experience, and construct elaborate metaphysical edifices using the conceptual bricks they have at hand. These may or may not be useful, but they are not to be confounded with the experience they are attempting to explain, which can allow for other alternative mechanisms. The experience is an immediate contact with the reality of experience, so that the distinction between the experiencing subject and the object experienced disappears. It needs no demonstration, no argument, no explanation. The explanation is not the mechanism.

The God Experience of Jesus

Jesus experienced God as unconditional love. He did this, probably, at his baptism by John, at a moment when, in a great act of solidarity he identified himself with sinful Israel (Mk 1:9-11). The experience irrupted into his life, shattering (as all such call experiences do) the ordinary patterns of existence, and impelling him to adopt the life of an itinerant charismatic preacher who announced in word and deed (in miracle and in parable, in table fellowship with outcasts and in aphoristic teaching), the imminent coming of the Kingdom of God, that is, of God's long-awaited definitive act of salvation. This God experience allowed Jesus to address God as "*Abba*" (loving parent), a name which is an invocation, not a description (as all divine names must be), and which tells us more about our own alienated situation and the way to redeem it than it tells us about the absolute mystery about God. *Abba* is the normal invocation Jesus henceforth used to address God, and to speak about God (Lk 10:21; Mk 14:36; Jn 11:41). In a religious tradition which stressed the transcendence of God to such an extent that his name was never spoken, this usage of Jesus was absolutely unique. God is never addressed as "Parent" in the Hebrew Bible. He/She is addressed as "Father" with a qualification ("Our Father in the heavens" or "Our Father our King") in rabbinic texts of the time of Jesus. But nowhere in Jewish tradition is God ever addressed simply as "Father," much less by the far more informal and intimate locution "*Abba*." The language of Jesus is unique and points to a unique experience of God.

Like every great religious teacher, Jesus shares this experience with his not always receptive followers. "No one knows the parent but the child," he says, "and those to whom the child has chosen to reveal the parent" (Mt 11:27). Jesus claims to "know" the Parent. In biblical language to "know" means to "experience," "to enter into an intimate relationship with," a relationship as intimate as that between man and woman in the closeness of the act of love (Gen 4:1). Jesus therefore experiences God as a loving parent, and he gifts this experience to those who follow him.

Indeed to be a follower of Jesus means precisely to share in this God-experience of his. What makes a person a Christian is not professing certain beliefs, nor practicing particular rituals, nor undergoing an initiation rite, nor belonging to a recognizable social group, nor even confessing the name of Jesus, though all these are inevitable stages in the evolution of a religious tradition. To be a disciple of Jesus means *to experience God the way that Jesus experienced God.* That is why one can say "Lord, Lord" and prophesy in the name of Jesus, or cast out demons in his name or do many mighty works in his name, and still not be acknowledged by him as his follower (Mt 7:21-24); and one may not have known Jesus at all and yet be recognized as one of his own, because one has fed the hungry, given shelter to the homeless, clothed the naked, cared for the sick, and visited those in prison (Mt 25:31-46). The routinization of charism, inevitable in the development of any movement, has transformed the community of disciples which Jesus gathered around him into a proliferating mass of competing (often squabbling) churches, defining themselves in terms of points of doctrine (*homoousios* or *homoiousios*), practices of ritual (communion under one species or under two), or issues of organization (monarchical papacy, collegial episcopacy or "democratic" presbyterate). In the process we have perhaps forgotten that the one thing necessary for Christian self-definition is the experience of God's love, which impels us to love in return and to reach out in effective compassion to those in need. But Jesus has not forgotten this. His fellowship is not limited to the churches which carry (and too often profane) his name. It reaches out to the many who will "come from east and west, and from north and south and sit at table in the kingdom of God" (Lk 13:29).

The Freedom of Jesus

The God experience of Jesus frees him. For love experienced always leads to a freedom from inner conditioning, that is, from the compulsions and fears that hold us in bondage. For are not such bondages the result of an absence of love? Are not the concupiscence of the eyes (our consumerism) and the concupiscence of the flesh (our eroticism) ultimately compensation mechanisms through which we strive to make up for the emptiness caused by the absence of love in our lives; and is not the pride of life (our macho assertiveness and craving for power) ultimately a defense mechanism through which we try to cover up the absence of self-worth we experience because we lack love? Is not the poverty of our people the result of such greed and the structures of exploitation it engenders? Is not their social rejection on grounds of race, caste, or gender, and the profound psychic scars this leaves a result of "patriarchy," the urge to dominate, and of the vast structures of domestic and societal oppression it creates? Does not our unfreedom make others unfree? Does not Mammon (personal bondage) generate (and is it not generated by) Satan (structured evil)? Love leads to freedom (to personal freedom and ultimately to structural freedom) because it frees us from the constraints and fears, the doubts and compulsions that paralyze us.

Jesus, who has experienced God as love, was supremely free. We marvel at his freedom. He was driven by no demons of greed or ambition. "The Son of Man has nowhere to lay his head," he said (Lk 9:58), describing the state of religious indigence that he had freely chosen. "The Son of Man has come not to be served but to serve and to lay down his life as a ransom for many," he announced (Mk 10:45), offering a neat and pointed summary of his life and mission. In a society that was politically colonized, socially patriarchal, and religiously conservative, he moved around with absolute freedom and authority. His freedom is all the more remarkable because he lacked position or power. Jesus had no religious prestige: he was not a priest born into a priestly family. He enjoyed no intellectual status: he was not a recognized theologian who had been trained in a scribal school (Jn 7:15). He commanded no political power. He did not enjoy the privileges of wealth. Yet he taught with authority in word and deed. "The crowds were astonished at his teaching," we are told on the occasion of the first miracle he performed (so Mk 1:2), and of the first "sermon" he delivered (Mt 7:28), "because he taught as one having authority and not as the scribes." The scribes of course had great authority, because of their patiently acquired knowledge of the Torah and of the oral traditions which had grown up around it. But the authority of Jesus was not like theirs. It was not "legal" authority based on learning and institutional sanction. It was charismatic and prophetic authority derived from his experience of God. The authority of Jesus (as he will explicitly affirm when challenged by the priests to justify his cleansing of the temple) is associated with his baptism by John; that is, it derives from his foundational experience of God (Mk 11:27-33).

This authority of Jesus (a significant christological element) enables him to confront the religious, social, and political establishment of his people with sovereign freedom. He reinterprets the Law with an authority that seems to parallel the authority of God. "It was said to them of old" (that is, "God said to our ancestors"), he announces, quoting not just rabbinic interpretations of the Law but the written Law itself (Mt 5:21, 27, 31, 33, 38), and then goes on to correct this with his "but I say to you" (Mt 5:21-48). No prophet has ever spoken like this. The prophets spoke in God's name, with God's authority, communicating God's message. "Thus says the Lord" was the prophet's way of speaking; but Jesus says: "I say unto you." Even if these antitheses of Matthew's Sermon on the Mount may be editorial compositions formulated at a time when Jesus was already interpreted as the founder of the new Israel standing over and against the formative Judaism of Jabneh representing the old, they carry the memory of the remarkable authority that Jesus must have shown in his interpretation of the Law.

Such authority is very evident in the Sabbath controversies which were a conspicuous feature of Jesus' ministry, attested to in all the Gospel traditions (Mt 9:18; 12:9-14; Mk 2:23-28; 3:1-6; Lk 13:10-17; Jn 5:1-18; 9:1-34). Jesus breaks the Sabbath whenever human need demands it, justifying his infringement of the sacred law of Sabbath rest with the radical principle that "the Sabbath is made for the human person not the human person for the Sabbath" (Mk 2:27). Every human institution or law (no matter how sacred) is thus subordinated to human need.

The pervasive law of purities which so restricted every aspect of Jewish life is abrogated by Jesus in the single striking observation that "nothing which enters anyone from the outside can make the person unclean: it is what comes out of the person that makes him or her unclean" (Mk 7:15). All purity lines are thus abolished in a stroke. Cleanness or uncleanness is a matter not of ritual purity but of the disposition of the heart. "Nothing in itself is unclean," as Paul rightly understands Jesus to have said (Rom 14:14). No *places* are of themselves holy, for God is to be worshiped not in Jerusalem or on Gerizim, but in spirit and in truth (Jn 4:21-23), wherever, that is, a community assembles in sincerity and love. No *person* is more sacred than another, for there is only one Parent God, and all humankind are brothers and sisters (Mt 23:8-10). There is here a radical desacralization of the cosmos, a radical dehierarchization of society (that is, a radical affirmation of the equality of humankind) and a radical shift from an ethics of observance (ritual and legal) to an ethics of love ("the heart").

In a patriarchal society where *women* were numbered with children and slaves as "minors" with diminished responsibility and a restricted role in worship and in public life, Jesus admits them into his movement as helpers and disciples. Not only do women follow him to take care of his needs (Lk 8:2), but Mary who sits at his feet listening to what he teaches (and so assuming the role of a disciple) is commended for having chosen the "better part" (Lk 10:38-42). Even in a tradition which has suffered heavy editing colored by patriarchal biases, the role of women in the Gospels is striking. Three conspicuous incidents in the ministry of Jesus, each heavy with theological significance, feature women (Jn 4:4-42; 7:36-50; Mk 14:3-9). In all these the women are not only occasions of significant teaching, but emerge favorably in comparison with their male counterparts. The spontaneous testimony of the Samaritan woman, who after conversing with Jesus proclaims him as the Christ to her people (Jn 4:28-30) contrasts with the embarrassed silence of the disciples who do not care to question Jesus (Jn 4:27); the moving love shown to Jesus by the woman who "had lived a sinful life" but shows by her loving actions that she is a forgiven sinner who has experienced God's forgiving love, is contrasted by Jesus with the indifference of Simon the Pharisee, whose unloving behavior shows him to be the real unforgiven "sinner," one who cannot love because he has not experienced forgiveness. The sensitive loyalty as shown to Jesus on the eve of his passion by the woman in Bethany contrasts sharply with the ideological fixation of the disciples and the disloyalty of Judas. This contrast is carried a great step further in the stories of the passion and resurrection, where the women disciples of Jesus are found at the cross and his tomb when the male disciples have all abandoned him and fled (Mk 15:40-41, 47; 16:1-8).

Where the Pharisees (the Jews of strict observance) and the Essenes of Qumran sought to renew their society through a rigorism that sought to enforce the observance of the Law as strictly as possible, Jesus opted for a *radicalism* which sought to realize as perfectly as possible the spirit of the Law, which he saw embodied in love (*agapē*), that is, in interhuman concern.

The Love (agapē) of Jesus

That is why Jesus can sum up his ethic in his love commandment (Mt 22:34-40), which he formulates by joining the great text of Judaism in Deuteronomy 6:4-5 ("The Lord your God is one God and you shall love the Lord your God with all your heart, with all your soul and with all your mind") to a little known text from the Holiness Code of Leviticus 19:18 ("You shall love your neighbor as yourself"). As understood by Jesus, this commandment does not ask us to love God and neighbor as if there were to be two different objects to our love. Rather Leviticus 19:18 is meant to be an interpretation of Deut 6:4-5. The content of Deuteronomy ("You shall love the Lord your God with all your heart") is spelled out by Leviticus ("You shall love your neighbor as yourself"). The love command of Jesus therefore reads: "You shall love the Lord your God with all your heart, with all your soul, and with all your mind; this means, you shall love your neighbor as yourself." To love God means, concretely, to love neighbor. The one commandment that Jesus gives us as the "great commandment," the one that founds and includes all the others is, then, that we *love God by loving neighbor.*

"Who, then, is my neighbor?" Is not this for Jesus a question as significant as that other christological question he will ask, "Who do you say I am?" In defining "neighbor" Jesus allows no distinctions of caste, race, gender, or class (Lk 10:30-37). For the love with which we love neighbor is not a human disposition (determined by human prejudices or preference), but it is the reflex of the experience of God's love for us. To the extent we experience God's love, we love neighbor the way that God loves us. But God loves us unconditionally. His love is not a response to our goodness. "God does not love us because we are good," as Augustine has somewhere said, "we are good because God loves us." God loves because God is love. God's love is not a reaction but an action. God loves the way the sun shines because it must. That is why our love for neighbor, which issues from (1 Jn 4:4) and images (Mt 5:43-48) God's love for us, can make no conditions and put no limits. It reaches out to the unrewarding, undeserving, even those hostile to us (Lk 6:32-36).

But by "love" Jesus does not understand friendship or fellowship or erotic passion, all the other human affects which (more or less correctly) are understood as "love" today. The *agapē* which the New Testament uses as its own very special term stands rather for an active, effective concern. It is best understood perhaps as the attitude of those who, because they have experienced God as Parent, experience (and not merely talk about) their fellow human beings as brothers and sisters and spontaneously respond to their needs. Like the Buddhist attitude of "mindfulness," the Christian attitude of *agapē* is thus an existential attitude deriving from a change in one's being. The change is not (normally) a sudden once-and-for-all transformation (as a "conversion" is usually understood to be), but a lifetime's process of growth. Christian life is a lifelong lesson in love.

Agapē then is effective love. The New Testament defines it as "doing good to" (Lk 6:35; 1 Thess 5:15) and understands this (as the parable of the Good Samaritan shows) as responding effectively to the real needs of the people we encounter. Love embraces the effective response to the whole spectrum of needs that we observe around us. Because it is increasingly evident that the effective response to many of our most urgent needs is necessarily a structural one, justice understood as a change of structures is an inescapable dimension of *agapē*.

Jesus and Justice

Jesus may not have been as aware as we are aware today of the structural origins of the evils of the society in which he lived. But he was committed to justice and to structural change because his proclamation of the Kingdom implied the vision of a new society. The Kingdom that he announced was the realization of the "alternative community" previsioned in biblical history at the Exodus, where Israel was liberated from bondage in Egypt that it might become God's people (Ex 6:2-7), and frequently invoked by the prophets who appear precisely when the monarchy has reversed the thrust of the Exodus (1 Sam 8:6-18; 1 Kgs 5:13) to protest against the perversion of the community that Israel was meant to be (Is 3:13-15; Am 2:6-8; Mic 2:1-2). The proclamation of the Kingdom by Jesus is both a promise and a summons, looking toward the ultimate realization of this alternative community, depicted in the core metaphor of "the family of God," which is implicit in all the teaching of Jesus.

As part of the realization of this vision, Jesus (who shares the apocalyptic worldview of the time) sees the coming of the Kingdom of God as the end of Satan's rule. Satan is the "prince of the world" (Jn 12:31), ruling the world through demons and demonic people. Satan stands for structured evil, organized might (the "legion" of Mk 5:1-20). It is this satanic power structure that Jesus combats through his controversies and his healings and exorcisms. The miracles of Jesus are therefore not to be taken as isolated actions of compassion (relief work). As such, the thirty or so healings and exorcisms that Jesus performed would not have amounted to very much. Rather they are an indication that God's rule has dawned and that Satan's rule has ended. "The strong man has been bound and his goods taken away" (Mk 3:27). The satanic power structure has been destroyed. The miracles of Jesus are thus the subversion of a power structure and so manifestations of a structural change.

Love as exercised by Jesus inevitably leads to conflict. This is because love, though it is universal in its object, is differentiated in its action. The *agapē* of Jesus reaches out indeed to all. But it affects people in different ways. The same love which prompts Jesus to say "Blessed are the poor" leads him to announce "Woe to you rich" (Lk 6:20-27). The concern he shows when he identifies his mission as the proclamation of the good news to the poor (Lk 4:16; Mt 11:5) is paralleled by the concern implied in his warning that "it is easier for a camel to pass through the eye of a needle than for the rich to enter the kingdom of God" (Mk 10:25). In an unequal world where class, caste, race, and gender conflicts exist, love must take sides. For nothing is more unjust (or more unloving), it has been said, than to divide equally among unequals, or treat oppressor and oppressed alike. The love of Jesus leads him to make (as the God of the Bible makes) an unambiguous option for the poor and the outcast, because they are as the Bible sees them, always victims of oppression.

Because of this self-defining option, the life of Jesus is lived out in the twin dimensions of *solidarity and conflict.* These are the complementary expressions of his God experience. The Gospels show Jesus living a life of progressive identification with the poor and of growing conflict with those who oppress them.

Solidarity with the Poor: Incarnation

Born into what we would call a *petit bourgeois* family (the class of artisans, who own the tools of their trade), Jesus de-classes himself by becoming an itinerant religious beggar with nowhere to lay his head (Lk 9:58). He breaks with his family to join the family of God, made up of all those who do the will of God, which is to love (Mk 3:31-35). He abandons himself wholly to God's provident care (Mt 6:28-34), depending for his livelihood on the casual help provided by sympathizing friends (Lk 8:1-2). A would-be religious teacher, he associates with outcasts, becoming an untouchable with the untouchables. He touches a leper (incurring ritual uncleanness) to welcome him back to human fellowship (Mk 1:40-42). He dines with the ritually unclean and socially ostracized tax collectors and sinners, incurring the hostility of the religious elite: "this man receives sinners," they say, "and eats with them" (Lk 15:2; Mk 2:16).

The solidarity of Jesus with the poor and the outcasts finds its christological symbol in the *incarnation.* This particular "mystery" of the confessional history of Jesus has been best expressed in the marvelous Johannine *sūtra:* "The word was made flesh (*sarx*), and dwelt (*eskēnōsen*) among us." The Word (whose identity is never disclosed except in Jesus) does not become a male (*anēr*); nor even a human person (*anthrōpos*). The Word becomes flesh (*sarx*). Flesh stands for humankind, indeed for all life, in its transience and fragility. "All flesh is as grass," says the prophet, "and its beauty is like the flower of the field; the grass withers, the flower fades, but the word of our God endures forever" (Is 40:3). The word of God's creation, challenge, and love, which endures forever, becomes fleeting flesh.

But flesh also stands for *solidarity and relatedness.* Man and wife become one flesh (Gen 2:24); members of a family are of the same "flesh and blood" (Gen 37:27); the poor and needy of our people are our own flesh (Is 58:7). Flesh stands for the solidarity of humankind, for the fact that humankind is not a collection of isolated individuals but an organic whole in which what happens to one happens to all. If the Word became flesh, it has graced, as Athanasius remarked, the whole human race. Humankind has now become the proper locus of our encounter with God. We meet God in neighbor; we love God by loving neighbor.

The individualism of Hellenistic philosophy, reinforced by the selfish individualism of bourgeois society, and legitimized by a psychology of personal fulfillment, which insists on the distinction between the "I" and the "you" ("I am I and you are you"), but forgets the oneness of the "we" ("you and I are we"), has made us forget this. We think of the incarnation only in its implication for Jesus as an isolated individual. Jesus is then made the God-Man (or even God appearing as a human being), who becomes the God of the Christians, much in the way that, say, Krishna is a God of the Hindus. The challenge of his human life is lost. He becomes the object of our devotion but no longer a paradigm for action so that Christian life comes to mean worshiping Jesus, not following him. But the incarnation (whatever its mechanism) must be seen primarily as a call to follow Jesus in his solidarity with humankind, expressed concretely through a consistent and progressive identification with the outcasts and the poor.

Conflict with the Powerful: The Cross

The solidarity of Jesus with these victims of economic, social, and political oppression is not merely a passive solidarity which assumes and endures their lot. It leads to a confrontation with the religious and political establishment which oppresses them, and to a struggle with Satan (structured evil) and Mammon (the mental causes of capitalism), which in his worldview are the ultimate sources of oppression. Jesus confronts the *theological establishment* (the scribes) to free people from a burdensome interpretation of the ritual and moral law (Mk 2:1-3:6); the *religious establishment* (the chief priests) and their misuse of the Temple, to protest against the exploitation of the people in the name of religion (Mk 11:15-19); and the *political establishment* (Herod), whose threat to kill him (a clear sign of the political impact of his ministry) he dismisses with contempt (Lk 13:31-33). The life of Jesus is thus riddled with conflict. Indeed conflict spills over even into the Gospel narrative of his infancy (Mt 2:1-23; Lk 1:27-32), and finds its resolution only with the death of Jesus on the cross.

The *cross* is no arbitrary intrusion into the life of Jesus. It is the natural outcome of a life of solidarity with the poor and the outcasts and of confrontation with the powerful who oppress them. Conflict with the rich and the powerful leads inevitably to the fatal confrontation which could only end with a foreseen and freely accepted death. And this death becomes the appropriate fulfillment of a life lived out with and for the poor and the outcasts. For on the cross Jesus is wholly poor and totally outcast. Identification and confrontation have here reached their furthest possible limits. Jesus is one with all the marginalized and all the martyred victims of the earth. The journey from the center to the periphery which, as Kosuke Koyama reminds us, was the basic movement of his life, now reaches its goal. A life of freedom and love expressing itself in a radical identification with the poor and the outcasts and a resolute confrontation with all the oppressive powers of the world arrives at its paradoxical outcome baffling all human calculation, where "[God's] power is made perfect in weakness" (2 Cor 12:9), and where "the foolishness of God is [shown to be] wiser than the human wisdom and the weakness of God stronger than human strength" (1 Cor 1:25). For the cross shows forth not just the death of Jesus but announces his resurrection as well.

The Goal of Life: The Resurrection

The resurrection, of course, escapes the net of history. Unless it is conceived as the resuscitation of a corpse, it is not an observable, locatable event that can be grasped by the historian's empirically oriented tools. It is, however, accessible through the two past historical traces it has left (the empty tomb and the appearances of Jesus to his first disciples), both of which can be reached (though not easily) through the confused, sometimes contradictory and not easily decipherable stories about them in the Gospels. But above all, the resurrection is accessible to us in our present experience of the living Jesus, which assures us that *Jesus is alive.* "The resurrection is not a doctrine that we try to prove or a problem that we argue about," Thomas Merton has said. "It is the life of Christ himself in us by the Spirit."

Rooted in the past event of Jesus, made actual in the present experience of his living presence among us, the resurrection grounds our hope for the future, turning, as Leonardo Boff would say, all our *utopias* ("nowheres") into *topias* ("somewheres"). But this faith experience which grounds our hope is available to us only in a life of love. Because it anticipates the end of history, the resurrection, God's final and overwhelming answer to our cry for life, "can be understood only through a praxis that seeks to transform the world" (Sobrino).

Indeed the mystery of Jesus can be grasped only through praxis, because Jesus is essentially the way. It is not in constructing theoretical models about his being that we "understand" Jesus (indeed these alienate us from him) but in following him in the life of solidarity and conflict that is his way to life. All true Christology is ultimately grounded on Christo-praxis. It is in communities walking this way that we shall discover (as Aloysius Pieris has already told us) the "names" that we are to give Jesus in the Third World today.

Because our understanding of Jesus emerges in the dialectic of the Jesus of faith and the cry for life, it is unlikely that in Asia and possibly Africa this understanding of Jesus will be an exclusive one. Jesus is a saving name for the Absolute Mystery as it is experienced by us. But the inexhaustible Absolute Mystery has, as Hinduism teaches, a thousand saving names. Is not the radical Freedom (the total silencing of all desire), which the Buddha realized through strenuous mindfulness, as much a name of God as the unconditional Love which was the name revealed to us in Jesus? For six hundred million people it is. Or the ongoing current of pulsing life received with awe and cherished with joy by the great indigenous religions of Africa—is not that too a name for God? Or again, the total harmony of the cosmos that the Chinese sages Confucius, or Lao-Tzu, or Mencius envisaged—does not that too name Absolute Mystery? All these names speak to us of the incredible richness of the religious experience of humankind, which throws up forms of religiosity as abundantly as the flowers in a forest. To fight about the superiority of one or the other of these would seem neither practical nor wise. Indeed the problem of the uniqueness of Christ as discussed in theology today seems to me an academic problem with little significance (for no one doubts that salvation exists outside the Christian community, and whether or not it is through "Christ" operating in some mysterious way, does not really seem to matter), and of much presumption (for it presumes to know the mind of God). In Asia at least, it is God (not Christ) who will always remain at the center. That is why perhaps Asians have produced no notable Christologies but many "theologies." The true "uniqueness" of Christ is the uniqueness of the way of solidarity and struggle (a way that is neither male nor female), that Jesus showed as the way to life. That uniqueness cannot be argued about but must be lived. We "follow" Jesus along this way because we have experienced the Absolute Mystery in him and have realized that his way is indeed the way of life. We invite others to walk along with us and share the experience we have had without affirming that this is the only way or the best one. "The whole world is pervaded by the glory of the Lord," says the *Īśā Upanishad*. It is when we forget this and reduce the Absolute Mystery to the dimensions of our own understanding that the saving name becomes a slogan, and Christology instead of being a way to life becomes an ideology of death.

"Fullness there; fullness here; fullness from fullness comes. Take fullness from fullness, fullness still remains" (*Īśā Upanishad*).

NOTES

1. For a useful survey of contemporary approaches to Christology, see Joseph A. Fitzmyer, *Scripture and Christology: A Statement of the Biblical Commission with a Commentary* (New York: Paulist, 1986), 54-96.

2. Although occurring for the first time in John in this clear and explicit form, the mystery of the incarnation is foreshadowed in Matthew's theme of Jesus as Emmanuel (1:23; 18:12; 28:20); in Paul's affirmation that "God was in Christ reconciling the world to himself" (2 Cor 15:15); and in Mark's eschatological *jus talionis* (sentence of holy law) which declares that a stance taken vis-à-vis Jesus will be sanctioned by corresponding eschatological consequence (Mk 8:38). A basic feature of the Jesus experience communicated in the New Testament is thus the conviction (expressed most clearly in the extreme and paradoxical form of the Johannine *sūtra*) that in Jesus we encounter God coming into our world.

3. W. H. C. Frend, *The Early Church* (Philadelphia: Fortress Press, 1982), 233.

4. M. Wiles, *Working Papers in Doctrine* (London: SCM Press, 1976), 39-40.

5. For a history of the christological controversies, see A. Grillmeier, *The Christian Tradition,* vol. 1, *From the Apostolic Age to Chalcedon* (Atlanta: John Knox, 1975), 153-554; J. Pelikan, *The Christian Tradition,* vol. 1, *The Emergence of the Catholic Tradition [100-600]* (Chicago: University of Chicago Press, 1971), 226-77; H. Lietzmann, *From Constantine to Julian: A History of the Early Church,* vol. 3 (London: Lutterworth, 1950), 94-136.

6. Grillmeier, *Christian Tradition,* 251: "A historico-political theology emerges: the appearance of the Messiah and imperial peace, Christianity and the empire are bound together in an indissoluble unity by the idea of providence. We already saw hints of this in Melito and Origen. Eusebius provides the theory."

7. Nicaea was attended by about 220 bishops from the East but only five from the West (Lietzmann, *From Constantine to Julian,* 116-17); Chalcedon in 451 by 520 bishops, of whom only the four papal legates were from the West (Frend, *Early Church,* 230). The first ecumenical councils had almost no Western bishops; those of the second millennium hardly any from the East.

8. Grillmeier, *Christian Tradition,* 1:547. [Editor's note: this endnote was missing in the *Spirituality of the Third World* version.]

9. The extent of Constantine's influence on conclusions of the council is disputed, but in spite of Grillmeier's elaborate *apologia* of the council's independence (*Christian Tradition*, 250-64), it was certainly considerable. Even the crucial expression *homoousios* (one in substance) with the father, which has become the basic expression of christological belief in the Christian tradition and a source of trouble in subsequent generations, appears to have been inserted into the council decrees at his behest (Pelikan, *Christian Tradition*, 1:201-2; Lietzmann, *From Constantine to Julian*, 118-19; Frend, *Early Church*, 140-41).

10. Frend, *Early Church*, 212-13. The different Christologies were based (as always) on different soteriologies, which Frend has neatly described as follows: "In the last resort the Antiochene Christ redeemed through his baptism and self-sacrifice on the Cross, 'drawing all men unto him,' the Alexandrian through the death-destroying power of the divine elements in the Eucharist" (p. 213).

11. Grillmeier, *Christian Tradition*, 1:544.

12. Pelikan, *Christian Tradition*, 1:263.

13. Ibid., 266.

14. Walter Bauer (*Orthodoxy and Heresy in Earliest Christianity* [London: SCM Press, 1972]) offers a now classic description of the origins of "orthodoxy" as representing the form of Christianity supported and actively propagated by the church of Rome, but never accepted elsewhere.

15. Pelikan, *Christian Tradition*, 1:266.

16. R. Panikkar, *Salvation in Christ: Concreteness and Universality, the Supername* (Inaugural Lecture at the Ecumenical Institute of Advanced Theological Study Tantur, Jerusalem, 1972), 1-81; see p. 3.

17. K. Rahner, "Basic Theological Interpretation of the Second Vatican Council," in his *Theological Investigations,* vol. 20 (New York: Crossroad, 1981), 77-79 [83].

18. K. Rahner, *Inspiration in the Bible* (New York: Herder, 1961), 47-50. As Rahner points out, it is precisely this fact—that they are the self-expression of the faith of the apostolic church—which makes the Scriptures inspired; inspiration is thus rightly seen as the quality of a text, not as some mysterious influence on an exclusive author.

19. Works on New Testament Christology are too numerous to be listed here. There is a useful discussion of recent New Testament Christology in *Semeia* 30 (1985), an issue on "Christology and Exegesis: New Approaches," and in Heinz Kremers, "Der Beitrag des Neuen Testaments zu einer nicht antijüdischen Christologie," in *Wie gut sind deine Zelte, Jaakow* [Festschrift Reinhold Mayer], ed. E. L. Ehrlich, B. Klappert, and U. Ast (Gerlingen: Bleicher, 1986), 196-207.

20. Raymond E. Brown, *The Birth of the Messiah* (New York: Doubleday, 1979).

21. On Jewish messianic beliefs in New Testament times, see Jacob Neusner, William Scott Green, and Ernest Frerichs, eds., *Judaism and the Messiahs at the Turn of the Christian Era* (Cambridge: Cambridge University Press, 1987).

22. For the future Christology of Q, see Edward Schillebeeckx, *Jesus—An Experiment in Christology* (London: Collins, 1979), 406-7.

23. J. D. G. Dunn, *Christology in the Making: An Enquiry into the Origins of the Doctrine of the Incarnation* (London: SCM Press, 1980), 258: "only with the Fourth Gospel can we speak of a full blown conception of Christ's personal pre-existence and a clear doctrine of incarnation" (p. 258). This is the basic thesis of Dunn's book. For a critical discussion of it, see *Semeia* 30 (1985): 65-121, with contributions by Carl Holladay, Alan Segal, Reginald Fuller, and Donald Juel.

24. Dunn, *Christology,* 196.

25. M. Casey, *From Jewish Prophet to Gentile God: The Origins and Development of New Testament Christology* (London: James Clarke, 1991).

26. Panikkar, *Salvation in Christ,* 24.

27. Edward Schillebeeckx, *Interim Report on the Books Jesus and Christ* (London: SCM Press, 1980), 14-15.

28. See J. Sobrino, *Christology at the Crossroads* (Maryknoll, N.Y.: Orbis, 1978), 1-16, for an excellent discussion on the starting point of Christology.

29. The old quest for the historical Jesus, which read the Gospels as biographies of Jesus colored by myth and sought to reconstruct a life of Jesus by removing mythical elements from the harmonized Gospel narratives, was brought to an end by Albert Schweitzer's *Quest of the Historical Jesus* (1906), which brilliantly demonstrated how the "historical Jesus" in every case turned out to be the historian's Jesus. The new quest initiated by Ernst Käsemann in 1954 after a period of Bultmannian skepticism when any quest for the Jesus of history was given up as impossible and illegitimate, gave up attempting to reconstruct a life of Jesus but was content to show some continuity between the "Jesus of history" and the "Christ of faith." It has died a quiet and unadvertised death. Though Jesus books continue to appear, no consensus has emerged about the "intention" of Jesus. The new "Jesus research" pretends to hold greater promise because it uses new evidence (from Nag Hammadi and Qumran) and new sociological methods for investigating the social setting of Jesus. But it has so far (in my opinion) been no more successful in disclosing the Jesus of history than previous attempts; see R. S. Sugirtharajah, "'What Do Men Say Remains of Me?' Current Jesus Research and Third World Christologies," *Asian Journal of Theology* 5 (1991): 331-37.

30. I have taken the distinction between "confessional" and "critical" history from G. von Rad, *Old Testament Theology,* vols. 1 & 2 (Edinburgh: Oliver & Boyd, 1965), 1:107.

31. See G. Soares-Prabhu, "The Historical Critical Method: Reflections on Its Relevance for the Study of the Gospels in India Today," *Theologizing in India*, ed. M. Amaladoss et al. (Bangalore: Theological Publications in India, 1981), 314-67 (esp. 340-41) and in *A Biblical Theology for India*, Collected Writings of George M. Soares-Prabhu, S.J., vol. 2, ed. Scaria Kuthirakkattel (Pune: Jnana-Deepa Vidyapeeth, 1999), 3-48.

32. Panikkar, *Salvation in Christ,* 33.

33. Mahatma Gandhi, in *Modern Review* (October 1964): 67, referred to in Panikkar, *Salvation in Christ,* 46, no. 1.

34. See especially M. K. Gandhi, *Christian Missions: Their Place in India,* ed. B. Kumarappa (Ahmedabad: Navjivan, 1957); and his *In Search of the Supreme*, vol. 3, ed. B. G. Kher (Ahmedabad: Navjivan, 1962), 313-42.

35. H. Staffner, *Baba Amte's Vision of a New India* (Sangamner: Nitre Prakash, 1990).

36. Bhagawan Shree Rajneesh, *The Mustard Seed,* vols. 1-2 (Pune: Rajneesh Foundation, l975); idem, *Come Follow Me,* vols. 1-4 (1976-77); idem, *I Say Unto You*, vols. 1-2 (1977-78). All three works contain the Bhagwan's discourses on the sayings of Jesus. The first on sayings taken from the *Gospel of Thomas;* the other two on sayings from the canonical Gospels.

37. Reflections about Jesus tend to be, to use a convenient distinction proposed by E. Schillebeeckx, either "theologies of Jesus" or "Christologies" proper. A theology of Jesus locates the saving event in the ministry of Jesus. It focuses on the human Jesus of Nazareth "experienced as a saving reality and interpreted as orientation and inspiration for Christian living." It finds in him "an inspiration and an orientation for working, not uncritically

but committedly, to achieve a better world here on earth, without expressly introducing any vista of a life eternal or an eschatological encounter with Christ, sometimes even expressly denying it." A Christology, on the other hand, locates salvation primarily (if not exclusively) in the death and resurrection of Jesus and so "celebrates and thematizes the Christ who is present in the ritual worship of the Church." It places, therefore, "a total emphasis on the God 'Jesus Christ,' the Lord exalted to the Father's side, who is active and alive among us even now, is celebrated in the liturgy and sheds upon us the spirit as pledge of an eternal life to come which is perpendicular, more or less, to our historical existence in this world, whereof the form passes away." See Schillebeeckx, *Jesus,* 29-30.

38. W. Baldensperger commenting on Jn 1:9-10, quoted in E. Käsemann, "The Prologue to John's Gospel," in his *New Testament Questions of Today* (London: SCM Press, 1969), 138-67.

6

RADICAL BEGINNINGS

The Jesus Community as the Archetype of the Church

If there is one thing that critical exegesis has made clear, it is that we can no longer hold that the Church was founded immediately by Jesus in its present institutional and highly structured form. It does not emerge fully armed from the pierced side of Jesus, like Athena from the head of Zeus! One might indeed speak of the dynamic foundation of the Church, in the sense that the structures which the Church gradually assumed in the course of its long and troubled history were continuous with or at least implicit in the intentions of Jesus.[1] This is a valid view, but it belongs, I suggest, to the confessional rather than to the critical history of the Church.[2] It is a faith understanding, not the fruit of critical investigation. For critical investigation shows up a great variety of church orders adopted by the different local churches of early Christianity so that its picture of the development of the Church is very different from the smooth and orderly progression from Peter and the Twelve through the supervisors (*episkopoi*) and elders (*presbyteroi*) of the Pastoral letters, to the monarchical bishop of Ignatius of Antioch, with which the confessional history of the church has familiarized us.[3]

It would, I believe, be very difficult to trace back any of these early Church orders to Jesus himself. For Jesus seems to have founded a wholly unstructured community of disciples without any differentiation of rank or ministry, in which he alone was Master and Lord (Mt 23:8-10). It is this community which is the starting point of the movement which later, as part of the inevitable routinization

This article first appeared in *Jeevadhara* 15 (1985): 307-81. It has also been published in *Theology of Liberation. An Indian Biblical Perspective,* Collected Writings of George M. Soares-Prabhu, S.J., vol. 4, ed. Francis X. D'Sa (Pune: Jnana-Deepa Vidyapeeth, 2001), 136-49.

of charisma to which every such movement is necessarily subject, emerges as the Church. Whatever, then, be the external structures that the Church adopts in the course of its history (and these, we have seen, have varied considerably even in the relatively short span covered by the New Testament), its spirit must be that of the Jesus community (the community of Jesus and his disciples) from which it originates. Origins are normative. We remain true to what we are, only by remaining true to our beginnings, when we become what we are. It is important, then, that we remain faithful to the spirit of the Jesus community, explicitly presented to us in the New Testament, and conspicuously in Matthew, as a paradigm for the Church.[4]

What was the Jesus community like? To understand it we shall have to look at both the *sociological milieu* in which it emerged, as well as at the *religious experience* of Jesus himself, which brought it into being. Both must be examined if the community of Jesus is to be properly understood. To insist on either one to the exclusion of the other would be misleading. "Sociological explanation," as Theissen notes, "can only apply to typical features and not to individual instances."[5] They can explain why certain forms of religious movements come into being at a particular time and place, but not the specific shape of any one of them. Why, for instance, should such different forms of religious reaction as the monastic withdrawal of the Qumran sectarians, the armed resistance of the Zealot guerrilla bands, the religious revivalism of the Pharisees, or the radical prophetic and charismatic movement of Jesus and his followers, have arisen in the same social setting, involving largely the same social classes?

But it would equally be naive to imagine that a religious movement can be explained merely in terms of the religious inspiration of its founder—as if religious life were lived out in a vacuum, isolated from other areas of experience. New Testament exegesis, which so far has shown little interest in the sociological background of the texts it studies (their proper *Sitz im Leben),* has now begun to be more sociologically aware, though it has yet to find a way of integrating sociological analysis into its exegesis.[6]

Both sociological and religious structures thus play a part in the origins and the development of the Jesus movement. Which of these is prior seems to me a question as academic as the one about the hen or the egg. The fact is that both sets of factors interact dialectically (each influencing and being influenced by the other), and both must be kept in mind when the Jesus community is discussed.

In attempting to understand the community of Jesus, whose "spirit" must animate our own, I shall therefore (A) begin with a description of the *sociological* milieu in which the community emerged, relating it as closely as I can to our situation in India, which in many ways is analogous to the situation of Palestine in the time of Jesus. I shall then (B) go on to discuss the *religious experience* of Jesus, which responding to this situation, gave rise to the Jesus community, with its specific features which are so significant for us today. My essay, then, is an attempt at history not (directly at least) at theology. I am not trying to spell out a New Testament ecclesiology, but merely attempting to understand the shape of the community of the historical Jesus. This attempt is, I believe, important. For even if we locate the foundation of the Church in the disciples' post-Easter experience of the Spirit, this post-Easter Church is not discontinuous with the community of Jesus. It is related to it, I suggest, as a tree is related to the seed from which it grows. For the risen Lord is, after all, not different from the earthly Jesus; and the spirit he communicates for the foundation of the Church is ultimately the Spirit of Jesus. There is a normativeness about the Jesus community, which the Church today (or at any time) ignores at its peril.

A. SOCIOLOGICAL MILIEU

Sociologically, the Jesus movement can be described as one of several responses to a deep-seated, pluriform crisis that was troubling Jewish society of its time.[7] This crisis, which affected all the areas of Jewish life (economic, political, cultural, and religious), was basically a crisis of colonialism. Five centuries of political domination, first by the Persians, then by the Greeks, and lastly by the Romans, had left deep scars in Jewish history and had led up to the profound crisis at the turn of our era, which among other things occasioned the Jesus movement. The crisis had several dimensions. We shall focus on three: the economic, the cultural, and the religious.

1. Economic Crisis

Economic exploitation is an inevitable feature of colonial rule, for no country occupies another for altruistic motives. Roman imperialism certainly imposed a heavy burden on Palestine at the time of Jesus—even though its economic exploitation was never anything quite as savage as that of the British in India, cold-bloodedly destroying a flourishing textile industry to make room for their Lancashire cottons;[8] or of the Western powers in China, forcing Bibles and opium (a combination that would have delighted Karl Marx) down the throats of a helpless and deeply humiliated people;[9] or of the United States in Latin America, impoverishing a rich continent by unleashing on it its big business backed up by its "big stick."[10]

The Romans exacted a tribute of six million denarii (about fifty million rupees) each year from Judea alone, apart from numerous toll fees and custom duties farmed out to unscrupulous tax collectors, whose rapacity and greed were proverbial.[11] Add this to the immense burden of heavy religious taxes (tithes of the harvest, the first fruits of the flock, stole fees for various rituals and sacrifices, and an annual Temple tax), which supported a huge, economically unproductive priestly class (some twenty thousand priests served in the Temple at the time of Jesus),[12] and maintained an enormously costly Temple liturgy, and one begins to understand the intolerable burden which lay on the people. So heavy a burden inevitably destroyed the economy of rural Palestine. Increasing rural indebtedness brought on by the heavy civil and religious taxation led to the selling off of the small land holdings, which had been the normal pattern of agricultural own-ership in Greek and early Roman Palestine, to large and often absentee landlords (Mk 12:1). These, while enjoying the urban amenities of cities like Jerusalem or Tiberius, ran their estates on hired labor through the intermediary of stewards (Lk 16:1-8). As a result there appeared a growing proletariat of dispossessed small farmers now become landless day laborers (Mt 20:1-16), who, when conditions took a turn for the worse, might take to banditry (Lk 10:30), join one of the rev-olutionary bands in the "hill country" engaged in guerrilla warfare against Rome (Mk 15:7), or flock to the cities to eke out a precarious living by begging. From the large crowds of the beggars, the sick, the crippled, the lame, and the "pos-sessed" that meet us in the Gospels it is clear that the poor made up a large part of the population of Palestine at the time of Jesus, and that it was from among these poor sections of society that the Jesus movement drew its main support.[13]

2. Cultural Crisis

Jewish society at the time of Jesus was also a culturally beleaguered society. Cultural imperialism (the attempt of the dominant power to impose its worldview and its values on subject peoples) joined to racism (the assumption by the colo-nizers of their innate superiority over the colonized) are the inevitable concomi-tants of colonialism. They lead to a deep culture shock and to a profound psychological trauma among the colonized peoples: less visible perhaps but more damaging than the economic devastation that colonialism causes. "The arrival of the white man in Madagascar," writes Franz Fanon, "shattered not only its horizons but its psychological mechanisms."[14] Colonialism creates a "colo-nized consciousness." When "millions of men . . . have been skillfully injected with fear, inferiority complexes, trepidation, servility, despair, abasement,"[15] then the colonized begin to see themselves and their world with the eyes of the colo-nizers. They interiorize the colonizers' contempt for the "native," his customs, his culture. They make their own his estimation of their worth. The psychological trauma that this produces goes hand in hand with a profound cultural insecurity. The "native" feels culturally threatened and may react either by an unconditional surrender to the culture of the colonizer, or by aggressive resistance to it, often in the form of a wholesale rejection, joined to an uncritical idealization of his own past.[16]

Such cultural imperialism and the racism that legitimizes and feeds on it are familiar to us from our experience of Western colonialism in Asia, Africa, and Latin America, which has been racist and imperialist to an unprecedented degree.[17] But they were part too of the Hellenization of Palestine at the time of Jesus. When one reads that Aristotle (that *anima naturaliter Christiana* so admired of Western theologians) could advise "the young Alexander to treat the Greeks as a leader would his men and the barbarians as a master would his slaves," that is, as "objects for exploitation"—for slaves in Aristotle's view were "implements" to be used[18] (can one imagine the Buddha saying this?)—then one begins to realize the tensions that must have been generated in Palestine at the time of Jesus, when such Greek/barbarian racism (watered down, no doubt, but by no means eliminated by the decline of Hellenistic power in the last two centuries preceding the Christian era) encountered the equally intransigent Jew/ gentile racism of Israel, based on its consciousness of being "the chosen people."

Racial tensions which are psychological translate sociologically into cultural tensions. Two wholly different cultures, the dualistic (matter, spirit), abstract, conceptual, contemplative culture of the Greeks and the holistic, concrete, symbolic, strongly action-oriented culture of the Jews, collided in the Palestine of Jesus' time,[19] engendering the typical reactions of the "colonized mind," which ranged from an unconditional surrender to the conqueror's way of life, to an outright and passionate rejection of it—from Herodianism to Zealotism, in Arnold Toynbee's celebrated classification.[20] A clash of cultures analogous to the conflict between tradition and modernity which we are experiencing in India today was thus a conspicuous feature of the world of Jesus.

3. Religious Crisis

Cultural tensions find expression in religious conflict, for religions are closely tied up with, if indeed they are not the animating force of, cultural systems. The religion of the colonizer threatens to overwhelm that of the colonized, particularly if, like Christianity or Islam, it is an aggressive missionary religion, making use of its position of political privilege to encourage proselytism. But, as Aloysius Pieris has pointed out, the major world religions (those with metacosmic soteriologies) are largely immune to such attack.[21] Neither Hinduism nor Buddhism has been seriously affected by the colonial Christian onslaught. Loss of membership to the colonizer's religion has been minimal—astonishingly so, given the highly privileged political and economic position that Christianity enjoyed.

The impact on Hinduism as a religion has been somewhat more pronounced, but not really significant. Hinduism's traumatic encounter with Christianity has led to syncretistic movements like the Brahmo Samaj, which soon died out, or to more successful modernizing attempts at renewal, like the Ramakrishna Mission, which borrowed some external forms from the language and the usages of Christianity (the Ramakrishna *mission,* the *gospel* of Ramakrishna) without capitulating to the Christian vision. Jesus was given an honored place among the religious figures of Hinduism, in sharp contrast to the systematic "demonizing" of Hindu deities by aggressive Christian missionaries. The Sermon on the Mount undoubtedly influenced Mahatma Gandhi, though it would be inaccurate to describe Gandhism (as I once did) as a synthesis of the "philosophy of the Upanishads with the ethics of the Sermon on the Mount."[22] For the nonviolent ethics of Gandhi derives not from the New Testament, but from the long Hindu-Jain tradition in which he grew up and whose best expression he found in the *Bhagavadgītā*. Values like liberty, equality, fraternity, social justice, and human rights (ultimately gospel values, which fit uneasily with the Hindu understanding of the human person as part of a hierarchical order [*caste*] and as bound by duties [*dharma*] rather than endowed with rights) have continued to leaven Indian society powerfully. But they derive not so much from the preaching of the Christian churches (which have generally ignored such issues when they have not opposed them), but from the spread of secular ideologies like the liberalism of John Stuart Mill (whose influence on the Indian intelligentsia has been prodigious) or the socialism of Karl Marx.

To all this Hinduism has reacted with remarkable vitality. It has begun to throw off the monstrous social evils which had developed during its dark ages under foreign rule (*sati*, the more blatant forms of untouchability and child marriage), has refashioned Vedanta into one of the great philosophical systems of our times, continues to produce a succession of gurus and god-men who attest to its abiding spiritual vitality, and still caters to the popular religiosity of the masses of India while providing a meaningful system for those whom secularism has alienated from popular religious rituals and beliefs. It has given rise too to militant revivalist movements which, unfortunately, have been infected by the narrow-minded aggressiveness of their opponents, just at a time when these have begun to learn tolerance from Hinduism! If Hinduism still remains a source of much repressive socialization and still legitimizes social injustice on an immense scale,[23] it has within itself the resources for its own healing. In spite of the defensive mentality of revivalist groups, it is no longer a threatened religion. Indeed it is doubtful if it ever really was so.

The Judaism of Jesus' time, a coherent, highly structured religion providing ethnic identity to a close-knit, fiercely nationalistic group, would obviously have been even more resistant to outside religious pressure than Hinduism has been. Syncretistic Jewish sects infected by Hellenism, the precursors of later Jewish Gnosticism, no doubt existed, but only as insignificant marginal groups.[24] All the main currents of Jewish religion were concerned rather with the preservation of their Jewish identity and "wanted the Torah to be observed more consistently than before."[25] If the Zealots insisted strongly on the *religious prescriptions* of the Torah, and particularly on its first commandment, which demands exclusive loyalty to the rule of God and so the rejection of all foreign rule, the Qumran sectarians and the Pharisees insisted on the observance of both its *religious and its social prescriptions*. But whereas the minute observance of the social prescriptions of the Law obliged the sectarians to withdraw into the wilderness, where alone, free from the contamination of the gentiles, such meticulous observance was possible, a highly developed casuistry allowed the Pharisees to interpret the Law in ways that made its rigorous observance possible in everyday situations. The rigorism of such groups, however, tended to accentuate rather than to resolve the religious crisis. For it created elitist groups of observants who rejected as outsiders all those who failed to live up to their own rigorous standards of conduct. The Zealots turned against all collaborators with foreign rule; the Pharisees despised the *ʿam hāʾareṣ* (the people of the land), that is "the rabble unlearned in the Law"; the Qumran sectarians lumped together as "children of darkness" all those who had not been predestined by God to join their privileged community of salvation. If the Jesus movement succeeded in avoiding such disruptive elitism, it is because it was not so much rigorous as radical. It insisted not on an exact observance of the detailed prescriptions of the Law (religious or social) but on a radical obedience to its spirit. The Law was understood to be a juridical formulation of the exigencies of love, that is, of that active concern (reflecting the concern of God himself) which reaches out to every human being in need (Lk 10:25-37). As Paul would say, "the whole Law is fulfilled in one word: 'You shall love your neighbor as yourself'" (Gal 5:14).

The radicalism of Jesus thus invites us to an interhuman concern that sets no limits but reaches out to the undeserving and the unrewarding (Lk 6:32-34)—to the collaborators with the Romans (the "tax collectors") so hated by the Zealots; the ʿam hāʾareṣ ("sinners," "little ones") despised by the Pharisees; the "children of darkness" (the "lost sheep of the house of Israel") written off by the sectarians of Qumran. The good news is truly for the "poor," for the destitute, the outcast, the sick, the crippled, the illiterate, the exploited, the oppressed (Lk 4:16-21).

The physician is for the sick (Mk 2:17). The shepherd goes after the one sheep that is lost (Lk 15:1-7). All occasion for elitist self-righteousness is thus ruthlessly eliminated, because when the Law is interpreted as a demand for an absolute and unconditional love which reflects the unconditional love of the Father (Lk 6:35), then no one can claim to have truly kept the Law, to be without sin (Jn 8:7), or to have the right to judge or to condemn (Mt 7:1-5).

B. RELIGIOUS RESPONSE

The success of the Jesus movement in responding to the religious crisis of its time was due therefore to its radicalism. The movement was radical because it originated in the new and radically liberative religious experience of Jesus. Jesus experienced God as *Abba* and communicated this experience to his followers (Mt 11:27). In their culturally colonized society, which sought security by "putting a fence around the Law," such an experience of God as unconditional love would have been shattering. It would have led to an authentic "conversion"—the dislocation of familiar patterns of perception and behavior and a shift to a radically new way of experiencing reality and responding to it. Such a conversion would inevitably mean the emergence of a new community with its own worldview and values, and with its own distinctive lifestyle in which these are expressed.[26] The Jesus community which emerged from and embodied the *Abba* experience of Jesus (and so became archetypal for all the Christian communities that would follow) was characterized, I suggest, by the following salient features, which must remain normative for every Christian community, no matter what concrete structures it may at any time adopt. It was a community that was free, all inclusive, open to sharing, prepared for service, and radically equal.

1. A Community of Radical Freedom

The experience of God's unconditional love frees the followers of Jesus from both internal compulsions toward greed and ambition and from the external constraints of a servile bondage to ritual and to law. For the experience of God's caring and provident love liberates them from anxiety about their daily sustenance (Mt 6:25-34) and from the need of affirming themselves by accumulating possessions or exercising power. They no longer "serve" (are the slaves of) Mammon (Mt 6:24). The followers of Jesus express this radical inner freedom through their radical renunciation of possessions (Mk 1:18; 10:28-30; Mt 10:9-10), of home (Mt 8:20), and of family (Mk 1:20; 3:31-35; Lk 14:26), thus showing themselves "radically detached from all the norms and traditions of the rural village society" of their time, where, as in all rural societies, property and family ties were particularly strong.[27]

Again the experience of God's forgiving and accepting love (Lk 15:1-31) frees them from guilt and from the need of straining after merit through the meticulous observance of innumerable ritual and moral laws. They cease to be "slaves" of the Law (Gal 4:21-31). Instead their ethos is so strongly centered on the human person, experienced not just as the image of God but as his child (and so as brother/sister) that both Law and cult are radically subordinated to human need. Love (ultimately the interhuman concern through which one expresses one's love for God) is "the basis of the law and the prophets" (Mt 22:40), and is "superior to all burnt offerings and sacrifices" (Mk 12:33).

Such a relativization of the Law and of cult is extraordinarily radical. That "the Sabbath is made for man not man for the Sabbath" (Mk 2:27), is one of the guiding principles of the Jesus community, whereby every institution is subordinated to human need. Equally radical and sweeping is the community's flat rejection of all the laws of ritual cleanliness (even those in the Old Testament) on the ground that good and evil are determined not by extrinsic factors (persons, places or things) but by the intentions of the heart alone: "There is nothing outside a man which by going into him can defile him; but the things which come out of a man are what defile him. . . . For from within, out of the heart, come evil thoughts" (Mk 7:15-23). With this, the separation of sacred and profane areas in the world, traditional to most religions, is wiped out at a stroke: "Nothing is unclean in itself," as Paul rightly understands Jesus to have said (Rom 14:14). No places are of themselves holy—for God is not to be worshiped in Jerusalem or on Gerizim but in "spirit and in truth" (Jn 4:21-23). No person is more sacred than another, for all are children of the one Father in heaven (Mt 23:8-9). The followers of Jesus are to be distinguished by the quality of their love, not by their possession of different degrees of sacral power.

So the early Church which grows out of the community of Jesus as a tree grows out of its seed has no special places of worship (no Temple, no synagogue, no church), no special cult objects to give physical expression to the deity (no *murti*, no ark of the covenant, no tabernacle), no special liturgical language (worship and instruction are in the common language of the people—Aramaic in Palestine, popular Hellenistic Greek in the Hellenistic world), and no sacral priesthood (for the ministers of the community are never called sacred persons [*hiereis*] in the New Testament, where Jesus alone is the one mediator and the one priest).[28] If such typical "religious" elements have crept into the later Church as part of its "inculturation" into the Hellenistic world, may it not be because the followers of Jesus have not always found it easy to live up to the radicalism of their Master?

2. A Community of Radical Universalism

The radical freedom of the followers of Jesus from their multiple alienation is a freedom for *universal* commitment. The experience of God as *Abba* implies experiencing all human beings as brothers and sisters, and so rules out all discrimination on any ground whatsoever. Jesus himself violates the caste distinctions of his people by "communing" with tax collectors and sinners (Lk 15:1-2) and by numbering an outcast customs official (Levi the tax collector of Mk 2:13) and an outlaw rebel against Roman rule (Simon the Zealot of Lk 6:15) among his closest followers. He makes women his disciples (Lk 8:1-2; 10:38-42), commends the faith of gentiles (Mt 8:10; Mk 5:34), and proposes a Samaritan as the model for the interhuman concern which for him is the essence of the Law (Lk 10:29-37). Such all-inclusiveness is pointedly formulated by Paul when he writes to the Galatians: "There is neither Jew nor Greek; there is neither slave nor free; there is neither male nor female, for you are all one in Christ Jesus" (Gal 3:28).

The Jesus community thus transcends all distinctions of race and culture (Jew/Greek), of caste and class (slave/free), or of gender and sex (male/female). Its unifying and identifying principle is being "in Christ Jesus," and this alone. No caste, race, or sex distinction can be made the specifying feature of the group. The community thus becomes radically "catholic." It is (potentially) catholic not just extensively, by geographical extension (as the British Empire was "catholic"), but *intensively* through its readiness and its ability to root itself in a variety of cultures (the way that Buddhism has been authentically inculturated in so many cultures of Asia today). Because it belongs to no single culture, the Jesus community is at home in all. All cultural imperialism is thus radically excluded from it. The Church of Jesus can never be an empire, however "holy" or "Roman." It is essentially a communion of local churches, each with a cultural identity of its own.

3. A Community of Radical Sharing

Such all-inclusiveness inevitably leads to tensions in the Jesus community between the diverse groups that constitute it and notably to the pervasive tension between the rich and the poor. Paul alludes to this when talking about the Eucharist at Corinth. Sharp class differences intervene even at this celebration of so basic a rite of Christian identity and oneness. "For in eating, each one goes ahead with his own meal, and one is hungry and another is drunk. What! Do you not have houses to eat and drink in? Or do you despise the assembly of God and humiliate those who have nothing?" (1 Cor 11:21-22).

The response of the Jesus community to such tensions is radical "sharing." This is to be understood not merely as doing works of social relief such as alms-giving (Mt 6:2-4), the care of widows (Act 6:1-4), or Paul's collection for the poor churches of Palestine (Rom 15:26-27; 1 Cor 16:1-3; 2 Cor 8:1-15)—though these were conspicuous ways in which sharing was actualized in the early Church. More basically, sharing means the assumption of responsibility by each member of the community for the welfare of all—an attitude which today might need far more radical forms of expression than were feasible in the infant Church.

A pattern of radical sharing is already evident in the life of Jesus and his dis-ciples, who lived as "wandering charismatics," that is, as itinerant preachers with healing powers, depending for their sustenance on the support of sympathizers and friends. The pattern continued into the early Palestinian church (*Didache* 11.3-6). Elsewhere too the early Church experimented with other forms of shar-ing, like the "love-communism" of the first Jerusalem community, which has been described for us in Acts (2:44-47; 4:32-37). If the language of Acts here echoes the stock description of ideal communities that we find in Jewish and in Greek literature,[29] this does not mean that its picture of the first Jerusalem com-munity is wholly fictitious. Rather it is probably (as so much in Luke-Acts) a "typical" description of many such attempts at living out the love-commandment of Jesus that must have been made by the early Christian communities. For as Troeltsch has rightly pointed out: "The command to love one another at least is bound to influence a small and intimate community on the economic side as well, which will lead it to make an attempt to realize this idea in practical life, that is, so long as external hindrances do not oppose it and make it impossible."[30]

4. A Community of Radical Service

Because the experience of God's unconditional love frees the followers of Jesus from their bondage to Mammon (greed, consumerism, "the concupiscence of the eyes"), they are able to form a community of radical sharing. Because it frees them from the craving for power (ambition, the need to dominate, "the pride of life"), they can form a community of service. In imitation of Jesus, who came "not to be served but to serve" (Mk 10:45), the Jesus community is essen-tially a community that serves. That is why to make oneself the "servant" (*diakonos*) or the "slave" (*doulos*) of all is perhaps the most urgent demand that Jesus makes of his followers (Mk 9:35f; 10:43f; Mt 23:11); and why "serving at table" (*diakonia*) is a standard description of Christian ministry in the New Tes-tament (Acts 1:17; 12:25; 21:19; Rom 11:31; 1 Cor 5:18; 2 Cor 4:17; 1 Tim 1:12).

Such a disposition for service will therefore define not only the attitude of the Church as a whole (so that its mission will always be understood as a service to the world and not as an expedition to conquer it) but also the attitude of individuals within the Church. There is no room in a Christian community for any desire for domination or for any ambition for power.

> You know that those who are supposed to rule over the gentiles lord it over them, and their great men exercise authority over them. But it shall not be so among you. Whoever would be great among you must be your servant, and whoever would be first among you must be the slave of all. For the Son of Man came not to be served but to serve, and to lay down his life as a ransom for many. (Mk 10:42-45)

The only hierarchy that Jesus will permit is thus a hierarchy of service—not a hierarchy of power.

5. A Community of Radical Equality

Indeed, so adamant is Jesus against the corrupting influence of power (for power does indeed corrupt and absolute power corrupts absolutely, as Lord Acton has pointedly put it), that he forbids even the assumption of titles that suggest the exercise of power. "But you are not to be called rabbi, for you have one teacher and you are all brethren. And call no man your father on earth, for you have one Father who is in heaven. Neither be called masters, for you have one master, the Christ" (Mt 23:8-10).

The community of Jesus is thus a radically egalitarian community. If all (Jew/gentile, slave/free, male/female) are truly "one in Christ Jesus" (Gal 3:28), they are all basically equal before the Lord. Differences of race, class, and sex do not affect their basic relationship with Jesus nor their basic worth as human beings who are children of the one Father in heaven. The Jesus community, then, will not tolerate any form of stratification (racist or caste) which touches the intrinsic worth of a person. Differences of status within the community will be differences of function, not of being. For if all are indeed (to use Paul's great metaphor) members of one body, then claims to superiority become meaningless—for no part of a body is "superior" to another and each is dependent on and at the service of the whole. "For by one Spirit we were all baptized into one body—Jews or Greeks, slaves or free—and all were made to drink of one Spirit" (1 Cor 12:13).

CONCLUSION

Of all the Jewish movements which arose in response to the multiple crises (economic, cultural, and religious) which afflicted Jewish society at the turn of our era, the Jesus movement was the one which weathered the crisis most successfully. It was able to do this because it provided a new and creative response to a critical situation. Its response was basically religious, deriving from a profound and genuine religious experience. The liberative experience of God as *Abba* called into being a radically free community, which could respond to the economic plight of the poor by "sharing," face cultural threat by abandoning defensive encystment for cultural pluralism, overcome the "will to power" through an unlimited readiness to serve, and confront the towering inequalities of a racist, sexist and slavish society by affirming the radical equality of all human beings. The movement was thus extraordinarily radical. Two thousand years after its emergence we still have to "realize" the radical vision of the Jesus community.

NOTES

1. Aelred Cody, "The Foundation of the Church: Biblical Criticism for Ecumenical Discussion," *Theological Studies* 34 (1973): 3-18.

2. I have borrowed this distinction from Gerhard von Rad, *Old Testament Theology*, vol. 1 (Edinburgh: Oliver & Boyd, 1962), 107-8; von Rad uses it for the Old Testament (the history of Israel). It applies equally to the New (the history of Jesus and for the Church).

3. James D. G. Dunn, *Unity and Diversity in the New Testament* (London: SCM Press, 1977), 103-23; Raymond E. Brown, *The Churches the Apostles Left Behind* (London: Chapman, 1984), 19-30.

4. See James P. Martin, "The Church in Matthew," in *Interpreting the Gospels*, ed. James Luther Mays (Philadelphia: Fortress Press, 1981), 97-114, esp. 107-9.

5. Gerd Theissen, *The First Followers of Jesus: The Sociology of Early Palestinian Christianity* (London: SCM Press, 1978), 97.

6. See Soares-Prabhu, "The Historical Critical Method," in *Theologizing in India*, ed. M. Amaladoss et al. (Bangalore: Theological Publications in India, 1981), 335-40, and in *A Biblical Theology for India*, Collected Writings of George M. Soares-Prabhu, S.J., vol. 2, ed. Scaria Kuthirakkattel (Pune: Jnana-Deepa Vidyapeeth, 1999), 3-48.

7. Theissen, *First Followers*, 97.

8. Ramesh Dutt, *The Economic History of India*, vols. 1 & 2 (Delhi: Publications Division, Government of India, 1960), esp. 1:xxv-xxvi.

9. See Elizabeth Peer, who in her review of Thomson, Stanley and Perry, "Sentimental Imperialism: The American Experience in East Asia" (*Newsweek*, September 14, 1981, 52), notes: "From the first contact in 1784 American traders deplored China's 'lack of dynamism,' missionaries' 'moral failure.' And both scrambled unblushingly for its business. On one expedition, the Rev. Dr. Gtuzlaff handed out Bibles from one side of a merchant ship, as from the other the crew unloaded contraband opium."

10. See Ronald Sider, *Rich Christians in an Age of Hunger* (London, Hodder & Stoughton, 1978), 125-26; Andre Gunder Frank, *Capitalism and Underdevelopment in Latin America* (Harmondsworth: Penguin, 1971).

11. Joachim Jeremias, *Jerusalem in the Time of Jesus* (London: SCM Press, 1969), 125-26; Frederick C. Grant, *The Economic Background of the Gospels* (London: Oxford Oxford University Press, 1926), 87-110.

12. Jeremias, *Jerusalem,* 205-6.

13. Soares-Prabhu, "Class in the Bible: The Biblical Poor a Social Class?," *Vidyajyoti,* 49 (1985): 322-46, and in *Theology of Liberation: An Indian Biblical Perspective,* Collected Writings of George M. Soares-Prabhu, S.J., vol. 4, ed. Francis X. D'Sa (Pune: Jnana-Deepa Vidyapeeth, 2001), 85-109.

14. Franz Fanon, *Black Skin, White Mask* (New York: Grove Press, 1967), 97.

15. Aimé Césaire, quoted in Fanon, *Black Skin,* 7.

16. A good example of this is the attitude of the celebrated Hindi novelist Premchand to Western culture; see Geeta Pandey, "Premchand and the West," *New Quest* 48 (1984): 34-54.

17. See C. R. Boxer on the Church's attitude to race relations in his *The Church Militant and Iberian Expansion, 1440-1770* (Baltimore: Johns Hopkins University Press, 1978), 138. This effectively explodes the myth of Latin racial tolerance, for it concludes: "There were exceptions in all times and in all places. But both Iberian empires remained essentially a 'pigmentocracy' . . . based on the conviction of white racial, moral and intellectual superiority—just as did their Dutch, English and French successors" (p. 38).

18. Aristotle, *Politica* I, 5 (1254 a), quoted in Martin Hengel, *Jews, Greeks and Barbarians* (Philadelphia: Fortress Press, 1980), 56.

19. Thorlief Boman, *Das hebräische Denken im Vergleich mit dem griechischen* (Göttingen: Vandenhoeck & Ruprecht, 1952). I am not convinced by Hengel's attempt to demonstrate that the Judaism of the Roman period was Hellenistic both in Palestine and in the Diaspora; see his *Judaism and Hellenism,* vols. 1 & 2 (Philadelphia: Fortress Press, 1974). The work depends on the study of literary texts which always reflect the mentality of a small literate minority. It shows little awareness of the dynamics of the encounter of cultures which anyone who has lived in India will be familiar with.

20. Arnold Toynbee, *A Study of History,* vol. 8 (London: Oxford University Press, 1954), 580-629.

21. Aloysius Pieris, "Towards an Asian Theology of Liberation," *Vidyajyoti* 43 (1979): 261-84.

22. Soares-Prabhu, "Mahatma Gandhi," in *Religious Hinduism,* ed. J. Neuner and R. De Smet (Allahabad: St Paul, 1964), 294.

23. Arun Shourie, *Hinduism: Essence and Consequence* (Ghaziabad: Vikas, 1979).

24. Marcel Simon, *Les sectes juives au temps de Jésus* (Paris: Presses Universitaires de France, 1960), 81-93.

25. Theissen, *First Followers,* 97.

26. When Dunn (*Unity and Diversity,* 106) advises us "to refrain from speaking of the community of Jesus or the community round Jesus," he is obviously thinking of a structured community.

27. Pheme Perkins, *Ministries in the Pauline Churches* (New York: Paulist, 1982), 14.

28. Raymond E. Brown, *Priest and Bishop* (London: Chapman, 1971), 13. I believe that this terminological limitation is more significant than Brown allows.

29. Cf. Soares-Prabhu, "The New Testament and the Economic Liberation of Man," *Jeevadhara* 32 (1976): 198-210, and in *Theology of Liberation: An Indian Biblical Perspective,* Collected Writings of George M. Soares-Prabhu, S.J., vol. 4, ed. Francis X. D'Sa (Pune: Jnana-Deepa Vidyapeeth, 2001), 126-35.

30. Ernst Troeltsch, *The Social Teaching of the Christian Churches,* vol. 1 (London: Allen & Unwin, 1931), 62.

Part II

THE PRAXIS OF JESUS

7

THE TABLE FELLOWSHIP OF JESUS

Its Significance for Dalit *Christians in India Today*

A recent study of Jesus describes his table fellowship with tax collectors and sinners as "one of the most conspicuous and controversial aspects of the renewal movement founded by him."[1] This echoes a long-standing consensus among scholars, all or nearly all of whom agree on the great importance of such table fellowship, even though they do not all explain its importance in the same way.[2] Eating with outcasts, says Günther Bornkamm in his classic work on Jesus of Nazareth, was "really the astonishing thing at which his enemies murmur."[3] It was the one feature of his life, thinks Geza Vermes, in his study of Jesus the Jew, in which Jesus differed most from both his contemporaries and his prophetic predecessors. "The prophets," he says, "spoke on behalf of the honest poor, and defended the widows and the fatherless, those oppressed and exploited by the wicked, rich and powerful. Jesus went further. In addition to proclaiming these blessed, he actually took his stand among the pariahs of his world, those despised by the respectable. Sinners were his table companions and the ostracised tax collectors and prostitutes his friends."[4] And Norman Perrin sees in such "regular table fellowship in the name of the Kingdom of God" between Jesus and the outcast Jews, a decisive factor which led to his violent death.[5]

Why is it that scholars give such importance to what would seem to us no more than a mildly scandalous behavior on the part of a would-be "holy man"? One reason for this is that intensive sociological and anthropological studies of first-century Palestine have taught us that in the social world of Jesus (so very different from the egalitarian, permissive postmodern society in which most of us

---

The article first appeared in *Jeevadhara* 22 (1992): 140-59.

live), a seemingly harmless practice like dining with outcasts would have been (as it would be in rural India today) an extraordinarily revolutionary act, fraught with radical consequences and holding important lessons for us who wish to follow Jesus in India today. In this article, which offers a reflection on what the Jesus of the Gospels has to say about the situation of the *dalits* in our country and in our Church, we need, then, to understand (1) what this revolutionary praxis of Jesus (his table fellowship with tax collectors and sinners) meant in the social world in which he lived; and (2) what it has to tell us about our own attitudes towards *dalit* Christians in the caste-ridden communities we live in.

A. THE TABLE FELLOWSHIP OF JESUS

1. *The Gospel Picture*

The Synoptic Gospels, which are our primary source for learning about the Jesus of history (that is, Jesus as he actually lived in an obscure Roman colony in Western Asia nearly two thousand years ago), contain many references to Jesus dining with tax collectors and sinners.

(1) Mark shows us Jesus sitting at table with tax collectors and sinners at the house of Levi, the tax collector whom he has just called to follow him. His table fellowship is resented by the purity-conscious religious leaders of his people ("the teachers of the Law who were Pharisees"), and they question his disciples: "Why does your teacher eat with tax collectors and sinners?" (Mk 2:15ff = Mt 9:10ff = Lk 5:29-30).

(2) A related Q saying (Mt 11:16-19 = Lk 7:31-35) shows Jesus complaining that his listeners are like discontented children playing at weddings or at funerals ("we played the flute for you and you did not dance, we wailed and you did not mourn"). They find fault with the Baptist for his asceticism and with Jesus for his association with the disreputable: "John came neither eating nor drinking, and they say, 'He has a demon'; the Son of Man came eating and drinking and they say, 'Look, a glutton and a drunkard, a friend of tax collectors and sinners'" (Mt 11:18ff). Jesus thus reports two related accusations made against him by his contemporaries ("this generation"). Unlike John, he does not lead the kind of ascetical life that befits a "holy man"; and worse still, he dines with "tax collectors and sinners."

(3) The same accusation ("This man welcomes sinners and eats with them") is used by Luke (15:1ff) to provide an introductory setting to his three parables of mercy (the Lost Sheep, the Lost Coin, and the Lost Son), which offer a significant theological comment on this praxis of Jesus (Lk 15:3-31). In a modified form ("he has gone to be the guest of a sinner") it interprets the story of the tax collector Zacchaeus (Lk 19:7), making it into a story which shows how "the Son of Man comes to seek and save what was lost" (Lk 19:7-10).

(4) Jesus refers to the charge of his association with "tax collectors and sin-

ners" in several of his parables and sayings. In these he does not deny the fact of such table fellowship, but justifies it on several grounds:

(a) The religious and social outcasts with whom he associates, Jesus points out, have not ceased to be part of God's people (Lk 19:9) nor the objects of God's loving concern (Lk 15:3-32). They must therefore be the object, indeed the special object, of his own mission too. "It is not the healthy that need the doctor," says Jesus, "but the sick" (Mk 2:17).

(b) Indeed, because of their readiness to repent, shown by their prompt acceptance of the teaching of John the Baptist (and eventually of Jesus himself), such "outcasts" are more open to the eschatological salvation he offers than are the religious elite. "Tax collectors and prostitutes (*dalits*)," Jesus tells the religious leaders of the Jews (as he might well tell priests, religious, bishops, and "respectable" lay people in the Indian Church today), "are going into the Kingdom of God ahead of you" (Mt 21:31-32).

(c) The ultimate reason for this is that the proper religious attitude which justifies a person (puts him or her into a right relationship with God) is not the reliance on one's own merits shown by the Pharisee in Luke's familiar parable of the Pharisee and Tax Collector at Prayer (Lk 18:9-14) but the readiness to trust in God's forgiveness shown by the tax collector. It is precisely this attitude of openness to conversion, which Jesus finds in the "tax collectors and sinners" (but not in their counterparts, the learned scribes and righteous Pharisees!), that justifies his table fellowship with them. As Joachim Jeremias sums it up, Jesus gives us three reasons for vindicating his proclamation of good news to the poor: (1) the need and the openness of "sinners"; (2) the self-assured religiosity of the righteous; and most of all (3) the compassion of a loving God.[6]

It is quite certain, then, that Jesus did habitually dine with the religious and social outcasts of his society, even though this behavior of his aroused sharp and sustained criticism from the religious elite. References to such table fellowship are found in all the commonly recognized strands of the Synoptic tradition, in Mk (2:16-17), in Q (Mt 11:16-19 = Lk 7:31-35), and in the special material of Luke (15:1ff) and Matthew (21:31ff). Such widespread reference to a subject which must have been a cause of considerable embarrassment to his first followers suggests that Jesus' table fellowship with the outcasts was not only a well-known, historically certain feature of his ministry, but a highly significant feature as well. What, then, did such table fellowship signify?

The Gospels (possibly echoing Jesus himself) explain it in terms of pastoral concern. Through his table fellowship with "tax collectors and sinners" Jesus reaches out to "the lost sheep of the house of Israel" (Mt 15:24), in order to bring them back to the fold. He goes to those who are in need of a physician (Mk 2:16); he seeks and saves the lost (Lk 19:7). His table fellowship with tax collectors and sinners is, as it were, the spiritual counterpart of his healing of the disabled and the sick. But such pastoral concern does not adequately explain the importance given by the tradition to this particular "deviant" behavior of Jesus, nor does it account for the immense hostility it aroused. Like his miracles (which are not just works of individual healing but signs of a radical structural change which put Satan's rule to an end, and ushered in a new cosmic and social order, God's Rule),[7] the table fellowship of Jesus is more than a form of individual pastoral care. It is the expression of a radically new (and therefore thoroughly disturbing) theological vision, rooted in a new experience of God and calling for a new kind of society.

2. The Jewish Background

A. THE MEAL AS AN EXPRESSION OF FELLOWSHIP

The theological vision implicit in the table fellowship of Jesus is intelligible only if we locate this table fellowship in the social world in which he lived. In this world the sharing of a meal was a sign of intimacy, communion, and fellowship. "Sharing a table," as Joachim Jeremias puts it, "meant sharing life."[8] This is true of most traditional societies, but it was especially true of Judaism, where table fellowship was always a religious affirmation of belonging. A Jewish meal was normally preceded by a blessing, in which the host blessed, broke, and shared a loaf of bread, to show that all those taking part in the meal shared in the blessing which had been pronounced over the unbroken bread. Table fellowship in Judaism meant, as Joachim Jeremias puts it, "fellowship before God."[9]

B. THE MEAL AS A PATTERN FOR COMMUNITY

But table fellowship in Judaism had other connotations as well. The communion it created had come to symbolize the shape and destiny of Israel itself. Fully liberated Israel, the end-time community, is therefore pictured in both the First and the Second Testaments, as a group of people enjoying table fellowship with God himself, by partaking in the eschatological banquet God has prepared for them (Is 25:6; Mt 8:1; Lk 22:30). This end-time community, it was believed, could be anticipated, made present here and now, in properly eaten festive meals. In the social world of Jesus, a meal had become (for some groups of Jews at least) "a microcosm of Israel's intended historic structure as well as a model of Israel's destiny."[10]

C. THE PHARISAIC MODEL: COMMUNITIES OF THE "HOLY"

This was certainly true of the Essenes of Qumran, who paid great attention to the arrangement of their meals, modeling them on what they believed would be the form of the messianic banquet (1QS 6:2-5);[11] and it was also, indeed very specially, true of the Pharisees. These "separated ones" (*pěrišayyā'*) were associations of pious laymen who lived a life of strict observance, adhering scrupulously to the rules of tithing and maintaining always the ritual purity required of priests actually serving in the Temple.[12] By 70 C.E. and possibly even earlier, the Pharisees had become, Jacob Neusner suggests, "primarily a society for table fellowship."[13] Table fellowship was "the high point of their life as a group,"[14] because their specific understanding of Israel's shape and destiny was expressed in the meals they ate together. These meals (not special meals, but their normal everyday meals) were always eaten with a great concern for ritual purity. "Members of a Pharisaic fellowship," writes Borg, "were committed to the tithing of all food and to eating every meal in that degree of purity observed by officiating priests in the Temple."[15] In this way the Pharisaic associations (*ḥăbûrîm*) used their meals to represent and prefigure the true Israel, which they believed was called to be a ritually pure community, "a kingdom of priests" (Ex 19:6).

The preoccupation of the Pharisees with observing strict ritual purity meant that their table fellowship was restricted to those who were ritually pure according to their own exacting Pharisaic standards. Only those were welcome to their tables who paid their tithes faithfully (Lk 18:12; Mt 23:23) and who scrupulously observed the rules of ritual purity incumbent on officiating priests, by avoiding contact with polluted people and things, and by always washing their hands before meals (Mk 7:1-4; Mt 23:25ff). Tax collectors (*telōnai*), who, because of their ongoing association with gentiles, were (like the "untouchables" in India today) judged to be in a permanent state of pollution, and notorious sinners (*hamartōloi*), those "who lived a flagrantly immoral life . . . or who followed a dishonourable vocation or one which inclined them strongly to dishonesty,"[16] could obviously have no place at the tables of these exclusive groups of the ritually pure.

Such exclusiveness was obviously a matter not of social snobbery but of religious zeal. Like the Essenes of Qumran, the Pharisees took seriously the basic thrust of the postexilic priestly code, neatly summed up in the command of Yhwh in Lev 20:26: "You are to be *holy* to me, because I, the Lord, am holy and I have *set you apart* from the nations to be my own." Holiness here is not to be understood merely as moral probity, but as integration into the "realm" of the divine, and therefore separation from the "profane" world. Postexilic Judaism, in imminent danger of being swamped by the dominant cultures of the imperial powers to which they were subject (Persia, Greece, Rome), adopted as a strategy of survival the policy of closing in upon itself and building defensive walls (purity lines) to separate itself from dangerous gentile influences. For the Essenes at Qumran the separation was complete. They kept themselves away from everything that could defile them by forming an isolated commune in the uninhabited "wilderness." For the Pharisees it was partial. They continued to live in the unclean world of a Roman colony, but tried to keep themselves uncontaminated by it and in a state of permanent priestly purity, by avoiding contact with polluted persons or things, and by faithfully performing the requisite purifying rituals when such contact had taken place. For both the Pharisees and the Essenes holiness was identified with *separation*. This has been well described by Asher Finkel in his comparative study of the teaching of Jesus and the Pharisees:

In the Pharisaic schools "holiness," the key word of the Priestly Codes, is identified with the word 'separation': separation from the heathens and foreigners in order to preserve the identity of the Jewish people; separation or classification among its own members, segregating the priests and the strict observers of the Code from the non-observers, the boorish and the common folk [the so-called *'am ha-aretz*]. Also among the Essene societies created by the Teacher of Righteousness—as the Qumran writings suggest—to achieve a status of holiness the community must stress the rules of separation and purity as prescribed in the "order of the Brotherhood" (*Serekh Hayyachad*). The words of Rabbi Pinhas ben Jair, a known Jewish saint of the early part of the third century A.D., reviews the important steps to be taken by the individual or the society in order to achieve a status of holiness or piety. He enumerates the steps as follows: heedfulness leads to diligence, diligence to cleanliness, cleanliness to separation and separation to holiness.[17]

3. The Meaning of the Table Fellowship of Jesus

Against the background of these exclusive meals of the Pharisaic associations (*ḥăbûrîm*) or the Essene community (*hayyaḥad*) at which "members only," that is, only those who satisfied the rigorous conditions for membership in the group, were welcome, the table fellowship of Jesus with "tax collectors and sinners," the religious and social outcasts of his time, stands out as a powerful challenge. It challenges the Pharisaic and the Essene ideal of Israel as a holy community, whose holiness is to be maintained by preserving a state of complete separation from all that is ritually unclean. It implies instead a radically new understanding of holiness, of community and of God.

A. A NEW UNDERSTANDING OF HOLINESS

This new understanding is revealed in a Q saying of Jesus (Mt 5:48 = Lk 6:36) which refers to a well-known text from the First Testament. The saying, in its probably more original Lukan form, urges us to "be *merciful* just as your Father is merciful" (Lk 6:36). This clearly echoes the key command of the Holiness Code of Leviticus: "Be *holy* because I, Yhwh, your God am holy" (Lev 19:2). But there is a significant difference. The "Yhwh your God" of Leviticus, becomes "Father" (*Abba*) in Luke; and so the point of reference shifts from God's "holiness" in Leviticus to God's "mercy" in Luke. Mercy, or interhuman compassion, rather than holiness in the sense of "otherness" or "separation" is now the content of our *imitatio dei,* so that the "mercy code" of Q (Lk 6:27-36) replaces the Holiness Code of Leviticus (Lev 17-26) as the norm of religious behavior.[18] True holiness is no longer defined by a "separation" from the world which would reflect the "otherness" of God; but by the "mercy" which imitates God's utterly unconditional love. Religion is no longer a matter of ritual purity or cultic competence but of interhuman compassion.

B. A NEW MODEL OF COMMUNITY

This implied for Jesus a profound change in his understanding of the structure and destiny of his people. The change is expressed in his forceful rejection of the purity rules, which, as we have seen, had largely determined the ethos of Judaism since the Exile. Because of their belief that holiness meant separation, a conviction accentuated by their threatened situation as a colonized people, Jewish theology after the Exile elaborated an intricate system of purity lines to define the boundaries which separated persons, places, and things considered "sacred" or "clean," that is, fit for use in the cult, from those regarded as "profane," "polluted," or "unclean," and so unfit for cultic use. Very generally, one might say that people, places, and things were defined as holy or unholy according to their relation to the Temple, the purity of their bloodlines, their bodily wholeness, and their congruence with the primal order imposed on the world (according to the priestly creation story) at its creation.[19] Thus:

(1) *Places* were holy in terms of their closeness to the Temple. Because the Temple was the "holy place" and its inner sanctuary the "very holy place" ("holy of holies"), Palestine was the "holy land," and the surrounding gentile world unholy, profane, demon-ridden territory. A list in the Mishnah elaborates on this, giving us ten degrees of holiness:

> There are ten degrees of holiness.
>> The Land of Israel is holier than any other land.
>> The Walled Cities of the Land of Israel are still more holy in that they must send forth lepers from their midst.
>> Within the Wall [of Jerusalem] is still more holy, for there only they may eat the Lesser Holy Things and the Second Tithe.
>> The Temple Mount is still more holy, for no man or woman that has flux, no menstruant, and no woman after childbirth may enter therein.
>> The Rampart is still more holy, for no gentiles and none that have contracted uncleanness from a corpse may enter therein.
>> The Court of Women is still more holy for none that had immersed himself the same day because of uncleanness may enter therein.
>> The Court of the Israelites is still more holy, for none whose atonement is incomplete may enter therein.
>> The Court of Priests is still more holy, for Israelites may not enter therein save only when they must perform the laying on of hands, slaughtering and waving.
>> Between the Porch and the Altar is still more holy, for none that has a blemish or whose hair is unloosed may enter there.
>> The Sanctuary is still more holy, for none may enter there with hands and feet unwashed.
>> The Holy of Holies is still more holy, for none may enter therein save

only the High Priest on the Day of Atonement at the time of the service.

(*m. Kelim* 1:6-9)[20]

(2) This grading of places already implies a grading of the *persons* associated with them. The Holy of Holies accessible only to the High Priest is holier than the Sanctuary accessible to priests. The court of the priests is holier than the court of Israelites, which in turn is holier than the court of women. The land of Palestine inhabited by the Jews is holier than other lands inhabited by gentiles. According to their standing with reference to the Temple we can therefore deduce a hierarchy of persons, descending from High Priest, to priest, to Levite, to lay male Israelite, to Israelite woman, to gentile. But several other factors also determined the purity rating of people, notably, the purity of their family lines, their bodily wholeness, and the nature of the occupation they were engaged in. Jews of dubious ancestry (such as bastards, orphans, or foundlings), those suffering from physical impairment (eunuchs, lepers, menstruating women, the mutilated or the maimed), and those engaged in polluting trades (gamblers, money-lenders, herdsmen, tax collectors) incurred impurity and were judged "unclean" (unfit for cult) in various degrees.[21] The Tosefta, an early (third century) supplement to the Mishnah, gives a list of people in Israel ranked according to its purity laws. The list is by no means exhaustive, but it offers a good illustration of how the various factors making for purity/pollution were combined to produce ranking. It grades the people in Israel as:

Priests—Levites—Israelites—Converts—Freed Slaves—Disqualified Priests (= illegitimate children of Priests)—Temple slaves—Bastards—Eunuchs—those with damaged genital organs. (*t. Meg.* 2.7)[22]

So an elaborate system of purity/pollution structured Jewish society at the time of Jesus, analogous to the caste system in India, which is also a system of purity/pollution but based on criteria which are totally different from those which determined the ordering of first-century Judaism.[23] For the Pharisees and the Essenes this system of purities was constitutive of Israel as God's "holy people." They therefore sought to implement it as perfectly as possible, believing that Israel's future lay in its attainment of perfect "purity." For Jesus, however, these purity regulations were a deviation to be removed; because for him, "holiness" meant not "separation" but "mercy." Jesus therefore rejected the whole system of purities with its distinctions of clean and unclean foods, holy and unholy places, pure and polluted people. This rejection, which he demonstrates in his table fellowship with the polluted tax collectors and sinners, his touching of lepers (Mk 1:41), his unconcern about eating with unwashed hands (Mk 7:2) or being touched by an "unclean" woman (Mk 5:25-34), was justified by him in a strikingly radical saying which totally rejects the purity regulations of Judaism.

"There is nothing outside a person which by going into him or her can make him or her unclean," says Jesus, explaining why he does not object to his disciples eating with unwashed hands, "but the things which come out of a person make him or her unclean" (Mk 7:15).

This emphatic, antithetically formulated saying, so typical of Jesus, does not refer only to the dietary regulations of Judaism as Mark seems to suggest, when he interprets it to mean that "Jesus declared all foods clean" (Mk 7:19; cf. Rom 14:4), but to the whole system of purities by means of which postexilic Judaism attempted to distinguish the sacred from the profane. Indeed it invalidates all systems of purity (including caste) that derive purity/pollution from any external factor whatever. *Nothing from the outside* (no place, no person, no thing) can pollute a person; for nothing is in itself unclean. There are no polluting persons, places, or things. The only source of pollution is the uncompassionate heart, which generates "evil thoughts," that is, harmful intentions which lead to injurious action. It is not the tax collectors and sinners (the *dalits*) with whom Jesus associates who are "polluted" but precisely the Pharisees (the so-called "clean castes") who treat them with contempt.[24]

Jesus thus radically redraws the purity lines of his social world. This redrawing abolishes the traditional distinctions between the sacred and the profane. There are now no intrinsically sacred places, persons, or things. All places and things are in themselves neutral (neither sacred nor profane), and every human person is in itself sacred because the human person as such, in its unadorned humanity, images the glory of God (Gen 1:27) and represents the person of Jesus himself (Mt 25:31-46). Aware that God is so with us, that the normal locus of our encounter with God is humankind,[25] the community that Jesus envisages will worship God neither in Jerusalem nor on Gerizim but in spirit and in truth, that is, wherever a human community comes together in sincerity and love (Jn 4:23). It will acknowledge no "father" except the "Father in heaven," no priest or teacher except the Christ (Mt 23:8-10), and admit no hierarchy of status (for all are brothers and sisters) but only a hierarchy of service and of love (Mk 10:42-45). It is unconcerned about Pharisaic purity rituals, like the washing of hands before meals, because it locates purity/pollution not in external factors but in the disposition of the heart (Mk 7:1-23), and measures holiness not in terms of separation but in terms of compassion. For it knows that it is by loving our brothers and our sisters that we "love God" (Mt 22:34-40),[26] and so enter into the "holy" realm of the divine.

C. A New Experience of God

Such a radical redrawing of the map of his social world is possible to Jesus, because he can draw on a radically new experience of God. God is not experienced by him primarily as "holy" (the source of numinous power, the "wholly other"), sharply separated from the "profane" world, and demanding that his people become a "holy" people, separated from other peoples by sharply defined purity lines, such as those elaborated in postexilic Judaism. Rather Jesus experiences God as "merciful," a God who reaches out in forgiveness and love to all people, across all the lines of separation that we like to draw (Jew/gentile, righteous/sinner, clean caste/*dalit*), and who summons his people to a similar compassion, that is, to an effective love that will reach out beyond the bonds of kinship, clan, and race to the outsider, the undeserving, the enemy (Lk 6:32-36).

It is this all-encompassing compassion of God that the table fellowship of Jesus reveals. His "communion" with tax collectors and sinners is an acted parable, through which he brings home to listeners his experience of God as *Abba,* the loving parent, and the "good news" of liberation (God's Rule) that this experience grounds. Like his healings and exorcisms, the table fellowship of Jesus with tax collectors and sinners becomes a strikingly effective enactment of the coming of God's Rule, that is, of the end-time salvation, whose imminent coming Jesus, on the basis of his God experience, forcefully proclaims. Such salvation, Jesus believes, will be brought about not (as the Essenes hoped) through armed conflict in which the "children of darkness" will be decisively overcome by the "children of light," nor (as the apocalyptists, many Pharisees among them, believed) by a cosmic catastrophe effected by God, which will bring to an end "this evil age" and usher in "the age to come," but by the free gift of God's loving forgiveness, reaching out unconditionally to all those who "repent," that is, who turn trustingly to God and accept his love.[27] The table fellowship of Jesus with tax collectors and sinners is therefore (like his miracles) a "sign," which translates his verbal announcement of God's Rule, the central message of his preaching (Mk 1:14-15), into visible action. His conduct thus becomes, as Ernst Fuchs has said, "the real framework of his proclamation."[28] Or as Joachim Jeremias sums it up:

> Jesus' meals with the publicans and sinners, too, are not only events on a social level, not only an expression of his unusual humanity and social generosity and his sympathy with those who were despised, but had an even deeper significance. They are an expression of the mission and message of Jesus (Mark 2:17), eschatological meals, anticipatory celebration of the feast in the end time (Matt. 8:11 par.), in which the community of saints is already being represented (Mark 2:19). *The inclusion of sinners in the community of salvation, achieved in table fellowship, is the most meaningful expression of the message of the redeeming love of God.*[29]

Through his table fellowship with the social and religiously outcast, Jesus thus demonstrates in a most convincing way that God's love is not conditional, not restricted to the religious elite who would like to monopolize it, but reaches out without exception to all. There are no outcasts for God.

B. THE TABLE FELLOWSHIP OF JESUS
AND THE CHRISTIAN DALITS

What is at stake in the table fellowship of Jesus with tax collectors and sinners is, therefore, the heart of the Christian message itself. Over and against the experience of God as "wholly other" and the image of community as "separated," which the exclusive meals of the Pharisaic *ḥabûrîm* present, Jesus, through his meals with the religious and social outcasts of his day, presents a new experience of God and a new understanding of community, in which there can be no "outcasts"—for God is experienced as a loving Parent, and every fellow Christian as a brother or a sister. To attempt, then, to maintain purity systems like caste, which refuse to accept sections of the community as brothers and sisters because they consider them "outcasts," is, plainly, to do violence to the basic message of Jesus. Caste discrimination in any form whatever is wholly incompatible with Christianity. It is frightening, then, to read in a recent study of two villages in India, that:

> More than two centuries of Catholic faith among the Reddys of these two villages have not been able to make any dent in their rigid attitude towards the caste system. By and large they are well integrated with Hindu Reddys and other Hindu communities in their villages. They have achieved this by keeping their caste systems intact and not integrating themselves with other Catholic communities including other Reddy Catholic subgroups. The Madigas, who became Catholics, could not improve their status. The Reddy Catholics are also against them and resent their conversions.[30]

What, one may wonder, is really Christian about these villages, where Christians, in their basic attitudes to people, remain exactly like the Hindus around them? Have they been "converted" at all? Or have they merely been "baptized" by earnest missionaries who compass land and sea for caste converts—as if it makes any difference to Jesus to what caste those he calls belong?[31] Can one speak here of a change of heart—or has there been just a change of label? Is such a change of label without a change of heart enough to make one a Christian? Can one, that is, claim to be a Christian without accepting, at least in principle, the basic Christian ethos? Is it possible to proclaim Jesus as Lord and refuse to share his experience of a God who admits no outcasts, or his understanding of a community in which all are brothers and sisters (and therefore of one caste), because they are children of the one Parent in heaven? Is it all right to say "Lord, Lord" and not "do the will of the Father who is in heaven" (Mt 7:21)?

The answers to these questions are surely obvious, and yet we know that the two villages spoken of above are by no means atypical in Christian India. In one form or the other caste even in its most virulent form of "untouchability" is rife in the Christian (and specially Roman Catholic) communities, particularly in the long-standing Churches of South India where one might have expected a centuries-old tradition of Christianity to have generated a stronger Christian sensibility. Surely there can be no clearer indication of the massive failure of Christian teaching in India (and specifically of the immense and costly system of education it has built up) than the fact that large sections of the Indian Church can still assume condescending caste attitudes, without even being conscious of the fact that they are guilty of serious sin.

When caste discrimination enters into the celebration of the Eucharist, the sin becomes sacrilege. The Eucharist has always carried the memory of Jesus' meals with tax collectors and sinners. Perhaps even more than the Last Supper of Jesus, what inspired the early Christian fellowship meals which developed into the eucharistic celebrations that we have today, was the memory of the meals that Jesus ate with his outcast disciples.[32] Indeed the Last Supper itself was the last of such meals,[33] bringing the faith in Jesus that inspired them, the hope they engendered as anticipations of the messianic banquet, and the loving fellowship they expressed, to their fullness. The eucharistic memorial of the life, death, and resurrection of Jesus is also the celebration of the community which that life, death and resurrection create. To celebrate the Eucharist while breaking up its participants into caste groups, and to treat fellow members of the one eucharistic community (the true "body of Christ") as outcasts, by consigning them to special parts of the church or to separate places in a communion queue, is therefore to parody the Eucharist. It is to turn the joyous, hope-filled, liberating meals of Jesus into caste meals, or the self-righteous celebrations of the Pharisaic *ḥăbûrîm.* What can it mean to speak of the "real presence" of Jesus in a situation where he is being openly humiliated in his brothers and sisters, and where the community that he founded by laying down his life as a ransom for all, is being fragmented and mocked? How is it that we who would be "scandalized" to see a priest celebrating mass without an alb, can comfortably tolerate or even take part in utterly scandalous Eucharists like these?

Paul's response to analogous situations is instructive. When Peter refused table fellowship with gentile Christians in Antioch, out of respect for the Jewish "caste system" (which was not even remotely as discriminating or as damaging as ours), Paul "opposed him to his face" (Gal 2:11-16). What disturbed Paul was, of course, not so much the discrimination Peter practiced against the gentile Christians (though this too would have figured in his reaction), as his concern that a return to the Law with its elaborate purity rules might dilute faith in Jesus, and weaken the conviction that salvation comes not by observing the law but by trusting in God's forgiving love revealed to us in Christ (Gal 2:15). But allowing for Paul's particular concern, one could interpret this early Christian dispute about table fellowship as a mirror image of the disputes between Jesus and the Pharisees. The Pharisees accuse Jesus of eating with tax collectors and sinners (Jews become "as gentiles");[34] Paul accuses Peter (become a Pharisee in his devotion to the Law) for not doing so! Basically the issue of table fellowship for

Paul and for Jesus is the same, that is, both see it as the affirmation of a community in which belonging is assured not by "righteousness" (or caste), that is, not by "works" (performed in this life or in a past one), but by grace. At stake is the basic value around which one structures one's world: is it "cleanness" or is it "love"?

This becomes clear when one comes to a properly eucharistic reference in Paul. His anger at the eucharistic abuses occurring in the community at Corinth is undisguised: "When you come together it is not the Lord's supper you eat, for as you eat, each of you goes ahead without waiting for anybody else; and one remains hungry while another gets drunk. Don't you have homes to eat and drink in? Or do you despise the Church of God and humiliate those who have nothing?" (1 Cor 11:20ff).

But what is happening in Corinth is surely no worse than what is happening in many Churches in India today. There in Corinth the eucharistic community was divided by class divisions, so that rich and poor coming together to affirm their oneness in Christ were kept apart by the different kinds of food they ate, or the different times or places in which they ate it.[35] But such class divisions are far less damaging than the caste divisions we have brought into our eucharistic communities. For these we know do immense psychic and spiritual harm, comparable only to the harm done by racism.[36] For what caste, like racism, does is to question the humanity of the *dalit* or the black, deny them human dignity, and by repeatedly affirming their inferiority, deprive them of their self-worth. Nothing can be more sinful than this. That is why I believe that the homologous systems of untouchability and apartheid (the institutional high points of the caste and of white racism) are the two most evil structures that exist in the world today. To bring either of these into the celebration of the Eucharist is surely to "despise the Church of God and humiliate those who have nothing" (1 Cor 11:22), and so "sin against the body and the blood of the Lord" (1 Cor 11:27).

The existence of Christian *dalits* with their inbuilt situation of inferiority (poignantly described by Antony Raj in the first article of this issue*) is a reminder to us of how deeply we have sinned. More, their existence makes us aware of the absurdity of our situation. For, properly speaking, the very expression "Christian *dalit*" is (like "square circle") a contradiction in terms. The brotherhood and sisterhood of humankind, as Adolf Harnack correctly perceived, is of the "essence of Christianity," even if it does not exhaust that essence.[37] For the "God of our Lord Jesus Christ" recognizes no one as outcast; and Jesus welcomes tax collectors and sinners to his table, and identifies himself with the least of his brothers and sisters, to model for us a community in which there are no "pure" or "polluted," no "great" or "small," because every one belongs to "the family of God" (Mk 3:31-35). There can be no "*dalit*" in a Christian community, for "in Christ" there is neither Jew nor Greek, neither slave nor free, neither male

---

* Editor's note. This article orginally appeared in *Jeevadhara* 22 (1992): 140-59, wherein Antony Raj's article appeared on pp. 95-111.

nor female, neither clean caste nor *dalit*—for all of us have "put on Christ" (Gal 3:28). The fact that Christian *dalits* do exist (and suffer) among us is a sign of how little Christian we are, and of how much we stand in a state of serious and, one suspects, unrepentant sin.

Evangelization 2000 could well begin at home!

NOTES

1. Marcus J. Borg, *Conflict, Holiness & Politics in the Teaching of Jesus* (New York: Mellen, 1984), 78-79.

2. While most authors interpret the tax collectors and sinners with whom Jesus associates as religious outcasts, who are not admitted to table fellowship by the pious because they are "unclean," E. P. Sanders (*Jesus and Judaism* [London: SCM Press, 1985], 174-211) questions this, on the grounds that "sinners" are not those who are ritually unclean but those who have violated the covenant. Ritual uncleanness does not, he argues, make someone a sinner. But Sanders, I feel, fails to take into account the importance of purity and pollution in traditional societies, like postexilic Judaism (or traditional India), in which the popular perception of purity and pollution may go well beyond the strictly juridical. What begins as merely cultic incompetence (this is how Sanders interprets pollution in the New Testament) soon becomes "social uncleanness" with moral overtones. See Jacob Neusner, *The Mishnah Before 70*, Brown Judaic Studies 1 (Atlanta: Scholars Press, 1987), 289. Had Sanders experienced the working of caste in India, he might not so easily have dismissed the significance of purity/pollution in the table fellowship of Jesus.

3. Günther Bornkamm, *Jesus of Nazareth* (New York: Harper, 1960), 80.

4. Geza Vermes, *Jesus the Jew* (London: Fontana/Collins, 1973), 224.

5. Norman Perrin, *Rediscovering the Teaching of Jesus* (London: SCM Press, 1967), 102-5.

6. See Joachim Jeremias, *New Testament Theology*, vol. 1, *The Proclamation of Jesus* (London: SCM Press, 1971), 119-20.

7. See Soares-Prabhu, "The Miracles as the Subversion of a Power Structure?" in *Jesus Today*, ed. S. Kappen (Madras: All India Catholic Universities Federation, 1985), 21-29.

8. Jeremias, *New Testament Theology*, 115.

9. Ibid.

10. Borg, *Conflict, Holiness & Politics*, 80.

11. Geza Vermes, *The Dead Sea Scrolls in English*, 3rd ed. (Sheffield: JSOT Press, 1987), 51-52.

12. Jeremias, *New Testament Theology*, 144.

13. Jacob Neusner, "Three Pictures of the Pharisees: A Reprise," in his *Formative Judaism: Religious, Historical, and Literary Studies, Fifth Series*, Brown Judaic Studies 91 (Chico, Calif.: Scholars Press, 1985), 76.

14. Ibid., 76.

15. Borg, *Conflict, Holiness & Politics*, 80-81.

16. Karl Heinrich Rengstorf, "*hamartōlos*," in *Theological Dictionary of the New Testament*, ed. G. Kittel (Grand Rapids: Eerdmans, 1965), 1:327. See Joachim Jeremias, *Jerusalem in the Time of Jesus* (London: SCM Press, 1969), 303-12, for a list of the

"despised trades" whose practitioners were not only looked down upon by the people, but in the case of those listed in *b. Sanh.* 25b 9 (among them tax collectors and publicans) were officially ostracized, "deprived of civil and political rights to which every Israelite had a claim, even those such as bastards who were of seriously blemished descent." As Jeremias remarks, "this makes us realize the enormity of Jesus' act in calling a publican to be one of his intimate disciples (Mt 9:9 par.; 21:3), and announcing the Good News to publicans and sinners by sitting down to eat with them" (pp. 311-12).

17. Asher Finkel, *The Pharisees and the Teacher of Nazareth: A Study of their Background, the Halachic and Midrashic Teaching, the Similarities and Differences* (Leiden: Brill, 1964), 43.

18. Borg, *Conflict, Holiness & Politics,* 127.

19. See Bruce Malina, *The New Testament World: Insights from Cultural Anthropology* (London: SCM Press, 1981), 122-52; Jerome Neyrey, "Idea of Purity in Mark's Gospel," *Semeia* 35 (1986): 91-128.

20. Quoted from Herbert Danby, *The Mishnah* (Oxford: Clarendon Press, 1933), 606ff.

21. Jeremias, *New Testament Theology,* 271-344.

22. Adapted from Neyrey, "Idea of Purity," 95-96.

23. Louis Dumont, *Homo Hierarchicus: The Caste System and Its Implications* (Delhi: Oxford University Press, 1988), 46-61.

24. Such a radical reversal of judgment is brought out with particular clarity in the story of the Pharisee and the Sinner in Lk 7:6-50. The point that the story makes is that the woman who has been labeled a "sinner" by Simon the Pharisee (v. 39) is, as her love for Jesus shows, a forgiven sinner. It is Simon who, in striking contrast to the woman, has shown no love at all (vv. 44-46), who reveals himself as an unforgiven sinner—that is, as one who has failed to experience the forgiving love of God. It is obvious that nothing has been forgiven him, because he has shown no love at all!

25. Soares-Prabhu, "The Sacred in the Secular: Reflections on a Johannine Sūtra, 'The Word was made flesh and dwelt among us' (John 1:14)," *Jeevadhara* 17 (1987): 133-36, and in *A Biblical Theology for India*, Collected Writings of George M. Soares-Prabhu, S.J., vol. 2, ed. Scaria Kuthirakkattel (Pune: Jnana-Deepa Vidyapeeth, 1999), 201-13.

26. Soares-Prabhu, "The Synoptic Love-Commandment: The Dimensions of Love in the Teaching of Jesus," *Jeevadhara* 13 (1983): 88-91, and in *Theology of Liberation: An Indian Biblical Perspective*, Collected Writings of George M. Soares-Prabhu, S.J., vol. 4, ed. Francis X. D'Sa (Pune: Jnana-Deepa Vidyapeeth, 2001), 110-25. See chapter 13 of this volume.

27. Soares-Prabhu, "The Kingdom of God: Jesus' Vision of a New Society," in *The Indian Church in the Struggle for a New Society,* ed. D. S. Amalorpavadass (Bangalore: National Biblical, Catechetical, and Liturgical Centre, 1981), 579-608, and in *Theology of Liberation,* vol. 4. See chapter 4 of this volume. I have suggested here that the central message of Jesus, "The Kingdom of God has come/repent" (Mk 1:15), ought to be paraphrased "God loves you/accept his love."

28. Ernst Fuchs, *Studies of the Historical Jesus* (London: SCM Press, 1964), 21.

29. Jeremias, *New Testament Theology,* 115-16.

30. G. Prakash Reddy, "Caste and Christianity: A Study of Shudra Caste Converts in Rural Andhra Pradesh," in *Religion and Society in South India,* ed. V. Sudarsen et al., A Volume in Honor of Prof. N. Subba Reddy, G. Prakash Reddy, and M. Suryanarayana (Delhi: B. R. Publishing Corp., 1987), 23.

31. Note the comment of Reddy in the article just cited ("Caste and Christianity"): "Some of the Catholic missionaries even disliked the conversion of untouchable castes and spoke openly against it. In this connection the comments of Fr. Clement Bonn, who was very popular among Telegu Christians around 1820 is [*sic*] revealing. He says that 'it is very difficult to convert the Pariahs; it is a waste of time to preach to them since much greater good can be done among the Sudras.'. . . The same attitude was evinced by them [the Catholic missionaries] to the recruitment of native clergy. Till 1950 there was an unwritten convention in the Catholic Church of India that except under extraordinary circumstances no untouchable Catholic should be admitted to priesthood. This convention was followed firstly to avoid displeasing the higher caste Christians, and secondly it was felt that an untouchable clergy would be at a disadvantage to deal with upper caste Christians" (119). How far such an "unwritten convention" was in fact operative needs, of course, to be studied.

32. Perrin, *Rediscovering the Teaching of Jesus,* 104-5.

33. Joachim Jeremias, *The Eucharistic Words of Jesus* (London: SCM Press, 1966), 204-5.

34. Borg, *Conflict, Holiness & Politics,* 84

35. The exact problem at Corinth is not easy to define from Paul's elliptical allusions to it. It has been suggested that divisions arose from one or more of three causes: (1) rich and poor ate at separate times, since the rich could begin their meal before the poor, who could come only after work; (2) rich and poor ate in separate places: the rich in the private room of the house, the poor in the outside atrium; (3) the rich and poor ate different kinds of food. See Gerd Theissen, "Social Integration and Sacramental Activity: An Analysis of 1 Cor 11:17-34," in his *The Social Setting of Pauline Christianity* (Philadelphia: Fortress Press, 1982), 145-74.

36. The psychological damage inflicted by caste has to my knowledge not been extensively studied. That inflicted by racism has. For a classic study, see Franz Fanon, *Black Skin, White Masks* (New York: Grove Press, 1971); and idem, *The Wretched of the Earth* (Harmondsworth: Penguin, 1967).

37. More accurately Harnack speaks of the Fatherhood of God and of our being children of God (and so of "the infinite value of the human soul") as basic elements of the message of Jesus. See Adolf Harnack, *What Is Christianity?* (Gloucester, Mass.: Peter Smith, 1978), 83.

8

THE MIRACLES OF JESUS TODAY

Compared to the miracles of well-known wonder-workers, from Apollonius of Tyana in the first century[1] to Satya Sai Baba in the twentieth,[2] or even to those attributed to the child Jesus by the apocryphal Gospels, like the second-century *Infancy Gospel of Thomas,* or the fourth-century *Gospel of Pseudo-Matthew,*[3] the miracles of Jesus reported in the canonical Gospels are conspicuous for their sobriety, altruism, and restraint. Jesus performs no spectacular stunts to impress the crowds, gives no frivolous exhibitions of arbitrary power, wreaks no acts of divine vengeance on those who oppose or slight him, works no miracles for himself alone.[4] His miracles, largely healings and exorcisms, are always performed in response to the clamoring needs of others. They are works of benevolence (better, acts of salvation),[5] largely unspectacular in character, and intended not as works of wonder but as proclamations in action of religious truths.

HOW JESUS UNDERSTOOD HIS MIRACLES

Indeed the Jesus of the Gospels steadfastly refuses to work wonders that might compel the admiration of the crowds. One function at least of the Temptation Story (Mt 4:1-11 = Lk 4:1-13)—a symbolic expression of undoubtedly real temptation experiences of Jesus, formulated in the form of a scribal disputation possibly by Jesus himself[6]—is to show how decisively he rejected the popular messianic expectations of his time, which looked to the Messiah to repeat the wonders once wrought for Israel in the wilderness, and to seize political power with supra-natural aid. All such expectation Jesus rejects as diabolic. "Signs and wonders" (marvels and prodigies) will be wrought by false messiahs and false prophets who will lead many astray (Mk 13:22). Jesus himself sharply refuses

This article first appeared in *Bible Bhashyam* 5 (1975): 189-204.

the request for a "sign from heaven," that is, for some suprahuman prodigy that would authenticate his mission. No such sign is to be given to this "evil and adulterous (i.e., faithless) generation," whose faithlessness is betrayed by its very demand for a sign (for a faith which looks for guarantees ceases to be faith)— except the sign of Jonah (Mt 12:38-42 = Lk 11:29-32). What is offered here is not really a sign, as the Jews wanted it, but a challenge. His own summons to conversion (Mt 4:17), he claims, ought to be as self-authenticating as Jonah's proclamation of repentance to Nineveh and should evoke the same unconditional response (Lk 11:30).[7]

Clearly, then, Jesus would not have regarded his miracles as "signs from heaven," as prodigies functioning as authenticating proofs of his mission. He saw them rather, to use the word in a different and Johannine sense, as "signs of the Kingdom." To the disciples of the Baptist who come querying whether he is indeed the expected Messiah, Jesus replies by referring them to all that they have seen and heard—how "the blind receive their sight and the lame walk, lepers are cleansed and the deaf hear, and the dead are raised up, and the poor have the good news preached to them" (Mt 11:2-4). This is not meant to be a catalogue of authenticating wonders, but is an impressionistic sketch, borrowing largely from Isaiah's lyrical description of the "last day" (Is 35:5-6 + 61:1), of the new order of salvation which Jesus inaugurates, and in which, significantly, the proclamation of the good news to the poor figures as conspicuously as physical healings, and comes indeed as their climax and crown. And when he is accused by his enemies of casting out demons by Beelzebub, the prince of demons, Jesus again describes his exorcisms as signs of the saving presence of God: "if it is by the spirit of God that I cast out demons, then the kingdom of God has come upon you" (Mt 12:28). He sees his healings and exorcisms (and these are the only miracles of his that he speaks about in any of his genuine sayings) not as "wonders," dazzling displays of his "divine" power (in this they differed little, Mt 12:27 suggests, from the healings and exorcisms of his contemporaries), but as "signs," intelligible indications, perceptible to those disposed to recognize them, that God is at work in him and that with him the promised age of definitive salvation has dawned.

THE MIRACLES OF JESUS
IN THE NEW TESTAMENT CHURCH

His understanding of his miracles is continued in the New Testament Church, though these miracles played there a much smaller part than is generally supposed.[8] Apart from the Gospels, which report some thirty-odd miracles worked by him,[9] and Acts, which refers obliquely to his miracles twice (2:22; 10:38)—while speaking frequently of miracles worked by the apostles in his name (4:30; 4:43; 5:12; 14:13)—the New Testament does not mention the miracles of Jesus at all. Paul is silent about them, and so are the deutero-Pauline Letters, the Epistles of Peter, John, James, and Jude and the Apocalypse. Even the

Gospels play down rather than emphasize the role of miracles in the ministry of Jesus, and are careful to insist not on the "wonder" character of the miracles they report, but on their theological meaning.

Words which underscore the "wonder" character of a miracle like *thaumazia* (amazing events), *paradoxa* (strange things), *aretai* (wonderful deeds) are avoided in the Gospels, even though frequent in the religious literature of the time. "Signs and wonders" (*sēmeia kai terata*), or, in the Synoptics, "signs" (*sēmeia*) alone, are the standard Gospel expressions of marvelous prodigies and are used not for the miracles of Jesus, but for the spectacular magic deeds he deplores (Mt 12:28; Mk 13:22; Jn 4:48). Instead the miracles of Jesus are called *dynamei*s (mighty works) in the Synoptics, a term which reminds us of the "mighty deeds" wrought by Yhwh to save Israel in the wilderness. It identifies his miracles as saving acts, while in John they are called *sēmeia* (signs)—not in the Synoptic sense of "prodigies," but with the specifically Johannine meaning of visible symbols of the saving activity of Jesus (2:11; 4:54), or *erga* (works), that is, expressions of an activity which continues the saving work of the Father on earth (5:17; 7:3; 9:3; 10:32). In every case it is the symbolic rather than the "wonder" character of the miracle that the term used expresses.[10]

It is for their theological meaning, then, rather than for their "wonder" character that the Gospels narrate the miracles of Jesus. This meaning is spelled out in the four Gospels, each of which takes up his understanding of his miracles as signs of "the Kingdom," and unfolds it, each in its own particular way.[11] Limitations of space prevent an examination of the miracle tradition of all the four Gospels, and so this enquiry is limited to the first two only (Mt and Mk), which treat of the miracles extensively enough to provide an adequate picture.

THE MIRACLES OF JESUS IN MARK

Mark interprets the miracles of Jesus in terms of the Jewish apocalyptic, which pictures the coming of "the Kingdom" as a massive cosmic conflict.[12] God's Rule can be established only to the extent that the rule of Satan (who is in effective command over the world in its "present age," its *kaliyuga* of hopeless subjection to injustice, sickness, sin, and death) is brought to an end. The "strong man" must be bound before he can be despoiled of his goods (Mk 3:27). The miracles of Jesus for Mark are plundering of the "strong man," who has been bound (rendered powerless, though not yet decisively defeated) by the coming of Jesus, and more specifically by the signal victory over Satan cryptically reported in Mark's story of the temptation (Mk 1:9-11).[13] That is why exorcisms are so conspicuous a feature of Mark's Gospel (1:23-27; 1:34-39; 3:11; 5:1-20; 7:26-30; 9:14-28), and why he begins his account of the ministry of Jesus with an exorcism, presented as a typical expression of the "authority" of Jesus (1:23-28), and why he can describe even a "nature" miracle like the stilling of the storm (4:35-41) as an exorcism, in which Jesus "threatens" (*epitiman*) the wind, and orders the sea to "be still" (*phimoun*), just as he had once (1:23-27) "threatened" (*epiti-*

man) the possessed man in the synagogue at Capernaum (1:23-27) and ordered him to "keep quiet" (*phimoun*). Natural catastrophes no less than sin, sickness, and death, are the "signs of Satan's rule," and with the coming of Jesus this rule is everywhere breaking down.

The miracles of Jesus in Mark are part of a great, poly-faceted process of liberation which Jesus comes to proclaim and achieve (cosmic, physical, psychic, social, religious) from Satan and all the adjuncts of his rule. For Jesus liberates not just from demonic possession (1:23-27) and sin (2:1-12), not only from sickness (1:29-31) and death (5:21-42), not merely from destructive forces of nature which threaten us (4:35-41), but equally, and indeed especially, from the ignominy of social ostracism (2:14-17) and from the crippling tyranny of a dead ritualism (7:1-6) and an oppressive law (2:23-27).

As elements in this total liberation the miracles are saving events. But the salvation they bring is partial and provisional. The decisive saving event, the final overthrow of Satan's rule, the definitive expulsion of the "strong man," is accomplished only with the death and resurrection of Jesus (15:38-39) and will be brought to completion only at the parousia (14:62). Meanwhile the miracles are anticipations of the new order which the death and resurrection of Jesus will bring, and they give us a foretaste as it were of a parousiaic existence.

It is to emphasize their provisional character, no doubt, that Mark ties up his accounts of the miracles with a puzzling demand for secrecy. Demons who proclaim Jesus' identity are harshly silenced (1:25; 1:34; 3:12), and those who have been healed are ordered not to make their healing known (1:44; 5:43; 7:36; 8:26). The meaning of this so-called messianic secret is much disputed,[14] but it is very probable that the secret is a device Mark uses to bridge the gap between his miracle-story tradition and its picture of Jesus as a triumphant wonder-worker, and his originally independent Passion narrative (it is Mark who first puts the two together and obtains a "Gospel"!)[15] with its wholly different picture of Jesus as the lowly but righteous sufferer. What Mark is telling us in his messianic secret, then, is that it is from the Passion rather than the miracles of Jesus, that we ultimately know who Jesus really is, so that it is only at the moment of his death in total abandonment that his true identity is officially disclosed, when the centurion proclaims him to be "the Son of God" (15:39). The followers of Jesus, then, are not to hanker after miracles, which are obscure signs only, but should follow him along the way of the Cross (8:34-9:1) through which alone the saving reality signified by the miracles is truly attained.

THE MIRACLES OF JESUS IN MATTHEW

The significance of the miracles is expounded by Matthew in a more elaborate and systematic way.[16] Miracle stories scattered all over Mark have been assembled by Matthew into a cycle of ten miracles (Mt 8-9), placed immediately after the Sermon on the Mount (Mt 5-7), with two identical summaries of the teaching and healing activity of Jesus (4:23 = 9:35) framing the two collections into a unity. Matthew begins his description of the Galilean ministry of Jesus with a diptych, a two-paneled portrait which shows him as the Messiah in his words (Sermon on the Mount) and in his works (the miracle cycle).

This first insight into the miracles of Jesus, which sees them as the works of the Messiah, closely associated with his words and, like them, serving as proclamations of "the Kingdom" (11:2-4), is deepened and further elaborated by Matthew in his miracle cycle (Mt 8-9), a masterpiece of theologically significant construction, brilliantly organized into a compact, informative treatise on what the miracles of Jesus mean.[17] The ten miracles of the group have been arranged into three groups of three miracles each, with a concluding miracle to round off the set. The sayings of Jesus (8:18-22) and "pronouncement" stories providing schematic settings for his sayings (9:9-17) separate one group from another and serve as pointers to the meaning of the group. Each group illustrates one particular theme of the miracle theology of Matthew, so that they successively present the miracles of Jesus as the works of the "servant messiah" prefigured in Isaiah (Mt 8:1-17), as the "mighty deeds" of the Lord who can protect his imperiled community from all destructive forces (the sea, Satan, sin) which threaten it, and so deserves its absolute trust (8:23; 9:8), and as works performed in response to the recipient's faith (9:18-31). It is the concluding miracle of the cycle, the healing of a dumb demoniac (9:32-34) which caps Matthew's teaching on the miracles of Jesus and forcefully expresses his attitude to the miraculous.

This concluding miracle is narrated so schematically that it is obviously intended merely as a setting for the double chorus with which the narrative (and indeed the whole miracle cycle) ends.[18] The crowds marvel: "Never was anything like this done in Israel"; the Pharisees complain: "he casts out demons by the prince of demons" (9:34). Clearly, the miracles of Jesus are not for Matthew compelling proofs of his mission. They decide nothing, but only provoke the same division that his other words and works (his proclamation of the Kingdom, his parables, his interpretation of the Law, his violations of the Sabbath, his table fellowship with social and religious outcasts) continually do. The miracles of Jesus do not create faith but presuppose it. Faith is needed in the recipient if Jesus is to work a miracle at all (9:22, 29, but especially Mk 6:6). Faith is necessary in the bystanders if the miracle is to be recognized for what it is—not an empty conjuring trick, nor an act of sorcery, but a sign of the power and the presence of God (7:34). The miracles of Jesus, like everything he is and does, are thus challenges to our faith. Each is a mini-gospel, a proclamation in action of the "good news" of salvation in Jesus, which like the proclamation of the "good news" in word, can be accepted in faith or rejected in unbelief.

THE MIRACLES OF JESUS TODAY

The New Testament shows the miracles of Jesus not as compelling "proofs" which decisively authenticate his person and mission from outside but as "signs," indications perceptible to those disposed to receive them (those enlightened by faith and instructed in the Scriptures) that God is truly at work in Jesus for the liberation of humans. Nowhere, indeed, does the New Testament attempt a miracle-based apologetic.[19] Instead it is to the prophetic authority of Scripture (Mt 8:17; 12:17-21; Lk 24:27, 44; Jn 12:38) and to the witness of the apostolic community (Acts 1:22; 2:32; 3:15; 1 Cor 15:3-11) that it appeals in order to justify its faith in Jesus, and the Gospel miracles become significant only in the context of this testimony.

This is inevitable, given the mentality of the early Jewish Christian communities in which the Gospel traditions first took shape. To these first Christians, who thought in terms of history rather than of nature, and for whom the universe was not so much a *cosmos* (an organized system of a strictly predictable natural causality) as a *creation* (a world dependent on and directed by the free activity of personal supra-natural forces: God, angels, and demons),[20] miracles were indeed unusual and striking, but not necessarily exceptional, and much less "supra-natural" events. Their particular "worldview" knew nothing of "nature." Miracles in fact were for them (as they are in an Indian village today) part of the normal order of things. Jewish exorcists cast out demons as successfully as Jesus did (Mt 12:28; Mk 5:38-41; Acts 18:31). Greek magicians like Simon Magus (Acts 8:9-10) worked wonders no less spectacular than those of the apostles. What mattered was not so much the occurrence of a miracle (this was "normal"), as its origin and meaning. Miracles were ambiguous in character (divine, magical, or diabolic), needing to be discerned. They guaranteed nothing, for they needed to be guaranteed themselves. The Gospel miracles do not authenticate Jesus but are authenticated by him! It is ultimately the character of Jesus and the accordance with Scripture of his words and works that ultimately guarantee his miracles as indeed deriving from the power of God.

This worldview of the Gospels determines not only their attitudes to the miraculous in general, but their understanding of the individual miracles as well. It is clear enough that the Gospel miracle stories reflect consistently a primitive cosmology, in which diseases are caused by demons, not germs (so Jesus "rebukes" a fever in Lk 4:39); in which the sea is the natural home of demonic powers of destruction (so Jesus exorcises the sea in Mk 4:39; on the other hand, the herd of possessed swine in Mk 5:13 run headlong into the sea, taking their demon back to his natural place, and so restoring the right order of things). In it cases of hysterical dumbness (Mt 9:32) or epilepsy (Mk 9:17-18) are attributed to possession.

Such a cosmology, indeed the whole apocalyptic worldview of New Testament times, is obviously quite alien to us today. For in spite of the growing fascination of the occult for us (finding its latest expression in the sick sensationalism of the *Exorcist*), and the explosive eruption of the charismatic movement with its easy familiarity with the miraculous, we today can scarcely picture the world as the battleground of conflicting supra-natural forces, divine and demonic. As citizens of a science-dominated space age, we experience it rather as an orderly, self-contained system of natural causality, operating according to strictly predictable patterns, which can be formulated in precise and utterly reliable laws.[21]

The vast success of science is due to its long experience which has been tested by sustained observation and experiment in regard to the absolute regularity of nature. All its dazzling success has depended on this. One could scarcely put a man on the moon if the flight of the space capsule were subject to the arbitrary whims of demons or gods! On it depends the growing ability of science to explain the hitherto inexplicable, so that yesterday's "miracles" are the commonplaces of today. All this makes it increasingly difficult to conceive of exceptions to the laws (as a miracle would be defined today)[22] and to recognize such exceptions if they do indeed occur. What now seem to be supra-natural events may well lie within the undiscovered potentialities of nature (for who can tell what nature can or cannot do?). Today's "miracles" may well have a simple explanation tomorrow. Science cannot rule out the possibility of miracles, for to do so it would have to transgress the limits of its competence and pronounce on the supra-natural, which is by definition outside the reach of its investigating techniques.[23] But it does make belief in miracles a good deal more problematic than in the uncomplicated days when the Gospels were written.

The problem is aggravated for the case of Jesus' miracles by the encroachments of history. A critical study of the Gospels has shown us how difficult it is today to establish the historicity of the miracles they narrate. Widely different versions of the same miracle confront us in the Gospels (compare the healing of the centurion's servant in Mt 8:5-13; Lk 7:1-10; and Jn 4:46-54), suggesting that the Gospel miracle stories were not handed down as scrupulously accurate reports of what actually happened, but are, like the rest of the Gospel material, sedimentations of a theologically loaded tradition, considerably touched up while being transmitted orally in a community before the Gospels were written, and again when it was written up in the Gospels, especially John.[24] While there is no doubt a solid historical nucleus of the Gospel miracle tradition—for the tradition is ancient, extensive, borne out by unusual sobriety and guaranteed by certainly genuine sayings of Jesus in which he claims to have cast out demons (Mt 12:28) and healed diseases (Mt 11:2-4)—it is by no means easy (nor always possible) to say what exactly happened on any given occasion, or to show that what did happen was, in fact, a miracle as we would understand it today.[25]

UNDERSTANDING THE MIRACLES OF JESUS

What then are we to make of the miracles of Jesus in this age of critical history and natural science? How should we interpret them so that they may become intelligible and religiously meaningful for man today? Not, surely, by going back to the miracle-based apologetic of "traditional" theology—the defensive, overabstract, largely unbiblical theology of the "siege years" from Trent to Vatican II—in which the miracles of Jesus (understood as divine interventions in the order of nature) were built up into unassailable credentials of his divine mission, if not irrefutable proofs of his divinity. An apologetic of this kind is hopelessly obsolete. It starts off with a distorted idea of faith, as if it needed, or were compatible with, "proofs" and uses a quite unbiblical concept of miracles, as if the Gospel miracles were prodigies perceptible in themselves without the illumination of faith. It breaks down wholly when faced with the historical uncertainties of the Gospel miracle tradition revealed by critical exegesis, or with the philosophical difficulty of recognizing a supra-natural miracle, given the open-ended progress of science and the new potentialities of nature it is continually revealing.

What really matters, then, is not the "how" of the miracles of Jesus (their physical structure), but their "why" and their "what" (their meaning). Here the accounts in the Gospels remain normal. The miracles of Jesus (no matter how we choose to explain them) are for us too "signs of the Kingdom." They announce and actualize (make present) the saving action of God, and reveal the particular form that it takes. For the miracles of Jesus are signs of the cosmic dimensions of the salvation he brings. They tell us that the Kingdom of God is not hidden in the privacy of a personal existentialist decision; it is not resolved by a flight from the cosmos; it does not come in a moment of gnostic enlightenment or at a peak experience of charismatic ecstasy. "The Kingdom" brings the total liberation of man from all the forms of unfreedom (cosmic, social, personal) that constrain him. "The Kingdom" means, the miracles of Jesus tell us, that the whole of man is wholly saved.

Signs, however, change. They age, grow dull with use, become obsolete, break down. Signs that speak out loud and clear to one generation are inarticulate in the next. The contemporaries of Jesus were conscious of their alienation, their state of unfreedom, their need for the liberating grace of God, primarily in their experience of utter helplessness in face of the dark ominous forces of nature that threatened them. They were continually menaced by the arbitrary violence of natural cataclysms, threatened by uncontrollable endemic diseases, paralyzed by a pervasive fear of the countless malignant demons with which they had peopled their world. They were exposed to sudden famines, lived always on the edge of want, and were ever anguished by the intractable finality of death. For them healings, exorcisms, raisings from the dead, the stilling of the storm, the multiplication of bread, would have been indeed reassuring signs that spoke tellingly of the gracious liberating presence of God and pointed to the new order of freedom and life which only God can give.

But are these appropriate signs today, for us who live in a world whose self-understanding is so vastly different from that of New Testament times? Demons have departed from our world, drummed out by the relentless march of a ruthlessly rationalist science;[26] and nature, though it still threatens, no longer terrifies, for we have learned to recognize its forces as challenges to be controlled, not malignant powers to be feared. Sickness yields to the growing assurance of a medicine that has learned to control leprosy and may soon eradicate infectious diseases from the earth. Cases of "possession" are successfully treated in psychiatric wards. The world finds itself at last with the means (if not yet the will) to adequately feed its poor. Human effort accomplishes today what was once looked for as a miracle from God.

It is not in sickness, then, or in hunger or the menace of storms or the fear of demons, that man, today, experiences his need for the liberating power of God. The signs of his helplessness are elsewhere: in his anguished loneliness, and in his desperate attempts to build up relationships, in his tragic sense of the meaninglessness of life, in his terror at the chilling immensity of the universe he lives in, in his helpless awareness of the infinite depths of his own selfishness and the flaring violence of his aggressions, in his despairing confrontation with the vast systems of injustice and oppression under which he suffers helplessly or to which he unwillingly belongs, in his silent raging at the absurd climax of death.

It is to these needs that today's signs of the Kingdom must speak. They are the *praeparatio evangelica* for man today, the propaedeutic which disposes him to long for, to recognize and to grasp at, the salvation freely offered to him in Jesus. Apocalyptic expectation has long given way to social concern. It is in the idiom of this new mood that the word of God must now speak. And indeed, were Jesus to appear among us today, would he, one wonders, come as a healer and exorcist, competing with the doctors and psychiatrists who have adequately assumed these functions? Would he not come rather as one who gives vision and purpose to a dispirited and drifting people, who sparks hope in a people driven to despair? Would he not open their eyes to the grim realities of injustice and oppression among which they blissfully live in stubborn blindness, rouse them from their paralyzed inaction and strengthen their sinews so that they may stand up for the poor to whom he proclaimed (how ironical it sometimes sounds!) the "good news" of salvation? Would he not exorcise the demons of self-righteousness, of intolerance, of the lust for power, of divisiveness, casteism and unconcern, which sit contentedly in the swept and empty spaces of their lives? Would he not start fashioning communities in which the outcaste would be welcome and the oppressed find relief, communities in which men would learn the courage to love, find the strength for commitment, and be given the truly supra-human ability to forgive? And would not these be "miracles" more potent than any he has wrought, "signs" more telling, because closer to the reality they signify, than any healing or exorcism speaking powerfully to us of the victory over evil which Jesus has won, and of the new life of freedom in the Spirit he has come to give? Should not these be the miracles we must look for today? For are they not ultimately the touchstone of the presence of Christ in our midst, and of the coming of God's Kingdom among us?

NOTES

1. Born at Tarsus in A.D. 20, Apollonius was the most celebrated wonder-worker of the Hellenistic world. His miracles, some strongly reminiscent of those of Jesus, are reported in the third-century *Life of Apollonius of Tyana,* a rather abridged translation of which is available in D. L. Dungan and D. R. Cartlidge, *Source Book of Texts for the Comparative Study of the Gospels* (Missoula, Mont.: Society of Biblical Literature, 1971), 259-96.

2. See H. Murphet, *Sai Baba: Man of Miracles* (Madras: Macmillan, 1971), for an impressive study of the apparently well-authenticated miracles of this colorful personality.

3. See E. Hennecke, *New Testament Apocrypha,* vol. 1 (London: Lutterworth Press, 1963), 388-402; 410-15.

4. In striking contrast to the miracles reported in the apocryphal Infancy Gospels, where the child Jesus makes clay sparrows which fly away (*Thom* 2:1), strikes dead a boy who bumps into him (*Thom* 4:1), and, during the flight into Egypt, makes a palm tree bend down to offer its fruit to his thirsty mother (*Ps-Mt* 20:2).

5. See L. Legrand, "Christ's Miracles as 'Social Work,'" *Indian Ecclesiastical Studies* 1 (1962): 43-64.

6. So J. Dupont, "L'arrière-fond biblique du récit des tentations de Jésus," *New Testament Studies* 3 (1952–53): 287-304.

7. Matthew's interpretation of the "sign" as a reference to Jonah's three-day sojourn in the whale's belly, prefiguring the burial and resurrection of Jesus (12:38-41), is certainly secondary. See E. Schweizer, *Das Evangelium nach Matthäus* (Göttingen: Vandenhoeck & Ruprecht, 1973), 188-89.

8. See A. Fridrichsen, *Le problème du miracle dans le christianisme primitif* (Paris: Libraire Istra, 1925), 16-46.

9. These comprise some 16 healings, 7 exorcisms, 3 resuscitations, and 7 nature miracles.

10. See R. H. Fuller, *Interpreting the Miracles* (London: SCM Press, 1966), 15-17; C. F. D. Moule, "The Vocabulary of Miracle," in *Miracles: Cambridge Studies in Their Philosophy and History,* ed. C. F. D. Moule (London: Mowbray, 1965), 235-38.

11. On the way in which the miracles of Jesus are handled in the four Gospels, see A. Richardson, *The Miracle Stories of the Gospels* (London: SCM Press, 1941), 100-22; A. Duprez, "Les récits évangéliques de miracles," *Lumière et Vie* 23 (1974): 49-69; and the issue of *Cahiers Evangiles* entitled *Les miracles de l'Evangile 8* (new series) (1974): 19-44.

12. See M. E. Glasswell, "The Use of Miracles in the Markan Gospel," in *Miracles: Cambridge Studies in Their Philosophy and History,* ed. C. F. D. Moule (London: Mowbray, 1965), 149-62; Moule, "Vocabulary of Miracle," 149-62. Other useful studies on the miracles in Mark are T. A. Burkill, "The Notion of Miracle with Special Reference to Mark's Gospel," *Zeitschrift für die neutestamentliche Wissenschaft* 50 (1959): 33-73; T. Snoy, "Les miracles dans l'évangile de Marc," *Revue Théologique de Louvain* 4 (1973): 58-101; and (the major work on the subject) K. Kertelge, *Die Wunder Jesu im Markusevangelium* (Munich: Kösel Verlag, 1970).

13. See J. M. Robinson, *The Problem of History in Mark* (London: SCM Press, 1957), 26-42.

14. For a brief survey of opinions, see W. G. Kümmel, *Introduction to the New Tes-*

tament (London: SCM Press, 1966), 66-67. For a more extensive study, see G. Minette de Tillesse, *Le secret messianique dans l'Evangile de Marc* (Paris: Cerf, 1968).

15. John too (independently?) fashions a Gospel by combining a collection of miracle stories (his "Signs Source") with a Passion narrative. On the implications of this for the development of the Gospel form, see J. M. Robinson, "The Johannine Trajectory," *Trajectories through Early Christianity*, ed. J. M. Robinson and H. Köster (Philadelphia: Fortress Press, 1971), 232-68.

16. On Matthew's theology of the miracles of Jesus, see the now classic work of H. J. Held, "Matthew as Interpreter of the Miracle Stories," in *Tradition and Interpretation in Matthew*, ed. G. Bornkamm et al. (London: SCM Press, 1963), 165-303. Also, more recently, K. Gatzweiler, "Les récits de miracles dans L'Evangile selon saint Matthieu," in *L'Evangile selon Matthieu: Rédaction et théologie*, ed. M. Didier (Gembloux: Duculot, 1972), 209-20.

17. See W. G. Thompson, "Reflections on the Composition of Mt 8:1-9, 34," *Catholic Biblical Quarterly* 33 (1971): 365-88; Held, "Matthew as Interpreter," 246-53.

18. The miracle in Mt 9:32-34 is probably an abbreviated version of the healing of the blind and dumb possessed person reported in Mt 12:22-25 = Lk 11:14-16, and duplicated here by Matthew just to provide his miracle cycle with an appropriate ending.

19. Traces of such an apologetic may perhaps be detected in some of the later writings of the New Testament (like Acts) which derive from a Hellenistic milieu. See G. W. H. Lampe, "Miracles in the Acts of the Apostles," in *Miracles: Cambridge Studies in Their Philosophy and History*, ed. C. F. D. Moule, 163-78.

20. See J. M. Court, "The Philosophy of the Synoptic Miracles," *Journal of Theological Studies* 23 (1972): 1-18; J. P. Ross, "Some Notes on Miracle in the Old Testament," in *Miracles: Cambridge Studies in Their Philosophy and History*, ed. C. F. D. Moule, 43-60.

21. The indeterminism of the subatomic world does not change this. For though, at the microcosmic level, the behavior of individual particles is determined by statistical laws (half a given number of photons will pass through a crystal grating in a given time, though we can in no way tell whether any one given photon will pass through or not), yet at the macrocosmic level, the level of human experience, the numbers involved are so great that the statistical probability amounts in fact to certainty. See E. and M. L. Keller, *Miracles in Dispute* (London: SCM Press, 1969), 159-80.

22. See the standard definition in traditional theological manuals: *"eventus sensibilis praeter communem cursum naturae divinitus factus*—an event beyond the ordinary processes of nature effected through divine agency. The definition, like most of the modern discussion on miracles, goes back to Hume, for whom a miracle could be accurately defined "a transgression of a law of nature by a particular volition of a deity or by the interposition of some invisible agent." For the serious philosophical problems which such an understanding of a miracle raises, see R. Swinburne, *The Concept of Miracle* (London: Macmillan, 1970).

23. Brilliantly demonstrated by I. T. Ramsey in his essay "Miracles: An Exercise in Logical Mapwork," published in the SPCK Theological Collection entitled *Miracles and the Resurrection* (London: SPCK, 1964).

24. See Soares-Prabhu, "Are the Gospels Historical?," *Clergy Monthly* 38 (March, April 1974): 112-24, 164-72, and in *Biblical Theology for India*, Collected Writings of George M. Soares-Prabhu, S.J., vol. 2, ed. Scaria Kuthirakkattel (Pune: Jnana-Deepa Vidyapeeth, 1999), 105-25.

25. See Fuller, *Interpreting the Miracles,* 18-39; R. Latourelle, "Authenticité historique des miracles de Jésus: Essai de critério logie," *Gregorianum* 54 (1973): 225-62.

26. The rejection of "demons," ultimately cosmological principles of animist origin, does not necessarily mean the denial of Satan, a personal power of evil. But Satan too is increasingly in theological trouble; see H. A. Kelly, *Towards the Death of Satan* (London: Chapman, 1968).

9

"AND THERE WAS A GREAT CALM"

A Dhvani *Reading of the Stilling of the Storm (Mk 4:35-41)*

A. *DHVANI* IN NEW TESTAMENT EXEGESIS TODAY

1. *Historical Criticism*

Anyone acquainted with recent parable exegesis will be aware of how closely the interpretations of a text through *dhvani* resemble recent attempts at understanding the parables of Jesus as metaphor.[1] These attempts are quite new. Ever since the scientific revolution of the sixteenth and seventeenth centuries, which ushered in the modern world, it is historical criticism that has been the dominant method of biblical exegesis. The scientific revolution, which gave rise to empirical science, brought in also new "scientific" methods for the study of literature and history. Historical criticism applies these methods to the Bible. Through the use of a series of rigorous techniques, the so-called "criticism" (text, literary, form, redaction and historical criticism) attempts to recover the original form of a biblical text and lay bare its original meaning.[2]

WHAT IS THE "MEANING" OF TEXT?

But just what is the "meaning of a text"? Is it what the author intended to say (*speaker or author meaning*), or what the text does in fact say whether the author intended it or not (*discourse or text meaning*)—for intent and expression need

---

This article first appeared in *Bible Bhashyam* 5 (1979): 295-308.

not always coincide, and an author may not fully express what he intended or even say more than he wished to. Or is it what his readers or listeners understood (or misunderstood) him to have said (*listener or reader meaning*)?[3] The problem becomes even more acute when we are dealing with texts like the Gospels, which are not the products of a writer's workshop—creative compositions of individual authors—but are the end products of a long and complex process of community tradition. Stories about and sayings of Jesus were handed down orally in the post-Easter Church for some thirty or more years before they were first incorporated into a continuous narrative, a Gospel. And in the course of their transmission these traditions were continually reinterpreted as they were handed down, acquiring new meanings as they were applied to new situations, until they received a fixed, final text meaning when they were edited into the Gospels.[4]

In his classic study on the parables of Jesus, Joachim Jeremias distinguishes three moments in their transmission.[5] The parables have a setting in the ministry of Jesus (*Sitz im Leben Jesu*), a setting in the life of the early Church (*Sitz im Leben ecclesiae*), and a setting in the Gospels (*Sitz im Leben evangelii*). In each new setting the parable is given a new form, fulfills a new function, and acquires a new meaning. Parables uttered by Jesus to throw light on concrete situations in his ministry were taken up by the early Church and adapted (often by allegorization or by the addition of "lessons") to new post-Easter contexts very different from the ones in which they were originally spoken. Parables from the oral tradition of the early Church were taken up by the evangelists and re-edited to conform to the specific perspectives of their Gospels.

The Parable of the Sower (Mk 4:3-9), spoken by Jesus to encourage his disciples disheartened by the failure of the Galilean ministry (its message being that spectacular success will follow large initial loss), is allegorized by the early Church (Mk 4:13-20) into a description of the dispositions that hinder the fruitful reception of the Word. The Parable of the Wicked Tenants (Mk 12:1-8) used by Jesus to drive home to the Pharisees the enormity of their hard-heartedness (like the wicked tenants, they are deliberately deaf to every possible appeal) becomes in Matthew (Mt 21:33-39) an allegory of salvation history, neatly illustrating a key theme of his theology—that the Jews by rejecting Jesus have lost their right to the Promise, so that it is the Church, made up of Jews and gentiles, which is now the true Israel. The Parable of the Dishonest Steward (Lk 16:1-8), through which Jesus summons his listeners to act as decisively as the steward does in the crisis they are in because of his proclamation of the Kingdom, is turned by Luke, through the addition of a series of lessons (Lk 16:9-13), into an illustration of the right use of riches.

WHAT DOES A PARABLE MEAN?

What, then, would be the true meaning of such parables which have undergone considerable reinterpretation in course of transmission in the early Church? Would it be what Jesus meant when he uttered them, or what his hearers understood him to have meant? Is it the meaning read out of the parable by the early Church, or that given to it by the evangelist when he edited it to express the theology of his Gospel? Or is it the meaning a preacher finds in the parable when he propounds it for an audience today?

For historical criticism the answer is clear. The real meaning of a parable is its "literal" meaning—that is, its original author-meaning, the meanings intended by Jesus when he first spoke to his listeners in Palestine. So historical criticism sets out to recover this meaning, working its way back through the layers of interpretation that may have accumulated around the parable during its oral transmission in the early Church and its integration into a Gospel. Historical criticism attempts to trace the history of the parable in order to recover its original form and meaning.

But it is precisely this preoccupation with history that is both historical criticism's strength and its weakness. If close attention to history is the source of the method's objectivity, it is also the source of its ultimate irrelevance. Focusing exclusively on their original author-meaning tends to rob the parables of significance for us today. For since the parables of Jesus were originally spoken in concrete situations very different from those we live in, their original meaning is not likely to say much to us.

But is the original meaning of a parable its true meaning? An increasing number of exegetes would question this. The historical-critical method, they would suggest, has misunderstood the parable form. It has failed to perceive that the parable (indeed the Bible as a whole) is a literary work, and like any literary work has a meaning which is not fully exhausted by what the author intended to say. The parables, that is, have a text-meaning which goes beyond their author-meaning, and which can be recovered by subjecting them to the methods used by literary critics for the study of creative literature. This is what rhetorical criticism, a new method that has been developed for the study of the Bible as creative literature, attempts to do.[6]

2. Rhetorical Criticism

Rhetorical criticism treats the parables as autonomous aesthetic objects. Like a painting by Amrit Sher Gil or a poem by Tagore, a parable can be appreciated and understood even if we do not know how and when it came to be. It has a meaning in itself, independent of its origin and its history. Parables, that is, have not only an author-meaning which historical criticism can discover, but a text-meaning which escapes historical criticism. For historical criticism treats a parable as a disposable container in which an original author's message is packaged, whereas in fact the parable is itself the message!

PARABLE AS METAPHOR

Rhetorical criticism expresses this by saying that a parable is a metaphor, using the word in the rather special sense it has acquired in modern literary criticism. Grammatically a metaphor is an expression comparing one thing with another in which the element of comparison is omitted. In this it differs from a simile, where the comparison is explicitly stated. To say that Ranjit Singh was as brave as a lion is to use a simile; to call Ranjit Sing "the lion of the Punjab" is to use a metaphor.

This apparently trivial difference is fraught with significance. For metaphor and simile function in very different ways. Whereas a simile "sets one thing against another; the less known is clarified by the better known," in a metaphor "we have an image with a certain shock to the imagination which directly conveys a vision of what is signified."[7] A simile, that is, illustrates; a metaphor reveals. A metaphor, then, does not embellish a proposition or illustrate a truth; it communicates an insight and evokes a new experience—indeed an experience so radically new that it can only be grasped within the metaphor itself.[8] Like a poem, a metaphor is "not equal to, but true"!

The rhetorical criticism of a parable will concentrate, then, on the parable itself taken as a metaphor, with little interest in its origin (who uttered the parable) or its effect (how was the parable understood by those to whom it was spoken). It will focus, that is, on the text-meaning of the parable, rather than on its author- or reader-meaning, thus avoiding both the *intentional fallacy* of judging a literary work in terms of the intention of its author, and the *affective fallacy* of judging it in terms of its audience effect.[9] Instead the rhetorical critic will try to "enter" into the parable itself, and resonate to the curious combination of realism and strangeness ("the disclosure of the extraordinary in the ordinary") through which the parable is able to evoke in us the "limit experience" of the Kingdom.[10]

As an extended metaphor evoking such a limit experience, a parable obviously cannot be conceptualized. One can never reduce it to a neat set of propositions or lessons. No one interpretation of a parable, not even a historical interpretation which would recover what Jesus meant when he first uttered it, will exhaust its meaning. For like any metaphor, a parable is open to the future and will continue to disclose an indefinite sequence of new meanings (all true!) as it is spoken in a succession of new situations. Each new situation will bring out a new understanding of the parable, because the meaning of a parable is not a fixed given to be unlocked by grammatical or philological keys, but is the actualization of its limitless revelatory potential through the perspective and perceptiveness of the reader/listener, in ever new ways.[11]

Such actualization is always personal, not intellectual. It involves the whole man. Unlike the proposition, which is grasped by the mind alone, a parable, because it is an aesthetic object, engages the whole man in the totality of his knowing-feeling, conscious-unconscious response. A parable, therefore, is to be understood not through intellectual abstraction but through imaginative participation. It is through the imagination that one enters into a parable, experiences that shock of the "dislocation of the familiar" that its story conveys, and is brought into a fleeting, vertiginous confrontation with the limits of one's world.[12]

The evocation of such a limit experience is effected in a parable through the tensions in its imagery. Parables are "riven with radical comparisons and dis-junctions."[13] Such disjunctions are of course the very essence of metaphor, which, until it is deadened by use, shocks the imagination by its juxtaposition of two realities (man and lion) that are not perceived as related until the metaphor joins them. The unexpected juxtaposition jolts the mind into a new insight into the reality compared, so that one moves through the metaphor to a new level of meaning.

METAPHOR AS DHVANI

Clearly, then, in interpreting the parables of Jesus as metaphor, rhetorical criticism is relying on *dhvani*—that is, on "that use of language which through either the primary or secondary meaning or through both of them takes the reader to a depth meaning which is experienceable but not expressible."[14] Metaphor, that is, functions much as *dhvani* does. Like *dhvani* it does not communicate a lesson, but evokes a limit experience—an experience of the transcendent which is so utterly beyond conceptualization that it can only be experienced as the limit of our "world." The evocation occurs only when the sensitivity of the reader is attuned to and resonates with the symbolic language of the metaphor. And it leads not to a communication of truths but to a communion of realities.

But unlike *dhvani*, which, since it functions through primary as well as sec-ondary meanings, can occur anywhere in a text, interpretation through metaphor would, strictly speaking, be confined to the explicitly figurative portions of the New Testament. There is, however, a growing awareness that the metaphorical process can occur beyond the boundaries of metaphor proper, and that the whole New Testament can in fact be treated metaphorically, since it is the story of Jesus who is "par excellence the metaphor of God."[15] The "familiar and mundane" story of Jesus is the way through which one arrives at the experience of God. This insight unfortunately has not been followed up, and we have hardly any example of a metaphorical or *dhvani* interpretation of non-parabolic New Testament texts. A fruitful field for exploration lies open here. We shall investigate its potentiali-ties by attempting a *dhvani* interpretation of a Gospel miracle story.

B. A DHVANI INTERPRETATION
OF MARK 4:35-41

The Stilling of the Storm in Mark (Mk 4:35-41) is a convenient subject for such an attempt. The story is compact, well structured (almost a perfect example of the miracle story form), and obviously rich in significance. Allusions to the Old Testament and the explicit use of technical exorcism terminology prevent us from reading it as a simple factual report of something which once happened. The story is obviously loaded with symbolism and riven with the tensions which suggest the straining of language called upon to express a limit experience. It thus lends itself admirably to an interpretation through *dhvani*. Before attempting such an interpretation, however, it will be useful to see how traditional historical-critical exegesis would go about interpreting it. This will throw our *dhvani* approach into sharper relief.

1. Historical-Critical Analysis

Historical criticism takes tensions in the story as indications of the conflation of sources or of the editing of underlying traditions by Mark. It thus sees the *introduction* to the narrative (vv. 35-36) as a largely redactional composition, which serves to integrate the originally independent story of the Stilling of the Storm (which came down to Mark as an isolated unit of tradition) into the context of the Gospel. This is obviously the function (a) of the typically Markan double time indication in v. 35a (cf. Mk 1:35; 14:12), which rounds off the parable discourse of Mk 4:1-34; (b) of the command of Jesus to "cross over to the other side" in v. 35b, which makes the episode part of a series of miracles narrated by Mark as occurring on the shores of the Lake of Gennesaret, repeatedly crisscrossed by Jesus (Mk 4:35; 5:1; 5:21); (c) of the dismissal of the crowds in v. 36a, which refers back to the beginning of the parable discourse when crowds gather around Jesus (Mk 4:1a); and (d) of the curious note that the disciples take Jesus "just as he was in the boat" in v. 36b, which makes sense only when we remember that the parable discourse in Mark is delivered by Jesus from a boat (Mk 4:1b).

The *narrative* itself (vv. 37-41) appears to have been taken by Mark from this tradition, but incorporates several *redactional* elements. Among these would be (a) the word of Jesus which stills the storm in v. 39, whose language clearly echoes the exorcism terminology (Jesus "threatens" [*epitiman*] the wind, and says to the sea "be muzzled" [*phimoun*]) of Mark's narrative of the healing of the demoniac in the synagogue of Capernaum (Mk 1:25); and (b) Jesus' rebuke in v. 40, which disturbs the flow of the narrative and contains the characteristically Markan theme of the disciples' lack of understanding and faith (cf. Mk 6:51; 8:17-18). The chorus in v. 41 is a natural response not to the rebuke in v. 40 (which is left unanswered and hanging in the air) but to the description of the stilling of the storm in v. 39. Verse 40 thus appears to be an intrusion. Its first half (v. 40a) may have been a secondary addition to the pre-Gospel tradition, occurring originally after v. 38; but v. 40b with its characteristic Markan theme is clearly redactional.

Other elements in the story appear to be *secondary but pre-Markan* additions inserted into the story during its transmission in the oral tradition of the early Church. This may be true (we have said) of the rebuke in v. 40a. It is probably true of the description of Jesus sleeping in v. 38a, which fits in ill with the miracle story form and unnecessarily delays the denouement of the story. Unless, then, we take it as a vestigial reminiscence of what actually happened (which is unlikely, given the strongly functional and formally stylized character of the

Gospel miracle stories), this odd little detail is probably a secondary addition to the primitive narrative.

Taking it as such, Ludger Schenke, in a remarkably thorough study of the narrative, is able to describe three stages in the history of its transmission.[16]

(a) In its original form (shorn, that is, of all its redactional and secondary elements) the story was formulated in the gentile-oriented mission preaching of Diaspora Judaism, where it functioned not indeed as a miracle story highlighting a miraculous event but as the story of an epiphany or manifestation, which focused on the figure of Jesus. Jesus was presented as the one in whom the awesome power of the Old Testament God, who stills the storm[17] and rescues the just man from threatening waters,[18] is made fully manifest. The story thus put Jesus before the gentile world as one superior to all their wonderworking "divine men" (*theioi andres*), and summoned it to a christological decision. That is why its concluding chorus took the form of a striking question ("Who then is this?"), which was meant to be not a catechetical question testing the knowledge of believers but a kerygmatic question inviting unbelievers to faith.

(b) With the addition of v. 38a (a secondary but pre-Markan insertion) the story is given a new meaning to respond to a new situation in the early Church. With the Church as an already established but persecuted community, living in imminent expectation of the parousia, concern for mission gives way to need for consolidation. The story now serves not missionary preaching but inner-community exhortation. It invites the community, tossed in the storms of persecution[19] and waiting apparently in vain for the appearance of its saving Lord who never seems to come, to an unconditional trust in Jesus, who even though "sleeping" can and will save them.

(c) Markan redaction, and in particular the addition of the rebuke in v. 40, gives the story a new point. Unconditional trust in Jesus could lead to a "divine man" soteriology, which would expect the risen Lord to save his persecuted community through a miraculous intervention. Mark's editing corrects this. The disciples are rebuked not because they are not reassured by the presence of Jesus even though he is sleeping, but because they are not willing to perish with him. They are not willing to, that is, follow him on the way of the cross as true disciples should (Mk 8:34), but look to be delivered by him through a miracle. Salvation, the story teaches us (along with the whole of Mark's Gospel), comes not through miracles but through the cross. For it is the cross rather than his miracles which is the true epiphany of Jesus.

Starting, then, from the many literary tensions in the story, historical criticism is able to detect various strata in it and reconstruct with some plausibility the history of the transmission. It shows us a story that was continuously reinterpreted as it was handed down in the tradition of the early Church, in order to meet the new needs that kept emerging as the Church developed. Such an analysis is obviously enlightening and useful. But it does not take us to the heart of the story—to the "limit experience" which the story as a religious text presumably enshrines. An interpretation through *dhvani* might take us there.

2. A Dhvani Interpretation

Unlike historical criticism, interpretation through *dhvani* is not interested in the history of a text but takes it as it now stands. As it now stands, the story of the Stilling of the Storm in Mark falls, we have seen, into two parts, each with its own particular finality and meaning. An introduction (vv. 35-36) leads up to a dramatic narrative rounded off by a comment of Jesus and the chorus of the awed disciples (vv. 37-41). Examining each of these in turn with an ear to the limit experience it evokes we find the following.

THE INTRODUCTION (VV. 35-36)

The introduction in vv. 35-36 prepares for the narrative that follows by disengaging Jesus from the situation in which he has been involved (the parable discourse of Mk 4:1-34) and freeing him for the action to follow. Every element in the introduction contributes to this. The time indication (v. 35a) rounds off the parable discourse by bringing to a close the day on which it was delivered ("when evening had come"). The command of Jesus to cross over to the other side (v. 35b) and the dismissal of the crowds (v. 36a) distances Jesus from the place where he had spoken and the people he had addressed. Only the mention of the "other boats with them" (v. 36b)—boats which subsequently vanish from the story—strikes a discordant note. Their mention serves no useful purpose in the story.

The result of such disengagement is the privatization of the miracle that follows. It is a miracle that is performed away from the crowds and before the disciples alone. The miracle mediates a revelation that is not accessible to public opinion but only to the faith of the believing community.

THE NARRATIVE (VV. 37-41)

The narrative that follows is sustained by three oppositions or tensions through which it mediates its meaning.

(1) The dominant opposition is that between the "great storm" (*lailaps megalē*) with which it begins and the "great calm" (*galēnē megalē*) in which it ends. The terse announcement: "and there was a great calm" (v. 39) rings out with impressive force after the vivid description of the storm (v. 37) and the clamor of the frightened disciples (v. 38b). One can almost experience physically the depth of the tranquil stillness and quiet it announces. The movement of the story is thus not circular but spiral. The great calm is not simply a return to a pre-storm quiet, but the attainment of a new depth of stillness, immeasurably greater than that obtaining during the anxious bustle that preceded the storm.

The movement from storm to stillness is effected by the mighty word of Jesus, who "threatens" (*epitiman*) the wind, and commands the sea to "be muzzled" (*phimoun*). The use of such exorcism terminology lights up a new and terrifying dimension to the story. We are suddenly made aware of the fact that the stilling of the storm is not just a spectacular work of wonder, a dazzling display of power over the forces of nature, but a rescue operation in which men are saved from the forces of destruction that continually threaten the world we live in. We experience vividly the precariousness of human existence lived out in a world teetering on the edge of chaos. The fragile boat of man's existence can at any moment be overwhelmed by the "sea," home of the great primeval monsters in biblical mythology (Gen 1:1; Ps 74:13-14; Is 27:1) and powerful symbol of the forces of destruction that always threaten the life of man (Rev 21:1).

(2) Yet even as we resonate to this evocation of the precariousness of human existence, we become aware of another tension in the story: the opposition between Jesus, who is asleep, and the disciples, who panic (v. 38). The significance of this opposition is again brought out by a word of Jesus, this time a word of rebuke: "Why are you afraid? Have you no faith?" (v. 40). Faith is opposed to fear. The peacefully sleeping Jesus (like the Psalmist in Ps 3:5 and 4:8) is a model of trusting faith, whose sleep reveals the ultimate stability that underlies the surface instability of human life. The frightened disciples are too disturbed by their panic to reach this level of awareness. They will experience it only if their fear gives way to faith.

(3) The focal point of this faith is revealed to us in the third of the oppositions that make up our story—that between Jesus, who is taken almost passively ("just as he was") in the boat (v. 36), and the Lord, who evokes the wondering cry: "Who then is this that even the wind and the sea obey him?" We move from the Master, who teaches in parables, to the Lord, who commands the wind and the waves. The wondering cry of the disciples evokes a great sense of awe. We experience the awesome yet immensely reassuring presence of the all-powerful Lord who has complete control over the demonic forces that threaten our lives. In his presence we overcome the paralyzing terror that grips us when we glimpse for a moment the fragility of human existence, always threatened by destruction and death. We recover our trust in the ultimate security and meaningfulness of life.

But our trust is not a return to a juvenile confidence in the benevolence of nature, or in the ability of our science to control it. It is only when we have experienced (as our world is beginning to) the terrible frailty of human life, lived out on a tiny planet spinning like a fretful midge in the vast emptiness of space and pulsing with titanic forces that threaten any moment to blow it apart, or when we have looked with terror into the caldron of savage violence and destructiveness that seethes in each human heart—it is only then that we can reach the great calm which recognizes behind the fragile patterns of human existence the unshakable stability of the ground of our being. It is this experience of ultimate stability behind the turmoil of our agitated and threatened existence that the story of the Stilling of the Storm evokes.

NOTES

1. See Robert Funk, *Language, Hermeneutic and the Word of God* (New York: Harper, 1969), 133-62.

2. See Edgar Krentz, *The Historical-Critical Method* (Philadelphia: Fortress Press, 1975).

3. See Vern Poythress, "Analysing a Biblical Text: Some Important Linguistic Distinctions," *Scottish Journal of Theology* 32 (1979): 113-37.

4. Soares-Prabhu, "Are the Gospels Historical?" *Clergy Monthly* 38 (1974): 112-24; 163-72; Joseph Pathrapankal, *Understanding the Gospels Today* (Bangalore: Dharmaram, 1977).

5. Joachim Jeremias, *The Parables of Jesus* (London: SCM Press, 1971).

6. See William Beardslee, *Literary Criticism of the New Testament* (Philadelphia: Fortress Press, 1970); George Petersen, *The Literary Critic and the New Testament* (Philadelphia: Fortress Press, 1978).

7. Amos Wilder, *Early Christian Rhetoric* (London: SCM Press, 1964), 80.

8. John Dominic Crossan, *In Parables: The Challenge of the Historical Jesus* (New York: Harper, 1973), 13. [Editor's note: "not equal to, but true" in the following sentence is from Archibald MacLeish's poem "Ars Poetica," *Modern American Poetry, Modern British Poetry: A Critical Anthology,* 5th ed., ed. Louis Untermeyer (New York: Harcourt, Brace & Company, 1936), 501.]

9. Dan O. Via, *The Parables: Their Literary and Existential Dimension* (Philadelphia: Fortress Press, 1967), 76-78.

10. Paul Ricoeur, "Biblical Hermeneutics," *Semeia* 4 (1975): 170-228.

11. See Susan Witting, "A Theory of Multiple Meanings," *Semeia* 9 (1977): 75-103.

12. Funk, *Language,* 143.

13. Sallie Te Selle, *Speaking in Parables* (Philadelphia: Fortress Press, 1975), 32-33.

14. See the article of F. X. D'Sa, "Dhvani as a Method of Interpretation," *Bible Bhashyam* 5 (1979): 276-94.

15. Te Selle, *Speaking in Parables,* 37.

16. Ludger Schenke, *Die Wundererzählungen des Markus Evangeliums* (Stuttgart: Katholisches Bibelwerk, 1975), 1-93; see also Karl Kertelge, *Die Wunder Jesu im Markusevangelium* (Munich: Kösel, 1970), 91-100.

17. Cf. Job 26:12; 38:8-11; Ps 104:6-9; Jer 5:22.

18. Cf. Ps 18:16; 32:6; 42:1-3; 69:1-2; 107:23-31; Is 43:2.

19. Cf. Ps 74:13-14; 89:10; Rev 13:1.

10

THE UNPREJUDICED JESUS AND THE PREJUDICED CHURCH

Gordon Allport begins his massive study on prejudice with a preliminary definition of the word, which can serve as a convenient starting point for our own reflections on the subject. He defines prejudice as "a feeling, favourable or unfavourable, towards a person or thing, prior to or not based on actual experience."[1] The heart of all prejudice is thus a prejudgment. This is usually the result of an unwarranted generalization from some particular set of experiences. Because we meet some Indians who are servile or some Englishmen who are snobs, we conclude that all Indians are servile and that all Englishmen are snobs—stereotypes common in India in the days of the Raj. We are, all of us, prone to such generalizations because of our need to categorize reality. We cannot possibly handle the immense mass of complex and confused information that is being beamed at us from our environment each moment, unless we learn to perceive things not in their bewildering individuality (no two seashells, no two trees, no two people are exactly alike), but as parts of large interrelated groups or categories. We *label* persons and things—and come to see not the things themselves but the standardized labels we have given them.

Categories work well until they harden into stereotypes. This happens when our labels become so clear-cut that no allowance is made for variations in their identifying features, so rigid that they are impervious to change even when contradicted by new inputs of information, and so simplistic that they divide up reality into polar opposites (good/bad, right/wrong, wise/foolish) with no intermediate types between them.

Stereotypes, which are oversimplified cognitive categories, generate prejudices, that is, affective attitudes, when they are associated with value judgments.

This article first appeared in *The Way* 27 (1987): 4-14.

This almost always happens because we rarely categorize without judging. Our categories are value-loaded in terms of our own personal or group systems of values and beliefs. "As partisans of our way of life," writes Allport, "we cannot help thinking in a partisan manner . . . so that the very act of affirming our way of life often leads us to the brink of prejudice"[2]—indeed usually carries us over the brink! Our value systems thus become significant sources of our prejudices. That is why religion, which is a primary source of our values, is a primary source of our prejudices too.

Religious prejudices are usually negative group prejudices. That is, they are "aversive or hostile attitudes" assumed by a person because he or she is the member of a particular group (their in-group), toward members of other rival groups (out-groups).[3] Such group prejudices too probably originate ultimately from the kind of unwarranted generalization of particular experiences that has been described above, but they are disseminated, that is, communicated to the members of the group, through its tradition. The tradition of a group, that is, the set of shared perceptions (group stereotypes), beliefs, and values which the group has made its own and which serve to distinguish it from other similar groups, thus becomes a fruitful source of its prejudices.

THE CHRISTIAN DILEMMA

Here precisely lies the dilemma of the Christian tradition. As a summons to experience "the Father of Our Lord Jesus Christ" as *Abba* (Mt 11:25-27), and therefore to experience humankind as brothers and sisters (Mt 23:8-10), Christianity can be understood as a sustained protest against prejudice of any kind. Paul in his letter to the Galatians quotes from an ancient baptismal liturgy to remind his readers that through baptism they have been initiated into the endtime community in which all ethnic, class, and sexist discrimination has been overcome (Gal 3:28). Because they have "put on Christ," that is, because they have undergone the radically transforming experience of having encountered Jesus, Christians are able to experience each other (and ultimately all humankind) as members of the same free, fraternal and non-exploitative community in which "there is neither Jew nor gentile, there is neither slave nor free, there is neither male nor female." People are no longer perceived nor experienced as "outcasts" or "outsiders," as "superior" or "inferior"—because all are experienced as "one (equal and united) in Christ." Christ, Paul might have said, is the end of prejudice—just as he has said that Christ is the end of Law (Rom 10:4).

But to the extent that the followers of Jesus become aware of themselves as a distinct religious group, they inevitably develop prejudices against rival groups—against the "perfidious" Jews (Mt 27:24-25) and the "depraved" gentiles (Rom 1:18-32). A strong anti-Pharisaic bias runs through the whole of Matthew's Gospel. It comes out very clearly in the "woes" against the Pharisees (23:3-36), which, in their sweeping and historically unjustified condemnation of a competing group, show all the marks (denigration, overcategorization, and inflexibility)[4] of a typically prejudiced judgment. Almost as prejudiced is Paul's indiscriminate condemnation of Hellenistic religion as a form of culpable idolatry, which leads to every kind of moral depravity (Rom 1:18-32). This is not how the Hellenistic cults would have appeared to a disinterested contemporary of Paul, less concerned than he was in drawing up a charge sheet against the pre-Christian world. Nor indeed do they appear like this to the Paul of Acts, who welcomes the insights of Hellenistic religion and is even prepared to justify the worship of "an unknown god" (Acts 17:22-23).

We find in the New Testament, then, the curious paradox of Christ proclaimed as the end of prejudice by an increasingly prejudiced Church. I propose to explore the implications of this paradox by reflecting on each of its two terms—on the "unprejudiced Jesus," who is the basis of our proclamation of Christ as the end of prejudice, and on the "prejudiced Church" which proclaims him.

THE UNPREJUDICED JESUS

Jesus appears in the Gospels as a person remarkably free from the individual and group prejudices of his people and his times. Unlike the Pharisees, the Jews of strict observance, Jesus shows no aversion toward "sinners," that is, toward notorious violators of the moral or ritual code; nor does he look down upon the *ʿammê hāʾāreṣ* ("the people of the land"), that is, the rural masses unschooled in the Law and so unable to observe its elaborate prescriptions fully. He shows special concern for the illiterate "little ones" (Mk 9:42) and is prepared to offend the respectable by "receiving tax collectors and sinners and eating with them" (Lk 15:1-2). Where even a liberal rabbi like Hillel could say, "no ignorant person (*ʿammê hāʾāreṣ*) is ever religious (*ḥāsêd*)"[5] Jesus tells the religious and the secular aristocracy of his people ("the chief priests and the elders") that "the tax collectors and the harlots go into the Kingdom of God before you" (Mt 21:31).

This clear option of Jesus for the poor and the outcast does not prejudice him against the elite, even though it brings him into open conflict with them. He engages in sharp controversy with the scribes and the Pharisees on a wide range of theological issues (Mk 2:1-3, 6; 12:13-40) but rarely if ever indulges in personal attacks on them. When he is shown doing this—conspicuously in Matthew (6:1-18; 23:3-36), rarely elsewhere (Mk 12:38-40)—these obviously prejudiced charges are usually not the words of Jesus himself. They are polemic formulations of early Jewish Christianity, struggling for self-definition against a hostile "normative" Judaism reconstituting itself after the great debacle of the Jewish revolt against Rome (66-74 C.E.). For the Gospels give us revealing glimpses of Jesus in such friendly association with the scribes and the Pharisees that it is impossible to think of him as "prejudiced," that is, as nursing an intransigent, generalized aversion toward them. He dines with a Pharisee, always in the East a sign of acceptance and friendship (Lk 7:36). He engages in a friendly and approving discussion with a scribe (Mk 12:28-34). He is warned by concerned Pharisees of Herod's threat to his life (Lk 13:31). The relations of Jesus toward the scribes and the Pharisees were obviously a great deal friendlier than an increasingly anti-Jewish Gospel tradition makes them out to be.

The close disciples of Jesus, the circle of the Twelve, chosen by him to symbolize the "new Israel," the end-time community that he intends to inaugurate, are drawn from an astonishingly wide range of ideological backgrounds. One of them is called "the Zealot" (Lk 6:15) and had obviously belonged (perhaps still belonged) to an extremist group engaged in preparing an armed revolt against Rome. Another may have been a customs toll collector (Mt 9:9), who, by profession at least, would have been a faithful collaborator with Roman rule. Many, like Jesus himself, had been followers of John the Baptist (Jn 1:29-51), a revivalist preacher who may have been connected with the dissident monastic group living in a commune on the desolate slopes of the Wadi Qumran, overlooking the Dead Sea.

Most of these disciples would have come from the poor artisan class to which Jesus himself belonged. With him they exercised their ministry among the poor of rural Palestine in the countryside (the *chōra*), away from the prosperous hellenized cities which Jesus rarely if ever visited.[6] Jesus and his disciples were thus a destitute group of itinerant preachers proclaiming the good news to the very poor. Yet, for all his severe warnings against the mortal danger of riches (Mk 10:23-27), which make a person godless (Lk 13:17-21) and heartless (Lk 16:17-31); and despite his implacable opposition to consumerism and greed, personified by him as *Mammon*, the great opponent of *Abba* (Mt 6:24), Jesus has time for rich sympathizers. Zacchaeus, the chief customs tax collector of the important township of Jericho, receives him as a guest (Lk 19:1-9); Joseph of Arimathea (Mk 15:43) and Nicodemus (Jn 3:1), wealthy members of the Jewish aristocracy, both of whom belonged to the Council, the supreme governing body of the Jews, are his friends.

Jesus shows an extraordinary appreciation for the Samaritans (Lk 9:51-56; 10:29-37; 17:11-19; Jn 4:4-42)—a people written off in the deutero-canonical Old Testament as a "foolish people" which is "no nation" (Sir 50:25-26), and treated as untouchable by the Jews of his time (Jn 4:9). Although he restricts his preaching to the Jews, he shows (unlike the Zealots or the sectarians of Qumran) no particular hostility toward gentiles. Indeed his appreciative references to them (Mt 8:10; Lk 13:29) suggest that his seemingly harsh refusal of the Syro-Phoenician woman's request for the healing of her daughter (Mk 7:27) is to be read not as a racist insult but as a provocative challenge to the woman's faith. Jesus' enthusiastic reaction to her quick-witted reply could not possibly have come from a prejudiced person.

Women too, who in the Judaism of his time were lumped together with children and slaves as people "inferior to men in mind, in function and in status,"[7] are accepted by him as disciples (Lk 8:1-2; 10:46-50). And, as the sole continuing witnesses of his death, burial, and resurrection (Mk 15:40, 47; 16:1-8), women play a significant role in furthering his mission. Nowhere in the words of Jesus do we ever find the slightest hint of any condescension toward women.

So Jesus comes across to us in the Gospels as unusually free from the ethnic, class, and sexist prejudices harbored by the people of his time. For him there was indeed "neither Jew nor gentile, neither slave nor free, neither male nor female"—for all were experienced by him as children of the one Father in heaven. The radical openness of Jesus toward all humankind is rooted in his radical experience of God as *Abba*, because to experience God as "father" implies that we experience all human beings as brothers and sisters who have a claim on our acceptance and our love. The *dharma* of Jesus—his understanding of existence and his way of life—is a *dharma* of unconditional and therefore of absolutely universal love. Such love will not tolerate prejudice.

THE PREJUDICED CHURCH

But prejudice flourished in the early Christian community, just as it flourishes in the Church today. The New Testament gives ample evidence of this. Sexist and class biases appear in the household codes of the deutero-Pauline letters (Col 3:18-4:1; Eph 5:21-6:9) and of the First Letter of Peter (1 Pet 2:13-3:12), which urge the submission of wives to their husbands, of children to their parents, and of slaves to their masters. They thus take up the class- and male-biased household regulations of contemporary upper-class Hellenistic society and legitimize them by making them expressions of God's will, exemplified in the conduct of Jesus (Col 3:18, 22-24; Eph 5:22-24; 6:5-6).[8] Narrow Jewish particularism not uninfected by a strong anti-gentile prejudice colors the sayings attributed to Jesus by early Palestinian Christianity, in which he limits the scope of his mission to the "lost sheep of the house of Israel" (Mt 10:5; 15:24) and refuses to give "children's bread" to "household dogs" (Mk 7:27). And anti-Jewish tendencies show up frequently, we have seen, in the Gospels of Matthew and of John.

Such prejudices are easily understood. They are symptoms of the early Church's capitulation to the "cultural nationalisms" of its time,[9] because of its inability to live up to the radical freedom of Jesus. The freedom of Jesus is grounded on the experience of a total love which casts out all prejudice. But the Church which is always of "little faith" (Mt 8:26; 14:31; 16:8) is also of little love. Poised between the "already" of the resurrection of Jesus and the "not yet" of his parousia, it is a community that is "living and partly living" the life of the Spirit, or (to change the image and the allusion), it is a pilgrim people that "must go always a little further."

But the real paradox of the unprejudiced Jesus and the prejudiced Church does not lie here. It is not these "prejudices of weakness"—prejudices that the

Church picks up from the world it inhabits because of its failure to live up to the love and freedom of Jesus—that are the problem. The problem lies in its "prejudices of strength"—that is, in those prejudices that appear in the Church precisely because it has succeeded in becoming a Church. For to the extent that the Church becomes "Church," that is, to the extent that it becomes aware of itself as a distinct religious group with its own specific identity and mission, and not merely as a reform movement within Judaism, it inevitably develops a competitive and hostile attitude toward other rival groups which contest its claims. It grows prejudiced against them.

We see this happening in the New Testament itself. The radical universality of the interhuman concern proclaimed by Jesus (Lk 10:25-37) is toned down by Paul into a preferential love for Christians. "Do good to one another and to all," he writes to the Christians of Thessalonica (1 Thess 5:15), distinguishing "one another" from "all"; and four years later, he tells the churches of Galatia even more clearly, to "do good to all human beings, but specially to those who are of the household of the faith" (Gal 6:10). The distinction between "one another" and "all" becomes alarmingly explicit in the First Letter of Peter, which urges its readers to "honor all men" but to "love the brotherhood" (1 Pet 2:17). And it is carried to its ultimate conclusion in the literature of the Johannine circle, whose specific formulation of the love commandment, "love one another as I have loved you" (Jn 13:34; 15:12; 1 Jn 3:23; 2 Jn 5), restricts the exercise of love to the Christian community ("one another") alone.

So we find in the New Testament a clearly defined tendency toward an in-group exclusivism. This may have been (partly) the result of the persecution suffered by the early Christian community (Mt 10:16-22), of the abundant charismatic phenomena it undoubtedly experienced (Acts 2:1-13; 1 Cor 12:1-31), and of the clear-cut dichotomies of the apocalyptic worldview to which it largely subscribed. For persecution tends to turn a group in upon itself; charismatic togetherness fosters in-group solidarity at the expense of those outside; and apocalyptic sees the world sharply divided into embattled camps of the good and the evil.[10] Not surprisingly "what had been after the fourth century the extreme racial exclusivism of the Old Israel became," Alan Watts suggests, "the extreme spiritual exclusivism of the New Israel—the inferiority complex of a repressed nation becoming that of a repressed religion."[11] Such exclusivism would in moments of stress generate attitudes of insecurity and hostility toward other competing groups. This would explain the violent "anti-Judaism" of Matthew and John, which then becomes the biblical justification for the vicious anti-Semitism which plagues the Christian churches of the West throughout their history, until it bears its last dreadful fruit in the stupefying horror of the Holocaust.[12]

Anti-Semitism is the most dramatic and publicized expression of Christian prejudice, but it is by no means its only one. The history of Western colonialism is scarred with the tragic fallout of many other of its catastrophic manifestations. Many factors, economic, social, cultural, and ethnic, obviously contributed to the colonial explosion of sixteenth-century Europe and influenced the way in which it developed. But there can be no doubt at all that Christianity played a major part in legitimizing Western colonialism and in shaping it. Papal bulls unleashed the dogs of colonial war (whether we identify the beginnings of the colonial movement with the Crusades in the twelfth century or the so-called Age of Discovery in the sixteenth century) and "established the guide-lines for subsequent European behaviour (or misbehaviour) in the tropical world";[13] and well-meant but highly damaging missionary propaganda played a significant part in creating the "benighted heathen" image of colored peoples, which was then explicated to justify "a wide range of prejudiced attitudes and policies" toward them.[14] For if the heathens were children of Satan, condemned to eternal fire, what claim had they to human rights? João de Barros, the sixteenth-century chronicler of the Portuguese conquest, is at pains to explain this. "The Moors and Gentiles," he tells us, "are outside the law of Jesus Christ—which is the law that everyone must keep under pain of damnation and eternal fire. If then the soul be so condemned what right has the body to the privileges of our laws?"[15] This may not have been the official policy of Church or State, but it was certainly a part of common colonial prejudice.

The results of such prejudice were deadly. The immediate outcome of the first encounter between the indigenous inhabitants of the Americas and Europeans was "an extermination of human beings in proportions that had never been seen before and had never been attained afterwards in spite of the efforts made in this regard in the twentieth century."[16] And like the spectacularly savage Portuguese onslaught on the "dazzling rich empires of the East," it stirred few Christian consciences. For to their Portuguese and Spanish (and later Dutch, French, English and German) conquerors, "these orientals [or Amerindians, or Polynesians, or Africans] were heathens, blacks, Moors, Turks, containing, as one of them wrote, 'the badness of all bad men.'"[17]

Prejudice and violence, as recent events in India have shown all too well, are not the prerogatives of any one people or religion. But it is, I think, certain that Christianity has been the most violent of all the great religions of humankind; and it is at least arguable that a Christian-inspired Western colonialism has been unparalleled in recorded human history for the sheer massiveness of the damage it has inflicted on the lives, the property and the psyche of its victims. In *The Sirian Experiments*, the third in a series of novels (*Canopus in Argos; Archives*) which attempts to construct a sort of cosmic history of the earth from an extraplanetary point of view, Doris Lessing has said this chillingly. Ambien II of Sirius is shown the future of Shikasta (the earth) by Klorathy of Canopus. A map of Shikasta appears on a blank wall, and running his finger along the edge of the great northern land mass (Eurasia today), Klorathy says:

Here, in the Northwest fringes, in these islands in this little space, a race is being formed even now. It will overrun the whole world, but all the world, not just the central part of it, as with the horsemen of the plains. This race will destroy everything. The creed of this white race will be:

if it is there, it belongs to us. If I want it, I must have it. If what I see is different from myself then it must be punished or wiped out. Anything that is not me, is primitive and bad . . . and this is the creed that they will teach to the whole of Shikasta.[18]

"Everything that is not me is primitive and bad": could there be a neater description of the Christian-colonial prejudice that inspired *conquistador* and missionary alike? Was not just this the attitude of Teilhard de Chardin, aspiring after "a white earth," and loving the "primitive" and "childish" Chinese "out of Christian obligation and by an effort, [what a desperate effort!] of will"?[19]

Do we not find here the hidden roots of the beery, bellicose, and unashamedly racist version of Christianity, loudly trumpeted by Chesterton and Belloc, textbook examples of the Catholic prejudice of their times? Does this not explain the glorification of Western colonialism as "the corruption of a great idea" by François Mauriac and the French *intégrists*, sighing after the civilizing mission of Europe amid torture in Algeria and terror bombing in Vietnam?[20]

The roots of the great tree of Christian prejudice run deep, and its fruits, to those who have tasted them, are bitter. We need to look at the tree squarely and ask ourselves how is it that the seed sown by the unprejudiced and nonviolent Jesus has grown to this? What evil force has nurtured its monstrous growth? Was it the native aggressiveness of the Western peoples, as Doris Lessing seems to say, or the implacable intransigence of their religion, as Alan Watts suggests? Perhaps a little of both. Certainly Christianity's awareness of itself as a "chosen people," with a privileged access to salvation and an exclusive claim on the truth, has not helped to reduce prejudice and violence. For religious intolerance breeds violence whether in Amritsar or in Belfast; fanatical Ayatullahs are not all that different from zealous Grand Inquisitors; and a "chosen people" is only a step away from a *Herrenvolk*.

NOTES

1. Gordon Allport, *The Nature of Prejudice* (Garden City, N.Y.: Doubleday, 1958), 7.
2. Ibid., 24.
3. Ibid.
4. Ibid., 32.
5. Mishnah, *Abot* 11:6.
6. Gerd Theissen, *The First Followers of Jesus* (London: SCM Press, 1980), 47.
7. C. G. Montefiore and H. Loewe, *A Rabbinic Anthology* (New York: Schocken, 1974), xviii.
8. E. Schüssler Fiorenza, *In Memory of Her* (New York: Crossroad, 1984), 251-70.
9. Choan-Seng Song, *The Compassionate God* (London: SCM Press, 1982), 127-41, which makes an excellent analysis of the "centrism" resulting from such a capitulation.
10. H. Montefiore, "Thou Shalt Love Thy Neighbour as Thyself," *Novum Testamentum* 5 (1962), 157-170.

11. Alan W. Watts, *Myth and Ritual in Christianity* (Boston: Beacon Press, 1968), 130.

12. Jon D. Levenson, "Is there a counterpart in the Hebrew bible to New Testament antisemitism?," *Journal of Ecumenical Studies* 22 (1985): 242-48. Levenson makes an illuminating distinction between New Testament anti-Judaism, which is a theological judgment, and anti-Semitism, which is an ethnic prejudice, and goes on to remark, correctly, that "the distinction between anti-Judaism and antisemitism is real, but so is the connection between them" (p. 244). Anti-Judaism serves as the religious legitimation for anti-Semitism.

13. C. R. Boxer, *The Portuguese Seaborne Empire, 1415-1825* (Harmondsworth: Penguin, 1969), 23.

14. Milton Singer, *When a Great Tradition Modernizes* (Delhi: Vikas, 1972), 21.

15. Quoted in K. M. Panikkar, *Malabar and the Portuguese* (Bombay: Taraporevala, 1929), 170-71.

16. Tzvetan Todorov, "The Morality of Conquest," *Diogenes* 125 (1984): 89.

17. J. H. Plumb, "Introduction" to C. R. Boxer, *Portuguese Seaborne Empire,* xxiii.

18. Doris Lessing, *The Sirian Experiments* (New York: Knopf, 1982), 292.

19. Quoted in a review of Claude Rivière, *En Chine avec Teilhard* (Paris: Éditions du Seuil, 1968, by Louis Allen in *New Blackfriars* 50 (1969): 726-27.

20. Quoted in Maurice Merleau-Ponty, *Signs* (Evanston: Northwestern University Press, 1964), 325. It is worth listening to Merleau-Ponty's comment: "But the idea is in François Mauriac's mind or in our history books. The Vietnamese themselves have above all seen the 'corruption' of it. It is in the precise sense scandalous that a Christian should show himself so incapable of getting outside himself and his 'ideas' and should refuse to see himself even for an instance through the eyes of others."

11

JESUS AND CONFLICT

Conflict plays a large part in the Gospel narratives of the ministry of Jesus. All four of our canonical Gospels describe the ministry of Jesus as a time of intense and mounting conflict, culminating in his death upon the cross. The conflict they describe is pluriform. Jesus is shown in conflict with Satan (Mt 12:28). In the apocalyptic worldview of the times Satan was "the ruler of the world" (Jn 12:31), who through his demons afflicted humankind with sickness (Jesus "rebukes" a fever in Lk 4:39), with natural calamities like storms (Jesus "rebukes" a storm in Mk 4:39), with mental illnesses which were then thought to be cases of spirit possession (Jesus heals an epileptic boy by freeing him from "a deaf and dumb spirit" in Mk 9:25). The miracles of Jesus are thus episodes in this cosmic conflict, indications that Satan's rule has been well and truly ended. Jesus is shown in conflict too with the religious leaders of his people, whose casuistic interpretation of the Law and whose thoroughly legalistic understanding of religion he opposes vigorously (Mt 5:21-48; Mk 7:1-23). He is in conflict with the crowds he draws, whose popular messianic, consumer expectations he refuses to gratify (Jn 6:15; 6:26); with his family whose preferential claims on him he firmly rejects (Lk 2:41-52; Mk 3:31-35); and with his disciples, whose persistent and exasperating misunderstanding of his teaching he must repeatedly correct (Mk 4:13; 8:14-21; 10:35-45). And he is in conflict with his own instinctive clinging to life and his natural aversion to suffering, when these threaten to come in the way of his Father's will (Mk 14:32-42; Mt 4:1-11). Conflict, then, is not a secondary dispensable element in the ministry of Jesus; it is of its essence. Not for Jesus the ecstasy of the frolicking Krishna who is beyond all conflict, nor the serene smile of the Buddha who is wholly untouched by it. His is a short and agitated ministry, ending in a violent and untimely death.

This article first appeared in *The Way* 26 (1986): 14-23.

Indeed so important is this theme of conflict in the Gospel narratives of the ministry of Jesus that it spills over into the more or less legendary traditions about his infancy that have grown up in the early Church. The infancy narrative of Matthew has been described appropriately by Adolf Schlatter, in a now classic expression, "the conflict of the Two Kings" (Herod and Jesus).[1] And though such sustained conflict is missing from the very different infancy narrative of Luke, conflict erupts powerfully into it when Simeon prophesies that "this child is set [like the "rock of stumbling" of Is 8:14 and the "precious corner stone" of Is 28:16] for the fall and for the rising up of many in Israel," and is to be "a sign that is spoken against" (Lk 2:34-35).

THE SOURCE OF CONFLICT:
THE GOD EXPERIENCE OF JESUS

Simeon's somber prophecy suggests that it is Jesus himself who is to be the focus and the occasion of the conflict that will invest his life. He is the stone on which people will stumble; he is the sign that will be spoken against. This becomes explicit in one of the rare I-sayings of Jesus in the Synoptic tradition: "Do not think that I have come to bring peace upon the earth: I have not come to bring peace but the sword" (Mt 10:34; Lk 12:51). The "peace" that Jesus does not come to bring is the peace that most of his followers seem to have opted for; the peace of a happy compromise with Mammon (Mt 6:24), and of a contented adjustment to a radically unjust and oppressive society, powered not by love but by greed. The "sword" that he brings is the sword of division (Lk 12:51), sharp enough to divide even the members of a closely knit oriental family into fiercely antagonistic groups who take up sides for or against him (Mt 10:35-36).

Such sharp divisions in which "a person's enemies are those of his own family" (Mt 10:36) are inevitable, because of the radically new experience of God which Jesus has, and which he communicates to his disciples as the foundational experience of his community (Mt 11:27). For the experience of God as *Abba* is not the soothing anodyne that long familiarity and centuries of the sentimentalizing of compassion by Christianity have made it.[2] It is a profoundly unsettling experience, because of the radical demands it makes on the self and on society.

THE UNIVERSALITY OF LOVE

To experience God as *Abba* is to experience people (and not just to speak or even think about them) as brothers and sisters. True, the "Father of Our Lord Jesus Christ" reveals himself as *Abba* to the followers of Jesus, to whom he communicates his spirit of "sonship," so that they can cry out in ecstatic prayer, "Abba, Father!" It is they (but surely not they alone) who experience God as unconditional, accepting, and forgiving love. But the compassion which this experience creates (1 Jn 4:7-12) is certainly not to be confined to the Christian community. Like the love of the Father himself it must reach out to all humankind, to "the evil and the good" and to "the just and the unjust" (Mt 5:45).

That such an attitude calls for a radical conversion, that is, a sharp dislocation of our normal patterns of perception and behavior, is obvious. We do not normally experience our fellow human beings in this way! Indians still spontaneously perceive their people as part of a complex, highly stratified system of caste. Africans, I am told, see them as members of a tribe. The Jews at the time of Jesus experienced their contemporaries as Jew or gentile; the Greeks as Greek or barbarian. The pale-faced overlords of the massive "pigmentocracies" which European colonialism built up all over the world perceived their subject peoples ("the lesser breeds without the law!") along a value-loaded spectrum of skin colors, ranging from white to yellow, red, brown, and black.[3]

To affirm, then, the radical equality of all human beings beyond all differences of sex, race, culture, class, rank, or caste is a profoundly radical and therefore conflict-provoking act. Jesus lived out such radicalism when he dined with tax collectors and sinners (Mk 2:15-17; Lk 15:1-2); called women to be disciples (Lk 10:38-42; Mt 28:9-10; Jn 20:11-18)[4]; held up a gentile as a model of faith (Mt 8:15) and a Samaritan as a model of compassion (Lk 10:29-37); renounced domination for service (Mt 10:35-45); and projected the vision of a community that would be free of all father, *Führer*, or guru figures, because it would acknowledge only one Father who is in heaven, and only one Master, the Christ (Mt 23:8-10).

THE PRIMACY OF LOVE

Other radical, conflict-laden consequences follow from the God experience of Jesus. To experience God as *Abba* is to grasp the absolute primacy of love. Interhuman concern as our appropriate response to God's love for us—"loving God by loving neighbor," as I would paraphrase the love-commandment of Jesus[5]—becomes the basis of all law (Mt 22:40), and takes precedence over all cult (Mk 12:33). Every institution then becomes subordinate to human need—for "the sabbath is made for the human person, not the human person for the sabbath" (Mk 2:27). "Mercy," that is, interhuman concern shown in concrete acts of active compassion toward the hungry and the outcast, is to be preferred to "sacrifice" (Mt 9:13; 12:7). Reconciliation with an injured brother or sister must precede reconciliation with God (Mt 5:23-24). Unlimited forgiveness of others is a necessary precondition for effective prayer (Mk 11:25; Mt 6:14-15). In a word, our relationship with God is mediated through our relationship with one another, for humankind is now the new Temple, the "sacred place" of our encounter with God.

To experience God as *Abba* is therefore to experience the "wholly other" in the give and take of human history. It is to realize the absolute closeness of the utterly transcendent God. This leads to the tearing down of the ritual barriers that religions tend to build up around God in order to safeguard his "holiness." The curtain of the Temple, which blocks the way to the Holy of Holies, is torn in two from top to bottom at the death of Jesus, allowing us untrammeled access to the Father (Mk 15:38). All the laws of ritual cleanliness are abrogated by Jesus (Mk 7:1-23), so that "nothing in itself is unclean" (Rom 14:14). The whole system of pollution which sets aside persons, places, and things as "untouchable" and "unclean," because they belong to the realm of disorder, formlessness, non-being, and death,[6] is abolished at a stroke.

THE CONFLICT OF LOVE AND OF LAW

Such radicalism would be disturbing in any traditional society. It would have been especially so in the Judaism of the time of Jesus, a Judaism scarred by its experience of the Exile and disfigured by three centuries of Greek and Roman rule. Colonial rule always distorts the social system of the colonized. To systematic economic exploitation it adds massive racist and cultural aggression, which creates deep psychic stress in the colonized peoples and drives them into rigidly defensive attitudes.[7] Not surprisingly, then, all the major religious movements of Palestine at the time of Jesus (the Pharisees, the Sadducees, the Qumran sectarians, and the Zealots) were movements of renewal which sought to affirm the ethnic, cultural, and religious identity of Judaism and insisted on the observance of the Torah more strictly than before.[8]

The radicalism of Jesus, who brushed aside the letter of the Law in order to grasp its spirit (radical obedience to God shown by radical concern for the neighbor), would have collided head-on with the rigorism of the sects. His universalism, with its sympathy for the outcasts within Jewish society and its openness to Samaritans and gentiles outside it, would have clashed with the particularism of the Jewish groups, whose bigoted insistence on the strict observance of the Law turned them into closed elitist or fanatical communities, which excluded from their fellowship not only gentiles but even Jews who failed to live up to their own exacting standards. The Pharisees looked down upon the "people of the land" (*'am hā'āreṣ*) as a "rabble who do not know the law" (Jn 7:49); the Qumran sectarians lumped together as "children of darkness" all those (Jews and gentiles) who did not belong to their dissident group (1QS 3:20-26); the Zealots were violently opposed to all collaborators with Rome. Jesus welcomed tax collectors and sinners into his movement and showed himself unusually appreciative of Samaritans and gentiles.

THE CONSEQUENCES OF CONFLICT: JESUS AND VIOLENCE

The conflict that the universalism and the radicalism of Jesus ignited among his people led inevitably to violence and culminated in his violent death on the cross. That Jesus foresaw such violence (though probably not its precise out-come) is clear from several of his sayings. Even if the Synoptic passion predictions (Mk 8:31; 9:31; 10:33-34) are not predictions made by Jesus, but early Christian references to the passion of Jesus formulated after the event, it is certain that Jesus did in fact reckon with a violent death as part of his prophetic mission (Lk 13:31-33). Indeed the fate of John the Baptist would have been for Jesus (as the death of Jesus ought to be for us) evidence enough of the violence that the authentic proclamation of the Kingdom inevitably arouses (Mk 9:9-14).

What is less clear is how such violence is to be met. Jesus, it would seem, met it nonviolently. In spite of attempts to associate him with the Zealots, it seems certain that Jesus did not initiate or support armed insurrection.[9] Instead of countering violence with violence Jesus overcomes violence by freely submitting to it (Mt 26:51-54). He thus becomes the "scapegoat" who, by taking upon himself all the innate violence of humankind, purges the world of violence and makes human reconciliation possible.[10] Faithful to his experience of God as the *Abba* who comes "not to carry out just revenge upon evil, but to justify sinners by grace, whether they are Zealots, tax collectors, Pharisees or sinners,"[11] Jesus commands his followers to love their enemies—and not just their personal enemies, hostile to them as individuals, but (and explicitly) their group enemies who "hate," "ostracize" and "persecute" their group (Lk 6:27-28). He urges them to accept uncomplainingly even extreme forms of personal injury—to turn the other cheek when struck a particularly insulting backhand blow on the right one, to give up one's cloak when one is sued for one's tunic (leaving oneself naked!), to carry a burden two miles when forced by a much-resented law of the occupying power to carry it one (Mt 5:39-41). Insistence on nonviolence could scarcely, it would seem, go further.

NON-RESISTANCE?

But the nonviolence of Jesus is more ambiguous than might, at first sight, appear. The examples of non-resistance that he gives are obviously not meant to be taken literally, for they are so extreme that they verge on the ridiculous. John Dominic Crossan has in fact suggested that they are meant to be case parodies which deliberately make fun of case law by juxtaposing sober, true-to-life cases ("if anyone would sue you and take your tunic") with solutions that are hilariously impractical ("give him your cloak also")! By doing this they prevent us from idolizing law, for they "remind us again and again that to abide with God is more fundamental than any case law and is itself fundamental ethics and morality."[12]

Even if we should find Crossan's fascinating explanation a shade too fanciful to be convincing, he is surely right in refusing to identify Jesus' instructions on non-resistance with "legal rules" which set down precise norms to be observed in designated situations. They are probably best taken as "focal instances": that is, as graphic examples of Christian behaviors in extreme and specific hypothetical situations, which, because of their "unreasonableness," shock us into becoming imaginatively aware of the kind of non-aggressive behavior that the following of Jesus implies.[13]

Such behavior certainly implies a refusal to retaliate. One does not return evil for evil—"an eye for an eye and a tooth for a tooth" (Mt 5:38). It does not, I believe, necessarily imply passive nonviolence, or the non-resistance to evil which a literal understanding of the "nonviolent" sayings of Jesus might suggest. Not only would such a literal understanding be untrue to the form of these sayings (which are, we have seen, "focal instances" not "legal rules") but it would conflict with the closely related and utterly basic command of Jesus that we are to love our enemies (Mt 5:43-48). For to love our enemies means to "do good" to them (Lk 6:27). It means not allowing ourselves to be overcome by their evil but overcoming their evil with good (Rom 12:21). To turn the other cheek might on occasion disarm the aggressor and convert him; but it is more likely to aggravate his violence. This would not be loving him. The Jesus of the Gospels, significantly, does not turn the other cheek when he is struck at his trial but sharply replies to the guard who strikes him (Jn 18:22-23). Paul is even less nonresistant. He reacts to a blow on the mouth by roundly abusing the High Priest who has ordered the blow (Acts 23:2-3)!

NONVIOLENT RESISTANCE?

Does Jesus, then, demand active nonviolence from his followers? Does he expect them to resist aggression—but always in a strictly nonviolent way? I am not sure that he does. The problem of the nonviolence of the Gospels is more complex than the spate of pacifist tracts pouring out of the Christian Churches of the West, under the threat of nuclear destruction and Third World revolution, would lead us to suspect. Before we subscribe to the blanket condemnation of violence that they pronounce, it might be worth reflecting on the frightening violence of the God of the Bible, and even of Jesus in the Gospels.

For to Asian sensibilities at least, Jesus is by no means a nonviolent person. Compared to the Buddha (always patient, never angry, always courteous and serene), or even to Mahatma Gandhi (who could say very hard things about his people and their colonial oppressors, but always in measured and dispassionate words), the Jesus of the Gospels is violent indeed. He may not have encouraged armed rebellion, but he certainly did not avoid inflammatory speech and action (Mt 12:34; Mk 11:15-19). His language is full of verbal violence, sometimes shockingly so (Mt 23:13-33), and betrays an assertiveness that sometimes seems to spill over into overt aggression. Only if we define violence narrowly, restricting it to mean merely lethal physical injury done to human beings—only then could Jesus be said to be truly nonviolent. But this is not how violence is understood in the non-Semitic religious traditions of Asia. In Hinduism, Buddhism, and Jainism (I cannot speak for Confucianism or Taoism, though I suspect that they too would not be very different), nonviolence (*ahiṃsā*) would exclude injury not just to humankind but to any living being, and not just in action but equally in thought and in word.[14]

LOVE AND VIOLENCE

This difference between the nonviolent Buddha and the violent Jesus is due to the different value systems to which they subscribe. For Buddhism (as indeed for all the great traditions of India) the supreme goal of life is the absolute and unconditioned freedom which results from the experiential realization of the ultimate relativity of the empirical self and of the world it inhabits. Such a "perceiving of the emptiness of the transitory" (*Dhammapada* v.92) results in the immediate dissolution of all binding attachments and leads to the state of "steadfast wisdom" (*sthita-prajña*). In this, the enlightened individual is supremely free, wholly untroubled by the "pairs of opposites" which he encounters in life, so that he holds "pleasure and pain, profit and loss, victory and defeat" to be exactly the same (*Bhagavadgītā* 2.38). Yet he is profoundly committed to the well-being of the universe, because he has acquired the basic disposition of the enlightened individual, "a passionate desire for the welfare of all beings" (*Bhagavadgītā* 5.25). Aggression of any kind toward any being whatsoever would be unthinkable in a person so disposed.

For Jesus, on the other hand, the supreme goal of life is not unconditional freedom but unconditional love. The basic religious experience that shapes his life and gives form to the movement he founds is the experience of God's unconditional love which empowers us (to the extent we experience it) to love our fellow human beings as unconditionally as God does (Lk 6:32-36). The fully "realized" follower of Jesus will be the person who fully loves. But love does not necessarily rule out violence. Indeed it may, as the life of Jesus shows us, demand violence for the defense or the correction of the person loved. The problem then is to determine just how much and what kind of violence love permits or requires in any given situation. In a world full of ambiguity and conflicting values this cannot be decided by blanket judgments on the use of violence issued from the outside, but only through agonizing discernment from within the situation of conflict.

In a world as overrun by violence as our planet earth today, such discernment might well lead to an option for nonviolence. It may be that the "politics of forgiveness" taught us by Mahatma Gandhi is the only way we have to break out of the spiral of violence that is threatening to tear our world apart. But such an option, if it is to be genuine, must come from the victims of unjust and oppressive violence, who in their sufferings and struggle learn to overcome violence through love. It cannot be preached to them from the outside—least of all by affluent First World Christians who, like it or not, have a vested interest in the massive systems of exploitation which the wretched of the earth are revolting against, and whose long complicity in violence has surely deprived them of the right to preach.

For whether or not Jesus taught nonviolence, Christians, from the time of Constantine at least, have been fiercely violent. With the exception of a few unfashionable and sometimes persecuted sects who have consistently and honorably practiced pacifism, and occasional off-beat individuals who have suffered in its cause, Western Christianity has not merely allowed "just wars" of defense ("the only defensible war," Chesterton reminded us, "is a war of defense"), but it has initiated aggressive Crusades (invoking the biblical tradition of the "holy war") and has provided incentive for and legitimation of the great marauding expeditions of Western colonialism which have devastated and depopulated large areas of our world.[15] That is why Gandhian *ahiṃsā*, which emerged from a long Hindu-Jain tradition of reverence for life and was proclaimed from within an exploited and struggling people by someone who shared in their lot, is consistent and credible. Passionate (even violent!) denunciations of violence addressed to Third World revolutionaries by Western Christians who have no constructive alternative to offer are, in my opinion, neither.

NOTES

1. A. Schlatter, *Der Evangelist Matthäus* (Stuttgart: Calwer, 1963), 25.

2. M. Fox, *A Spirituality Named Compassion and the Healing of the Global Village: Humpty Dumpty and Us* (Minneapolis: Winston Press, 1979), 4-6.

3. C. R. Boxer, *The Church Militant and Iberian Expansion* (Baltimore: Johns Hopkins University Press, 1978), 38.

4. The "better part" which Mary chooses in Lk 10:38-42 is not a "contemplative" as opposed to an "active" life. This would have made little sense at the time of Jesus or of Luke. Rather it is a life of a "disciple" who sits at the feet of the master, rather than that of a "sympathizer" who merely serves him (cf. Lk 8:1-2).

5. G. M. Soares-Prabhu, "The Synoptic Love-Commandment: The Dimensions of Love in the Teaching of Jesus," *Jeevadhara* 13 (1983): 87-91, and in *Theology of Liberation: An Indian Biblical Perspective*, Collected Writings of George M. Soares-Prabhu, S.J., vol. 4, ed. Francis X. D'Sa (Pune: Jnana-Deepa Vidyapeeth, 2001), 110-23. See chapter 13 of this volume.

6. F. Belo, *A Materialist Reading of the Gospel of Mark* (Maryknoll, N.Y.: Orbis, 1981), 37-39.

7. F. Fanon, *Black Skin, White Masks* (New York: Grove Press, 1967).

8. G. Theissen, *The First Followers of Jesus: A Sociological Analysis of the Earliest Christianity* (London: SCM Press, 1980), 80.

9. M. Hengel, *Was Jesus a Revolutionist?* (Philadelphia: Fortress Press, 1971).

10. R. Schwager, *Brauchen wir einen Sündenbock?* (Munich: Kösel, 1978), 143-231, which applies René Girard's "scapegoat" theory for the origins and the resolution of violence in human society to the Bible.

11. J. Moltmann, *The Crucified God* (London: SCM Press, 1974), 142.

12. J. D. Crossan, "Jesus and Pacifism," in *No Famine in the Land: Studies in Honor of John L. McKenzie,* ed. W. Flanagan and A.W. Robinson (Missoula, Mont.: Scholars Press, 1973), 195-208.

13. R. C. Tannehill, "The Focal 'Instance' as a Form of New Testament Speech: A Study of Matthew 5:39b-42," *Journal of Religion* 50 (1970): 372-85.

14. U. Tähtinen, *Ahiṃsā: Non-violence in Indian Tradition* (London: Rider, 1976), 50-69.

15. C. R. Boxer, *The Portuguese Seaborne Empire, 1415-1825* (Harmondsworth: Penguin, 1973), 2-24, which shows how the papal bulls legitimizing Spanish and Portuguese colonial expansion "established guide-lines for subsequent European behaviour (or misbehaviour) in the tropical world" (p. 23).

Part III

THE TEACHING OF JESUS

12

THE DHARMA OF JESUS

An Interpretation of the Sermon on the Mount

It is not easy to spell out the precise meaning of a widely used religious term like Dharma. Like so much traditional religious vocabulary, the word has acquired a variety of overlapping meanings. Its semantic edges have become blurred through use. Dharma, Kuppuswamy tells us, "stands for religious observance, righteousness, justice, conformity in law, conformity to custom, obedience to the social order, sense of duty, etc., and thus has religious, moral, ethical as well as legal significance."[1] And Kane, collating the various dictionary definitions of the word, describes Dharma as "ordinance, usage, duty, right, justice, morality, virtue, religion, good works, function or characteristic."[2] The term then is thus "all comprehensive."[3] It is both religious and ethical. Dharma is what I believe in (Hindu-*dharma,* Christian-*dharma*): it is also what I am *supposed* to do (*kula-dharma* or *jāti-dharma,* i.e. my family or caste obligations). Yet it is clear from the descriptions given above that the primary thrust of the term is in fact ethical. The definitions collated by Kane are almost all legal and juridical terms, and Dandekar, for all his insistence on the "all-comprehensive" character of Dharma, defines it "broadly speaking" as comprising "precepts which aim at securing the material and spiritual sustenance and growth of the individual and society."[4]

Traditionally, in fact, Dharma has often been identified with *varṇāshrama dharma,* the code describing the obligations of the four ideal castes of society (*varṇas*), and the four stages (student, householder, hermit, and wandering ascetic) which should ideally define the life of every "twice-born" individual in each of the three upper classes (*āshramas*). So Dharma "in spite of its compre-

This article first appeared in *Bible Bhashyam* 6 (1980): 358-81.

175

hensive character . . . was in its most common connotation limited to two principal ideas, namely the organization of social life through well defined and well
regulated classes (*varṇas*), and the organization of an individual's life within
those classes into definite stages (*āshramas*)."[5]

But from the time of the *Bhagavadgītā* at least, this narrow understanding of
Dharma has been leavened by the notion of *svadharma* or "natural law." Better
one's own Dharma (*svadharma*) however unglamorous, urges the concluding
chapter of the *Gītā*, than the Dharma of another (*paradharma*), however well
done.

> *Śreyān sva-dharmo viguṇah para-dharmāt svanuṣṭhitāt*
> *svabhāva-niyataṃ karma kurvan n'āpnoti kilbiṣam*

> Better one's own *dharma* though without merit
>   than the *dharma* of another well performed;
> Doing the *karma* inhering in one's nature
>   one does not incur defilement.
>
>   (*Bhagavadgītā* XVIII, 47)

Although the *svadharma* of the *Gītā* has usually been interpreted as a spec-
ification of *varṇa dharma,* that is, as a label for the specific obligations of the
particular caste to which an individual belongs,[6] it is probably better to understand it more radically as describing the pattern of behavior that flows from the
intrinsic tendencies of one's being. *Svadharma* is *svabhāvaniyata-karma,* the
doing of action that inheres in one's own nature. It implies "the individual finding his own *svabhāva* and developing accordingly."[7]

Even in its ethical dimension, then, Dharma is not an extrinsic norm impos-
ing a strained and artificial code of conduct on an individual, but is an indication
of his natural behavior. Ideally this behavior would spring from the inner depths
of his personal spontaneity. In practice it is too often the result of interiorized values which function as an "eternal law taken into the psyche," and so enable a
dominant minority to control the community through "hegemony," that is,
through "a permanently organized consent."[8] In Hinduism Dharma has only too
often functioned in this way. Arun Shourie has put it forcefully:

> The ideological superstructure of ancient India represents one of the
> most highly articulated, one of the best worked out hegemonic systems.
> The world-view was highly developed, the myriad elements were
> worked out in fine detail, each element perfected to reinforce others.
> And with the world-view went an elaborate and fully perfected mode
> for ensuring—through rules of family life, ritual, religion and social
> conduct—that the details were internalized.[9]

But Dharma need not always be this kind of legitimating ideology serving to create a "permanently organized consent." It can be the outcome not of internal val-

ues which domesticate, but of the liberating exigencies of human freedom. This, F. X. D'Sa has suggested, is in fact true of the original Dharma of the *Gītā*.[10] It is certainly true of the original Dharma of Jesus—however much this too has been transformed into a legitimating ideology by an increasingly aggressive Christendom.[11]

The Dharma of Jesus, that is, the complex of religious insight and ethical concern (of experience, worldview, and value) which determines the lifestyle that Jesus proclaimed and practiced, has been conveniently formulated for us in the Sermon on the Mount (Mt 5-7). These three chapters of Matthew's Gospel, which like the *Gītā* went "straight to the heart" of Gandhiji,[12] are everywhere accepted in non-Christian India as the "essence of Christianity." In a sense they are. For they present in a brief and striking aphoristic way a pattern of existence appropriate to a follower of Jesus, because it is in fact a replica of the kind of life which Jesus himself lived. The Sermon on the Mount thus gives us the authentic Dharma of Jesus—the pattern of existence he lived by and proclaimed.

WHAT IS THE SERMON ON THE MOUNT?

Yet the Sermon on the Mount was never really preached by Jesus as such. It is not a "sermon" proper, but an edited collection of the sayings of Jesus, made by the early Christian community and then greatly expanded by Matthew. For Matthew's Sermon on the Mount has a close though much abbreviated parallel in Luke's Sermon on the Plain (Lk 6:17-49), the whole of which is found in Mt and in much the same order as in Mt!

Mt 5:1-7, 28		Lk 6:17-49
5:3-12	*Beatitudes*	6:20-23 (24-26)
5:38-48	*Law of Love*	6:27-36
7:1-5	*On Judging*	6:37-38 (41-42)
7:18-20	*The Two Trees*	6:43-45
7:24-28	*The Two Houses*	6:46-49

Both "sermons," then, probably go back to a common source, written or oral, which must have had an inaugural discourse of Jesus roughly similar to the "sermon" in Lk.[13] But even this original discourse was not the text of any real sermon preached by Jesus. A quite cursory reading of the Gospels will show that it would have been far too short and much too disorganized to qualify for this. For a slow reading of Luke's Sermon on the Plain does not take more than a few minutes (scarcely enough for a "sermon"); and it gives us not a systematically developed theme but a collection of individual and largely unrelated sayings loosely strung together. This primitive collection of sayings (found now in Luke's "sermon") has been expanded by Matthew, who has added, theme-wise, other isolated sayings of Jesus current in his tradition. Some of these sayings are found elsewhere in Lk (and so are part of the common sayings' source Mt and Lk may have shared);[14] others are peculiar to Mt.[15] The Sermon on the Mount as we have it now is thus an editorial composition of Matthew. It is Matthew's presentation of the Dharma of Jesus. The presentation is accurate enough, since it agrees with other New Testament formulations of the basic thrust of Jesus' proclamation, notably with that of Paul! But it remains Matthean—colored by Matthew's specific Jewish Christian concerns, and intelligible only in the context of his Gospel.

Matthew's Gospel is arguably one of the most carefully constructed books in the New Testament. Written in a "Jewish Style" it has carefully arranged and skillfully structured its material to produce precise literary and theological effects.[16] The *context* of the Sermon on the Mount (the place it occupies in the Gospel) and its *structure* (the arrangement of its parts) will thus provide significant clues to its *meaning*.

THE CONTEXT OF THE SERMON OF THE MOUNT

As part of the Gospel of Matthew the Sermon on the Mount has a whole range of significant contexts. These emerge successively as we look at the Sermon with an ever narrowing focus, shifting our attention from the place of the Sermon in the Gospel as a whole to the place it occupies in its immediate setting. At least four such contexts appear as we zoom in, each with its own contribution to the Sermon's meaning.

(1) Seen against the background of the Gospel as a whole, the Sermon on the Mount appears as the first of the five great discourses (Mt 5-7; 10; 13; 18; 24-25) which form the structural backbone of the Gospel. Each discourse concludes with a stereotyped formula: "and it happened that when Jesus had finished (*kai egeneto hote etelesen ho Iēsous*)" (7:28; 11:1; 13:53; 19:1; 26:1), a clear indication that the discourses are meant to be parts of the architecture of Matthew's Gospel. Their role in the Gospel is indicated in the grand finale with which the Gospel triumphantly ends (28:16-20). The solemn and powerful proclamation of the risen Lord, in this his concluding Christophany, gives us the key to Matthew's theology. For here we are told that Christian existence as Matthew understands it means *discipleship* of the risen and ever-present Lord ("make disciples of all nations"), and that each discipleship is achieved through *baptism,* an external rite through which one is initiated into the community of the Father, the Son, and the Spirit ("baptizing them in the name of the Father and the Son and the Holy Spirit"), and through the faithful observance of *the teachings of Jesus* ("teaching them to observe all things that I have commanded you"). These teachings are set out in the five discourses of the Gospel. The discourses, then, and the Sermon on the Mount among them, set out for us, it would seem, the conditions of Christian discipleship.

(2) Looked at more closely in the context of its more immediate setting, the Sermon on the Mount is seen to be part of a diptych, a two-paneled picture of Jesus with which Matthew begins his narrative of the ministry of Jesus. For the

Sermon is preceded by a summary of the activity of Jesus (preaching-teaching-healing) in Mt 4:23 which is identical to a similar summary in Mt 9:35. The two summaries thus form an inclusion which frames the Sermon on the Mount of Mt 5-7 and the Miracle Cycle (a collection of ten miracle stories put together by Matthew) in Mt 8-9 into a single unit.

Sermon on the Mount / Miracle Cycle
4:23 _____ 5-7   8-9 _____ 9:35

This unit has obviously served to introduce us to the messianic proclamation ("preaching") of Jesus, exemplified by his "teaching" (the Sermon on the Mount) and of his "healing" (the Miracle Cycle). It gives us, that is, a representative sampling of the messianic words and works of Jesus. The Sermon on the Mount thus appears as the New Messianic Law, proclaimed by Jesus, in intimate association with his messianic activity, as a Law that is to transform the world.[17]

(3) A still closer look shows us that the Sermon on the Mount has been placed by Matthew immediately *after* his programmatic summary of the Galilean preaching of Jesus ("Repent, for the Kingdom of the Heaven is at hand") given in Mt 4:12-17. The Sermon thus follows the proclamation of the Kingdom. It spells out concretely what the "repentance" demanded by the Kingdom means in practice. The Sermon on the Mount is to be understood, then, as a description of man's response to the Kingdom.

(4) Finally, a look at the Sermon itself reveals a significant tension between its beginning and its end. The Sermon begins (Mt 5:1-2) by showing Jesus as a rabbi solemnly instructing his disciples *ex cathedra* in the tenets of the "new law" ("and when he sat down his disciples came to him, and he opened his mouth and taught them, saying . . ."). It ends (Mt 7:28) with a picture of Jesus as a charismatic prophet addressing enthusiastic crowds with characteristic prophetic authority ("the crowds were astonished at his teaching, for he taught as one who had authority and not as the scribes"). Clearly, then, Jesus the new Moses speaking on the new Sinai is both scribe and prophet, and his Sermon is not just an esoteric lesson addressed to a select few, but teaching for the people at large.

These are some of the insights into the significance of the Sermon on the Mount thrown up by an examination of the *context* into which Matthew has set it in his Gospel. Other insights will emerge from an examination of its *structure*. Together these will throw light on the meaning of the Sermon and on what it has to tell us about the Dharma of Jesus.

THE STRUCTURE OF THE SERMON ON THE MOUNT

Although Matthew has not composed the Sermon on the Mount freely, but has compiled it by adding sayings of Jesus to an already existing collection, he has been able to impose a recognizable structure on his material. An *introduction* describing the sort of people to whom the Sermon is addressed (5:3-16) leads on to an explicit statement of the *theme* of the Sermon presented as the fulfillment of the Law and the Prophets (5:17-20). This is followed by the *Sermon proper* (5:21-7:20), articulated into *three sections* according to the three parts of Mt 5:20—a verse which gives us the key to the structure of the Sermon. "Unless your righteousness is greater than that of the Scribes and the Pharisees," Mt 5:20 announces, "you will never enter the Kingdom of the Heavens." The Sermon, then, (1) shows us how our righteousness must exceed that of the scribes, the moral theologians of the day, by proposing a better morality than theirs (5:21-45); (2) describes a righteousness better than that of the Pharisees, the pious people or "religious" of the times, by sketching out a more authentic piety (6:1-19); and (3) gives us a number of somewhat random prescriptions, both negative and positive for entering the Kingdom of the Heavens (6:20-7:20). These prescriptions are rounded off by a *conclusion* which urges its listeners to effective action (7:21-27), and the whole Sermon is framed by an *introductory setting* which shows Jesus as the new Moses instructing disciples and crowd on the new Sinai (5:1-2), and a *concluding comment* which joins the stereotyped formula with which Matthew ends each of his five discourses to a comment on the enthusiastic reaction of the crowds to the teaching they have just received (7:28). The structure of the Sermon on the Mount can therefore be outlined as follows:

THE SERMON ON THE MOUNT

—*Introductory Setting* (5:1-2): Jesus the New Moses
A. INTRODUCTION (5:13-16): The addressees of the Sermon
    1) The Beatitudes (5:3-12)
    2) Two Similes (5:13-16)
B. THEME (5:17-20): Fulfillment of the Law and the Prophets
C. SERMON (5:21-7:20): Righteousness Greater Than That of the Scribes and the Pharisees to Enter the Kingdom of the Heavens (cf. 5:20)
    1) Righteousness Greater Than That of Scribes
       —6 Antitheses (5:21-47)
       —Concluding Principle (5:48)
    2) Righteousness Greater Than That of Pharisees
       —Introductory Principle (6:1)
       —3 Illustrations (6:2-19)
    3) Entering the Kingdom
       —5 Prohibitions (6:19-7:6): "Do Not"
       —3 Recommendations (7:7-20): "Ask-Enter," "Beware"
D. CONCLUSION (7:21-27): Deeds Not Words
    1) Principle (7:21-23)
    2) Illustration (7:24-27): The Two Houses
—*Concluding Comment* (7:28): The Astonishment of the Crowds.

WHAT DOES THE SERMON ON THE MOUNT MEAN?

What, then, are we to make of the Sermon on the Mount in the light of the insights gained from an examination of its context and its structure? At first sight it might seem that Matthew intends us to understand the Sermon as the proclamation of the Messianic Torah, of a new and more perfect Law which is to replace the now obsolete Law of Moses. This is suggested by the strongly juridical language of much of the Sermon (cf. 5:21-48); by its setting on a "mountain" in an obvious attempt to identify Jesus with Moses giving the Law on Sinai; by its place in the Gospel as one of five discourses which set down the norms of discipleship (cf. 28:18-20); and by its theme, explicitly spelled out as the fulfilment of the Law and the Prophets (5:17). Yet if the Sermon on the Mount were to be understood in this way it would contain a Dharma of the most extrinsic kind: an external set of prescriptions, a new "tradition of the elders," a sort of extended *kula-dharma* for the Christian community as a whole.

But it is unlikely that the Sermon on the Mount, for all its strongly juridical form, should be a set of prescriptions of this kind. If it were it would constitute a thoroughly utopian law, one whose demands cannot really be fulfilled. Like all such impractical laws, which bring Law itself into disrepute, it would then be worse than no law! Interpreting the Sermon on the Mount in this way would, besides, fly in the face of the constant Christian tradition that Christ has freed us from the weight of law. "Christ is the end of law, that every man who has faith may be justified," Paul reminds us in Rom 10:4, and though not all New Testament writings take off from Paul's particular problematic, there is in all of them the awareness that Jesus has brought a new religious consciousness (and with it a new Dharma) which runs counter to the legalism which formed a substantial part of the Pharisaic tradition that was taken up by the "normative" Judaism reconstituted after the fall of Jerusalem at Jamnia.[18]

How, then, are we to reconcile the juridical form and (to judge from its context and its theme) the juridical intent of the Sermon on the Mount with the clearly non-juridical, personal attitudes that inform so much of the Sermon itself (cf. 5:44-48; 6:25-31; 7:7-12) and certainly most of the Gospel in which it is set (cf. 11:25-27; 18:23-35; 25:31-46)? The problem is not a new one, and H. K. McArthur has listed no fewer than twelve different attempts at its solution.[19] Of these three are significant because of the large echo they have found in the traditions of the churches and the works of critical scholarship. Traditionally, Roman Catholics have treated the Sermon on the Mount as a *counsel of perfection* meant not for all but for an elite few. Traditional Protestants follow Luther in understanding it is a *praeparatio evangelica* (preparation for the Gospel), that is, an unattainable ideal put before the Christian to drive him to a profound sense of his radical inadequacy and so prepare him for the Gospel, that is, allow him to acknowledge his radical dependence on the salvation freely given by Jesus. And Albert Schweitzer, one of the earliest scholars to appreciate the significance of eschatology in the teaching of Jesus, has described the Sermon as an *interim ethic* meant for a community which is awaiting the imminent coming of Jesus, and so because of the crisis in which it is living, is able to rise to the Sermon's utopian demands.[20] But none of these solutions is wholly satisfactory. The Sermon on the Mount, as Matthew gives it, is addressed not to a select few but to the crowds at large, and so is not really proposed as a counsel of perfection. Nothing in it suggests an imminent *parousia* so that it cannot be an *interim ethic*. And it is not a *praeparatio evangelica* because it has not been set before us as some unattainable ideal, but as a way of life which Jesus clearly expects his disciples (all of them) to follow (7:21-27).

A solution, then, must be sought elsewhere. We find it in Jesus' attitude to the Law, the traditional Dharma of his people. This attitude is described for us in the Sermon on the Mount itself, where Jesus states categorically that he has come not to "abolish" (*katalysai*) the Law and the Prophets, but to "fulfill" (*plērōsai*) them (5:17). This addition of the Prophets to the Law (the two together signifying the whole Old Testament way of salvation), and the meaning which *pleroun* regularly has in Mt ("to fulfill," "to bring to perfection," "to realize in a new, unexpected, higher way"), shows that Matthew is thinking here of a fulfillment which is neither *ethical* ("I have come not to break the Law but to observe it"), nor *legal* ("I have come not to abrogate the Law but to sanction it"), but one of which is *prophetic* ("I have come not to frustrate the purpose of the Law but to realize it in a higher way"). The Law is to be fulfilled in the way that the Prophets have been fulfilled by the words and works of Jesus (cf. the fulfillment quotations 1:23; 2:15; 4:14; 8:17; etc.). That is, the purpose, goal, and movement of the Law are to be realized in a new, altogether unexpected "more excellent way" (1 Cor 12:31). "The law was given by Moses," as John puts it, "grace and truth came through Jesus Christ" (Jn 1:17). A new Dharma replaces the old one and fulfills it.

Just how this new Dharma proclaimed by Jesus in the Sermon on the Mount fulfills the Dharma of the Old Testament (much as the Dharma brought by Krishna in the *Bhagavadgītā* "fulfills" the *kula-* and *jāti-dharma* by which Arjuna stands)[21] can be shown by means of three *sūtras* or aphorisms. Together these give us a good if impressionistic idea of the thrust of the Sermon on the Mount.

A. Sūtra 1: The Sermon on the Mount Is Not Law But Love

The way in which the Sermon on the Mount "fulfills" the Law and the Prophets is illustrated in the six antitheses of the Sermon (Mt 5:21-48). These result in (1) an *interiorization* of the Law, a shift in emphasis from external performance to interior intention (5:21f; 5:27f); and (2) in its *simplification,* that is, in the reduction of the multiplicity of its many precepts into the unity of a single fundamental attitude. For the antitheses all climax in the core demand of the Sermon: "You must, therefore, be perfect as your heavenly Father is perfect" (5:48). This core demand sums up for us the "essence" of the antitheses, indeed of the whole Sermon itself. For to be "perfect" (*teleios*) does not mean here to be "flawless" or "without imperfections" (as in the Greek understandings of the word), but, in line with *tāmîm* or *šĕlĕmîm,* its Old Testament equivalents, it means to be "wholehearted" or "undivided" in one's love.[22] The core demand of the Sermon, then, is that we be as wholehearted and undivided in loving God (and neighbor, for in the New Testament the two are inseparably united), as God is undivided in loving us.[23] The antitheses are given as illustrative examples of this basic attitude of love. The Sermon on the Mount, then, is not to be read as a collection of precepts (law) but as an invitation to and an illustration of the basic Christian attitude of obedience (love of God) and radical concern (love of neighbor). For elsewhere in the Gospel too these have been proposed as the basis of "the Law and the Prophets": "on these two commandments depend all the law and the prophets" (Mt 22:40).

B. Sūtra 2: The Sermon on the Mount Is Not Law But Gospel

This attitude of obedience and concern is not to be understood as a condition for, but rather as the consequence of, Christian discipleship. For the Sermon on the Mount follows the proclamation of the Kingdom. Matthew has put the Sermon *after* his account of the proclamation of the Kingdom by Jesus and of the call to repentance that goes with it: "Repent, for the Kingdom of the Heavens is at hand" (4:17). The Sermon on the Mount is thus a spelling out of the concrete modalities of "repentance" (*metanoia*)—of that turning of the whole person to God which is the unforced response of anyone who has listened to the proclamation of the Kingdom and experienced the unconditional love of the Father which this proclamation announces.[24] The love (*agapē*) to which the Sermon urges us is thus "not a virtue among other virtues to which a man can aspire"; rather it is "that total attitude which is brought about by exposure to the love of God" as it is experienced in Jesus.[25] As John puts it: "we love because He first loved us" (1 Jn 4:19), telling us, as Dodd rightly comments, that "we are capable of love, of *agapē* at all, only because we are first its objects."[26] The Sermon on the Mount, therefore, is no arbitrary code imposed on us from outside. It is a description of the "natural" lifestyle of a Christian. It sets down the pattern of life that will be spontaneously lived by a follower of Jesus to the extent that he has been gripped by the proclamation of the Kingdom and has experienced the unconditional love of God made visible to us in Jesus. The Dharma projected by the Sermon on the Mount is the Christian *svadharma*.

C. Sūtra 3: The Sermon on the Mount Is a Goal-Directed Norm

As Christian *svadharma* the Sermon on the Mount is goal-directed. For Christian existence is not a static condition acquired once and for all, but a "way" along which we must walk "following" Christ. None of us *is* really a Christian (only Jesus is that!); we are all *becoming* Christians. For the eschatological tension of the "already and the not-yet" is mirrored in our lives too. The Sermon on the Mount thus sketches out (in exemplary and impressionistic outline) the life pattern toward which we must grow. Rather than obliging us to this or that particular action, the Sermon on the Mount obliges us to move in a given direction. For "the law of Christ is essentially concerned" not so much with the nature of an action, as Dodd tells us, but "with the *quality* of the act and the direction in which it is moving."[27]

THE DHARMA OF THE SERMON ON THE MOUNT

From what has been said it is clear that the Sermon on the Mount proposes a distinctive Dharma, a Dharma of grace and growth and of freedom and concern. The Sermon on the Mount does not lay down a static code of conduct (like the Law of Moses, or the code of Manu), but spells out a pattern of eschatological existence toward which we are to walk. But our walking is a walking in grace. We are not to be impelled toward our goal by the external pressures of Law or by an inner compulsion to achieve, resulting in a striving after "works." Rather we are to be urged on by a power from within, welling up from an experience of God's unconditional love, and producing "fruits" of love, in its turn. "Fruits," the spontaneous outcome of our *svabhāva,* of what we truly are ("every good tree produces good fruit" [Mt 7:17]), and not "works," actions strained after under the goad of guilt or of greed ("no one will be justified by the works of the law" [Rom 3:20]) are what the Dharma of the Sermon on the Mount requires from us.

For the Sermon on the Mount is grounded on an experience of God's unconditional love. Jesus' own life was totally determined by his own experience of God as *Abba*—a foundational experience probably associated with his baptism by John.[28] His ministry was a sustained attempt to evoke this experience in his disciples and in the crowd through word and deed. In his parables, his healings, his concern for the de-communitized (the lepers and the possessed), his table fellowship with outcasts—indeed in all the various ways in which he proclaimed the Kingdom of God (a symbol for Israel's hopes of liberation, "fulfilled" by Jesus through his revelation of God's liberating love),[29] Jesus draws on and communicates his *Abba* experience. "No one knows the Son except the Father," says Jesus, "and no one knows the Father except the Son and he to whom the Son chooses to reveal him" (Mt 11:27). "To know" the Father (in the biblical sense of "knowing," which implies not just abstract knowledge of, but intimate personal communication with) is a prerogative of Jesus, but one which he communicates to his disciples by evoking in them the same *Abba* experience. The Dharma of the Sermon on the Mount spells out a man's response to this communication.

But the experience of God as Father has as its inseparable obverse the experience of man as brother. "A man's relationship with God the Father and his relationship with his brother are so linked together," says Vatican II (*Nostra Aetate,* 5), "that the Scripture says 'he who does not love does not know God' (1 Jn 4:8)." The double commandment of love formulated by Jesus (Mk 12:28-34 par) is thus not a happy coincidence, an accidental juxtaposition of two unrelated Old Testament texts (Deut 6:4f and Lev 19:18), but is the natural outcome of an experience in which love of God and neighbor are held indissolubly together.[30] Rooted in this experience of sonship and brotherhood (God *experienced* as Father, man experienced as brother), the Dharma of the Sermon on the Mount (an authentic expression of the Dharma of Jesus) shows three features which derive directly from its root experience. It is *a* Dharma of freedom, of sonship, and of concern.

A. *A Dharma of Freedom*

Because it was formulated in opposition to traditional Jewish legalism, the Dharma of Jesus was experienced by the first Christians as a Dharma of freedom, liberating them from the oppressive burden of the Law (Mt 11:28-30; Lk 11:45-46).[31] For Jesus proposes a new understanding of the Law which is both more radical and more liberating than the formalistic legalism of his Pharisaic contemporaries, at least as this is described in the New Testament (Mk 2:23-28; 7:9-13; Mt 23:23). Jesus radicalizes the Law. Its demands now reach down to the innermost intentions of the "heart" (Mk 7:14-23; Mt 5:21-47). They embrace a man's life in its entirety (his whole heart, always and everywhere) and not only those areas and moments in it which come under legislation—for a man stands always and everywhere under God's love and must respond to it, always and everywhere, by *discerning* what is the most loving thing to do. And they require not just the avoidance of evil ("thou shalt not") but a positive never-to-be-ended endeavor to love which aspires to the undivided, wholeheartedness of the love of God himself (Mt 5:48).

Yet these demands of Jesus are liberating demands. For they are not prescriptions imposed arbitrarily on a man from the outside, but merely spell out for him the implications of the radical obedience and the radical concern which are his spontaneous, grace-given response to the experience of God's love made present through him in Jesus. So the "law of Christ" (Gal 6:2; 1 Cor 9:21) of which Paul speaks is the "law of the Spirit of life in Christ Jesus" (Rom 8:2). That is, it is not a code of law but a new interior principle of love (the Spirit), which in the Dharma of Jesus takes the place of Law.[32] "*Principaliter lex nova est ipsa gratia Spiritus Sancti quae datur Christifidelibus*," says Aquinas, affirming that "the new law is primarily the grace of the Holy Spirit given to Christians" (*Summa Theologica* I-II, 106, 1). Christian law codes are only expressions of this Spirit of love and are always subordinate to the Spirit they express.

What, then, is the place of law in Christian life? The Dharma of Jesus allows for Law—but only as a concession to the imperfect, "pilgrim" condition of human existence. Ideally law as an external code of conduct should be completely replaced by the Spirit, the interior principle of loving action. And as one who ushers in the eschatological age of the Spirit, Jesus is truly "the end of the Law that everyone who has faith may be justified" (Rom 10:4). But the eschatological age has not yet come to its fullness, so that for us poised between the "already" of the resurrection and the "not yet" of the parousia the tension between Law and Spirit (like that between institution and charism, structure and freedom, conservation and change) remains an authentic element of our Christian existence. We need law because we have not yet (individually and collectively) attained the fullness of eschatological existence. Yet we have been freed from the constraint of the Law because we live in the light of the liberating event of the resurrection. "Christ has set us free that we may be free men" (Gal 5:1).

Law, then, belongs to the as yet unchristianized areas of our life. For "the Law was not made for the just but for the unjust" (1 Tim 1:9). So "if all Christians were just there would be no need to constrain them with laws," for "the Law intervenes only to repress an existing disorder."[33] To the extent that this disorder disappears, and the "un-Christian" areas of our lives are eliminated by the flooding in of the Spirit of love, so does our dependence on Law diminish. The quality of Christian life, then, is not to be measured by the multiplicity of its "observances" but by the extent of its conformity to "the mind which was in Christ Jesus" (Phil 2:5). Christian Dharma is ultimately not so much a matter of obeying laws as of following Christ, whose own life from what we know of it was the clearest possible embodiment of the Sermon on the Mount. Such following becomes possible because of an inner transformation resulting from an experience of God's love—that is, of the gift of the Spirit given to us not as a spirit of slavery to call us back into fear, but as the Spirit of sonship which enables us to cry out "*Abba,* Father" (Rom 8:15).

B. A Dharma of Sonship

Ultimately it is this experience of sonship which is the heart of the Dharma of Jesus. His own extraordinarily liberated attitude toward the Law derives from his experience of God as *Abba,* an experience very different from that of his Pharisaic contemporaries. They experienced God not as a loving Father but as a just *Judge,* and this was the source of their strongly legalistic Dharma.[34] In this Dharma, Law assumes a preponderant role, because as a just Judge God can relate to man only through Law. Law thus becomes the *mediator* between God and man. It exercises a descending mediation by revealing to man God's will for him—the only aspect of God to which man can relate in a legalistic system—and it exercises an ascending mediation by revealing to God man's obedience, which in such a system can only be measured in terms of his observance of the law. Since the primary attribute of God is his justice, God's attitude toward man in a law-based Dharma will not be love (a judge does not love the man he is trying) but *conditional approval.* He will reward those who keep the Law and punish those who infringe it. There is no room here for forgiveness, graciousness, or unconditional acceptance. Everything goes strictly according to *merit,* for the perfect justice of God is the absolute value which must always be strictly maintained.

In such a Dharma man's attitude will obviously be one of formal obedience, the disposition to do externally only what is formally commanded. This is the only sort of obedience that law requires and which a Dharma based on law can demand. For such a Dharma has no place for the enthusiasm of love—for the reckless folly of a Francis of Assisi or the driving "magis" of an Ignatius. All it can do is to encourage the avoidance of sin (conceived not as a betrayal of love but as the transgression of a law) and the performance of "good works" prescribed by the Law, in order to pile up merit, which will enable one to claim (in strict justice!) his due reward from God. For the man who, like Paul (Rom 7:15-24), finds himself unable to do this, such Dharma becomes a source of endless anxiety, of deep-rooted guilt and ultimately perhaps of that agonizing scrupulosity which is the characteristic pathology of a Dharma based on Law. For the man who, like the Pharisee in the Gospel (Lk 18:11f) thinks he is successful, his Dharma leads to self-righteousness. For in a legalistic Dharma where merit is self-achieved, one quite rightly attributes one's righteousness to oneself, and is naturally contemptuous of those who have not come up to the level of one's own observance. These are some of the features of the legalistic Dharma which Jesus consistently opposed as a deep perversion of the proper disposition of man toward God. The fact that they evoke so many familiar resonances in our own spiritual experience warns us how far the Dharma *of* Christians (particularly in the more law-prone Christian communities) has drifted away from the Dharma of Jesus.

For the Dharma of Jesus is of a very different kind. Grounded on an experience of God as the "dear Father" (*Abba*) who forgives recklessly (Lk 15:11-31) and like an "unjust" judge "justifies the ungodly" (Rom 4:5), the Dharma of Jesus proposes as the primary attribute of God not his justice but his *love*. God's attitude to man is not then conditional approval ("I will love you if you are good") but wholly *unconditional love* ("I love you"; "experience this and you will be good"). Law can no longer mediate between God and man, for a man's relation to God is not now determined by his observance of a law. Instead the mediator is now *Jesus,* who reveals both God's unconditional love for man and man's radical obedience to God. For in the life of Jesus, with its unlimited acceptance of others (Mk 2:13-17), its limitless compassion for the suffering and the sick (Mk 6:34), its total availability for service (Mk 1:35-39), its openness to death for others (Mk 10:45), God's unconditional love is made visible in the history of a human life. Looking at this life, we know what God is like; and looking at this life we know too what man can be like. For in Jesus' unswerving fidelity to his "way" (Mk 8:27-33) and in his refusal to abandon his Father's will even at the cost of life itself (Mk 14:36) we get a glimpse of what man's obedience should be.

For to God's unconditional love man can only respond with a truly *radical obedience,* which is not content with the external performance only of what is commanded, but which places the whole heart everywhere and always at the service of the Father's love. Such obedience will not be sin-centered, preoccupied with avoiding sin, but God-centered, concerned with being perfect as the heavenly Father is perfect—that is, with becoming as undivided, wholehearted and unconditional in one's love as one can possibly be. Aware that this concern is not to be a moralistic striving after "perfection" but a walking in love in which he is carried by his experience of God's "absolute paternal care that will not leave us, but protects us everywhere," the follower of Jesus loses his deep-seated anxieties. He does not worry about the future, striving desperately to keep his record clean so that, like the one-talent servant in the parable (Mt 25:14-30), he might be "safe" before an exacting God. Rather, conscious of his sinfulness and his need, he yet faces the future with serenity, aware that he has been unconditionally forgiven (even before he sinned!) and that he is fully accepted by God as a "son." His concern, then, is not to bargain with God, on whom he knows he has no claim whatever (Lk 17:7-10), but to live out his sonship with the "love, joy, peace, patience, kindliness, goodness, faithfulness, gentleness and self-control" which are the "fruits of the Spirit" (Gal 5:22f), and so the unmistakable marks of those who are genuinely following the Dharma of Jesus.

C. A Dharma of Concern

Because "sonship" in the New Testament is inseparably linked with "brotherhood" (to experience God as Father is to experience man as brother) the Dharma of Jesus is inevitably a Dharma of concern (*agapē*). Concern for the brother looms so large in the Sermon on the Mount (Mt 5:43-48, 7:12), and indeed all through the New Testament (Mt 22:34-40; Jn 13:34; Rom 13:8; 1 Cor 13:1-13; 1 Pet 4:8; Jas 2:8; 1 Jn 3:23; 2 Jn 5) that it is arguable that the double commandment of love propounded by Jesus (Mt 22:34-40) urges us not so much to love God *and* neighbor, as to love God *by loving* neighbor.[35] When Jesus combines Deut 6:4f ("you shall love the Lord your God with all your heart, with all your soul and with all your mind")—the *šĕmaᶜ yiśrāʾēl,* which rabbinic Judaism would have unhesitatingly judged the most important text of the Old Testament—with the obscure and little quoted passage from Lev 19:18 ("you shall love your neighbor as yourself"), he may have been interpreting the first text by means of the second. He would then have been saying that to love God with all one's heart means to love one's neighbor as oneself. This is at least how the New Testament seems to have understood him. For elsewhere the New Testament scarcely ever speaks of loving God. "Loving God" is mentioned in it only about eight times, and then too mostly either in the stereotyped formula "those who love God" (Rom 8:28; 1 Cor 2:9; 8:3; Jas 1:12; 2:5) or in texts which relate love of God to love of neighbor (1 Jn 4:20f; 5:1f; Heb 6:10). Only thrice, and that too in an ambiguous and indirect way, do we find an exhortation to love God (Lk 11:42; Jn 5:42; 2 Thess 2:45). Instead we find a steady stress of clear and powerful directives to love neighbor running all through the New Testament (Mt 19:19; Rom 13:8; Gal 5:14; Heb 13:1; 1 Pet 2:17; 4:8; Jas 2:8; Jn 13:34; 15:12; 1 Jn 2:7f; 3:23; 4:21; 2 Jn 5). Lev 19:18 (explicitly quoted in Mt 19:19; Gal 5:14; and Jas 2:8) thus becomes the *šĕmaᶜ* of the community of Jesus, replacing Deut

6:4f, which except in the love commandment of Jesus is never mentioned in the New Testament again!

Concern for the neighbor is thus central to the Dharma of Jesus. Such concern is understood by the New Testament in a most radical way. It must be absolutely *universal,* reaching out to anyone in need (Lk 10:29-37), even to those who are hostile to us (Lk 6:35f). It must be wholly *gratuitous,* looking for no reward whatever (Lk 6:32-34; 14:12-14). In a word it must be as *unconditional* as the love of the Father from which it ultimately derives (Mt 5:44f). For all love comes from the Father: "beloved, let us love one another, for love is of God" (1 Jn 4:7). And the love of the sons must be like the love of the Father: "love your enemies and pray for those who persecute you, so that you may be the sons of your Father who is in heaven; for he makes his sun rise on the evil and the good, and sends his rain on the just and on the unjust" (Mt 5:44f).

This concern of the Dharma of Jesus which emulates the love of the Father is an *affective* concern, responding affectively (as the Father's love does) to human need. It shows itself not so much in the attitudes of warmth and acceptance that so color our highly psychologized understanding of love today, as in concrete acts of material and social sustenance. To love according to the Dharma of Jesus means not only to forgive enemies (Mt 5:23f), to accept persons non-judgementally (Rom 14:1-4), to be patient, kind, magnanimous, and tolerant (1 Cor 13:3-7); it means also (and indeed primarily) to sit at table with outcasts and untouchables (Mk 2:15-17), to give food to the hungry and clothing to those who have nothing to wear (Mt 25:35; Jas 3:14-17), to visit people in prison (Heb 13:3), to console the lonely and the sick (Mt 25:36). For as 1 John, a compact but profound treatise on Christian love, put it: "if anyone has the world's goods and sees his brother in need, yet closes his heart against him, how does the love of God abide in him? Little children, let us not love in word or in speech, but in deed and truth" (1 Jn 3:17f).

This strongly materialistic orientation of Christian concern is so striking in the New Testament that it probably brings out a specific element in the Dharma of Jesus. Rooted strongly in history and focusing sharply on man (Mk 2:27), experienced not as an "embodied spirit" but as an "animated body," and understood not as the center of an individual destiny but as part of the history of a people, the Dharma of Jesus looks forward to building up a universal and fraternal community of sharing and love. Such a community is prefigured in the description of the first Christian church of Jerusalem. We find in Acts: "the company of believers were of one heart and soul, and no one said that any of the things which he possessed was his own, but they had everything in common," so that "there was not a needy person among them" (Acts 4:32-34 = Acts 2:44-45). And its promise is celebrated continually in the central action of the Christian cult, the Eucharist, in which a community is created symbolically through the sharing of bread, in memory of a life that was lived out and laid down ("shared") for others.

This eschatological vision of the end-time community gives order and consistency to all the other concerns of the Dharma of Jesus. *Svadharma* now becomes the fulfillment of one's individual destiny not for itself but as part of the universal destiny of man; *lokasangraha* looks to the welfare of the community, seen not as a collection of individuals who will realize their fulfillment in isolation from each other, but as a community where the welfare of each can only be achieved through the health of the whole. Such a vision of "the family of man" adds a structural element to the Dharma of Jesus which gives it a strong revolutionary thrust. Committed to the building of a genuinely fraternal community, the Dharma of Jesus will be compelled by its own inner dynamism to oppose all social, economic, political or religious structures which hinder the emergence of such a community. Institutional forms of this Dharma have doubtless played in the past (as they continue to play today) an ideological role, legitimizing the structures of society that happened to be dominant and dominating. For feudalism, absolute monarchy, colonialism, and (most shockingly) even slavery have found (as international capitalism and neo-colonialism continue to find) official "Christian" support.[36] But the concern for man that lies at the heart of the Dharma of Jesus cannot be silenced and has broken out in movements of protest and relief that have so greatly marked Christian history. Is it an accident that the great revolutions of freedom in our times—the proclamation of the political equality of all men ("liberty, equality, fraternity") by the bourgeois revolutions of the eighteenth centuries or the violent protests against the ruthless oppression of early capitalism by the socialist movements of the nineteenth should all have occurred in that segment of mankind which has long been leavened (however imperfectly) by the Dharma of Jesus? In these, as in the struggles for liberation now being waged by the oppressed masses of the national security states aided by international capitalism, we hear directly or indirectly echoes of the voice that spoke so firmly of the immeasurable worth of man, loved as he is unconditionally by God his Father.

NOTES

1. B. Kuppuswamy, *Dharma and Society* (Delhi: Macmillan, 1977), 16.

2. P. V. Kane, *History of Dharmashastra,* vol. 1, part 1 (Poona: Bhandarkar Oriental Research Institute, 1968), 1.

3. R. N. Dandekar, "Dharma, the First End of Man," in *Sources of Indian Tradition,* ed. W. T. de Bary (Delhi: Motilal Banarsidass, 1963), 218.

4. Ibid.

5. Ibid.

6. Note how R. C. Zaehner, in his *Bhagavad-Gītā* (London: Oxford University Press, 1973), 394, translates *sva-dharma* as "one's own (caste) duty."

7. Kuppuswamy, *Dharma and Society,* 23.

8. Arun Shourie, *Hinduism: Essence and Consequence* (Ghaziabad: Vikas, 1979), 1, quoting A. Gramsci, *Selections from Prison Notebooks* (London: Lawrence & Wishart, 1971), 80.

9. Shourie, *Hinduism,* 2.

10. See F. X. D'Sa, "Dharma as Delight in Cosmic Welfare: A Study of Dharma in the Gita," *Bible Bhashyam* 6 (1980): 335-57.

11. See R. M. Grant, *Early Christianity and Society* (London: Collins, 1978), 13-43, for a balanced account of ideological approval given to the Roman imperial rule by the early Christians; and F. Houtart, *Religion and Ideology in Sri Lanka* (Bangalore: Theological Publications in India, 1974), 108-32, for the ideological role played by Christianity in the Portuguese conquest of Sri Lanka.

12. M. K. Gandhi, *An Autobiography: The Story of My Experiments with Truth,* in *Selected Works of Mahatma Gandhi,* vol. 1 (Ahmedabad: Navjivan, 1969), 101.

13. Although H. T. Wrege (*Die Überlieferungsgeschichte der Bergpredigt* [Tübingen: Mohr, 1968]) has attempted to show that the material common to the two sermons derives from an oral tradition, most scholars would locate it in "Q," a written collection of the sayings of Jesus supposedly used by Matthew and Luke.

14. Cf. Mt 5:13 = Lk 14:34f; Mt 5:14 = Lk 11:33; Mt 5:25 = Lk 12:57ff; Mt 6:5 = Lk 18:10ff; Mt 6:24 = Lk 16:13; etc.

15. Cf. Mt 6:1-4; 5:17-20; 6:1-6; 6:16-18; etc.

16. See P. F. Ellis, *Matthew: His Mind and His Message* (Collegeville, Minn.: Liturgical Press, 1974), 10-22, 27-98, for a good initiation into the meticulous composition of Matthew, who has "put together his gospel with the precision of a Swiss watch" (p. 27).

17. See L. Ridez, *Die Bergpredigt: Menschsein nach Jesus* (Zurich: Benziger, 1979), 28-29. The book offers an excellent catechetical introduction to the Sermon on the Mount, with excellent comments on its structure.

18. While there was a tendency in the past to exaggerate the difference between "legalistic" Pharisaism and "personalistic" Christianity, some postwar Western scholars suffering from guilt over "the Holocaust" have swung over to the other extreme and deny all difference between them. But Jesus was not a Pharisee and proclaimed a liberative message that was radically new. See J. Jeremias, *New Testament Theology,* vol. 1 (London: SCM Press, 1975), 204-18.

19. H. K. McArthur, *Understanding the Sermon on the Mount* (New York: Harper & Row, 1960), 105ff.

20. See Joachim Jeremias, *The Sermon on the Mount* (Philadelphia: Fortress Press, 1965), Indian reprint by Theological Publications in India, Bangalore, as the first of three booklets of Jeremias printed together as Facet Books.

21. D'Sa, "Dharma as Delight in Cosmic Welfare."

22. See Jeremias, *New Testament Theology,* 1:212.

23. Soares-Prabhu, "The Love Commandment: The Jesus Way as a Way of Revolutionary Concern," *Anawim* 21.

24. See Jeremias, *New Testament Theology,* 1:113-21.

25. C. H. Dodd, *Gospel and Law* (Cambridge: Cambridge University Press, 1951), 44.

26. Ibid.

27. Ibid., 77.

28. Jeremias, *New Testament Theology,* 1:55f.

29. Soares-Prabhu, "The Central Message of Jesus: A Contemporary Interpretation of Mk 1:14-15," *Nirjhari* (Annual of the Adhyatma Vidyapitham, Carmelaram, Bangalore, 1978-79), 58-72 .

30. V. P. Furnish, *The Love Command in the New Testament* (London: SCM Press, 1973), 63: "Loving the neighbour is no less an act of obedience than loving God and is part of the *total* response to the sovereign claim of God under which man stands."

31. C. Spicq, *St Paul and Christian Living* (Dublin: Gill, 1964), 66.

32. Ibid., 68.

33. S. Lyonnet, "Christian Freedom and the Law of the Spirit according to St. Paul," *The Christian Lives by the Spirit*, ed. S. Lyonnet and I. de La Potterie (New York: Alba House, 1974), 45-74, esp. p. 164.

34. What we give below are two theoretical "types" of Dharma, not two descriptions of the way in which the Pharisees and the followers of Jesus actually lived. The New Testament description of the legalism of the Pharisees is polemic, and the caricature inevitable in any such description has been accentuated by Christian interpreters anxious to demonstrate the superiority of the Christian love ethic. In fact neither type is ever realized in full. The practical Dharma of all people is a combination of both. There were loving Pharisees as there are legalistic merit-oriented Christians! But there is no doubt that the love-based Dharma of Jesus does stand in opposition to the merit-oriented Dharma of Pharisaic Judaism, though the opposition may have been more a matter of emphasis than of an absolutely new affirmation.

35. See Soares-Prabhu, "The Love Commandment," *Anawim* 21, where this has been argued in detail.

36. It is a sobering thought that official Roman Catholic teaching right up till the middle of the last century, and Catholic moral theologians right up to the middle of the present one (Lehmkul, Prümmer, Genicot, Zalba among them) decreed and defended the morality of slavery. See P. F. Kaufman, "An Immoral Morality?," *Commonweal* 107 (1980): 493-97; Kaufman refers us to two studies by J. F. Maxwell, "The Development of Catholic Doctrine Concerning Slavery," *World Justice* 11 (1969); 12 (1970); and *Slavery in the Catholic Church* (London, 1975).

13

THE SYNOPTIC LOVE COMMANDMENT

The Dimensions of Love
in the Teachings of Jesus

Any attempt to explore the dimensions of love in the teaching of Jesus will begin inevitably with the love commandment of the Synoptic Gospels (Mt 22:34-40 = Mk 12:28-34; Lk 10:25-37). For the command to love God with all one's heart and to love one's neighbor as oneself is surely the most comprehensive and powerful statement of Jesus that we have in the New Testament on the significance of love in human life. The three Synoptic Gospels which report this love commandment of Jesus recognize its importance. The commandment is presented by Matthew as one on which "depend all the law and the prophets" (Mt 22:40); by Mark as that which is "more than all whole burnt offerings and sacrifices" (Mk 12:33); and by Luke as the way through which one can "inherit eternal life" (Lk 10:25; 28).

Each of the Synoptics thus presents the significance of the love commandment in its own specific way, as part of its particular theological perspective. This is inevitable. For the Gospels, as Victor Paul Furnish reminds us in his excellent study of the love commandment in the New Testament, "do not just *exhibit* Jesus' teaching, but rather receive, transmit, and apply it in specific ways relevant to the needs of the Church in the writers' own times."[1] The differences in their presentation of Jesus' love command have been carefully spelled out by Furnish. He has shown convincingly how Mark has presented the love command as part of the early Church's missionary preaching in Hellenistic society—in order to demonstrate the oneness of God over against the many gods of Hellenism (cf. "You are right, Teacher, you have truly said that he is one, and there is no other but he"

This article first appeared in *Jeevadhara* 13 (1983): 85-103.

[Mk 12:32]), and the primacy of love over against the cult ritual of Greeks and Jews ("to love him with all one's heart . . . and to love one's neighbor as oneself is much more than all whole burnt offerings and sacrifices" [Mk 12:33]); how Matthew has presented it as the epitome of the Law, in a polemic against the absolutization of the Torah and of all its parts by rabbinic Judaism ("on these two commandments depend all the law and the prophets" [Mt 22:40]); and how Luke has presented it as an exhortation to the Christian community, for he insists not so much on the love commandment itself (which is assumed to be known—note how it is the lawyer and not Jesus who pronounces it), as on the need to put it into practice ("*Do* this, and you will live" [Lk 10:28]; "Go and *do* likewise" [Lk 10:37]).[2]

But behind these different Synoptic presentations, kerygmatic, polemic, and parenetic, lies the teaching of Jesus. Jesus has certainly inspired the Synoptic love commandment, at least in the sense that the Synoptic formulations of it are wholly in his Spirit;[3] and it is very likely, indeed I believe quite certain, that it is Jesus who has, in its essentials, also formulated it.[4] For who else but Jesus could have brought together Deut 6:5 (love of God) and Lev 19:18 (love of neighbor)—texts associated nowhere else in Jewish literature[5]—into so creative and even scandalous a combination? And how else except by recognizing this combination as an authentic saying of Jesus are we to explain the importance given to the love commandment in the Synoptic Gospels, or to account for the fact that it is found in the two earliest sources (Mk and Q) of the Synoptic tradition? For it is very likely that Matthew and Luke do not here depend on Mark, but have edited an earlier Q version, parallel to Mark's source.[6] And if Lev 19:18, a relatively neglected text in Judaism, has become the *mahāvākya* of the New Testament—presented expressly as a summary of the Decalogue by Matthew (19:19); as the fulfillment of the Law by Paul (Rom 13:8-9; Gal 5:14); and as the "law of the Kingdom" by James (Jas 2:8)—this surely could only have happened because it was Jesus himself who put this obscure text on to a level with the *šĕmaʿ* (Deut 6:4-5), the great confession of Israel's faith, which was to become the key text of rabbinic Judaism.

In the Synoptic love commandment, then, we stand face to face with Jesus' teaching on love. An examination of this commandment in the earliest form available to us, that found in the Gospel of Matthew (Mt 22:34-40),[7] will thus (1) provide us with a convenient starting point for our exploration into Jesus' teaching on love. Investigation of the love commandment will lead inevitably (2) to the command to love our enemies (Mt 5:43-48), which Matthew presents precisely as a *midrash,* or interpretative comment, on the love commandment. Having studied this, we shall be able (3) to draw conclusions about the significance of love in the teaching of Jesus (cf. Mt 25:31-46; Lk 10:29-37); and (4) to locate its basis in his *Abba* experience, as this has been communicated to his disciples (Mt 11:25-27; 5:45-48). We shall thus be able to discern in broad outline the dimensions of love in the teaching of Jesus.

1. TO LOVE MEANS TO LOVE NEIGHBOR
(MT 22:34-40)

The love commandment is formulated by Jesus in Matthew's Gospel in response to a question put by a "lawyer" (*nomikos*) about which is the "great" commandment in the Law—one, that is, that ranks above all the others, is the fundamental principle from which they can all be derived, and which can be understood as their sum and summary. The question is presented by Matthew as a malicious one ("testing him"), because no such great commandment is conceivable in rabbinic Judaism. Occasional references by rabbis to some one prescription summarizing the others (cf. Rabbi Hillel's version of the golden rule,[8] or Rabbi Akiba's commendation [under creation influence?] of Lev 19:18 as "the most comprehensive rule of the Law"),[9] or the analogies to the Synoptic "double commandment" of love that occur in the *Testaments of the Twelve Patriarchs* (and only there)[10] are not presented as "great commandments," summarizing or representing the rest. They draw attention to one or other precept of the Law, without invalidating the obligation that one has to fulfill also all the others. The obligation to follow the whole Law in all its parts is always implied in rabbinic writings, and indeed is usually asserted in explicit terms.[11]

1.1. Love Is the Basis of the Law

Rabbinic Judaism understands the Law "formally"—that is, as being, in its precise formulation, the revelation of God's will. As such, the Law is binding in its totality and in all its parts, even the minutest. For its obligation derives not from what is commanded but from the *will of God* who commands: and this touches equally all its prescriptions. Each commandment, then, is in principle as important as every other, and no one commandment can be singled out as greater or of more importance than the rest.[12] "Woe to us that Scripture attaches the same weight to the easy as to the hard," laments Rabbi Johanan ben Zakkai;[13] and as Rabbi Jehuda ha-Nasi explains: "the lightest precept is to be fulfilled with the same care as the gravest, because each expresses the divine will."[14]

Jesus cuts right through such a formal understanding of the Law by proposing in reply to the lawyer's question a "first and great commandment": "You shall love the Lord your God with all your heart, and with all your soul, and with all your mind. This is the great and first commandment. And a second is like it, you shall love your neighbor as yourself. On these two commandments depend all the law and the prophets" (Mt 22:37-40).

So not only does Jesus, in the teeth of the rabbinic understanding of the Law, propose a "great commandment," expressly presented as one on which "all the law and the prophets" depend (*kremetai*),[15] but he proposes this core command as a double commandment of love, in which love of God and love of neighbor are set side by side. The love commandment, then, is proposed as the "soul" of the Law, its constitutive principle, of which its individual legal prescriptions are concrete expressions. And this love commandment is presented as the double commandment in which love of neighbor is placed on a level with love of God. For "first" and "second" in the Words of Jesus are meant to be indications not of a rank but of sequence. Love of neighbor is not the second commandment, subordinate to the first: it is a second command which is "like" (*homoios*), that is, similar in character and equal in importance to, the first.[16]

1.2. Neighbor Is the Focus of Love

Such "horizontalism" would have been quite shocking to the contemporaries of Jesus—as it continues to shock his followers today, for they have never found it easy to adjust to the radicalism of their Master. Yet it is quite certainly what the love commandment of Jesus means. "To love one's neighbor is a commandment equal to the precept of love of God," says Ceslas Spicq in his monumental study of love (*agapē*) in the New Testament,[17] and after having discussed the meaning of the word "like" (*homoios*), he concludes: "Such uses of the word 'like' suggest that the second commandment has the same nature or value as the first. It is analogous to the first so that, without being strictly equal, the two commandments constitute a special category of precepts completely distinct from all others. They have a common excellence and universality; the nature of the two loves is identical."[18]

Indeed if anything, Jesus, according to the Synoptic tradition, stresses love of neighbor even more than he does love of God. It is significant that loving God is seldom urged in the New Testament. Apart from its single occurrence in the Synoptics, the love command, Deut 6:4-5 (so significant for rabbinic Judaism) appears nowhere else in the New Testament, while Lev 19:18 is quoted or implied in nearly every strand of the New Testament tradition. Indeed "there is only one other Synoptic passage [other than the love commandment] which speaks at all of man's love for God (Luke 11:42: the Pharisees "neglect justice and the love of God"), and the idea appears only rarely elsewhere in the New Testament (cf. Rom 8.28; 1 Cor 2:9; 8:3; 16:22; Eph 6:24; 1 Jn 4:20-21)."[19] But the whole New Testament is spilling over with endlessly repeated exhortations to love neighbor (cf. Mt 7:12; Lk 6:32-36; Jn 13:34; 15:12-17; Rom 13:8-9; 1 Cor 13:1-13; Gal 5:14; Eph 5:1-2; Phil 2:1-5; Col 3:14; Jas 2:8; 1 Pet 2:17; 1 Jn 3:23; 4:7-12; 2 Jn 5), and with concrete indications of how that love is to be exercised (Mt 18:10-37; 24:31-46; Mk 10:42-45; Lk 10:29-37; 14:12-14; Jn 13:1-14; Acts 2:44-47; 4:32-35; 1 Cor 16:1-4; 1 Jn 3:17-18; 2 Jn 5-7; Jas 2:1-7).

Equally significant is the way in which Jesus in his teaching consistently subordinates religious observance to human need.[20] Mercy or interhuman concern, Jesus tells us, quoting Hos 6:6, is always to be preferred to cult (Mt 9:13; 12:7); so that one must not engage in an act of worship without first being reconciled with an offended brother (Mt 5:23-24). The Sabbath is made for man, not man for the Sabbath (Mk 2:27), and the duty to care for one's parents overrides the obligations of a religious vow (Mk 7:9-13). It is the observance of the commandments of the Decalogue, which prescribe one's duty to one's fellow human beings rather than of those which speak of one's duty to God, that are recommended to the rich young man as a way to eternal life (Mk 10:17-19), just as it is effective concern for the needy (the hungry, the ill clad, the prisoners, and the sick) that will entitle the just to receive their eternal reward (Mt 25:31-46).

1.3. God Is Loved When Neighbor Is Loved

This of course does not mean that the New Testament brackets out the love of God, or that it reduces religion to philanthropy. Rather, the comparative neglect by the New Testament authors of "the command" to love God is best explained by supposing that (1) the early Christian tradition has preferred to use words other than "love" with which to express humankind's relation to God[21]— possibly because "love" implies a reciprocal relation among equals, and so can be applied only analogically (if at all) to God, particularly in its primary New Testament meaning of "doing good to"; and that (2) the New Testament has (following Jesus) developed its own specific understanding of loving God, in which to love God is to love neighbor. For the association of Deut 6:4-5 (love God) with Lev 19:18 (love neighbor) is not a mere juxtaposition of two relevant Old Testament texts, but is a combination made according to the well-known rabbinic technique of interpretation (the *gĕzērâ šāwâ*), in which passages with similar wording ("thou shall love") are brought together on the strength of their "analogy of words," so as to mutually interpret each other.[22] Lev 19:18 has thus been added to Deut 6:4-5 in order to serve as an interpretative comment on it. To love God with all one's heart, Jesus is saying, means to love one's neighbor as oneself. One loves God by loving neighbor. Loving neighbor is the concrete actualization of one's love for God.[23]

It is just this intimate pairing of the love of God and the love of neighbor that constitutes the specificity and the uniqueness of the teaching of Jesus. Interhuman concern is obviously an element in all religious traditions. The liberated Buddha sends out his disciples on a mission, "for the profit of many, out of compassion for the world, for the bliss of the many, for the welfare, the profit, the bliss of Gods and humankind" (*Mahāvagga* I 10:32), and the *Bhagavadgītā* makes "passionate delight in the welfare of all beings" (*sarvabhūtahite ratāḥ*) the mark of the truly liberated person (v. 25). The Old Testament too, both in its legal codes and in its prophetic exhortations, abounds in prescriptions that urge concern for one's fellow human beings and which prohibit the exploitation of the powerless.[24] But interhuman concern here is always a secondary attitude which follows from a prior religious experience (liberation) or a primary commitment to God (the Covenant). It is only with Jesus that the ethical attitude becomes, as it were, an integral part of the religious experience itself, for to experience God as "Father" is to experience the neighbor as "brother." The horizontal is thus inseparably welded into the vertical, and love of neighbor is brought onto a level with love of God.

2. TO LOVE NEIGHBOR IS
TO LOVE YOUR ENEMY

The striking emphasis on interhuman concern which is so characteristic a feature of Jesus' teaching on love is paralleled by an equally striking insistence on the universality of that concern. The love of neighbor demanded by Jesus reaches beyond all limits of personal preference, of class or caste solidarity, of religious or racial oneness. The neighbor we are to love is anyone in need (Lk 10:25-37), indeed especially the unrewarding (Lk 6:32-34; 14:12-14), and even those who are hostile to us (Lk 6:35-36).

Such loving of one's enemies is not a uniquely Christian demand, as is sometimes suggested. It probably features in some form or other in all religions and is certainly strikingly conspicuous in Buddhism. "Hatred is never stilled by hatred in this world," says the Dhammapada, "only by non-hatred is hatred stilled—this is the eternal law" (1:5). And this "eternal law" is vividly illustrated by the Buddha in a touching story which tells of how the prince of Kosala spares the life of his enemy the king of Kashi (who had slain his parents and annexed his kingdom), because, just when about to strike him down, he recalls the words uttered aloud by his father as he was being led to his execution, as a last instruction to his son following him at a distance: "Do not look long [i.e. do not let your hatred last long], do not look short [i.e. do not be quick to fall out with your friends]; for hatred is not appeased by hatred, hatred is appeased by non-hatred alone."[25] Indeed the "love command" of Buddhism (and Hinduism) is in a sense more comprehensive than that of the Christians, for it reaches out to all sentient beings and not to humankind alone. Christianity with its curious insensitivity to non-human life—its tolerance of bull-fighting and blood sports, of the ruthless hunting down of animals for fun, and the reckless extermination of whole species of living things for "profit," has a lot to learn from the Hindu-Buddhist tradition of reverence for life.

Yet there is something particularly impressive in Jesus' command that we love our enemies. This appears in Matthew's Gospel as an interpretation of Lev 19:18, formulated to serve as the sixth antithesis of his Sermon on the Mount: "You have heard that it was said: 'You shall love your neighbor and hate your enemy.' But I say to you: 'Love your enemies and pray for those who persecute you, so that you may be sons of your Father who is in the heavens: for he makes his sun rise on the evil and on the good, and sends rain on the just and on the unjust'" (Mt 5:43-45).

The antithetical form of the passage is very likely the result of Matthew's editing of his Q-source (cf. the parallel in Lk 6:27-28), but the injunction to love one's enemies is certainly from Jesus, probably in its Lukan form, whose synonymous parallelism and underlying rhythm are characteristic of Jesus' sayings.[26] It is likely too that Jesus did in fact pronounce the saying (as Matthew suggests) as a homiletic comment on Lev 19:18—possibly during a synagogue service when this Old Testament text had been read.[27]

Loving enemies is thus for Jesus an explication of loving neighbor. In its original Testament setting (Lev 19:18), of course, "neighbor" means no more than a "fellow Israelite." For the text in its immediate context reads: "You shall not hate your brother (ʾāḥ) in your heart. But you shall reason with your fellow tribesman (ʿāmît); You shall not take revenge nor bear a grudge against the sons of your own people (bĕnê ʿammêkā), but you shall love your neighbor (rēʾâ) as yourself" (Lev 19:17-18).

The neighbor to be loved as oneself is thus the "son of your own people," the "fellow-tribesman," the "brother." Even the extension of this command to the "stranger" (gēr) in Lev 19:34 does not make an essential difference. For a "stranger" (gēr) in the Old Testament is not usually a non-Israelite—generally designated there as an "alien" (nokrî), or as the "gentiles" (gôyîm)—but a "dispossessed Israelite," living in a territory where he has no property or tribal rights, or later and by extension, a Canaanite fugitive who has been "adopted" into Israelite society.[28] Eventually the gēr comes to signify a "proselyte" or convert to Judaism, and it is doubtless that in this sense it was understood in the time of Jesus.[29] Jewish tradition at the time of Jesus, then, would not have been familiar with the idea of loving enemies—particularly when such enemies were understood not just as personal adversaries but as members of an alien and hostile group. And if no Old Testament or rabbinic text speaks *of hating* one's enemy, the exhortation to the Qumran sectaries in their *Manual of Discipline* to "love all the sons of light, each according to his lot along the council of God, but to hate all the sons of darkness, each according to his guilt in the vengeance of God" (1QS 1:9) shows that Matthew's formulation of the traditional understanding of Lev 19:18 ("you shall love your neighbor but hate your enemy") was not altogether unfounded.

Sayings like this illustrate the sharp religious and political tensions (Pharisee against Sadducee, Zadokite against Hasmonean, Jew against Roman) that tore up Jewish society in the time of Jesus, and give particular point to his sayings on love. How shocking Jesus' demand to love enemies must have appeared in a society where love was largely restricted to the confines of a tightly knit ethnic or religious group, and where hatred of the foreign oppressor was preached with religious fervor. For what Jesus asks for is not just the resolution of personal antagonisms within the group, but for the acceptance of members of alien and hostile groups as well. "It seems clear," notes Furnish, "that the enemies envisioned in both Synoptic versions of the commandment are those who oppose God's people (and therefore God), and whose opposition is expressed in direct personal ways: as persecution, cursing, abuse."[30] The love command of Jesus is thus radically comprehensive. Political and religious antagonisms as well as personal ones are the objects of his command.

Understood in this way, the command to love one's enemies becomes the most challenging and radical of Jesus' demands. No barriers of personal antipathy, religious disharmony, class conflict, or caste or race prejudice can be allowed to impede the imperative of love. Love must determine not just our personal conduct but our public life as well. This is to be urged not only on black Africans struggling against the unspeakable indignities of *apartheid* or on the Latin American *campesinos* opposing utterly repressive military regimes, or Dalit Panthers confronting the terrible reality of the caste atrocities—but equally on Polish trade unionists fighting for their rights, or on Afghan nationalists resisting foreign aggression! No one, capitalist or Communist, is outside the pale of love!

Such love for our enemies ought not, of course, to hold us back from an active and effective resistance to the exploitation and oppression of the "poor" that these "enemies" engender. If Jesus, in the Sermon on the Mount, invites us not to resist one who is evil (Mt 5:39), he is not advocating passivity in the face of injustice, but is inviting us not to "retaliate" or "re-act" to evil, but to overcome it through constructive action. Aggression is not to be met with aggression nor with servility but with constructive assertiveness.[31] Jesus' own life of vigorous protest (Mt 23:1-30; Mk 2:23-28; 7:1-15; Lk 6:20-26) is strong evidence for this. Indeed a struggle for justice is a necessary and integral part of Jesus' love commandment.

3. TO LOVE MEANS TO DO JUSTICE

The reason for this is that "love" in the teaching of Jesus is not merely an affective emotion—the experience of "pleasure in proximity, a desire for fuller knowledge of one another, a yearning for mutual identification and personality fusion."[32] It is primarily an effective concern: "an active, effective love." Seitz has called it, "operating with singular tenderness."[33] The Gospels of course know about and approve of the affective love of friendship, for which they generally use the Greek word *philia*. This is the love for one's parents which the follower of Jesus must transcend (Mt 10:37), the love which binds friends together (Lk 11:5; 28:12), or the love which Jesus had for his disciples (Lk 12:14), for Lazarus and his sisters (Jn 11:3-5), for the "disciple whom he loved" (Jn 20:2).

3.1. Love Aids and Affirms

But it is not to such an affective love of friendship (*philia*)—which of its very nature is limited to a closed circle of friends—that Jesus urges his followers in his love commandment or in his command to love enemies. Here, and indeed overwhelmingly in the New Testament, we meet with a different kind of love— a specifically "Christian" love, active in character and utterly universal in scope, for which the New Testament has its own special word, *agapē*.[34] Such love is primarily a love of affective concern which shows itself in "doing good to" the neighbor (Lk 6:35), by responding actively to his concrete needs (Lk 10:29-37). But the effective concern of *agapē* should not be mistaken for an impersonal doling out of benefits, with scant respect for the person to whom one gives. Such condescending giving is far from Christian love. For the effective concern of *agapē is* rooted in a Christian experience which recognizes in the neighbor a brother or a sister. Christian love affirms the neighbor as "brother" even as it reaches out to aid him in his need.

Because *agapē* experiences the neighbor as brother, it responds to the *totality* of his needs. Its expressions are thus manifold—spiritual, material, personal, and societal. Love as taught by Jesus means indeed forgiveness (Mt 18:21-22), reconciliation (Mt 5:23-24), self-forgetful service (Mk 10:42-45), the non-judgmental acceptance of persons (Mt 7:1-5), a wholly disinterested concern for the unrewarding (Lk 6:32-34), and a willingness to reach out to and to help even those who are hostile to us (Lk 6:35-36). But it means too "doing good to" the neighbor in his material and social needs—sharing one's bread with the hungry and one's clothes with those who do not have enough to wear (Mt 25:31-46; Lk 3:11); visiting prisoners (Heb 13:13) and "communicating" with the outcasts and untouchables of society (Mk 2:13-17; Lk 15:1-10); sheltering the homeless and caring for the sick (Mt 25:36), proclaiming the "good news" of liberation to the "poor" (Mt 11:5) and setting free the oppressed (Lk 4:16-21). And because the biblical tradition understands the human person to be a living *body* rather than a *soul* temporarily and somewhat accidentally inhabiting a body, it gives special importance to these "corporal works of mercy."[35] Indeed it is precisely such expressions of social concern that are proposed most frequently and most explicitly by Jesus and his followers as the most authentic criteria of genuine Christian love (Mt 20:31-46; 1 Jn 3:17-19; Jas 2:1-7, 14-17).

3.2. Love Strives after Justice

In a community that has arrived at a structural understanding of society,[36] such expressions of social concern will not be limited to a privatized sharing but will take the form of action for justice—that is, for the transformation of those social, economic, and political structures which hinder the emergence of a just and fraternal society. Aware of the extent to which such structures (the economic, political, and social systems which control the distribution of property, power, and social rank in any given society) determine the configuration of a society and even the consciousness of its members,[37] a structural understanding realizes that the situations of poverty, unfreedom, and oppression that are so much a part of our social experience in India and elsewhere are not just the hazards of history, nor the consequences of ill-will of a few "wicked men," who need only to be converted for all our troubles to end. They result from the working of an impersonal system of property, power, and social relationships, which operate almost independently of the people who serve them. A change of hearts is not enough. Nothing less than a change of structures is needed if exploitation and oppression are truly to end.

Effective love (*agapē*), then, will respond to the needs of the exploited and oppressed neighbor by engaging in action for the removal of the structures that are responsible for such exploitation and oppression. In an unjust society *agapē* inevitably becomes a struggle for justice: it strives "to set free the oppressed" (Lk 4:18). For as the second general assembly of the Synod of Roman Catholic Bishops has affirmed with unusual firmness and clarity, "Love implies an absolute demand for justice, namely a recognition of the dignity and rights of one's neighbor. Justice attains its inner fulness only in love."[38]

3.3. Love Tolerates Violence?

Does love permit the use of violence in its striving after justice? The question is a complex one.[39] Denunciations of violent revolution (but not, be it noted, of the structural violence that provokes them, nor, until recently, of the massive stockpiling of nuclear weapons under the pretext of "deterrence" [a euphemism for nuclear terror], nor even of the right to a first, preemptive nuclear strike which could devastate half the world)[40] continue to emerge from First World churches secure in their positions of alliance and power. They sound empty and unconvincing in a tradition which, since at least the time of Constantine, has not only tolerated violence as a legitimate form of defense (the just war theory), but has initiated aggressive wars of great ruthlessness and brutality. Can we so easily forget the centuries of violence unleashed by the Crusades, which even today can be hailed by a loyal Christian like Henri Daniel-Rops as "one of the outstanding achievements of the mediaeval church"?[41] Or can we (its victims) fail to remember the massive colonial expeditions which set out from Europe, duly legitimized by papal bulls, whose stupendous violence, which wiped out whole peoples from the face of the earth, led to the enslavement of millions and to the impoverishment of whole continents, is blithely dismissed by François Mauriac (a pillar of Roman Catholicism) as merely "the corruption of a great idea"?[42]

How does one reconcile the love commandment of Jesus with opinions like these? Or is it only violence against the "Unyoung, the Uncolored and the Unpoor" that Christians find wrong?[43] It may be of course that our perception of Christian love has changed so radically in the past fifty years that the violence that was encouraged then[44] has become unacceptable today. Perhaps. But may it not also be that the love of enemy proposed by Jesus does not necessarily exclude opposition, even if need be violent opposition, to the evil that this "enemy" does particularly when this evil is directed against a brother whom also I must love and protect?

A structural understanding of society may throw some light on this. Such an understanding locates the root causes of oppression and exploitation not in the ill-will of individual oppressors but in the operation of the exploitative economic and political system to which they belong, and of which they themselves are often the unconscious victims. By distinguishing between the oppressive structure (always to be contexted), and the "oppressor" (always to be loved), such an understanding of society allows us to struggle even violently against an oppressive system, without necessarily ceasing to love those who operate it—particularly since the system dehumanizes both the oppressor and the oppressed, and its destruction is the liberation of both. Paulo Freire is worth listening to on this subject:

> Yet it is paradoxical though it may seem precisely in the response of the oppressed to the violence of their oppressors that a gesture of love may be found. Consciously or unconsciously, the act of rebellion by the oppressed (an act which is always, or nearly always, as violent as the initial violence of the oppressors) can initiate love. . . . As the oppressed, fighting to be human take away the oppressors' power to dominate and to suppress, they restore to the oppressors the humanity they have lost in the exercise of oppression.[45]

4. TO LOVE MEANS TO BE A CHILD OF OUR FATHER IN HEAVEN

But whatever be our response to the tangled question of violence, we cannot evade the obligation of loving our enemies—even when we feel justified in opposing them with violence! The obligation to love every human being, without any exception whatever, is an integral part of our Christian existence. For our Christian existence is constituted by our experience of the Father's unconditional love revealed to us in Jesus. "No one knows the Father," says Jesus, "except the Son and anyone to whom the Son chooses to reveal Him" (Mt 11:27), and Paul can tell the Christians of Rome: "You have received the Spirit of Sonship, [for] when we cry '*Abba!* Father!' it is the Spirit himself bearing witness with our spirit that we are children of God" (Rom 8:15-16). But to be a child of God means to be "like God"—not indeed by aspiring to a divine knowledge of "good and evil," an act of human *hubris* which leads to the destruction of humankind, not to its divinization (Gen 3:1-21), but by loving as God loves. "Love your enemies," Jesus tells us, "so that you may be sons of your Father who is in heaven; for he makes his sun rise on the evil and the good and sends his rain on the just and the unjust" (Mt 5:45). As children of the Father in heaven we love as unconditionally and as universally as he does.

The prescriptive form of this saying can be misleading. It might suggest that our divine childship is somehow conditioned by our ability to love our enemies. "Love your enemies . . . 'so that' (*hopōs*) you may be the sons of your Father who is in heaven" (Mt 5:45). But this is to misunderstand the subtle Greek construction. What is really being said is that by loving our enemies we show ourselves to be children of our Father in heaven: our love for our enemies is an indication that we are indeed God's own. There is a close parallel to this in Luke's story of the sinful woman who anoints the feet of Jesus in the house of Simon the Pharisee (Lk 7:36-50). "Therefore I tell you," Jesus tells the Pharisee, "her sins, which are many, are forgiven, for (*hoti*) she has loved much" (Lk 7:47). As the parable of the Two Debtors which Jesus has just narrated shows, this is not to be understood as meaning that the woman has earned her forgiveness by her love: so that much has been forgiven her *because* she loved much. Rather the great love she is able to show is a sign that her many sins have indeed been forgiven. As the Jerusalem Bible correctly, if somewhat awkwardly, translates it: "For this reason I tell you that her sins, her many sins, must have been forgiven her, or she would not have shown such great love" (Lk 7:47). Her great love thus proves that her many sins have been forgiven—just as the little love shown by Simon the Pharisee shows how little forgiveness he has received. It is he (and this is the sharp, ironical point of the story) who is in need of forgiveness, and not the woman whom he has so contemptuously dismissed as a "sinner."

Ultimately, then, our *agapē* is rooted in our experience of God as *Abba;* for to experience God as Father is to experience every human being as brother or sister. Our love for neighbor is a consequence of our experience of God's love for us. As 1 John has put it with marvelous concision: "We love because he first loved us" (1 Jn 4:19).

The love taught by Jesus, then, is a love which comes from the Father and can indeed come only from him. God alone is the source of love, of all love— "every sort of love, the highest and the lowest, the poorest and the richest, the most ridiculous and the most sublime, all sorts of love," as David, the author, in Ingmar Bergman's great film *Through a Glass Darkly* explains to his alienated son at the film's end.[46] This is a cinematographic transposition of what 1 John has to say in what is perhaps the most profound comment ever made on Jesus' teaching on love: "Beloved let us love one another; for love is of God and he who loves is born of God and knows God. He who does not love does not know God; for God is love" (1 Jn 4:7-8). Here we have the ultimate, depth dimension of love in the teaching of Jesus.

NOTES

1. Victor Paul Furnish, *The Love Command in the New Testament* (London: SCM Press, 1973), 23.

2. Ibid., 24-25; also Günther Bornkamm, "Das Doppelgebot der Liebe," in his *Geschichte und Glaube I* (Munich: Kaiser, 1968), 27-45.

3. Rudolf Bultmann, *The History of the Synoptic Tradition* (Oxford: Blackwell, 1963), 55.

4. See Furnish, *Love Command,* 62; Rudolf Pesch, *Das Markusevangelium,* 2 (Freiburg: Herder, 1977), 247.

5. Furnish, *Love Command,* 62.

6. Klaus Berger, *Die Gesetzesauslegung Jesu,* Teil I: *Markus und Parallelen* (Neukirchen-Vluyn: Neukirchener Verlag, 1972), 203; Pesch, *Markusevangelium,* 244-45.

7. If Mark gives us a considerably expanded version of his original source (a variant of the one used by Matthew) adapted to the needs of a Jewish Hellenistic community (see Pesch, *Markusevangelium,* 244), Luke has slightly abbreviated his Q-source (which he

has in common with Matthew) to provide an introduction to his parable of the Good Samaritan (see Bultmann, *History,* 23).

8. See *b. Shab.* 31a: "What is hateful to you do not do to your fellow: that is the whole law; all the rest is explanation; go and learn!" (quoted from C. G. Montefiore and H. Loewe, *A Rabbinic Anthology* [New York: Schocken, 1974], 200).

9. *Sifra* on Lev 19:18, quoted in George Foot Moore, *Judaism in the First Centuries of the Christian Era, II* (New York: Schocken, 1971), 85.

10. See Andreas Nissen, *Gott und der Nächste im antiken Judentum* (Tübingen: Mohr, 1974), 230-44, esp. 240.

11. Ibid., 236-37.

12. Gerhard Barth, "Matthew's Understanding of the Law," in *Tradition and Interpretation in Matthew,* ed. G. Bornkamm et al. (London: SCM Press, 1963), 77-78; and Nissen, *Gott und der Nächste,* 337-42, for a detailed presentation of the evidence.

13. *B. Hag.* 5a, quoted in Barth, "Matthew's Understanding," 78 n.1.

14. *Aboth* II, I in the explanatory paraphrase of R. Traders Herford, *The Ethics of the Talmud: Sayings of the Fathers* (New York: Schocken, 1962), 39.

15. Not in the sense of exegetical dependence, as if the whole Law could be exegetically deduced through the love commandment, but in the more basic sense that love is the "essence" of all the commandments. The Law thus "hangs" on the love commandment as a door hangs on its hinges (Barth, "Matthew's Understanding," 77-78).

16. Furnish, *Love Command,* 31.

17. Ceslas Spicq, *Agape in the New Testament,* vol. 1, *Agape in the Synoptic Gospels* (St. Louis: Herder, 1963), 28.

18. Ibid., 27-28.

19. Furnish, *Love Command,* 27.

20. Spicq, *Agape,* 137: "It is perhaps surprising to realize that the duty of loving one's neighbor seems to prevail over duty toward God."

21. Furnish, *Love Command,* 27.

22. Ibid., 28; Berger, *Gesetzesauslegung Jesu,* 170.

23. Soares-Prabhu, "Love Commandment."

24. See G. Van Leeuwen, *Le développement du sens social en Israël avant l'ère chrétienne* (Assen: Van Gorcum, 1955), for a comprehensive and perceptive account of Israel's social concern.

25. See Paul Carus, *The Gospel of Buddha: According to Old Records* (Tucson: Omen Press, 1972), 90-94.

26. O. J. F. Seitz, "Love Your Enemies," *New Testament Studies* 16 (1969–70), 39-54, esp. 52. See also Heinz Schürmann, *Das Lukasevangelium, I* (Freiburg: Herder, 1969), 345-46, for a closely argued demonstration of priority of the Lukan form of these verses.

27. Seitz, "Love Your Enemies," 42.

28. Martin Noth, *Leviticus* (London: SCM Press, 1965), 144; D. Kellermann, "*gur,*" in *Theological Dictionary of the Old Testament,* ed. G. J. Botterweck and H. Ringgren (Grand Rapids: Eerdmans, 1974–), 2:443.

29. Seitz, "Love Your Enemies," 48.

30. Furnish, *Love Command,* 48.

31. Assertiveness involves "standing up for personal rights and expressing thoughts, feelings and beliefs in direct, honest and appropriate ways which do not violate another person's rights." It thus implies "respect for oneself, that is, expressing one's needs and

rights, as well as respect for the other person's needs and rights" (Arthur J. Lange and Patricia Jakubowski, *Responsible Assertive Behaviour* [Champaign, Ill.: Research Press, 1976], 7). The ministry of Jesus is of course a superb example of responsible assertive behavior; so is Gandhi's *satyāgraha.*

32. Karl Menninger, quoted in Furnish, *Love Command,* 16.

33. Seitz, "Love Your Enemies," 138.

34. The verb *agapan* ("to love") occurs in the New Testament 141 times, the noun *agapē* ("love") 117 times. This alone shows how significant the word is for the New Testament teaching on love. Whether this large use of *agapē* is indeed special to the New Testament, and whether the word as used in the New Testament has consistently a specific meaning which never coincides with that of *philia,* are disputed questions. See the well-documented discussion in Ceslas Spicq, *Notes de lexicographie néotestamentaire, I,* Orbis Biblicus et Orientalis 2211 (Fribourg: Editions Universitaires, 1978), 15-30.

35. See Gerhard von Rad, *Genesis* (London: SCM Press, 1972), 77; Hans Walter Wolff, *Anthropology of the Old Testament* (London: SCM Press, 1974), 10.

36. See the excellent analysis of "the two basic perspectives for looking at social affairs, *actor-oriented* and *structure-oriented,* in Johan Galtung, *The True Worlds: A Transnational Perspective* (New York: Free Press, 1981), 41-44.

37. "It is becoming more and more evident that the structures of our society are among the principal formative influences in our world, shaping man's ideas and feelings, shaping their most intimate desires and aspirations; in a word shaping man himself." These words from Decree 4, no. 40 of the 32nd General Congregation of the Society of Jesus (Dec. 1974–Mar. 1975) express a truth now a commonplace in sociology, but which has been rarely expressed with such clarity and vigor in an ecclesiastical document.

38. *Justice in the World* (Statement of the Second General Assembly of the Synod of Bishops, November 1971), n. 34, quoted in Joseph Gremillion, *The Gospel of Peace and Justice* (Maryknoll, N.Y.: Orbis, 1976), 520.

39. See J. G. Davies, *Christians, Politics and Violent Revolution* (Maryknoll, N.Y.: Orbis, 1976), for a sound theological discussion; John Ferguson, *The Politics of Love: The New Testament and Non-Violent Revolution* (Cambridge: James Clarke, 1973), for a "pacifist" interpretation of the New Testament evidence; and Jean-Michel Hornus, *It Is Not Lawful for Me to Fight: Early Christian Attitudes Toward War, Violence and the State* (Scottdale, Penn.: Herald Press, 1980), for a serious study of Christian attitudes toward violence in the pre-Constantine Church.

40. On structural violence, see the comment of Galtung, *True Worlds,* 107: "We assume that structural violence is tremendously significant because of its two major forms of expression . . . *repression* (or uniformity, as the opposite of diversity, pluralism, freedom) and *exploitation* (as the opposite of equity). In extreme cases structural violence may be so repressive that it virtually leads to the psychological death of the people exposed to it, or so exploitative that it may lead to their physical death by keeping them well below the limit of fundamental need satisfaction." Another and perhaps more familiar term for structural violence is "institutional violence."

41. Henri Daniel-Rops, *Cathedral and Crusade: Studies of the Medieval Church* (London: Dent, 1957), 481.

42. Quoted in Maurice Merleau-Ponty, *Signs* (Evanston: Northwestern University Press, 1974), 324. As Merleau-Ponty bitingly remarks: "But the idea is in François Mauriac's mind . . . the Vietnamese themselves have above all seen the 'corruption' of it"

(ibid.). Significantly "good" Catholics like Mauriac have consistently been avid defenders of Western imperialism.

43. See Colin Morris, *Unyoung Uncoloured Unpoor* (London: Epworth Press, 1969)—a fascinating polemic against the attitudes of the Western Christian "establishment."

44. J. Derek Holmes in his *The Papacy in the Modern World* (New York: Crossroad, 1981) gives a telling example. "After the defeat of the Abbyssinians [in a particular dirty colonial war, waged with great barbarism—including terror bombing and the use of poison gas—against a defenceless and wholly inoffensive people, who posed no threat whatever to their invaders], the Archbishop of Rhodes was sent to Addis Ababa as Apostolic Visitor and celebrated a Pontifical Mass during which he 'saluted all the heroic soldiers of the Italian army which the world admires, but at which Heaven has no need to marvel since it is their ally.'" One could hardly hope for a clearer legitimation of a nakedly aggressive war (p. 70).

45. Paulo Freire, *Pedagogy of the Oppressed* (Harmondsworth: Penguin Books, 1972), 32.

46. Quoted in Robert E. Lauder, *The Love Explosion: Human Experience and the Christian Mystery* (New York: Living Flame Press, 1979), 26.

14

SPEAKING TO "ABBA"

Prayer as Petition and
Thanksgiving in the Teaching of Jesus

"Christianity," Lucien Cerfaux reminds us, "did not come into the world as an explosion of prayer."[1] The world of Jesus, both the Jewish world in which he lived and the larger Hellenistic world of which it was an integral but unassimilated part, was rich in the forms and formulae of prayer. The New Testament had little to add to this. It contributed nothing to the splendid sacrificial liturgy of the Second Temple, nor to the immense "treasure house of prayers of imperishable worth,"[2] stored up in the Psalter of the Hebrew Bible, nor to the secret but profoundly moving rites which led the initiates of the mystery religions to their blissful experience of salvation. Compared to all this (and even more when compared to the vast wealth and variety of the rituals, meditation techniques, and forms of prayer that Hinduism has to offer),[3] New Testament teaching on prayer is meagre indeed!

1. GETTING TO KNOW THE TEACHING
OF JESUS ON PRAYER

This teaching goes back to Jesus, whose own experience of prayer is the basis of what the New Testament teaches. For in spite of the great variety of traditions in the New Testament, orientations on prayer remain strikingly unchanged all through the book. John has obviously (re-)formulated the prayers of Jesus in the light of his own theology of glory. We see this when we look at the typically Johannine vocabulary of the prayer of Jesus at the tomb of Lazarus (Jn 11:41-42), or when we compare the "Johannine Gethsemane" (Jn 12:27f) with that of the Synoptics (Mk 14:36), or Jesus' prayer of thanksgiving in John (Jn 17:1-26)

This article first appeared in *Concilium* 229 (1990): 31-43.

with his thanksgiving in Matthew (Mt 11:25f). Both of the Synoptic prayers of Jesus (petition and thanksgiving) are thus to be found in John, though in an altered form! Again, John gives an explicitly christological coloring ("in my name") to Jesus' instruction that we ask God for what we need (Jn 14:13; 15:16; 16:23). But the Johannine sayings are clearly related to those in the Synoptics, because their basic form (the "ask and you will receive" of Jn 16:24) obviously echoes the "ask and it will be given to you" of the Synoptics (Mt 7:7 = Lk 11:9).[4] In Paul too, though the emphasis shifts from petition to thanksgiving,[5] the basic structure of Christian prayer (moving from confident petition to joyous thanksgiving) remains unchanged. And the instructions on the efficacy of petitionary prayer that we find in 1 Jn 3:22 ("we receive from him whatever we ask"), and in Jas 1:5 ("if any one of you lacks wisdom, let him ask God . . . and it will be given to him") are so similar to the Q saying in Mt 7:7 = Lk 11:9 ("ask and it will be given to you") that we surely have here a tradition which has been transmitted with great fidelity all through New Testament times.

We find in the various books of the New Testament, then, a unified and consistent teaching on prayer, and this is best explained by assuming that this teaching is the result of a developing but basically undistorted tradition that goes back to Jesus himself. Access to the origins of this tradition (the teaching of Jesus) is provided by the Synoptic Gospels, whose teachings on prayer reproduce a very early stage of it. We may with some confidence, then, rely on the Synoptic Gospels to tell us what Jesus taught about prayer.

The Synoptic Gospels give us (1) the text of three prayers recited by Jesus at peak moments in his life: his glad cry of thanksgiving at the return of his disciples from their successful mission (Lk 10:21-22 = Mt 11:25f); his anguished petition for a reprieve from his approaching death at Gethsemane (Mk 14:36 = Mt 26:39 = Lk 22:42); and his cry of abandonment on the cross (Mk 15:34 = Mt 27:46).[6] They also describe (2) a model prayer which Jesus taught his disciples as "their" prayer (Lk 11:2-4 = Mt 6:9-13). And they hand down (3) instructions on prayer (sayings and parables) given by Jesus, in which Jesus does not spell out a method for praying (as an oriental *guru* would do) but tells us what to pray for, and what attitude to adopt when praying. We are to pray for the Kingdom (Lk 11:2), which comes as the fulfillment of all our needs (Mt 6:33); and we are not to pray ostentatiously like the Pharisees (Mt 6:5-6), nor wordily like the gentiles (Mt 6:7-8), but with an attitude of faith (Mk 11:24 = Mt 21:22), of forgiveness (Mk 11:25), of tireless perseverance (Lk 18:1-8) and of oneness in community (Mt 18:19-20).

2. THE BASIS OF THE TEACHING OF JESUS ON PRAYER

Here, precisely, lies the distinctive feature of Jesus' teaching on prayer. Jesus does not give us a new form of prayer—except for the Lord's Prayer, which is more a model than a formula. He himself and his followers after him, continue (to this day) to use the prayer forms of the Hebrew Bible, especially the Psalms. Nor does he elaborate new techniques for praying. Prayer techniques are poorly developed in Christianity (as compared to, say, Hinduism or Buddhism), and where they exist they are usually merely the accumulated experience of generations of praying Christians, put together without much vigor.[7] Instead, what Jesus gives us is a new attitude in prayer, emerging out of a new experience of God. All Jesus' prayer and all his teaching on prayer flow out of his experience of God as *Abba*. It is this which explains the specific orientation of the prayer of Jesus, and its disconcerting neglect of "technique" in favor of "attitude."

For Jesus experiences God not as the all-pervading Absolute (*brahman*) who is the real "self" (*ātman*) of the cosmos and of every individual thing in it, but as the loving Parent (*Abba*) who has gifted itself in love to humankind. God is therefore to be encountered not through "meditation," that is, through a sustained introspective awareness that leads to the perception of "the Self in the self" (*Bhagavadgītā* vi.20), but through "prayer," that is, through an interpersonal "conversation" with God, in which love is experienced and given, and relationships of intimacy founded.[8] Meditation may need highly refined techniques. But techniques are not usually helpful in a conversation, except perhaps at the start, to set the conversation going. Once that is done the dynamics of personal interaction take over, and what is needed is not a technique but an attitude of mutual openness and trust.

The basic attitude which Jesus looks for in his followers at prayer has been imaged by him in the figure of a child. "Truly I say to you," he says solemnly, "whoever does not receive the Kingdom of God like a child, shall not enter it" (Mk 10:15 = Lk 18:17). To receive the Kingdom of God like a child means to accept God's saving love with the openness, the trust, the freedom, and the spontaneity with which a child responds to life. It means to accept fully (as children do) the giftedness of life—not to count on one's merits like the Pharisee at prayer in the parable of Jesus (Lk 18:9-14), nor to cling to one's possessions like the rich man who wants to follow Jesus in the Gospel story (Mk 10:17-22),[9] but to be simple, unself-righteous, trusting, and free.

Jesus requires this attitude of his followers because it is the obverse side of the specific experience of God he has given them. To the foundational Christian experience of God as a loving Parent (*Abba*), there corresponds (dialectically) the basic Christian attitude of receiving the Kingdom like a child. To the ongoing Christian experience of God's absolute paternal, or better, maternal care (for it is the mother not the father who feeds and clothes) there corresponds (dialectically) the continuing Christian attitude of a care-free and childlike trustfulness that does not worry about the morrow (Mt 6:25-34). Experience and attitude are thus related to each other dialectically. God is experienced as a loving and a caring Parent only when we receive the Kingdom of God (God's saving love) like a trusting child; but we can receive the Kingdom of God like a child only when we have experienced the provident love of God.

It is from this dialectic of experience and attitude that Christian prayer emerges. Because the Christian experiences God as a loving Parent and relates to God as a trusting child, Christian prayer will be a child's prayer. Such prayer will be primarily a prayer of petition and of thanksgiving, because asking and thanking (specially asking) are normal forms in a child's conversation. We understand, then, why the teaching of Jesus on prayer, as revealed in the Synoptic Gospels, insists so strongly on petition and (to a lesser extent) on thanksgiving.

3. PETITION IN THE TEACHING OF JESUS

3.1. The Lord's Prayer

When his disciples ask Jesus to teach them to pray (Lk 11:2), he does not give them a technique for praying, but, typically, teaches them a prayer of petition (Mt 6:9-13 = Lk 11:2-4). In its original form, as uttered by Jesus, the prayer would have probably sounded as follows:[10]

> *Abba!*
> May your name be holy,
> May your kingdom come;
> Our bread for tomorrow, give us today;
> Forgive us our debts as we now forgive our debtors;
> And do not allow us to fall away from you.

The prayer begins by addressing God as *Abba*, and so setting the tone for the familial mood of the "conversation" which is to follow. The confidence expressed and engendered by this intimate form of address leads smoothly to the five petitions of the prayer. Of these the first two, the so-called "you-petitions," ask the Father to make his name holy and to allow his Kingdom to come—parallel ways of saying the same thing. They prepare for the three so-called "we-petitions" that follow. This they do in two ways. The first of the "you-petitions" ("may your name be holy") can be read as a form of acknowledgment and praise, which in a prayer of petition could serve to dispose God to respond favorably to the petitions that follow. More significantly, the second "you-petition" ("may your kingdom come") prays for the realization of God's eschatological salvation, whose concrete dimensions are then spelled out in the three "we-petitions" that follow. In these we pray for our "bread for tomorrow" (that is, for physical and spiritual sustenance); for the forgiveness which we acknowledge is dialectically related to our forgiving people who have injured us (that is, for a right relationship with God and with "neighbor"); and for preservation from the threat of apostasy (that is, for lasting fidelity to God). In the three "we-petitions" we thus pray for the concrete realization of the new eschatological existence in love given to us by Jesus (the Kingdom), in the economic, social, and religious areas of our lives. It would be difficult to find a prayer which says so much so briefly. The prayer is short, simple, comprehensive, and profound.

This extraordinary prayer taught by Jesus to his disciples is truly the "Lord's Prayer"! It reveals the structure of Jesus' own understanding of what prayer is. All his teaching on prayer must therefore be understood in its light. But the Lord's Prayer, like all Jesus' teaching and preaching, in word and in deed, is centered wholly on the Kingdom. It is in terms of the Kingdom, then, that the prayers Jesus says and the instructions of prayer that he gives are to be understood.

3.2. *Jesus' Instructions on Prayer*

In the Synoptic Gospels, the instructions of Jesus on prayer (as distinct from the prayers he says, or the model prayer he gives) can be put together in four groups. There are: (1) three Lukan parables (the Friend at Midnight in Lk 11:5-8; the Importunate Widow in Lk 18:1-8; and the Pharisee and the Tax Collector in Lk 18:9-14), which urge us to pray insistently, and with humility, in the confident assurance that our prayer will be heard, because it is addressed to a God who cares for us much more than any human friend; (2) a pair of sayings in Mark which teach the need of praying with faith if our petition is to be heard (Mk 11:24 = Mt 21:22), and with forgiveness if our own sins are to be forgiven (Mk 11:25); (3) a saying in Matthew (Mt 18:19f) which assures us that the "Father in heaven" will grant anything asked for by "two or three" gathered together in the name of Jesus; and (4) two sayings from Q, one of which (Mt 9:37 = Lk 10:2) is an apocalyptic exhortation urging us to pray that God may send us helpers for the promising eschatological mission entrusted to us, while the other (Mt 7:7-11 = Lk 11:9-13) is a well-formulated wisdom admonition recommending petitionary prayer.

Of all these it is the last, the Q wisdom admonition, that is the most interesting and important, because it provides us with a compact but comprehensive summary of Jesus' own teaching on prayer of petition. The prayer parables in Luke (which probably also go back to Jesus himself) give us powerful confirmatory illustrations of what the admonition teaches, but they add nothing new. Nor do the sayings on prayer in Matthew and Mark (probably community creations), because they are merely concrete applications of this teaching to specific situations in the early Church. It is the admonition in Matthew's Sermon on the Mount (Mt 7:7-11 = Lk 11:9-13) that tells us most clearly what Jesus has to say about petitionary prayer.

In its original form the Q admonition would probably have read:[11]

A. Ask and it will be given to you
   Seek and you will find
   Knock and the door will be opened to you.

B. For everyone who asks receives,
And one who seeks, finds,
And to the one who knocks the door will be opened.

C. Who is the person among you,
Who when his son asks him for a loaf of bread will give him a stone?
Or when he asks him for a fish will give him a snake?
If then you, being evil, know how to give good gifts to your children,
How much more will your Father in heaven give good things to those
who ask him?

The passage is beautifully structured. It begins (A) with a thrice-repeated exhortation (ask-seek-knock) to petitionary prayer. The exhortation is motivated (B) through a thrice-repeated assertion that petition will always be answered. Exhortation and motivation are parallel but not tautologous, because the emphasis shifts from petition ("ask") in A to the concession of the petition ("you will receive") in B. The admonition concludes (C) by setting out the ultimate theological basis for the efficacy of petitionary prayer. Two parallel illustrations from everyday life, formulated as a pair of rhetorical questions, build up an *a fortiori* argument, which argues from the experienced benevolence of human parents (Who would give their children a stone instead of a loaf of bread, or a snake instead of a fish?) to the much greater readiness of God to give "good things" to those (God's children!) who ask for them.

With its well-rounded structure, its authoritative tone, its rootedness in the experiences of God as *Abba*, its parabolic form and rhythmic style, and its close agreement with the social and linguistic milieu of pre-70 C.E. Judaism, this wisdom admonition is a unit which has all the marks of being an authentic saying of Jesus. It draws our attention to the great importance given to petition in the teaching of Jesus on prayer. Indeed, almost all the sayings on prayer reported in the Synoptic Gospels are about prayer of petition; so that "to pray" (*proseuchesthai*) in the Gospels is almost synonymous with "to ask" (*aitein, deisthai, erōtan, parakalein*). Such prayer, Jesus assures us, is always effective. Its effectiveness is affirmed repeatedly in formulations which shock us by their forcefulness. "Everyone who asks receives," says Jesus, with a categorical firmness that allows no restriction of limit or condition. His affirmation that prayer is heard is as universal and as absolute as it could possibly be.

Elsewhere in the Gospels conditions are sometimes placed on prayer: rarely in the Synoptics (Mk 11:24; Mt 18:19-20), generally in John (Jn 14:13; 15:16; 1 Jn 3:22).[12] These are usually prudential comments of the early Church, which tone down but do not take away the radicalness of Jesus' affirmation. What they tell us is that the efficacy of petitionary prayer is enhanced by insistent perseverance in prayer (Lk 18:1-8), carried out in the attitude of a faith so trusting that it believes that the petition prayed for has already been granted (Mk 11:24), and supported by a community consensus (Mt 18:19-20). But the efficacy of petitionary prayer is not dependent on these dispositions of the person praying. It derives, ultimately, wholly from the benevolence of God, who because God is *Abba*, gives "good things" to all those who ask. The dispositions mentioned in the Gospels as "conditions" for efficacious prayer do not, in fact, dispose God to give: they dispose the one who asks to receive.

3.3. *The Problem of Unanswered Prayer*

Such teaching on prayer of petition poses a problem which is experienced by all those who pray and which has often been expressed with great poignancy in the prayers of mystics and saints. It is the problem of unanswered prayer. If everyone who asks receives, how is it that so many (often those most in need) do not get what they pray for? Is not the teaching of Jesus unrealistic here—the expression of a primitive, childish naiveté, rather than of a mature if childlike faith, appropriate to a world come of age? In part, an answer is given by Jesus himself. For his prayer in Gethsemane is a dramatic example of unanswered prayer. The way Jesus prays here suggests that all the prayer of petition he commends contains (like his own prayer) an unstated condition: "not what I will but what you will" (Mk 14:36). We respond to God's unconditional love for us by placing in God a trust so absolute that our prayer is always: "Your will be done." For God's will, we believe, is indeed our peace.

To put it in another way, all Jesus' teaching on petitionary prayer is to be understood in the light of the Lord's Prayer, which, I have suggested, determines the horizon of Jesus' own understanding of prayer. But the Lord's Prayer is wholly prayer for the Kingdom. When therefore Jesus exhorts us to ask, to seek, and to knock, it is not for casual "favors" that he wants us to pray. He is urging us to pray for the Kingdom of God (his sole preoccupation), which, as the new existence in love gifted to us by God, does in fact fulfill every aspiration of human life. Like the petitions of the Lord's Prayer, all our petitions are ultimately paraphrases of the one great petition: "May your kingdom come." As such, they are always answered—but in God's way, not in ours, as Mahatma Gandhi has aptly said.[13] God does indeed give "good things" (the blessings of the Kingdom) to all those who ask (Mt 7:11).

4. THANKSGIVING IN THE TEACHING OF JESUS

Prayer, understood as petition, is often associated with thanksgiving in the New Testament. This is especially so in Paul. His letters almost always begin with a thanksgiving, which is part of the normal form of a letter in the Hellenistic world, but which Paul usually expands well beyond conventional limits to express his overflowing gratitude (Phil 1:3-11; 1 Thess 1:2-10). And his letters often end with an exhortation to "pray constantly" and "give thanks in all circumstances" (1 Thess 5:17-18; cf. Phil 4:6; 1 Tim 2:1), through which he attempts to draw his readers into his spirituality of continual petition and thanksgiving.

This association of petition and thanksgiving is not accidental. It reflects the close relationship that exists between these two streams of prayer, both of which emerge from the same basic attitude of childlike faith, with which the followers of Jesus respond to the revelation of God as *Abba*. This attitude implies both an awareness of our powerlessness to merit love (so that we are driven to "ask" for the Kingdom), and the awareness that love has been freely gifted to us by God (so that we are moved to thank God for the "good things" we have been given). Prayer of thanksgiving in the New Testament, then, is to be seen not merely as an occasional episode, celebrating petitions that have been answered, but (as is clear from Paul) as the expression of an abiding attitude which is constitutive of the Christian life.

4.1. Thanksgiving in the Gospels

It is, then, surprising that Jesus' teaching on prayer, which has so much to say about petition, is so poor on thanksgiving. True Aramaic, the language spoken by Jesus, has (like Hebrew) no special word for "thanks." But the Hebrew Bible is rich in thanksgiving, which is expressed in specialized literary forms like the thanksgiving song (*tôdāh*); or through appropriate formulae like "to bless (*bārak*) the Lord." Such Jewish turns of phrase do in fact occur in the Synoptic Gospels (Mk 6:41; 8:7; Lk 1:46-55, 64, 68-79; 2:28), together with occasional occurrences of the Greek *eucharistein* ("to thank") and its cognates (Mk 8:6; 14:23; Lk 17:16; 18:11). But they are infrequent. What the Synoptic Gospels have to say about thanksgiving is meagre.

The Infancy Narratives in Luke have two early Christian canticles, typically Jewish songs of thanksgiving, which celebrate key moments in saving history: the birth of the Baptist (Lk 1:68-79), and the conception of Jesus (Lk 1:46-55). All three Synoptics (following Mark) show Jesus pronouncing (as a good Jew would) thanksgiving over food in the two feeding miracles (Mk 6:41; 8:6), and at the Last Supper (Mk 14:22-23). Matthew and Luke give us a prayer of thanksgiving recited by Jesus (Mt 11:25-26 = Lk 10:21). And Luke alone has a saying of Jesus on thanksgiving (the only such saying in the Synoptic tradition), in which Jesus complains that of the ten lepers he had healed, only a Samaritan has come back to give him thanks and so find not just healing but salvation (Lk 17:17-19).

We might be inclined to take the description of the institution of the Eucharist at the Last Supper of the Lord (Mt 26:26-29; Mk 14:22-25; Lk 22:17-20) as the most important reference to thanksgiving in the Gospels. For the Eucharist, as its name indicates, is for us the great rite of Christian thanksgiving. But it is doubtful whether the Eucharist had this significance in the Gospels. There the giving of thanks is not central to the rite, but is merely a customary grace before meals which prepares for the "breaking of bread" which follows. It is this gesture of oneness and sharing which is central and serves to designate the Eucharist in New Testament times (Acts 2:42, 46; 20:7; 1 Cor 10:16). It is not the Gospel texts on the institution of the Eucharist, then, nor their foreshadowing in the two accounts of the feeding miracle worked by Jesus (both of which have been edited to conform to the Institution Narrative)[14] that will teach us what Jesus has to say about thanksgiving. For this we must turn to the prayer of thanksgiving attributed to him in Matthew and in Luke (Mt 11:25-26 = Lk 10:21) and supplement what we learn there by what is said about thanksgiving in the canticles of Lk 1-2, and in the saying on thanksgiving which concludes the Lukan story of the Ten Lepers (Lk 17:17-19).

4.2. The Thanksgiving Prayer of Jesus

As reconstructed by Siegried Schulz from its almost identical versions in Matthew and Luke (Mt 11:25-26 = Lk 10:21), the prayer would have read:[15]

> In that same hour Jesus said: "I praise you Father, Lord of heaven and earth, because you have hidden these things from the wise and understanding, and revealed them to babes. Yes, Father, for such was your gracious will."

With its concluding "Yes, Father . . . ," which forms an inclusion with the "I praise you Father . . ." of the opening address, the prayer is a rounded unit, complete in itself. It was originally distinct from the revelatory word ("no one knows the Son except the Father") to which it has been attached in Q (Mt 11:27 = Lk 10:22). In itself and separated from the revelatory word—the Hellenistic vocabulary and explicit Christology make it unlikely that the revelatory word was pronounced by Jesus—the prayer of thanksgiving could well be authentic. It is thoroughly Jewish in form, and its content reflects both the attitude of Jesus, with its clear option for the poor, as well as the situation of his mission, which was successful among the "little ones" but not among the religious and intellectual elite. The sharpness of the opposition between the "babes" to whom "these things" (the presence of eschatological salvation in the words and deeds of Jesus) have been revealed and the "wise and understanding" from whom they have been hidden, recalls the uncompromising radicality of so much of the teaching of Jesus which inevitably leads to the separation of conflicting groups. Jesus thus opposes God and Mammon (Mt 6:26), poor and rich (Mt 6:20-24), tax collector and Pharisee (Lk 18:9-14), old law and new (Mt 5:21-48), defilement from outside and defilement from within (Mk 7:15), observance of law and practice of love (Mk 3:1-5). The Q prayer of thanksgiving thus stands well within the specific perspective of Jesus, and may safely be attributed to him.

The prayer begins (as all the prayers of Jesus do) by addressing God as

"Father" (*Abba*). The qualification "Lord of heaven and earth" which follows is (like the addition to the invocation in Matthew's version of the Lord's Prayer) an insertion by the Jewish Christian community, using a typical rabbinic formula. Yet the insertion is appropriate to the mood of the prayer. For in it Jesus thanks God not for personal favors done to him, but for the form which God's saving action takes in history. The thanksgiving of Jesus is thanksgiving for salvation history!

In this Jesus stands well within the biblical tradition. All through the Hebrew Bible, "thanksgiving responds to the unique work of God. More or less confusedly, every particular kindness of Yahweh is always felt as one moment of a grand history in the process of realization. Thanksgiving carries biblical history and prolongs it in eschatological hope."[16] This orientation continues through Jesus into the Christian community. We find it in the canticles of the Infancy Narratives of Luke, which are good examples of early Jewish Christian piety. In them, Zechariah gives thanks to God not just for the birth of a son, but because this birth shows that the "Lord God of Israel has visited and redeemed his people" (Lk 1:68). And Mary's song of thanksgiving too, which begins by thanking God for the favor done to her (Lk 1:46-49), goes on to thank God for the definitive liberation of his people which this gracious act of God has started (Lk 1:50-55).

The story of the Ten Lepers in Luke (17:11-19) adds a further dimension to this. The Samaritan who returns to thank Jesus is told: "Rise up and go, your faith has brought you salvation" (Lk 17:19). Thanksgiving is here identified with saving faith. The story with its double saying of Jesus, and its distinctively Lukan vocabulary, has little likelihood of being historical. As it stands it is largely a Lukan composition. But what it says about thanksgiving is fully consonant with the teaching of Jesus. For the point it makes is that, being an expression of faith, thanksgiving (like petition) is a constitutive element of Christian life.

4.3. The Problems of Prayer and Action

There is a danger, obviously, that such a life, built on petition and thanksgiving, could lead to passivity and fatalism. Prayer of petition can easily become a substitute for effective action, and thanking God in all things can easily lead to a passive acceptance of unjust situations. But this did not happen to Jesus or to Paul. When Jesus urges us to ask for all things with childlike trust, and when Paul invites us to thank God continually, they are not exhorting us from the security of a cloister, but speaking out of the turmoil of intensely active and conflict-filled lives. If prayer was not for them an excuse for inaction, it is because they understood prayer (petition and thanksgiving) as always related to the Kingdom of God and to its realization in history.

For the Kingdom of God is both a gift and a task. God's love for us is shown precisely in its profound respect for human freedom, and in its challenging summons to humankind to assume responsibility for its history. The love of *Abba* is not paternalistic or maternalistic, but a love that fosters responsibility and growth. To pray for the Kingdom means therefore to assume responsibility for our part in the personal, communitarian, and societal revolution that the Kingdom brings. To thank God for salvation history is to acknowledge the demands that history makes on us. And, adapting slightly a well-known maxim of Ignatius of Loyola, to pray as if everything depended on God is also to act as if everything depended on ourselves alone.

NOTES

1. L. Cerfaux, *Recueil Lucien Cerfaux,* Tome 3 (Gembloux: Duculot, 1962), 253.

2. J. Herrmann, in *Theological Dictionary of the New Testatment,* ed. G. Kittel (Grand Rapids: Eerdmans, 1965), 2:798.

3. See M. Dhavamony, "Hindu Prayer," *Studia Missionalia* 24 (1975): 185-92; and K. Mitra, "Cultic Acts in Hinduism," in *Offenbarung als Heilserfahrung im Christentum und Buddhismus,* ed. W. Strolz and A. Ueda (Freiburg: Herder, 1982), 127-44.

4. J. Caba, *La oración de petición: Estudio exegético sobre los evangelios sinópticos y los escritos joaneos,* Analecta Biblica 62 (Rome: Biblical Institute Press, 1974), 310-16.

5. Statistics indicate this. The verbs *aitein* and *deomai,* the two main verbs used for petition in the New Testament, are found (as prayer) about thirty times in the Gospels and fourteen times in Paul. In contrast, *eucharistein* ("to thank") is found only eleven times in the Gospels as against twenty-four times in Paul; and the cognate noun *eucharistia* ("thanksgiving") is not found in the Gospels at all, though it occurs twelve times in Paul.

6. Of the two other prayers attributed to Jesus in the Synoptic Gospels, Lk 23:34 is textually doubtful. Even if authentic, it would, like Lk 23:46, be a Lukan composition formulated to make the death of Jesus as paradigm for Christian martyrdom.

7. Even the *Spiritual Exercises* of Ignatius of Loyola, one of the more technical treatises on prayer in the Christian tradition, would appear curiously unfinished to an Indian reader, accustomed to the meticulous instructions on diet, posture, breathing, and methods of concentration that are detailed in Indian texts on meditation.

8. See F. X. D'Sa, *Gott der Dreieine und der All-Ganze: Vorwort zur Begegnung zwischen Christentum und Hinduismus* (Düsseldorf: Patmos, 1987), 79-95, for a comparison between Christian prayer and Indian meditation.

9. The saying on receiving the Kingdom like a child is found in Mark and Luke attached to the story of Jesus blessing little children (Mk 10:13-16 = Lk 18:15-17). This is found immediately before the story of the Rich Young Man in Mk (10:17-22) and in Luke (18:18-23) and immediately after the parable of the Pharisee and the Tax Collector in Luke (18:9-14). In these Gospels, then, the Pharisee of the parable and the rich man of the story serve as negative illustrations of what it means to be a child. They show how a person does not receive the Kingdom of God.

10. J. Jeremias, *The Prayers of Jesus* (London: SCM Press, 1967), 82-107.

11. S. Schulz, *Q: Die Spruchquelle der Evangelisten* (Zurich: Theologischer Verlag, 1972), 161-62.

12. Caba, *La oración de petición,* 310-11.

13. M. K. Gandhi, quoted in S. R. Tikekar, *Epigrams from Gandhiji* (Delhi: Publications Division, 1971), 124.

14. See A. Heising, *Die Botschaft der Brotvermehrung,* Stuttgarter Bibelstudien 15 (Stuttgart: Katholisches Bibelwerk, 1966), 61-68.

15. Schulz, *Q: Die Spruchquelle,* 213-14.

16. A. Ridouard and J. Guillet, "Thanksgiving," in *Dictionary of Biblical Theology,* ed. X. Léon-Dufour (New York: Seabury, 1973).

15

"AS WE FORGIVE"

Interhuman Forgiveness
in the Teaching of Jesus

An Indian reader who leafs through the New Testament endeavoring to catch the specific savor of its spirituality, will, I suspect, be struck by two features in its teaching. He will be impressed by its repeated insistence on active concern for our fellow human beings, and by its frequent invitation to forgive. Neither feature will appear to him as altogether new. Compassion for our fellow human beings, indeed for the whole of creation—*sarvabhūtahite ratāḥ* (passionate delight in the welfare of all beings) in the *Bhagavadgītā's* marvelous formulation (V, 25 XII, 4)—is a mark of the fully liberated individual in both the Hindu and the Buddhist traditions; and nowhere have I found the lesson of forgiveness inculcated so forcibly as in the Buddhist story of the Dīghāvu, the prince of Kosala, who, when he has the murderer of his family and the usurper of his kingdom in his power, spares his life, because he remembers his father's dying advice: "Do not look far (i.e., do not let your hatred last long), do not look near (i.e., do not be quick to fall out with your friends), for hatred is not appeased by hatred; hatred is appeased by non-hatred alone" (*Mahāvagga* X.ii.3-20).[1]

Yet the Indian reader would at once identify active concern and forgiveness as the two poles, positive and negative, of the Dharma of Jesus—of that complex blend of worldview and values, of beliefs and prescriptions, which "holds together" the followers of Jesus, and integrates them into a recognizable community. For if these are not exclusively Christian attitudes, the importance given to them in the teaching of Jesus and the concrete forms they assume in the New Testament give them a specifically Christian significance.

This article first appeared in *Concilium* 184 (1986): 57-66.

Active concern, expressing itself not only in spiritual attitudes of patience, forbearance, acceptance, and benevolence (1 Cor 13:1-5) but in concrete ways of caring for the material needs of the "neighbor" (Mt 25:31-46; 1 Jn 3:17; Jas 1:27), is proposed by the New Testament as the supreme rule of Christian life (Mk 12:28-34; Rom 13:7; Gal 5:14; Jn 13:33; 1 Jn 3:23; 2 Jn 5; Jas 2:8), while forgiveness of those who have injured us (Mk 11:25; Mt 6:14-15) and reconciliation with those whom we have injured (Mt 5:23-24) are laid down as indispensable preconditions for Christian prayer and worship.

1. FORGIVENESS IN THE LORD'S PRAYER

Not surprisingly, then, both active concern for the needs of our neighbor and forgiveness of those who have injured us figure conspicuously in the Lord's Prayer (Mt 6:9-13; Lk 11:2-4)—a prayer given by Jesus to his disciples as a model prayer that would express their distinctive identity as the eschatological community of salvation (Lk 11:1). The prayer thus offers a brief but lucid compendium of the Dharma of Jesus. In its original form as reconstructed by Joachim Jeremias the prayer would probably have read as follows:[2]

> *Abba*!
> May your name be holy,
> May your Kingdom come;
> Our bread for tomorrow, give us today;
> Forgive us our debts as we now forgive our debtors;
> And do not allow us to fall away from you.

The invocation of the prayer (*Abba*) evokes the specific and unique God experience of Jesus (the foundation of his Dharma), which he communicates to his disciples (Mt 11:25-27), so that they too may experience God (and not just name or conceptualize him) as a parent who loves with a caring, unconditional, and all-forgiving love (Mt 6:25-34; Lk 15:11-31). The two you-petitions that follow both pray for the central concern of Jesus, the Kingdom of God, for God's name is made holy when and to the extent that the Kingdom comes. Two we-petitions then spell out two complementary aspects of the Kingdom: they ask for the bread of life and for eschatological forgiveness. The concluding petition reminds us of the precarious conflict situation in which we pray; for our life as disciples of Jesus is lived out in a violent, acquisitive, power-hungry world, which engenders hunger and scorns forgiveness, and which tirelessly attempts to lure or pressurize us away from the values which inspire our prayer.

The two petitions for bread and for forgiveness belong closely together. They take up the two complementary aspects of the Dharma of Jesus (effective concern and reconciliation) that we mentioned above. For the petition for bread images in a concrete symbol our active concern for our brothers and sisters, while the petition for forgiveness expresses our readiness for reconciliation with them. True, the "tomorrow's bread" (*arton epiousion*) for which we pray is not just material bread but the "bread of life," that is, the gift of eschatological salvation. But this includes too the "daily bread" we need to sustain life here and now. For biblical eschatology is not exclusively spiritual or other-worldly; it does not negate history: it fulfills it. And because the Kingdom is not just the paternalistic doling out of benefits (for God is a nurturing, not an indulgent, parent), but is both gift and responsibility, so to pray for bread is to commit ourselves to sharing our bread with and working for bread for all those without bread; just as to pray for the eschatological gift of God's pardon is to commit ourselves to forgive those who have injured us.

The promise to forgive those who have injured us stands out strikingly as the sole reference to human activity in the Lord's Prayer. This, evidently, strongly highlights the significance of forgiveness in the Dharma of Jesus. The ability to forgive is clearly not just one of several items in a repertoire of qualities desirable in a follower of Jesus drawn up by the New Testament! It is rather an absolutely necessary dimension of Christian existence, as eschatological existence in the end-time community. For without such a readiness to forgive (and be forgiven) no eschatological community is possible. God's eschatological pardon (like God's caring love) becomes effective in fashioning a community of forgiveness only when those who have experienced this forgiveness are able to forgive. There can be no "bread of life" unless there is also forgiveness.

2. THE RELIGIOUS DIMENSION OF FORGIVENESS

The readiness to forgive demanded by the Lord's Prayer is therefore not just a happy trait of character or an acquired psychological disposition. It is a religious attitude rooted in the core Christian experience of an utterly forgiving God. The New Testament therefore consistently relates our forgiveness to God's forgiveness. This relation is formulated in several different and sometimes seemingly contradictory ways. Mark seems to make our forgiveness a precondition for God's forgiveness when he exhorts us: "Whenever you stand praying, forgive if you have anything to forgive in order that (*hina*) your Father who is in heaven may forgive you your transgressions" (Mk 11:25). Luke's version of the Lord's Prayer suggests the same in a somewhat more nuanced way: "Forgive us our sins, for we ourselves also (*kai gar autoi*) forgive everyone indebted to us" (Lk 11:4). Matthew formulates this petition of the prayer in an even weaker way: "Forgive us our debts as (*hōs*) we also now forgive our debtors" (Mt 6:12). Our forgiveness now is no longer a condition for meriting God's pardon, but a paradigm for it, or rather a concomitant of it. But in his commentary on the prayer which immediately follows, Matthew singles out this petition for forgiveness, to reformulate it in such a way that the need to forgive in order to be forgiven is emphasized even more strongly than in Mark: "For if you forgive human beings their transgression your heavenly Father will forgive you also; but if you do not forgive people neither will your Father forgive your transgression" (Mt 6:14-15). But the letter to the Colossians reverses this! It makes our forgiving not a condition for but a consequence of the forgiveness we have received from Jesus, whose forgiveness is to be a model for ours: "As the Lord has forgiven you, so you must also forgive" (Col 3:13).

2.1. Human Forgiving and Divine Pardon

How, then, does human forgiving relate to the forgiveness of God? The rather confused and seemingly conflicting formulations of the New Testament (which because they are theologically non-technical formulations are not to be pressed too closely) indicate, I believe, a relation of dialectical interdependence rooted in the unlimited forgiveness of God. All forgiveness, like all love, of which it is a particular form, originates from God, who has loved and forgiven us first (1 Jn 4:7, 21; Lk 7:47; Mt 18:23-35). When we love (and forgive) our neighbor, God's love (and forgiveness) is made perfect in us (1 Jn 4:12). That is, our experience of God's loving forgiveness is intensified, and our capacity to love and to forgive is augmented. Should we refuse to forgive our neighbor, we shall no longer experience the forgiveness of God—not because God ever ceases to love or forgive (he cannot because he *is* forgiving love), but because our failure to respond to his forgiveness by forgiving our neighbor closes us up to his forgiveness and his love. The sun shines always, for it cannot but shine; it is we who hide ourselves away from its warming rays or close our eyes to its light.

Forgiving neighbor as an appropriate response to our experience of God's forgiveness thus sets in movement a spiral of forgiveness. Human forgiveness, originating from the experience of God's love, feeds back into this experience, creating new possibilities of forgiveness. Human forgiveness is thus both a consequence of our being forgiven by God, and (at a second level) a condition for it. That is why New Testament formulations on forgiveness are seemingly contradictory and confused. They describe different moments in the cycle of forgiveness, different segments of the spiral.

2.2. Forgiving and Being Forgiven

It is clear from the New Testament, then, that our forgiveness of our brothers and sisters cannot be the result of a strained effort undertaken in the hope of earning God's forgiveness or for fear of losing it. It is always the outcome of experiencing the free and gracious forgiveness of God: only one who has experienced forgiveness can truly forgive, just as only one who has experienced love can truly love (Lk 7:36-50).

Being forgiven is thus a precondition for forgiving. Jesus' injunction that prayer be preceded by forgiveness (Mk 11:25) is balanced by his instruction that worship, no matter how solemn, be interrupted as soon as the memory of an unresolved conflict intrudes (Mt 5:23-24). This instruction of Jesus is striking. Offering a gift at the altar is a particularly solemn act of worship. Yet Jesus tells us that this is to be stopped at once, the moment one remembers that one has done an injury to a brother or sister—even though an injury so casually and inopportunely remembered could scarcely have been a serious one![3] We are back here at the bedrock of the Dharma of Jesus, in which relationships with God are normally mediated through relationships with our fellow human beings. History is the locus of humankind's encounter with God. We love God by loving neighbor (Mk 12:28-34); we experience God's forgiveness as we forgive our brothers and sisters who have injured us (Mt 6:14-15); we seek reconciliation with God only when we have been reconciled with those whom we have injured (Mt 5:23-24).

Forgiveness in the New Testament thus comprises both a readiness to forgive those who have injured us and a readiness to seek pardon from those we have injured. Both are necessary if our forgiveness is to be genuine, and not degenerate into a typically religious manifestation of self-righteous condescension. For we learn to forgive in a genuine and unforced way only when, acknowledging our own sinfulness, we allow ourselves to experience God's forgiveness by asking for and accepting forgiveness from our brothers and sisters. Inability to accept forgiveness indicates an inability to forgive. In psychological terms, we forgive others only when we have learned to forgive ourselves.

3. THE PSYCHOLOGICAL DIMENSION OF FORGIVENESS

The way to a self-forgiveness that would empower us to forgive others is the cultivation of a non-judgmental attitude toward ourselves and others. Forgiveness is, in fact, equated with non-judging in a significant collection of sayings at the heart of Luke's Sermon on the Plain (Lk 6:36-38):

Be compassionate, even as your Father is compassionate.
Do not judge, and you will not be judged;
Do not condemn and you will not be condemned;
Forgive and you will be forgiven;
Give and it will be given to you. . . .

An unusually pointed formulation of the Christian imperative ("be compassionate [*oiktirmōn*] as your Father is compassionate") is here spelled out concretely in four formally similar sayings. Each has been constructed as a "sentence of holy law," that is, as a form of a divine *lex talionis* in which human behavior in the present is sanctioned by a corresponding divine action (note the theological passive!) in the eschatological future.[4] A pair of parallel prohibitions ("do not judge," "do not condemn") balances a pair of commands ("forgive," "give"), which remind us of the two basic we-petitions (bread and forgiveness) of the Lord's Prayer. Forgiveness is thus linked to a refusal to condemn.

3.1. We Dare Not Condemn Because We Are All Sinners

How, then, are we to arrive at such a non-judgmental attitude that refuses to condemn? Obviously we shall be reluctant to condemn those who have injured us if we realize that we are as sinful as they. The universal sinfulness of all humankind, making all of us without exception debtors to God's forgiving grace, is strongly insisted on by the New Testament (Rom 5:12-21; 1 Jn 1:8-10). Such consciousness of sin is not so much the expression of a pessimistic view of human nature as the result of an extremely radical understanding of what human behavior should be. Jesus has so radicalized the norms of right human conduct (love), that all claims to sinlessness are effectively foreclosed. This is brought home to us impressively in the first two antitheses of Matthew's Sermon on the Mount (Mt 5:21-32). Unlike the next three (Mt 5:33-48) these do not lead up to a prohibition or a command. Instead each ends in a principle stating that anger is equivalent to murder (Mt 5:21-22), and that a lustful look is the same as adultery (Mt 5:27-28). But if such spontaneous expressions of human aggressiveness and sexuality as anger and erotic fascination can bring us onto a level with murderers and adulterers, then truly no one can claim to be without sin and venture to cast the first stone (Jn 8:2-11).[5] We dare not presume to remove the speck in our brother's eye, because we all have a log in our own (Mt 7:3-5).

3.2. We Dare Not Judge Because We Cannot Read Hearts

Ultimately, however, our refusal to condemn those who have injured us is part of a more comprehensive and radical attitude demanded by Jesus, who invites us to refrain from judging altogether: "Do not judge that you may not be judged" (Mt 7:1).[6] All judging is here excluded, because only God knows the heart where alone the ethical quality of an action is determined (Mk 7:14-23).

In an age which has been alerted to the hidden motives of human behavior, personal and social, by the great "masters of suspicion," Nietzsche, Freud, and Marx,[7] the logic of Jesus' prohibition becomes obvious, even if its practice remains as difficult as ever. We forgive because we have no right to judge, and we have no right to judge because we have no means of looking into the heart. In the uncertainty that results from this lack of insight into human motivation, love will indeed prompt the follower of Jesus to justify rather than to condemn. "Father, forgive them, for they do not know what they are doing" (Lk 23:34), says Jesus of his executioners, giving his followers an example of forgiveness that goes beyond non-condemnation to a positive extenuation of the fault!

But what is basic to the teaching of Jesus is the absolutely radical prohibition to judge anyone in any way whatsoever. This will be particularly appreciated by an Indian reader, because in his tradition too non-judgmental awareness is the beginning (and the end) of wisdom and the heart of all forgiveness. "If I want to understand something," writes Krishnamurti, "I must observe, I must not criticise, I must not condemn, I must not pursue it as a pleasure or avoid it as a non-pleasure. There must merely be the silent (that is to say, the non-judgmental) observation of a fact."[8] "Teach me to forgive," asks the disciple of his master in an ancient Indian story. "If you never condemned," comes the reply, "you would never need to forgive."[9]

4. THE POLITICAL DIMENSION OF FORGIVENESS

Avoidance of judgment on persons ought not of course to lead to a condoning of the evil that they do. Forgiveness of sinners is not the approval of sin, whether personal or social. For forgiveness in the New Testament does not excuse or tolerate evil; it overcomes it (Rom 12:21). Like the love of enemies (Lk 6:34-35) for which it is merely another name, forgiveness is a thoroughly dynamic, even an "aggressive" act.[10] It is not just affective but effective. Not only does it imply a change in the disposition of the person who forgives; it also leads to a change in the situation of the person forgiven.

4.1. Forgiveness and Repentance

This is brought out symbolically in the Gospel story of the healing of the paralytic at Capernaum (Mk 2:1-12). For here the forgiveness of the sins of the paralytic ("your sins are forgiven") is made visible as it were by the cure of his paralysis ("take up your bed and walk"). The forgiveness of the paralytic leads to and is manifested by his healing. True, the story as we have it now in the Synoptic Gospels is meant to be an apologetic justification of the authority of Jesus and of his community to forgive sins, grounded in the power of Jesus to heal. But this is clearly a secondary meaning imposed on the original miracle story (Mk 2:1-5, 11-12) by the insertion of a controversy dialogue (Mk 2:6-10) into it. But the insertion of the dialogue has not been arbitrary. It has probably been latched onto as an explanatory expansion to a reference to the forgiveness of sins already part of the original healing story, or at least implicit in it.[11] For, as signs of the Kingdom, "all of Jesus' healings are symbols of . . . the forgiveness of sins which restores men to the fellowship with God."[12] The healing of the paralytic is thus also meant to be a visible manifestation of his being forgiven. Forgiveness, that is, leads to healing.

A similar lesson is taught in the story of Simon the Pharisee and the sinful woman (Lk 7:36-50). The love which the sinful woman shows Jesus is a sign "that her many sins have been forgiven" (Lk 7:47). It is her experience of being forgiven them that empowers her to love. Forgiveness changes her. Simon, on the other hand, is not changed, because he does not allow himself to experience forgiveness. He remains the unforgiving, judgmental person he always was. It is he, not the woman, who is the real (unrepentant and unforgiven) sinner. The experience of being forgiven thus empowers one to love.

For Zacchaeus also (Lk 19:1-10), the experience of the forgiving acceptance of Jesus radically changes his life. "Half my goods I give to the poor, and if I have defrauded anyone of anything I restore it fourfold" (Lk 19:3). Experiencing forgiveness leads to his repentance (*metanoia*).

The New Testament thus postulates a dialectical relationship between forgiveness and repentance (Lk 24:47), which parallels the dialectic between divine and human forgiveness that we spoke of above. Genuine forgiveness, genuinely accepted, leads to the repentance of the person forgiven—which in turn feeds back into and energizes the original act of forgiveness. If this spiral of interhuman forgiveness breaks down something obviously has gone wrong. Either our forgiveness has not been genuine, or the person to whom the forgiveness is directed does not want to be forgiven.

4.2. The Politics of Forgiveness

It is important to remember this in situations of structural sin. When those who maintain the vast structures of exploitation, oppression, and discrimination (racial and sexist) that reduce two thirds of humankind to hopeless misery, demand forgiveness while refusing to surrender anything of their wealth, privilege, and power, they are obviously being perverse. "What are we to say," as James Cone remarks, "to a people who insist on oppressing us but get upset when we reject them?"[13]

The answer may lie in the active and persistent forgiveness which Mahatma Gandhi practiced and preached. Because he spoke from within an exploited and struggling people and did not exhort them from a position of comfort, security, and connivance outside, his words carry weight. Nonviolence (which for him always implied "enlightened forgiveness"), Gandhi tells us, "does not mean meek submission to the will of the evil doer, but it means putting one's whole soul against the will of the tyrant."[14]

Such active forgiveness, evidently, can best be practiced from a position of strength rather than from one of weakness. "Abstinence (from retaliation) is forgiveness," Gandhi again reminds us, "when there is the power to punish; it is meaningless when it pretends to proceed from a helpless creature. A mouse hardly forgives a cat when it allows itself to be swallowed by her."[15] Obviously, then, authentic forgiveness will not be fostered by emasculating revolutionary movements among the "wretched of the earth," through a partisan and palliative interpretation of the teachings of Jesus. For it is only when the exploited have discovered their strength by becoming aware of their dignity as human beings, by experiencing the massive strength of their solidarity, and by coming to realize the creative role that they are called upon to play in history—it is only then that they will be in a position fully and authentically to forgive.

When such forgiveness meets the repentance of the exploiter, moved to conversion by the pressures of an energetic and unrelenting, forgiving and demanding love, then the spiral of forgiveness begins to function. This spells out the dynamic of Gandhi's *satyagraha* (active, nonviolent struggle, grounded on truth), which is the most consistent and effective method that has yet been elaborated to practice the politics of the forgiveness, implicit in the Gospel. In it lies, I believe, hope for the future in an increasingly violent and unforgiving world. For only the spiral of active forgiveness can break the spiral of violence that is tearing our world apart.

NOTES

1. Quoted in Paul Carus, *The Gospel of Buddha* (New Delhi: National Book Trust, 1969), 85-88.

2. Joachim Jeremias, *The Prayers of Jesus* (London: SCM Press, 1967), 82-107.

3. Ernst Lohmeyer, *Das Evangelium des Matthäus,* 3rd ed. (Göttingen: Vandenhoeck & Ruprecht, 1962), 122-23.

4. On the "sentences of holy law," see Ernst Käsemann, *New Testament Questions of Today* (London: SCM Press, 1969), 66-81. Note that Käsemann explicitly excludes the sayings in Luke 6:37-38 from the form he has so brilliantly described (ibid., 99). But I do not find the reasons he gives for the exclusion convincing.

5. Gerd Theissen, *The First Followers of Jesus* (London: SCM Press, 1978), 105-7.

6. As its context in Matthew shows, this saying was transmitted independently of the others that have been appended to it in Luke 6:37-38. Because of its extreme radicalism, it has good claims to be an authentic saying of Jesus. See Herbert Braun, *Spätjüdisch— häretischer und frühchristlicher Radikalismus,* Zweiter Band (Tübingen: Mohr, 1969), 92-93.

7. Paul Ricoeur, *The Conflict of Interpretations: Essays in Hermeneutics* (Evanston: Northwestern University Press, 1974), 148.

8. Jiddu Krishnamurti, *The First and the Last Freedom* (London: Gollancz, 1954), 179.

9. [Editor's note: This is a slightly modified version of] Anthony de Mello, *One Minute Wisdom* (Anand: Gujarat Sahitya Prakash, 1985), 167 [in the 1996 edition, p. 170].

10. Luise Schottroff, "Non-Violence and the Love of One's Enemies," in L. Schottroff et al., *Essays on the Love Commandment* (Philadelphia: Fortress Press, 1978), 9-32.

11. Leonhardt Goppelt, *Theology of the New Testament,* Volume One (Grand Rapids: Eerdmans, 1981), 131-32.

12. Eduard Schweizer, *The Good News According to Mark* (Richmond, Va.: John Knox Press, 1970), 60.

13. James H. Cone, *God of the Oppressed* (Maryknoll, N.Y.: Orbis, 1975), 226.

14. M. K. Gandhi, in *Young India,* August 11, 1920, reprinted in *The Collected Works of Mahatma Gandhi* (New Delhi: Publication Division, 1965), 133.

15. Ibid., 131.

16

GOOD NEWS TO THE POOR

The Social Implications of the Message of Jesus

We live today in a world of the very poor. Of the 604 million inhabitants in India today, some 247 million live on or just above the poverty line (that is, they can just about afford to buy the minimum food they need to lead a normal human life); while some 247 million more are *below* this line and cannot even afford this minimum. Only some 10 million or so are adequately housed, clothed, and fed.[1] Such poverty leads, of course, to massive malnutrition. Possibly 70 percent of the people of India are undernourished, both qualitatively and quantitatively: they lack not only the special *kinds* of food (proteins and vitamins), but even the minimum *amount* of food (1,500-2,000 calories a day) necessary for healthy growth and functioning. So some 500,000 children succumb each year to diseases brought on by severe malnutrition,[2] and perhaps 60 percent of all children in India between the ages of three and five suffer from some form or other of retarded growth.[3] The price that has to be paid for such poverty in terms of hunger, weakness, impaired ability for sustained work, diminished resistance to disease, retarded intellectual growth—to say nothing of the daily heartbreak of those who must watch helplessly while those they love hunger, sicken, wither away and die—is truly frightening.[4]

Do we in this grim situation of savage and dehumanizing poverty dare to proclaim the message of Jesus as "good news for the poor"? Jesus apparently expects us to do so. He himself claims in the Gospel of Luke (4:16-21) that he has been anointed by the Spirit precisely to proclaim good news to the poor

This article was first published in *Bible Bhashyam* 4 (1978): 193-212. Obviously the demographic figures today would be substantially higher.

(*euaggelisasthai ptōchois*); he refers to this proclamation of good news to the poor (*ptōchoi euaggelizontai*) as the clearest indication of his messianic identity (Lk 7:18-23); and he solemnly announces that the poor are blessed (*makarioi hoi ptōchoi*), because the Kingdom of God which he has come to proclaim is truly and exclusively theirs (Lk 6:20-26). How, then, are we to understand these astonishing sayings of Jesus? Who are the poor he is proclaiming blessed? Is he thinking of the *spiritual poverty* of detachment from material and consumer goods, or of the oppressive poverty of destitution we have spoken of above? How are the poor blessed? What is the "good news" that is being proclaimed to them?

These are complex questions,[5] and any answer at all adequate would have to take into account Jesus' attitude to riches too. For his almost obsessive preoccupation with the dangers that riches bring (cf. Mt 6:19-24; Mk 10:17-27; Lk 12:16-21; 16:19-31) is the obverse side of his proclamation of good news to the poor (Lk 4:16-21; 7:18-23; 6:20-26). We shall survey briefly, then (focusing mainly on Mk 10:23-27), Jesus' warning against riches, before going on to explore at some length (through a detailed study of Lk 4:16-21 and Lk 6:20-26) what exactly Jesus meant when he announced that he had been sent to proclaim good news to the poor.

I. DANGER OF RICHES

A. How Hard for the Rich

That an attachment to, indeed the mere possession of, riches can be an obstacle to following Jesus is affirmed repeatedly by him in the Gospels. Just how great an obstacle they can be is shown by the story of the Rich Young Man (Mk 10:17-22), who for all his high principles and irreproachable conduct (10:20), is deterred from following Jesus simply because he cannot tear himself away from his large property (10:22).[6] Not even the sign of affection which Jesus gives him (10:21)[7] can persuade him to give away his possessions to the poor and experience the exhilarating liberation of a life lived in total freedom from attachment to consumer goods and in loving dependence on God.

So important is the lesson of this story that Mark has made it explicit by adding to the story a dialogue between Jesus and his disciples (Mk 10:23-27), in which this lesson is emphatically spelled out and proclaimed as a general principle applicable to all. The dialogue, probably composed by Mark from one or more genuine sayings of Jesus,[8] has been skillfully structured to bring out the relevant point.

Mark 10:23-27

A v. 23 And Jesus looking around said to his disciples, "With what difficulty will those who have riches enter the Kingdom of God."

B v. 24 And the disciples were amazed (*ethambounto*) at his words. But Jesus said to them again,

A   "Children, how difficult it is for those who trust in riches to enter the Kingdom of God."

C   v. 25   "It is easier for a camel to go through the eye of a needle than for a rich man to enter the Kingdom of God."

B   v. 26   And they were exceedingly astonished (*perissōs exeplēssonto*) and said to one another,

         "Who, then, can be saved?"

   v. 27   Jesus looking at them said,

A   "With men it is impossible, but not with God; for all things are possible with God."

The dialogue obviously follows a roughly concentric pattern, centering on the striking hyperbolic saying of v. 25. Jesus comments twice, in almost identical words, on the danger of riches (vv. 23 and 24b), only to meet each time with the incredulous astonishment of his disciples (vv. 24a and 26). His concluding reassurance (v. 27), introduced with the same reference to "Jesus looking" as his opening comment (v. 23),[9] brings the dialogue to its appropriate close.

The saying in v. 25 about a camel passing through the eye of a needle is thus the structural and thematic center of the dialogue and expresses in a single striking image all that the dialogue has to say. In its fanciful, almost grotesque imagery, the saying is quite typical of Jesus, who delights in such creative paradoxical flights of fancy (cf. Mk 8:35; 9:43; Mt 10:34; 15:14). Attempts to water it down by suggesting, for instance, that the "eye of a needle" was the name given to a small gate in the walls of Jerusalem (a detail first mentioned in a ninth-century commentary!),[10] or that the word *kamēlos* ("camel") in the Greek text of Mark be read *kamilos* ("ship's rope"),[11] miss the point; for this saying of Jesus is meant to be exaggerated and fanciful. It deliberately juxtaposes the largest known animal (the camel) with the smallest known opening (the eye of a needle),[12] in order to shock its hearers into a stunned awareness of the unpalatable truth that riches are an insuperable obstacle to salvation. "It is easier for a camel to pass through the eye of a needle than for a rich man to enter the Kingdom of God"—that is, the salvation of a rich man is (humanly speaking) impossible.

B. God and Mammon

Just why should riches be for Jesus so great an obstacle to salvation? Putting together his many sayings on the subject, one could suggest the following two reasons:

(1) Riches make a man godless. The accumulation of wealth leads to covetousness or greed (*pleonexia*),[13] and the covetous man spends his life piling up treasures on earth, to the total neglect of treasure in heaven (Mt 6:19-21). That is, the rich man ceases to have values other than the pursuit of the material comfort and the power that his money brings. He is like, indeed he *is*, the Rich Fool of Jesus' parable (Lk 12:16-21), preoccupied wholly with the piling up of material

resources that will enable him to "eat, drink and be merry" for many years to come. Like him the man who is rich soon forgets the pointed warning of Jesus (so startlingly relevant to our consumer society today) that the security (and quality) of a man's life is not to be measured by the abundance of his possessions (Lk 12:15). God ceases to have a place in his life. He becomes a practical atheist, and so, in biblical parlance, a "fool" (*aphrōn*), for it is the fool (*aphrōn*), the Psalmist tells us, who "says in his heart, 'there is no God'" (Ps 14:1).

(2) Riches make a man heartless too, insensitive to the needs of his fellow men. This seems to be at least one of the lessons of the puzzling parable of the Rich Man and the Beggar in Lk 16:19-31. As the parable now stands it has two clearly distinct and possibly originally independent parts,[14] each with its own particular point. If the *second part* of the parable (vv. 27-31) warns against a craving for "signs," by pointing out how even the testimony of a dead man come back to life again would not convert someone who has been deaf to the Scriptures, that is, to the normal vehicle of God's revelation,[15] the *first part* (vv. 19-26) again affirms the exclusion of the rich from the Kingdom—this time because of their massive neglect of the poor.

For the parable begins with a nicely balanced description of the sharply contrasting conditions of an unnamed rich man, clothed in fine linen and feasting sumptuously every day (16:19), and a poor beggar named Lazarus,[16] who lies at his door, covered with sores and hungering for the crumbs that fall from the rich man's table (16:20-21).[17] And it then goes on to tell of the dramatic reversal of their condition that takes place when they die (16:22-26). Not only is the beggar carried to paradise while the rich man roasts in hell, but their respective roles have been precisely reversed. For it is the desperately thirsty rich man who now looks on longingly as the once starving beggar feasts contentedly at Abraham's table.

Clearly, then, this sudden and dramatic reversal of roles is the main point of this first part of the parable, which is best understood as an attempt to arouse the listeners of Jesus to an awareness of the drastic revision of values (cf. Lk 6:20-26) which the irruption of the Kingdom must inevitably bring.[18] But the parable teaches another lesson too. Implicitly at least it draws our attention to the rich man's unfeeling neglect of the poor beggar at his door. None of Jesus' audience would have missed this. For to a Jew a rich man dining sumptuously every day with a starving beggar at his door would have been "the very epitome" of anti-social behavior, clearly and repeatedly condemned by the Law.[19] The parable suggests, then, though it does not explicitly say so, that the rich man was condemned to hell because of his large neglect of the poor. It thus becomes a forceful warning against the callous insensitivity to which riches can lead.[20]

So riches are for Jesus an insuperable obstacle to the Kingdom, because they make a man godless and heartless. They monopolize his attention, become his overriding value, and lay hold of his "heart"—for "where your treasure is, there will your heart be also" (Mt 6:21). The dreadful inhumanity that this can lead to has been well described by Dom Helder Camara, bishop of Recife in North Brazil:

> I used to think when I was a child that Christ might have been exaggerating when he warned about the dangers of wealth. Today I know better. I know how very hard it is to be rich and still keep the milk of human kindness. Money has a dangerous way of putting scales on one's eyes, a dangerous way of freezing people's hands, eyes, lips and hearts.[21]

Riches are deadly. That is why Jesus affirms with such uncompromising firmness against every desperate evasion of affluent Christians living in our consumer capitalist society and striving mightily to make the best of both worlds, that "no man can serve two masters . . . you cannot serve God and mammon!" (Mt 6:24).

II. THE CHALLENGE OF THE POOR

Jesus' uncompromising stand against *riches* (but not against the rich!)—that is, against an attachment to or even the possession of superfluous wealth as source of comfort and power—is balanced by his equally intransigent commitment to the *poor* (but not to poverty!)—that is, to all those who are deprived of the material and social goods needed for an authentically human life. Such a commitment to the poor is proclaimed by Jesus as the essence of his mission in the inaugural sermon with which (in Luke's Gospel) he begins his public ministry (Lk 4:16-30), and its significance is spelled out with great force and clarity in the set of beatitudes with which (again in Luke's Gospel) he opens his great public discourse, the Sermon on the Plain (Lk 6:20-26). It is through a study of these two texts, then, that we shall come to know Jesus' attitude toward poverty and the poor.

A. *To Proclaim Good News to the Poor (Lk 4:16-30)*

Luke begins his narrative of Jesus' ministry with the description of a solemn inaugural sermon delivered by Jesus in the synagogue of his hometown, Nazareth (Lk 4:16-30), and he describes this not just as the first act of a crowded preaching tour, but as an inaugural act. The sermon at Nazareth launches the ministry of Jesus and gives us its meaning. For it is the occasion of a stirring manifesto through which Jesus announces his own understanding of his mission and proclaims the significance of all that he is to do.

Attending the Sabbath service of the synagogue (as he had so often done before), Jesus stands up to read and is handed the scroll of the prophet Isaiah.[22] He unrolls it to the oracle of Is 61:1-3 and reads out the moving words in which Trito-Isaiah announces his prophetic calling.[23] He then hands back the scroll to the "attendant" of the synagogue and sits down to expound the text he has just read. And then into the expectant silence of the waiting congregation of his townsfolk, whose eyes are all "fixed intently" on him, he announces with the force of a thunderclap: "this day this scripture has been fulfilled in your hearing" (4:20).

The proclamation is startling. For what Jesus tells his audience is that at that very moment, even as they listen to him, the salvation announced (but not decisively effected) by Trito-Isaiah[24] is in fact being realized. Even as he speaks, the age of God's definitive salvation begins to dawn. The real spirit-filled herald of the good news to the poor is thus not the prophet of five hundred years ago, but Jesus himself, who, having just received the fullness of the Spirit at his baptism (Lk 3:21-22), now declares Trito-Isaiah's mission to be his own.

The scope of the mission which Jesus assumes is as startling as the proclamation that has now begun. For the manifesto which he makes his own (Lk 4:18-19) is formulated in language of astonishing earthiness and actuality. Jesus announces his task as that of "evangelizing" (proclaiming the good news of liberation to) the poor, of heralding freedom to captives, sight to the blind, liberty to the oppressed, and so of inaugurating a time of salvation prefigured by the Jubilee year of Old Testament legislation, when debts were to be remitted, ancestral property returned, and slaves set free (Lev 25:8-17, 25-28).[25] His is thus a *social manifesto* with little that is "spiritual" about it. Indeed its social thrust is intensified by the deliberate changes the Lukan Jesus makes in the Old Testament text he quotes.

For in quoting Is 61:1-2 Jesus uses not the original Hebrew text but its "official" Greek translation, the Septuagint (LXX), which at Is 61:1b has, like Luke, "recovery of sight to the blind" in place of the "opening of prison to those who are bound" of the Hebrew. And Jesus quotes the LXX with two significant changes in the text. A half-verse ("to bind up the brokenhearted") is left out from Is 61:1; and another ("to set free the oppressed") is added from Is 58:6.

Lk 4:18-19	*Is 61:1-2 (LXX)*
The Spirit of the Lord is upon me Because he has anointed me. To announce good news to the poor he has sent me;	The Spirit of the Lord is upon me Because he has anointed me. To announce good news to the poor he has sent me; To *heal the brokenhearted;*
To proclaim to prisoners freedom; And recovery of sight to the blind. To *set the oppressed free* To proclaim (*kēryxai*) a year acceptable to the Lord.	To proclaim to prisoners freedom, And recovery of sight to the blind To declare (*kalesai*) a year acceptable to the Lord.

These changes can scarcely be fortuitous. Luke at Is 61:2 has "proclaim" (*kēryxai*) instead of the LXX's "declare" (*kalesai*) an acceptable year, obviously because of the pressure of Christian terminology, in which "to proclaim" (*kēryssein*) has become a much-used technical term for the proclamation of the "good news." The omission of the "brokenhearted" from Is 61:1 and the intrusion into it of the "oppressed" from Is 58:6 are probably intended as preventive measures against the kind of spiritualizing interpretation of a text which has led to Matthew's religious rendering ("Blessed are the poor in spirit") of Jesus' originally strongly social beatitude ("Blessed are you poor").[26] Commentators have been slow to recognize this,[27] but it is difficult to see why else Luke should have omitted the one line in Is 61:1-2 ("to bind up the brokenhearted") open to such spiritualizing, and have brought in an expression from Is 58:6 ("to set free the oppressed"), whose strongly social thrust is plain.

Given, then, the setting of Is 61:1-3, an oracle addressed originally to the miserable, poverty-stricken remnant of Judah, freshly returned from exile,[28] the socially oriented directives of the Jubilee year of Lev 25 to which the prophecy expressly refers, and Luke's deliberate effort to forestall through his editing any spiritualizing of the text—there can be little doubt that the manifesto of Jesus in Lk 4:18-19 is to be understood in a strongly social sense. The salvation Jesus announces here is primarily a liberation from the pressures of social, economic, and societal oppression.[29] He has come indeed to announce "good news" to the "poor."

Scholars are largely agreed that this inaugural sermon of Jesus in the synagogue of Nazareth (Lk 4:16-30) is a Lukan composition which Luke has fashioned by rewriting Mark's story of the rejection of Jesus at Nazareth (Mk 6:1-6), and by combining it with other traditions known to him.[30] Yet, and in spite of the fact that concern for the poor is a peculiarly Lukan theme, the social thrust of this manifesto of Jesus is not just Luke's interpretation. Luke is here reflecting the intentions of Jesus himself. For the same "social" understanding of his mission (in terms of Is 61:1-3) is to be found in other sayings of Jesus which are certainly genuine—notably in Jesus' reply to the question posed by the Baptist about his identity in Lk 7:18-23 = Mt 11:2-6; and in the beatitudes with which Jesus begins his "sermon" to the crowds in Lk 6:20-26 = Mt 5:3-12. It is in these beatitudes in particular that the extent and significance of Jesus' commitment to the poor become clear.

B. How Happy the Poor! (Lk 6:20-26)

Luke's Sermon on the Plain opens with a set of four beatitudes (and four corresponding woes) of which the first three form a close-knit group, differing conspicuously from the fourth and last beatitude in Luke and significantly from their parallels in Matthew too.

Lk 6:20-23	Mt 5:3-12
V. 20 Blessed are you poor for yours is the Kingdom of God	V. 3 Blessed are the poor in spirit for theirs is the Kingdom of Heaven.
V. 21 Blessed are you that hunger now for you shall be satisfied.	V. 4 Blessed are those that mourn for they shall be comforted.
	V. 5 Blessed are the meek for they shall inherit the land.
Blessed are you that weep now for you shall laugh.	V. 6 Blessed are those that hunger and thirst after righteousness for yours is the Kingdom of Heaven.
V. 22 Blessed are you when men hate you and when they exclude you, and revile and cast out your name as evil on account of the Son of Man.	V. 11 Blessed are you when men revile you and persecute you, and speak all kinds of evil against you falsely, on my account.
V. 23 Rejoice in that day and leap for joy, for behold your reward is great in heaven; for so their fathers did to the prophets.	V. 12 Rejoice and be glad for your reward is great in heaven; for so men persecuted the prophets who were before you.

The fourth Lukan beatitude (6:22-23) obviously differs strikingly from the other three. It is repetitive and wordy and refers so clearly to a problem of the post-Easter community (the expulsion of the Jewish Christians from the Synagogue),[31] that it is almost certainly a composition of the early Church. The first three Lukan beatitudes, on the other hand, with their crisp, rhythmic style and their strongly prophetic content are utterly characteristic of Jesus, and are certainly his authentic words. They are in fact more likely to be the authentic utterances of Jesus than their parallels in Matthew (5:3-6). For appearances suggest that it is Matthew who is secondary, for he has:

(a) spiritualized the three original beatitudes of Jesus by changing "poor" into "poor *in spirit*" (5:3), by toning down "you that hunger now" into "those who hunger and thirst *after righteousness*" (5:6), and by replacing "you who weep now" (i.e., who give concrete and external signs of distress) with the more abstract and spiritual "those who *mourn*" (5:4);

(b) rearranged the beatitudes in the order (poor-mourn-hunger) in which their key words occur in Is 61:1-3;

(c) added a fourth beatitude parallel to the first (5:5) by recasting Ps 37:11 ("the meek shall inherit the land") into a beatitude form—so as to get the two sets of four rhythmic beatitudes each with which he begins his Sermon on the Mount.[32]

In the first three Lukan beatitudes, then, we hear the authentic voice of Jesus himself—though it is possible that Jesus spoke them in the third person (as in Matthew) rather than in the "you"-form which Luke gives. For Old Testament beatitudes and woes are normally in the third person (cf. Ps 1:1; 31:1; 41:1; Is 5:8-12); and Luke's "you" could well be an editorial adaptation restricting the beatitudes to the particular Christian community for which he wrote. But whatever their grammatical form, it is clear that the three beatitudes of Luke are not meant to be three independent proclamations—as though the poor, the hungry, and the weeping whom Jesus successively addresses were three distinct categories of people; or as though the blessing of the "Kingdom" were different from the promise of being "filled" (at the messianic banquet), or the hope of "laughing" (with messianic joy). The three beatitudes are in fact expressions of a single beatitude, *the* Jesus-beatitude: "blessed are the poor for theirs is the Kingdom of God."

I. WHO ARE THE POOR?

What, then, does this beatitude mean? Who are the "poor" whom Jesus calls "blessed"? Just why are they called "blessed"? In what exactly does their blessing consist? The Greek text of Luke's first beatitude reads *makarioi hoi ptōchoi* ("blessed the poor"), whose *ptōchos* suggests not just poverty but destitution. For unlike the milder *penēs* ("poor"), which describes a man who has no property, lacks superfluities, and has to work for his living, *ptōchos* ("destitute") designates one who lacks even the necessities of life and must beg in order to live.[33] The "poor" in Jesus' beatitude, it would seem then, are those who are utterly needy, desperately in want; so that one would be tempted to formulate the Jesus beatitude as: "Blessed are the *destitute,* for theirs is the Kingdom of God."

But it is doubtful whether Jesus himself meant quite this. For Jesus spoke in Aramaic, not in Greek. And the Aramaic ʿinwānayyāʾ or ʿinwĕtānayyāʾ that he must have used (more familiar to us no doubt in their Hebrew forms of ʿănîyyîm or ʿănāwîm) would have had a much broader connotation. It would have stood for all those who were in any way oppressed, and so reduced to a condition of diminished worth or capacity. So the "poor" addressed by Jesus would have included not only the economically straitened (the destitute) but also the socially outcast (the tax collectors and sinners of Mk 2:15-17 or Lk 15:1-2), the religiously simple and unlettered (the "little ones" of Mt 18:10), the mentally ill (epileptics and "demoniacs" like those in Mk 9:14-29 and 5:1-20), and the physically handicapped (all the blind, the deaf, the crippled, the sick shown flocking to Jesus in Mk 1:32-34; 3:7-12; 6:53-56), whose sufferings would have been accentuated by the shame and guilt resulting from the then prevalent belief that their illness or deformity was a punishment for sin (Jn 9:2). In a word, the "poor" for Jesus comprised the ʿammê hā-ʾāreṣ ("the peoples of the land")—a contemptuous designation by which the religious and social elite of his time labeled the "rabble ignorant of the Law," that is, the poor, the unschooled, the socially unacceptable, the religiously defiled, the sick.

In postexilic times the term ʿānāwîm began to acquire a religious connotation and was used to describe the pious and faithful Israelites ("the poor of Yahweh"), whose poverty and helplessness had taught them to rely absolutely and exclusively on God.[34] Echoes of this development resonate doubtless in Jesus' understanding of the "poor" and these have been taken up and explicit in Matthew's "poor in spirit" (Mt 5:3). But the primary reference of Jesus' beatitude is surely not religious but social. The Jesus beatitude is the beatitude of *the oppressed.*

So among the "poor" addressed by the Jesus beatitude today we shall find the Harijans*, daily victims of inhuman atrocities and of an utterly dehumanizing discrimination practiced against them (incredibly!) even in allegedly Christian communities. We shall find too the pavement dwellers of our slum-ridden cities, who have literally no place where to lay their heads; the crippled beggars who swarm around us at our bus stops and railway stations; and the vast masses of our landless laborers, who, like the shades in sheol, eke out a twilight existence in hopelessness and exhaustion. These are the people whom Jesus calls "blessed"!

2. WHY ARE THE POOR BLESSED?

But why does Jesus call them blessed? Surely not because their poverty is in itself a good thing! Poverty is sometimes hailed as a blessing (usually by those who are curiously reluctant to share in this "blessing" themselves) because, it is said, it makes men spiritually docile, open to God. It is the poor man, keenly aware of his helplessness, who turns trustingly to God. This may be true of *spiritual poverty*, the non-attachment to material things which Jesus demands as a necessary disposition for salvation. But that *oppressive poverty*, which is ultimately dehumanizing, is a religious value may be doubted. Jesus certainly never proclaims it as such. Rather, he proclaims the poor "blessed," not because their poverty is a good thing, but precisely because it is an evil which he is about to bring to an end. The poor are blessed because they are to be poor no more—"blessed are you that hunger now for you shall be filled"! The poor, that is, are blessed because they are to be the beneficiaries of the *total revolution* ("blessed are you poor—woe to you rich") that the Kingdom of God will bring.

Behind this proclamation of Jesus lies a whole Old Testament tradition of God's predilection for the poor.[35] Because he is King, charged with the protection of the weak,[36] the God of the Old Testament champions the cause of the poor and the oppressed, who are the victims of an injustice which the just God must redress. So innumerable passages in the Old Testament speak of Yahweh's concern for the defenseless—exemplified by the *widow, the orphan, and the refugee,* types of utter helplessness in a pre–welfare-age society (Deut 10:17-19; Ps

---

* Editor's note: Harijan, people of Hari/God, an expression used by Gandhi to designate the casteless and "untouchables" of India.

68:5)—and of his vindication of the *oppressed* of the earth (Ps 76:9; 146:5-9). And because Yahweh is concerned about the poor, he demands with deadly earnestness (Ex 22:21-24) a similar concern from his people (Deut 24:17-18; Jer 7:5-7; Ps 82:1-4) and from their king (Jer 22:1-5); and he condemns through his prophets every kind of oppression with violent anger (Am 2:6-8; 4:1-3; 6:4-7; 8:4-10; Hos 2:1-3; Mic 2:1-3; Is 3:13-17; 5:8-10; 10:1-4; Jer 5:26-29; 34:17-21; Ezek 34:1-24). Israel's oppression of the poor will lead, warns Amos, to a famine of "hearing the words of the Lord," that is, to Yahweh's total abandonment of his people (Am 8:11-12). To "know God," proclaims Jeremiah, is to practice "justice" (Jer 22:13-17). A cult that becomes an alibi for neglect of the poor, say Isaiah (58:6-9d) and Hosea (6:6), is wholly unacceptable to God.

3. WHAT IS THE BLESSING PROMISED TO THE POOR?

The Jesus beatitude is the concentrated expression and the crowning of this long tradition of God's concern for the "poor." In it Jesus announces that through him God is at work (the Kingdom has come!) reaching out to liberate the oppressed of the earth. The liberation he proclaims is not be spiritualized away, as though those who are poor now on earth will be "rich" in heaven. Such a "pie-in-the-sky-when-you-die" interpretation fails to do justice to the strongly this-worldly character of the Kingdom which Jesus proclaims. For the Kingdom is, after all, God's intervention into *history*.

Rather, what Jesus promises is God's revolution, which will liberate all men (both the rich and the poor) from the whole range of oppressions personal and societal that constrain and diminish them. It will free men not only from the dehumanizing structures of an oppressive poverty which grinds them down, but equally from the compulsions to possession and power which lead men to oppress one another. For Jesus has not come to make the poor "rich," and turn the oppressed into new oppressors. He intends rather to bring about both *a change of heart* (freedom from attachment to riches) and *a change of structures* (liberation from oppressive social systems); for it is this combination alone that can lead to the new humanity which is the ultimate goal of the long process of total liberation that Jesus has begun.

To the extent, then, that the Kingdom of God comes; to the extent, that is, that we are open to the liberating revelation of God's unconditional love in which the Kingdom ultimately consists; to the extent that we are prepared to live by the values of Jesus and commit ourselves to the building up of the kind of community of freedom and fellowship that he envisioned—to that extent spiritual poverty (anti-consumerism) will flourish and oppressive poverty (destitution) will vanish from our lives (Rev 21:1-4). For in a community that is truly Christian there can be no greed and no destitution, as the experiment in Christian living attempted by the Jerusalem community ("and there was not a needy person among them") clearly shows (Acts 2:44-45; 4:32-35).

The existence of consumerism and destitution among us is thus a measure of the failure of our Christianity. The fact that there should be rich (and greedy) Christians in a hungry world is a towering scandal which no amount of private devotions or much publicized almsgiving can take away. For ultimately our greed is a sign of our godlessness, and the presence of the destitute in our midst is the mark of our infidelity to Jesus. God has set himself squarely against Mammon (Mt 6:24); and, in a paroxysm of concern, Jesus has identified himself with the poor (Mt 25:31-46). Our consumerism, then, is an option against God; our neglect of the poor is a neglect of Jesus.

NOTES

1. D. Barreto, *The Indian Situation* (Bangalore: Centre for Social Action, 1976), 14.

2. K. N. Pandey, "Malnutrition: A Major National Problem," *Indian Express,* August 5, 1977, 6.

3. Barreto, *Indian Situation,* 19-20.

4. For a deeply moving description of what it means to live in poverty in a (Brazilian) slum, see Carolina Maria de Jesus, *Child of the Dark* (New York: Signet Books, 1962).

5. No really thorough study has yet been made of Jesus' attitude toward poverty and the poor, but useful material may be gathered from the following studies: R. Batey, *Jesus and the Poor* (New York: Harper & Row, 1972); M. Hengel, *Property and Riches in the Early Church* (London: SCM Press, 1974); R. J. Sider, *Rich Christians in an Age of Hunger: A Biblical Study* (New York: Paulist Press, 1977); H.-J. Degenhardt, *Lukas, Evangelist der Armen* (Stuttgart: Katholisches Biblwerk, 1965); J. Dupont, *Les Béatitudes,* tomes I-III (Paris: Gabalda, 1958-69). See also G. Mangatt, "Jesus' Good News to the Poor," *Jeevadhara* 3 (1973): 300-317.

6. The Greek text has *ktēmata* here, a word which describes landed property rather than money and possessions (cf. the *chrēmata* of 10:23). The rich man of the story is (as would be expected in the Palestine of Jesus' time) a rich landlord.

7. The *ēgapesen auton* of the Greek could indicate a loving gesture made by Jesus, even a kiss given by him. See E. Lohmeyer, *Das Evangelium des Markus* (Göttingen: Vandenhoeck & Ruprecht, 1967), 211; R. Pesch, *Das Markusevangelium,* vol. 2, Herders Theologischer Kommentar zum Neuen Testament (Freiburg: Herder, 1977), 140.

8. See E. Schweizer, *The Good News According to Mark* (London: SPCK, 1971), 209-10; Pesch, *Das Markusevangelium,* 136-37.

9. As in v. 21, the "looking" of Jesus serves to draw attention to what he says and may also express his affectionate concern for his disciples (addressed only here in the Gospels as "children"), who are finding it difficult to swallow so hard a saying on riches.

10. Schweizer, *Good News According to Mark,* 213.

11. W. Grundmann, *Das Evangelium nach Markus,* Herders Theologischer Kommentar zum Neuen Testament (Freiburg: Herder, 1973), 213.

12. Compare the similar saying from the Babylonian Talmud: "You come indeed from Pumbeditha, where an elephant is made to pass to through the eye of a needle" (*b. B. Meṣi'a* 38b). J. Jeremias (*The Parables of Jesus,* 3rd ed. [London: SCM Press, 1972], 195) points out that the elephant was the largest animal known in Mesopotamia, as

the camel was the largest known in Palestine. The image in the Talmud is thus the exact Babylonian equivalent of that used by Jesus.

13. From the frequency with which *pleonexia* occurs in the many New Testament lists of sins (Mk 7:22; Rom 1:29; Eph 5:3; Col 3:5; 2 Pet 2:14) it is clear that the early Church followed the lead of Jesus in regarding greed (the motive power of our consumer capitalistic society!) as a deadly evil.

14. See John Dominic Crossan, "Parable and Example in the Teaching of Jesus," *Semeia* 1 (1974): 79-81. Against Jeremias (*Parables,* 186), where the parable as a whole is classified as one of the four double-edged parables used by Jesus, Crossan believes that its second part (vv. 27-31), with its obvious echoes of Lk 24, is an addition of the early Church, "in the line of an allegorical allusion to the Jewish refusal to accept either Moses and the prophets as witnesses to the resurrection of Jesus or the risen Lord himself" (p. 80). The original parable uttered by Jesus would then have comprised only vv. 19-26.

15. So, J. Ernst, *Das Evangelium nach Lukas* (Regensburg: Pustet, 1977), 477; Jeremias, *Parables,* 187: "He who will not submit to the Word of God, will not be converted by a miracle."

16. The fact that the beggar is named while the rich man is not is significant, given the importance that names have in the Bible. God "knows" the beggar as it were "by name." The name given to him is itself significant. For *Lazaros* is the Greek form of the Hebrew *Laʾzār,* a rabbinic abbreviation of *ʾĕlîʿezer,* which means "God helps."

17. Luke's description of Lazarus, "longing to be filled (*epithymōn chortasthēnai*) with what fell from the rich man's table" and licked by unclean dogs (16:21), parallels that of the Prodigal Son in exile, who also lived with unclean swine and "kept on longing to be filled (*epethymei chortasthēnai*) with the husks on which the swine used to feed" (15:16). Both are images of extreme physical need and humiliating social rejection.

18. The revolution expressly formulated in the beatitudes of Lk 6:20-26 (see below) is anticipated in Mary's Magnificat: "He has filled the hungry with good things, but the rich he has sent away empty" (1:53). So the poet Wilfred Meynell can say of Mary:

This is very she who sings,
  "The poor God filleth with good things";
And rebel she who dares to say:
  "But empty sends the rich away."

19. J. D. M. Derrett, "Fresh Light on St. Luke XVI:II: Dives and Lazarus and the Preceding Sayings," *New Testament Studies* 7 (1960–61): 373.

20. So ibid.: "Failure to deal righteously with *mammon* leads to 'Hell'"—so that the parable is seen as the mirror image of that of the Unjust Steward in Lk 16:1-10. For Ernst (*Das Evangelium nach Lukas*) too, the parable contains an implicit exhortation, urging its listeners not just to almsgiving but to effective care for the needy brother (p. 476). Against this, Jeremias (*Parables,* 187), sees the point of the parable in its "epilogue" which teaches the lesson that "the demand for a sign is an evasion and a sign of impertinence," while Crossan ("Parable and Example," 81) locates it in the dramatic reversal of the situations of the rich man and Lazarus, through which "the kingdom's disruptive advent could be metaphorically portrayed and linguistically made present." All these meanings are doubtless to be found in the parable, for like any symbolic form it is not to be interpreted too narrowly.

21. Helder Camara, *Revolution through Peace* (New York: Harper & Row, 1971), 142, quoted in Sider, *Rich Christians,* 39.

22. The synagogue service at the time of Jesus would have included the following elements: (a) a confession of faith (the *šĕmaᶜ*), which consisted of the recitation of Deut 6:4-9; 11:13-21; Num 15:37-41; (b) prayers of praise (the *tĕfillāh*) which by the time of Jesus had been more or less standardized into the *šĕmōneh ᶜeśrēh,* the Eighteen Benedictions; (c) a reading from the Pentateuch or Law (the *pārāšāh*) by one or more readers, each reading at least three verses; (d) a second reading from the Prophets (the *haphtārāh*); (e) a homily on the readings by the president of the synagogue or an invited guest; (f) a concluding prayer by the homilist. See G. F. Moore, *Judaism in the First Centuries of the Christian Era,* vol. 1 (New York: Schocken Books, 1971), 291-307. Luke describes only the last part of the service, but his description as far as it goes (Jesus standing up to read, handing the scroll to the "attendant," sitting down to deliver his "homily") is accurate enough.

23. See C. Westermann, *Isaiah 40-66* (London: SCM Press, 1969), 365.

24. In contrast to Deutero-Isaiah, whose promise of a blessing "looks on the change as already brought about as far as God is concerned," Trito-Isaiah announces a "turning in grace which God is to make a reality in an indeterminate, although near, future" (Westermann, *Isaiah 40-66,* 367).

25. On the Jubilee year, see R. de Vaux, *Ancient Israel* (London: Darton, Longman & Todd, 1961), 175-77.

26. See the discussion on the Lukan beatitudes below.

27. Grundmann (*Das Evangelium nach Markus,* 120-21) offers no explanation for the changes. Ernst (*Das Evangelium nach Lukas,* 170) believes that Is 58:6 has been added as an interpretative comment on "to proclaim to prisoners freedom" of Is 61:1c. This is scarcely a satisfactory explanation, for it does not tell us how Is 58:6 "interprets" an expression at least as clear as itself, nor why Luke should have dropped the immediately preceding line about the "brokenhearted." Equally unsatisfying is the explanation offered by H. Schürmann, *Das Lukasevangelium,* I, Herders Theologischer Kommentar zum Neuen Testament (Freiburg: Herder, 1969), 229, who suggests that "to bind up the brokenhearted" was dropped (not by Luke but by a later copyist of the Gospel, for he accepts as genuine the reading supported by a few manuscripts in which the expression is kept), because it was thought to be inconsistent with the fact that Jesus worked no miracles in Nazareth, while Is 58:6 was added (by Luke) to further elaborate the idea of the Jubilee year accounted in 61:2. But "to bind up the brokenhearted" does not imply the working of miracles, so that there is no reason why it should have been dropped merely because Jesus is not shown working miracles in Nazareth. And the idea of a Jubilee year surely does not need the reinforcement that Is 58:6 allegedly gives it. Ours is in fact the only explanation which makes sense if the two changes in the quoted text (the omission of Is 61:1c and the addition of Is 58:6) are seen as parts of a single meaningful editorial operation.

28. See Westermann, *Isaiah 40-66,* 295-96.

29. Ernst, *Das Evangelium nach Lukas,* 171.

30. See especially R. C. Tannehill, "The Mission of Jesus," in *Jesus in Nazareth,* ed. W. Eltester (Berlin: de Gruyter, 1972), 51-75, who accounts for Lk 4:16-30 in terms of Luke's editing of Mk 6:1-6 (in 4:23-24), his use of non-Markan traditions (in 4:25-27) and his own free composition (in 4:16-21 and 4:28-30). But H. Schürmann ("Zur Traditionsgeschichte der Nazareth Perikope," in *Mélanges Bibliques en hommage au R.P. Béda Rigaux,* ed. A. Descamps and A. Halleaux [Gembloux: Duculot, 1970], 187-205) believes that Lk 4:16-30 is substantially a pre-Lukan narrative belonging to the Q tradition, formed by the addition (at a pre-Lukan stage) of vv. 17-21 and vv. 25-27 to a core narrative

(vv. 16, 22, 23-24, 28-30) which was in fact an earlier form of the rejection story of Mk 6:1-6.

31. See Ernst, *Das Evangelium nach Lukas,* 219.

32. See Dupont, *Les Béatitudes,* vol. 1, for a very thorough study of the literary relationships between the beatitudes of Matthew and Luke.

33. See W. Barclay, *The Plain Man Looks at the Beatitudes* (London: Fontana, 1963), 16-19.

34. See A. Gelin, *The Poor of Yahweh* (Collegeville, Minn.: Liturgical Press, 1964).

35. Powerfully presented by J. P. Miranda, *Marx and the Bible* (New York: Orbis Books, 1974), 35-108.

36. On the role of the king as the protector of the "poor" in the ancient Middle East and Israel, see Dupont, *Les Béatitudes,* 2:53-90. This role was not altogether unlike that ascribed to the king in the laws of Manu, one of which states: "If the king did not untiringly inflict punishment on those to be punished, the stronger would roast the weak like a fish on the spit" (Manu VII, 20), quoted from *Hindu Polity (The Ordinances of Manu),* trans. A. C. Burnell (Ludhiana: Kalyani Publishers, 1972), 150.

Part IV

THE MISSION OF JESUS

17

EXPANDING THE HORIZON OF CHRISTIAN MISSION

A Biblical Perspective

The aim of this paper is to offer insights from the Bible that may help us to develop an understanding of mission appropriate for the Christian community in India today. Working toward such an understanding of mission is, as I see it, the task of this seminar. As I have argued elsewhere, missiology, like theology, is historically and culturally conditioned.[1] There is no uniform, unchanging, universal understanding of mission valid always and everywhere, any more than there is a uniform, unchanging, and universal understanding of the Christian faith which is always and everywhere the same. It is part of the finitude and historicity of Christian existence that our understanding of mission (like our understanding of the Christian faith) should vary in place and grow in time.

This has in fact been so from the beginning, as any history of mission will show.[2] The mission to the Jews of the first Palestinian followers of Jesus was radically different from the centrifugal gentile mission initiated by the Jewish Hellenistic Christian communities of the Diaspora, and Paul's understanding of mission was very different from that of John.[3] Mission in the Middle Ages was not the same as mission in the violent world of European colonialism; and mission in a post-colonial world, for which European culture is no longer the normative culture, nor European religion the normative religion of humankind, cannot replicate the missionary beliefs, attitudes, and strategies of the colonial age, in which non-European peoples were dismissed as subhuman "natives,"[4] and their religions written off as demonic forms of "idolatry."[5] The Indian Church must therefore develop its own understanding of mission, responsive to its post-conciliar and post-colonial situation.

This article was originally a contribution to a seminar on mission and was published along with the other papers in *Paths of Mission in India Today*, ed. A. Kanjamala (Bombay: St Pauls, 1997), 33-48.

It is as a contribution to this challenging task of spelling out the meaning of Christian mission in India today, that I offer the following reflections from the Bible. These reflections are not meant to be exhaustive nor definitive. It would be presumptuous, indeed absurd, to pretend that they are either. The task of theology is not to proclaim definitive and exhaustive formulations of doctrine but to promote an ongoing critical and creative reflection on the faith that underlies these. What I offer here, then, are tentative suggestions from the Bible, which, when integrated into the teaching of the post-conciliar Church, and the hard reality of post-colonial India will, hopefully, help us to move toward a meaningful and relevant understanding of mission in India today.

1. THE BIBLE AS STORY

What, then, does the Bible tell us about mission? As soon as we put this question we realize how difficult it is to answer it. For the Bible, we know, is a large and complex work. In its Catholic version it contains seventy-three different books, in the Protestant version sixty-seven. These books were written in three different languages (Hebrew, Aramaic, and Greek), over a period of more than a thousand years (from 1000 B.C.E. to about 100 C.E.), in a great varieties of cultural worlds (Canaanite, Babylonian, Assyrian, Egyptian, Persian, Greek and Roman). No other sacred text (except possibly the Buddhist Scriptures) has been influenced by so many different cultures as the Bible. Other sacred texts (like those of Hinduism, Islam, Confucianism, or Taoism) have generally grown up within the confines of a single cultural world.

Yet for all its diversity the Bible is one work. It is one because (1) it expresses the unique God experience of a single developing religious tradition, and (2) it does this in the form of one story. The Bible is thus one in its content, and one in its form. The unity of its form is related to the unity of its content, because the form of the Bible is in fact the outward expression of its basic content. It is because the specific God experience of biblical religion is the experience of a God active in history that the literary expression of this God experience takes the form of a story.

It is important, then, that we grasp firmly this overarching unity of the Bible as a story. The Bible contains many laws but it is not (unlike the *Manusmriti*) a book of laws. The Bible contains much doctrine, but it is not (unlike the *Upanishads*) a book of doctrine. The Bible contains many hymns but it is not (unlike the *Rgveda*) a book of hymns. Laws, doctrines, and hymns are all parts of the one story the Bible tells.

This story begins with the creation of the "heavens and the earth" (Gen 1:1) and ends with the appearance of "the new heavens and the new earth" (Rev 21:1). It is therefore the story of creation understood not as a once and for all event, but as Teilhard de Chardin understood it so well, as an ongoing process of evolution.

The Bible tells us the story of the "evolution" of humankind and the cosmos in their journey toward wholeness (*shalom*).

This story is obviously not to be read as a scientific report of how the world came to be, nor as a critical history of the progress of humankind. The history that the Bible tells is not critical but confessional history.[6] Such history tells us not about what actually took place in the history of the cosmos and of humankind, but (to use the telling expression of John Marsh) it tells us about "what went on in what took place."[7] That is, biblical history is concerned not so much about what exactly happened, but about the significance of what happened. The biblical story tells about the meaning of the world, of human history, of personal life. Christian mission is part of this meaningful story. A closer look at the biblical story will show us how.

2. MISSION IN THE BIBLICAL STORY

The shape of the biblical story is shown in the diagram given on the following page. This diagram shows us that the story develops in three cycles. It moves (a) from chaos to creation to sin (the cycle of creation); (b) from sin to Israel to the Exile (the cycle of Israel); and (c) from the Exile to Jesus to the new heavens and the new earth, where the story ends (the cycle of Jesus). Each cycle except the last rises to a peak before collapsing into a trough. This last ends in a peak (or a rising plateau) which is both the climax of the story and (in a sense) a return to its beginning.

This pattern shows us that the biblical story is a story of conflict. Creation is a continuing struggle against disintegration (entropy). Each step in it involves two moments: a negative moment of being freed from bondage (liberation) and a positive moment of consolidation in the freedom achieved (salvation). This dynamic of liberation/salvation structures each cycle of the story.

The three peak moments of the story (Creation-Israel-Jesus) are related, as are its three low points (chaos-sin-exile). That is, they are seen by the Bible as qualitatively similar and are therefore depicted in overlapping imagery. Israel is understood to be a new creation (Deut 32:6; Is 43:1-7) as is Jesus (Jn 1:1). Creation is sometimes described in the imagery of the Exodus: it becomes a rescue operation in which God "saves" the world from the waters of the abyss just as Yhwh saves his people from the Red Sea (Is 51:9-11). The return from the Exile is a replay of the Exodus (Is 43:16-21). The three cycles are thus coiling circles of a spiral in which the same story of the continuing struggle between the creative power of God and the entropy of chaos is played out at new levels, until a breakthrough is achieved with Jesus, who ushers in the new age that is to lead to the ultimate triumph of creation in the new heavens and the new earth (Rev 21:1).

Christian mission has a significant part to play in this triumph. What this part is will become clear when the three cycles of the story are looked at in detail.

The Bible and Mission

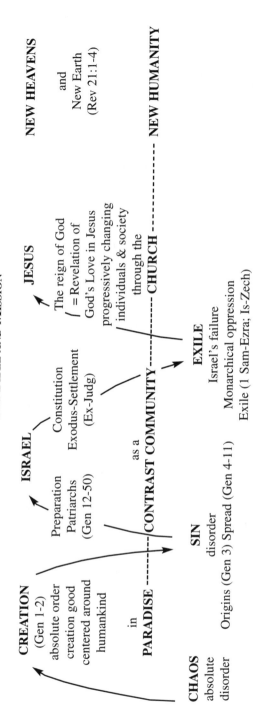

CHAOS
absolute disorder

CREATION
(Gen 1-2)
absolute order
creation good
centered around
humankind

in

PARADISE -------- **CONTRAST COMMUNITY** -------- **CHURCH** -------- **NEW HUMANITY**

as a

SIN
disorder
Origins (Gen 3) Spread (Gen 4-11)

ISRAEL
Preparation
Patriarchs
(Gen 12-50)
Constitution
Exodus-Settlement
(Ex-Judg)

EXILE
Israel's failure
Monarchical oppression
Exile (1 Sam-Ezra; Is-Zech)

JESUS
The reign of God
= Revelation of
God's Love in Jesus
progressively changing
individuals & society
through the

NEW HEAVENS
and
New Earth
(Rev 21:1-4)

The story of the Bible is a story of the progressive LIBERATION-SALVATION of humankind and the cosmos.

The World is freed from	CHAOS	to become	COSMOS	at CREATION (Gen 1-2)
Israel is freed from	BONDED LABOR	to become	GOD'S FREE PEOPLE	at the EXODUS (Ex 6:2-7)
Humankind is freed from	SIN AND DEATH	to become	CHILDREN OF GOD	at the RESURRECTION of Jesus (1 Cor 15)

Taken as a whole the biblical story reveals the three dimensions (cosmic-social-personal) of all mission.

2.1. The Cycle of Creation

The biblical story starts with the creation of the universe (Gen 1-2). "In the beginning," we are told in the opening words of the Bible, "God created the heavens and the earth" (Gen 1:1). But creation as described by the Bible is not creation from nothing. God does not call the world into being from nothingness. Instead God organizes a preexisting chaos into a cosmos. The proper translation of the first words of Genesis is not the traditional translation: "In the beginning God created the heavens and the earth." Instead, the first verses of Genesis should be translated as follows: "When God began to create the heavens and the earth— the earth being formless and empty, with darkness over the surface of the deep and a terrible storm agitating the water—then God said, 'let there be light, and there was light'" (Gen 1:3).[8] Chaos, a state of total disorder, precedes God's act of creation. Creation means bringing order into this disorder. God organizes chaos by separating light from darkness, the waters above from the waters below, dry land from sea, earth from sky (Gen 1:3-10). God then fills the domains so delimited with forms of life appropriate to each (Gen 1:1-25); and God finally crowns the whole of creation by creating humankind (*hāʾādām*) in God's image, that is as God's representative charged with taking care of the cosmos that has just been created.[9]

But the harmonious cosmos created by God is destroyed by sin, which takes the world back into the disorder of chaos. The Book of Genesis describes this powerfully in a marvelously evocative story about the "fall of humankind" (Gen 2:4b-3:24). The story does not mean to tell us about how sin began (this is not its point), but about what the sin really is.[10] Sin, we learn, is not so much an act of disobedience (as the story at first sight seems to suggest) but is rather an attitude of distrust toward God. For what underlies our first parents' "disobedience" is the fact that they do not believe that their welfare lies in trusting God's plans for them. Humankind tries to achieve fulfillment through an autonomous technocratic control of its own destiny. But, as Brueggemann warns us, "failure to trust God with our lives is death."[11]

Lack of trust in God leads to distrust in people and to the collapse of our harmony with nature (Gen 3:8-19). The result of this disintegrating harmony is the explosion of violence, exemplified in the tragic story of Abel and Cain (Gen 4), and in the growth of oppression described in Gen 5-11. "The sins of Adam and Eve, Cain, Lamech, the angel marriages, the Tower of Babel," von Rad points out, "are stages along that way which has separated man [*sic*] farther and farther from God."[12] Creation lapses increasingly into chaos.

2.2. The Cycle of Israel

It is at this point of its story that the Bible introduces a new initiative of God to restore creation. Primal history (Gen 1-11) passes over into patriarchal history (Gen 12-50) as God begins the genesis of Israel, a people through whom creation is to be restored. The shaping of Israel is described in two steps: (1) the patriar-chal history of Gen 12-50 shows how God prepares for the emergence of a new people; (2) the story of the origins of Israel in Exodus through Judges shows how this people comes into being.

From the very first, the universal dimensions of God's renewal project are clear. All the peoples of the earth, we are told, will find a blessing in Abraham (Gen 12:3).[13] So, as Brueggemann notes, "the call to Sarah and to Abraham has to do not simply with the forming of Israel but with the re-forming of cre-ation."[14] This is because Sarah and Abraham are called to be the ancestors of a special people. This people is to be a contrast community, whose presence will renew creation by transforming all other nations into its own image.

The biblical story shows us how Israel is explicitly constituted a contrast community from its beginnings. It is liberated from bondage in Egypt in order to become Yhwh's people (Ex 6:6-7). Its shape as Yhwh's people is spelled out in the great codes of the Bible, notably the Covenant Code in Ex 21-23, the Holi-ness Code in Lev 17-26, and the Code of Deuteronomy in Deut 12-26. These make it clear that unlike neighboring societies (the Canaanite city-states or the great empires of Egypt, Babylon, or Assyria), the societal structures of Israel are not to be oppressive and exploitative, but just—indeed, marked by a special con-cern for the care of the needy and the protection of the powerless (the widow, the orphan, and the refugee).[15] And this contrast community is meant to transform other communities in the world into its own image. "It is the hope of God," as Brueggemann puts it, "that in this new family all human history can be brought to the unity and the harmony intended by the one who calls."[16]

But Israel fails to become the contrast community it is meant to be. Its fail-ure becomes evident when, in emulation of its powerful neighbors (like Third World societies hungering to join the First World today), it chooses to become a monarchy, assuming all the oppressive structures that this social system implied (1 Sam 8). Israel is now no longer a contrast community. It is a state like any other state. It supports an army and a court at the expense of its laboring people. It turns an egalitarian peasant community into a hierarchical society dominated by a military aristocracy and an institutionalized priesthood. It confines its radi-cally free and freeing God, who till now had no fixed abode but would appear and disappear at will, into a temple (the King's temple), where Yhwh now becomes the legitimating deity of the monarch.[17] Worse still, we are told that Solomon conscripts forced laborers (thirty thousand of them) throughout Israel (1 Kgs 5:13). Nothing could be more poignant than this. God had fashioned Israel as a contrast community by liberating people from bonded labor in Egypt. Now Israel's king has brought back bonded labor into Israel. Israel has been taken back into Egypt. The Exodus has been reversed.

Significantly, it is precisely at this moment in the biblical story that the great writing prophets begin to appear. Amos, the first of them, taught in the northern kingdom around about 760 B.C.E. The prophets form a protest movement, which, by appealing to the covenant, attempts to call Israel back to its original vocation and to remind it that it is meant to be a contrast community. That is why the preaching of the prophets focuses on two basic themes: the denunciation of idolatry (Jer 11:9-13; Ezek 14:1-11) and a passionate condemnation of social injustice (Is 3:13-15; Am 2:6-8; 8:4-8; Mic 2:1-11). The two themes are related. To worship Yhwh, the God of liberation, implies that we do justice to people; to go after the Baᶜals of the fertility cults is to approve of the oppressive regimes they legitimize. The "prophetic imagination" thus counters the "royal consciousness" (so like the consciousness of consumer society today) in which (as Brueggemann puts it) an "economics of affluence" (1 Kgs 4:20-23) depends dialectically on a "politics of oppression" (1 Kgs 5:13-18; 9:15-22), and both are legitimized by a "religion of immanence," that is, by a religion in which God has been integrated as it were into the structures of society (1 Kgs 8:12-13). Brueggemann diagrams this as follows:[18]

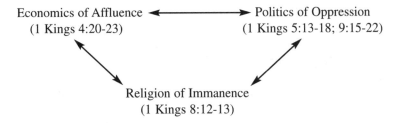

Economics of Affluence ⟷ Politics of Oppression
(1 Kings 4:20-23) (1 Kings 5:13-18; 9:15-22)

Religion of Immanence
(1 Kings 8:12-13)

By challenging the domestication of Yhwh and reasserting his strong socio-ethical demands, the prophets call for an economics of compassion and a politics of justice. Biblical prophetism thus becomes Yhwh's continuing call to Israel to fulfill its destiny as a contrast community.

2.3. The Cycle of Jesus

Because Israel does not heed the warnings of the prophets, it suffers the ultimate catastrophe. A series of crushing military defeats results in the fall of Samaria in 722 and of Jerusalem in 587 B.C.E. Yhwh's people are led into exile. The Holy City is profaned. The dynasty of David, in which the hopes of restored creation had been firmly anchored (Is 11:1-9), disappears from history. God's project of renewing creation through Israel appears to have come to an end.[19]

But the biblical story does not end here. God is faithful even if God's people are unfaithful (Is 49:14-16; Jer 31:31-34; Mic 7:18-20). Exiled Israel returns home (Ezra, Nehemiah), and from this impoverished and oppressed remnant, living in subjection to a succession of imperial regimes (Persian, Greek, and Roman), God, according to the Christian Bible, raises up Jesus, through whom (we believe) creation has once and for all been redeemed.

This decisive saving act of God is described in the language of the times as the arrival of the Kingdom or (more accurately) the Reign of God. We have here a rather misleading translation of an Aramaic idiom (*malkût dî šĕmayyāʾ*) which stands not for a *place* or a community ruled by God, but for the decisive salvific *action* through which God, finally "liberating" creation, reveals God's self as King.[20] By the time of Jesus, the "Reign of God" had become a standard formula for expressing Israel's hopes of liberation.[21] When, therefore, Jesus announces the arrival of God's Reign (Mk 1:14-15), he is claiming that with his coming Israel's hopes of liberation have been definitively fulfilled. God's decisive act of salvation has come. The long-awaited liberation of the world has been once and for all achieved. Creation has been restored; paradise regained!

Such an affirmation appears at first sight to be nonsense. For nothing seems to have changed with the coming of Jesus. The hopes of liberation felt so intensely by Jews of his time (a time of shaming colonial occupation and massive impoverishment, punctuated by violent outbursts of savagely repressed revolt)[22] were, apparently, in no way realized by him. Jesus does not free Israel from the yoke of the Romans, as the Zealots would have wished him to do. He does not lead the "children of light" to victory over the "children of darkness" in the eschatological triumph which the sectarians at Qumran were awaiting. He does not satisfy the hopes of the priesthood by renewing the Temple and its cult, but proclaims instead their imminent destruction. He does not proclaim a new messianic Torah whose observance would bring about (as the Pharisees believed) the "Kingdom of God"—or if he does it is through a radicalization of the law that is quite unacceptable to them. No one's hopes are realized by Jesus, whose own proclamation of the Kingdom ends with the shattering failure of the cross. Was Jesus, then, no more than a failed messianic pretender, or a disappointed visionary who hoped for a divine intervention in history but died in despair when it failed to come?

For us Christians, of course, this is not the case, because we believe that the story of Jesus does not end with the cross. His claims are vindicated by his resurrection from the dead. This emergence of life from death, this dramatic reversal of entropy, guarantees the ultimate triumph of God's act of creation. The resurrection validates Jesus' proclamation that the Reign of God has come, but in doing so it reinterprets the traditional understanding of that Reign. God's salvation, it tells us, comes not through the exercise of coercive power, whether it be political or moral or magical (all of which options Jesus steadfastly refuses),[23] but through the revelation of God's love. For what Jesus proclaims in word and in deed, in his sayings and his parables, in his miracles and his table fellowship with tax collectors and sinners, in his living out his life in availability and service and his laying it down in a freely accepted death (Mk 10:45), is always God's absolute and unconditional love for us—a love he himself has experienced in his foundational experience of God as *Abba*. In announcing the Reign of God, Jesus announces that God loves us, and in inviting us to "repent" he invites us to accept that love and to entrust our lives wholly to it, thus reversing the distrust of sin.[24]

But the Reign of God which Jesus brings is, the New Testament tells us, both present and future. It is, as scholars say, "already and not yet." Jesus compares it to a mustard seed that grows into a great tree (Mk 4:30-32) or to leaven that slowly leavens the huge mass of dough into which it has been put (Mt 13:33). The Reign of God is therefore a process which has begun but has not yet ended. The awareness of God's love has come into the world through Jesus and is at work among us transforming hearts and structures, and so liberating people from both *Mammon* (greed) and from *Satan* (structured evil). This process of liberation is taking us toward the "new heavens and the new earth," the end-time community which God will bring about in the fullness of time, not as an arbitrary act which ignores human history, but as the crowning act of creation which brings that history to its fullness.

In this process we too have a role. Because God's Reign is both a gift and a task, the act of God which ushers in the new heavens and the new earth and brings creation to its fullness is not without its human side. We are not passive receptors of God's Reign but active collaborators in its growth. It is here that Christian mission comes into the biblical story.

The task of mission is to enter into the process of the Reign of God inaugurated by Jesus and to further its movement toward the end-time community. That is, Christian mission is concerned with fostering what Vatican II has called "the body of a new human family, a body which even now is able to give some kind of foreshadowing of the new age."[25] Because the Church is the community of Jesus which continues his active presence in the world and is entrusted with his mission, its primary task is to further the process inaugurated by Jesus and to help bring the Reign of God to its fullness. It does this by becoming the symbol and the servant of God's Reign.[26] As such it is the new contrast community, which by living out the values of Jesus makes God's love present in the world and so prepares it for its transformation into the new heavens and the new earth. The primary mission of the Church, the biblical story tells us, is to lead humankind and cosmic history to its fulfillment, in the full realization of God's Reign.

3. MISSION TODAY

It is against this vast panorama of human and cosmic history sketched out by the Bible that the Church in India must understand its mission. Its primary mission, as we have seen above, is that of promoting the growth of the Reign of God, which, Vatican II tells us, is "already present on this earth in mystery," but which, "when the Lord returns, will be brought to full flower."[27] The Church will fulfill this mission *by making God's love present in whatever way it can.* This simple formula, I believe, describes adequately and accurately the primary mission of the Church: for where God's love is present, there the Reign of God grows.

But making God's love present can take a variety of forms. The love (*agapē*) proclaimed by Jesus as the soul of God's Reign is an effective love. It means "doing good" to people by responding effectively to their needs.[28] Since we can do this in many different ways, the mission of the Church will always be a pluriform mission. It will certainly include proclamation and conversion where these are appropriate, that is, when they are offered and accepted as gifts of love, not as the expressions of "conquest" or of "sale."[29] But the Church's mission is certainly not to be restricted to this. To identify mission with Church growth would be to impoverish and distort it. For Church growth is a typically institutional preoccupation, which the Church, because it is also an institution, rightly shares, but which must not be allowed to become its primary concern. For the Church, while it needs its institutional shell in order to survive, is not primarily an institution but a living community whose life is love. Like Jesus (Mk 10:45), it lives not for itself but for others. It is, therefore, wholly at the service of the world. The Church is not the Reign of God, but only the symbol and the servant of God's Reign. Mission, therefore, is not service of the Church, but the Church's service of the Reign of God.

Christian mission, therefore, must not forget the primacy of God's Reign, and so the ultimate primacy of God. Like all Christian life, Christian mission too is theocentric, not Christocentric—much less ecclesiocentric.[30] It is always God and God's Reign that is the goal (1 Cor 15:28), Christ who is the way (Jn 14:26), and the Church that is the concrete locus ("the body") of this way in our world (1 Cor 12:27). The concerns of Christian mission therefore extend beyond the interests of the Church to embrace all the manifold demands of the Reign of God.[31] The cosmic, historical, and spiritual dimensions of the biblical story must enter into Christian mission so that its horizons are as large as the cosmos (for God the Redeemer is also God the Creator, who does not abandon creation), and its concerns embrace (like the biblical story) every aspect of human and cosmic liberation.

NOTES

1. Soares-Prabhu, "Missiology or Missiologies?," *Mission Studies* 3, no. 2 (1986): 85-87.

2. See especially Julian Saldanha, *Patterns of Evangelization in Mission History* (Bombay: St Pauls, 1988).

3. Lucien Legrand, *Unity and Plurality: Mission in the Bible* (Maryknoll, N.Y.: Orbis Books, 1990), 107-30.

4. As Yacob Tesfai ("Invasion and Evangelization: Reflections on a Quincentenary," *International Review of Mission* 81 [1992]: 525-41) notes: "The Indians and blacks were denied the status of human beings; they were branded barbarians. They had no culture worthy of human beings" (p. 539).

5. Walbert Bühlmann (*The Chosen Peoples* [Slough, U.K.: St. Paul's, 1982]) gives a telling quotation from Willibald Wanger's adult catechism, written in Africa (for Africans!) in 1912. "This terrible error, called paganism," the catechism informs us, "is from the Devil who wishes to be as God, and from the stupidity of human beings who, deceived by the Devil, pass on to their children the lies of their fathers" (p. 104). Closer

to home we find Francis Xavier writing that "the inhabitants of India have no culture at all. It is hard to live among a people that knows not God, nor hears its own reason because its life is so steeped in sin" (p. 110). He is echoed three hundred years later by Bishop Athanasius Hartmann: "The people are on the lowest rung of breeding and development, and steeped in the rawest idolatry. They lack the most primitive qualities of social life—namely constancy, veracity, and enterprise. And we heard this from one end of India to the other" (p. 110). Such quotations do not tell the whole story of the colonial mission, but they catch a significant feature of the missionary's prejudiced attitude to "pagans" and "paganism."

6. Gerhard von Rad, *Old Testament Theology*, vol. 1 (Edinburgh: Oliver & Boyd, 1962), 108.

7. John Marsh, *The Gospel of John*, Pelican Gospel Commentaries (Harmondsworth: Penguin, 1968), 18.

8. Richard Clifford and Roland E. Murphy, "Genesis," in *The New Jerome Biblical Commentary*, ed. Raymond E. Brown, Joseph A. Fitzmyer, and Roland E. Murphy (Bangalore: Theological Publications of India, 1990), 10. I have adapted the translation given there, replacing its "a wind of God sweeping over the waters" with "a terrible storm agitating the water"—which I believe is a more appropriate rendering of the *rûaḥ ʾĕlōhîm mĕraḥepet ʿal pĕnê hammāyîm* of the original. See Gerhard von Rad, *Genesis*, Old Testament Library (London: SCM Press, 1972), 49-50; E. A. Speiser, *Genesis*, Anchor Bible (New York: Doubleday, 1964), 3-5.

9. Von Rad, *Old Testament Theology*, 1:60: "Just as powerful earthly kings, to indicate their claim to dominion, erect an image of themselves in the provinces of their empire where they do not personally appear, so man is placed upon earth in God's image as God's sovereign emblem. He is really only God's representative, summoned to maintain and enforce God's claim to dominion over the earth. The decisive thing about man's similarity to God, therefore, is his function in the non-human world."

10. Gordon J. Wenham, *Genesis 1-15*, Word Biblical Commentary (Waco, Tex.: Word Books, 1987), 90.

11. Walter Brueggemann, *Genesis*, Interpretation (Atlanta: John Knox, 1982), 54.

12. Von Rad, *Old Testament Theology*, 1:152.

13. The *nibrĕkû* of the Hebrew original can be read as a passive, as a reflexive, or as a middle. So all the peoples of the earth "will be blessed" (*passive*—so NIV, JB), "will bless themselves" (*reflexive*—so RSV, NEB), or "will find a blessing" (*middle*—so NAB) in Abraham. Wenham (*Genesis 1-15*, 277) makes a good case for the middle sense. Gen 12:1-3 would then, as he points out, give us a progressive insight into the "blessing" of Abraham: (1) Abraham alone is blessed (v. 2b); (2) his name will be used as a blessing (v. 2c); (3) those who bless Abraham will be blessed (v. 3a); (4) all the peoples of the earth will find blessing in him (v. 3c). Whatever reading we adopt, the universal significance of the call of Abraham is clear.

14. Brueggemann, *Genesis*, 105.

15. See Soares-Prabhu, "Class in the Bible: The Biblical Poor as a Social Class?," *Vidyajyoti* 49 (1985): 322-46, esp. 338-39, and in *Theology of Liberation: An Indian Biblical Perspective*, Collected Writings of George M. Soares-Prabhu, S.J., vol. 4, ed. Francis X. D'Sa (Pune: Jnana-Deepa Vidyapeeth, 2001), 85-109.

16. Brueggemann, *Genesis*, 105.

17. Soares-Prabhu, "The Temple of Jerusalem: Its Religious and Political Significance in the Old Testament," *Jeevadhara* 23, no. 134 (1993): 130-32, 144-49.

18. Walter Brueggemann, *The Prophetic Imagination* (Philadelphia: Fortress Press, 1978), 35-38.

19. As Walter Brueggemann notes (*Hopeful Imagination: Prophetic Voices in Exile* [Philadelphia: Fortress Press, 1986], 1), the Exile and the end of Israel "could be understood politically as the result of the Babylonian expansionism or theologically as the end of Yahweh's patience with this people. While biblical literature is not unaware of the former political explanation, it focuses deliberately and almost exclusively on the latter theological point. Thus, Babylonian expansionism is subordinated to and explained in terms of Yahweh's judgment (Jer 25:9; 27:1-6)."

20. See G. M. Soares-Prabhu, "The Kingdom of God: Jesus' Vision of a New Society," in *The Indian Church in the Struggle for a New Society,* ed. D. S. Amalorpavadass (Bangalore: National Biblical Catechetical and Liturgical Centre, 1981), 591-93. See chapter 4 in this volume.

21. Norman Perrin, *Jesus and the Language of the Kingdom* (London: SCM Press, 1976), 32.

22. G. M. Soares-Prabhu, "Jesus and the Poor," in *Poverty in India: Challenges and Responses,* ed. J. Murickan (Bangalore: Xavier Board, 1988), 262-64, and in *Theology of Liberation: An Indian Biblical Perspective*, Collected Writings of George M. Soares-Prabhu, S.J., vol. 4, ed. Francis X. D'Sa (Pune: Jnana-Deepa Vidyapeeth, 2001), 173-97.

23. Cf. the temptation story in Mt 4:1-11 = Lk 4:1-13 and its echoes in Mk 8:11-12 (Jesus refuses to give a sign from heaven); Mt 16:22-23 (Peter is rebuked as *Satan* for "tempting" Jesus away from the way of the cross); and Jn 6:15 (Jesus avoids being made king by a crowd enthused by his feeding miracle).

24. Soares-Prabhu, "Kingdom of God," 597-600.

25. *Gaudium et Spes* (Pastoral Constitution on the Church in the Modern World), no. 39, quoted from Walter Abbott, *Documents of Vatican II* (London: Chapman, 1966), 237.

26. See Michael Amaladoss, "Religious and Mission," *SEDOS Bulletin* 25 (1993): 208.

27. *Gaudium et Spes,* no. 39.

28. G. M. Soares-Prabhu, "The Synoptic Love-Commandment: The Dimensions of Love in the Teaching of Jesus," *Jeevadhara* 13, no. 74 (1983): 85-103. See chapter 13 in this volume.

29. "Conquest" and "sale," I have suggested, are the metaphors that have determined the aggressive missiologies and the sinful missions of the colonial and neo-colonial age. See Soares-Prabhu, "Missiology," 86-87.

30. G. M. Soares-Prabhu, "The Church as Mission: A Reflection on Mt 5:13-16," *Jeevadhara* 24 (1994): 280, and in *Biblical Themes for a Contextual Theology for Today,* Collected Writings of George M. Soares-Prabhu, vol. 1, ed. Isaac Padinjarekuttu (Pune: Jnana-Deepa Vidyapeeth, 1999), 22. See chapter 18 of this volume.

31. On this, see also G. M. Soares-Prabhu, "Following Jesus in Mission: Reflections on Mission in the Gospel of Matthew," in *Bible and Mission in India Today*, Forum of Indian Missiologists Series 1, ed. J. Kavunkal and F. Hrangkhuma (Bombay: St Pauls, 1993), 84-87. See chapter 19 of this volume.

18

THE CHURCH AS MISSION

A Reflection on Matthew 5:13-16

The so-called Great Commission (Mt 28:16-20) which concludes the Gospel of Matthew has become a foundational text for the aggressive missiology underlying new evangelical movements in the sects and mainline churches. But to be properly understood the text is to be read in its setting in the Gospel of Matthew and particularly in the light of another, largely neglected mission command (Mt 5:13-16) which Matthew has inserted at a crucial point in the Sermon on the Mount. Reflection on this text offers a corrective to a flawed understanding of the so-called Great Commission and draws attention to forgotten dimensions of mission which are of particular relevance to the Church in India. Mission, the text reminds us, is not just Christocentric (making disciples of the risen Lord) but theocentric (giving glory to God by building up God's Kingdom); and the way to this mission is not so much individual proclamation as community witness. Unless the Church lives as Church, that is, as the symbol and servant of the kingdom it cannot engage in authentic mission.

For Christians interested in mission, the Gospel of Matthew is significant primarily for its so-called Great Commission (Mt 28:16-20), which is probably the most used and abused mission text in recent times.[1] This marvelous finale to what is arguably the most meticulously constructed of the New Testament writings (Matthew) offers a summary of the Gospel in a carefully crafted composition, whose theological density rivals that of the prologue of John. The text is therefore to be read as part of the Gospel it so brilliantly concludes. Instead, it is (especially in evangelical tracts) often taken out of its context and read as an autonomous decree which speaks directly to our own situation. An editorial masterpiece which weaves together the christological (28:18), ecclesiological

This article first appeared in *Jeevadhara* 24 (1994): 280-92.

(28:19-20a), and eschatological threads (28:20b) of the Gospel into a theological text of great power is now read as a simple (even simplistic) Great Commission, purporting to come from Jesus himself.[2]

Such a reading of the text is based on questionable exegesis and can lead to a damaging missiology. It is based on questionable exegesis because it ignores the results of the critical study of the Gospels, which has shown convincingly that Mt 28:16-20, as it now stands, is a composition of the evangelist, not a saying of Jesus, and does not encourage the simplistic, aggressive proselytizing often derived from it.[3] It can lead to a damaging missiology because it gives rise to a distorted understanding of the practice of mission. Mission is no longer understood as the spontaneous and joyous communication of the experience of the risen Lord, as it always is in the New Testament.[4] It is now looked upon as a "duty" to be imposed on a reluctant people, who, because they have not been fired by the spirit of Jesus, must be prodded to proclaim the "good news" through guilt. Mission thus becomes not gospel but law.

Worse still, a mission fueled by such triumphalistic "commands" easily degenerates into a "conquest" (with or without a "holy alliance" with aggressive colonial or neo-colonial powers), where the numerical expansion of the missionizing Church or the political or economic advancement of its patrons can become more important than the welfare of the "evangelized" people. Mission then ceases to be an act of service and becomes a selfish and therefore sinful exercise of institutional survival, expansion, or power. The consequences of this are plain for anyone who cares to reflect on what five hundred years of colonial mission have done to the Third World, or on the panic reactions that Christian missions still evoke in India.[5]

A corrective to this understanding of mission can be found in another mission text in the Gospel of Matthew (Mt 5:13-16), whose significance for the New Testament theology of mission has been largely overlooked. This text gives us an understanding of mission which complements that offered by the Great Commission. In it mission is described not so much in terms of verbal proclamation as of witness. Such a description, I hope to show, is not only more appropriate to the postcolonial situation of India today, but is also truer to the New Testament understanding of mission, than is the narrow, one-sided proclamation missiology derived from the Great Commission. For mission, as the New Testament understands it, is always integral mission.[6] It includes not only verbal proclamation but healing action as well (Mt 4:23 = 9:35), and it strives not just for "Church growth" (as if the Church were an end in itself) but for the wholeness of creation, that is, for the total and integral liberation of human and cosmic history into the fullness of the eschatological Kingdom (Mt l0:7). These dimensions of mission form the backdrop to all the mission texts of the New Testament. They find a conspicuous expression in the other mission command of Matthew's Gospel, the mission command of the Sermon on the Mount (Mt 5:13-16), which though less known is probably richer in its overall missiological content than the much quoted Great Commission (Mt 28:16-20). It is this mission command that I propose to study here, hoping to find in it an appropriate starting point for a reflection on mission in India today.

1. THE SETTING OF MT 5:13-16

Mt 5:13-16 is part, indeed a crucial part, of the Sermon on the Mount, the first and most important of the five discourses (Mt 5-7; 10; 13; 18; [23] 24-25) which form the structural backbone of Matthew's Gospel. This inaugural discourse gives us a sort of compendium of Christian life. It does this not in the form of a set of rules which are to be rigorously observed (the Sermon on the Mount is no way Canon Law!), but as a series of "goal directed norms,"[7] illustrated by "focal instances,"[8] which together indicate the attitude of radical obedience and radical concern which a follower of Jesus must develop.[9] The attitude demanded by the Sermon on the Mount is, however, not merely an inner disposition but is an attitude of effective love (*agapē*), which shows itself in "doing good to" anyone in need (Mt 5:45; 1 Thess 5:15). Like the rest of the Gospel the Sermon is strongly oriented toward "doing" (Mt 7:21-27).

This "doing" which the Sermon recommends is not, formally, missionary praxis. Matthew, who has arranged the sayings of Jesus into discourses themewise, has kept his instructions for mission in the Mission Discourse of Mt 10. But because mission is an essential dimension of discipleship for Matthew, the whole praxis of the Sermon on the Mount is in fact oriented toward mission.

This orientation is given by Mt 5:13-16, a link text which joins the solemn and joyous opening of the Sermon (the beatitudes of Mt 5:3-12) to the definition of its theme (the I-saying of Mt 5:17-20). The beatitudes form a kind of overture to the Sermon. They offer as it were a preliminary outline of Christian life whose details will be filled out by what follows. The I-saying, on the other hand, defines the purpose of the Sermon. The Sermon, it tells us, is meant to "fulfill" the economy of the First Testament by proposing a form of righteousness (Christian Dharma) which is better than that practiced by the religious leaders of traditional Judaism, the learned scribes and the pious Pharisees (5:20). The "mission command" (5:13-16), which comes in between the two, gives the whole Sermon a missionary orientation, by pointing out the effect that living out the Sermon will have on the liberation of the world. If the beatitudes tell us the "how" of Christian Dharma (how Christian life is to be lived), the I-saying tells us its "what" (namely, that Christian Dharma is the "fulfilment of the Law"), and the mission command tells us its "why" (showing us that living out this Dharma is significant for the liberation of the world). The beatitudes (5:1-12) are thus addressed strictly to the followers of Jesus; the I-saying (5:17-20) relates their following to the religiosity of the Jews; the mission command of the Sermon (5:13-16) relates it to the salvation of the world.

BEATITUDES	MISSION COMMAND	I-SAYING
(5:3-12)	(5:13-16)	(5:17-20)
How	Why	What
	of	
	Christian *Dharma*	
(Christians)	(world)	(Jews)

2. THE MEANING OF MT 5:13-16

This crucial mission command of the Sermon on the Mount is a carefully composed text which reads as follows:

v. 13 You are the salt of the earth.
      But if salt has lost its taste, how can its saltiness be restored?
      It is no longer good for anything,
      but is thrown out and trampled under foot.
v. 14 You are the light of the world.
      A city built on a hilltop cannot be hid.
v. 15 No one after lighting a lamp puts it under the bushel basket,
      but on the lamp-stand, and it gives light to all in the house.
v. 16 In the same way, let your light shine before others,
      so that they may see your good works
      and give glory to your Father in heaven.

It is only the last verse (v. 16) of this carefully structured text with its lone imperative ("let your light shine") which, strictly speaking, is a "mission command." But this verse concludes the whole preceding section (5:13-15). It rounds it off and gives it its orientation. It is, as Ulrich Luz comments, "the summarizing key of the pericope."[10] The whole pericope has been shaped by Matthew, from originally independent sayings,[11] into a coherent, closely knit unit which comes to its point in v. 16. The pericope as a whole, then, is to be taken as a "mission command," in which vv. 13-15 motivate the command while v. 16 articulates it.

The mission command makes two striking assertions about the followers of Jesus. "You are the salt of the earth," it says, and "you are the light of the world." These terse indicatives, remarkable in themselves, become all the more striking in their context. The "you" in them which is emphatic ("*You* are . . .") links them to the verses that precede (5:11-12), in which the third person of Matthew's first eight beatitudes ("Blessed are the . . ." in 5:3-10) changes suddenly into the second person ("Blessed are you . . ." in 5:11-12). It is this "you" of the ninth beatitude, that is, the followers of Jesus, blessed because they are persecuted, slandered, and reviled, who are now declared to be the salt of the earth and the light of the world. The assertions of 5:13-16 are, then, as Davies and Allison note, "strikingly paradoxical," because they claim that "the world is saved precisely by those it persecutes."[12]

The claim made in these assertions is even more striking. The persecuted followers of Jesus are said to be "the salt of the earth" and "the light of the world." Images that in the Bible are usually reserved for the Torah, or for Israel, or for the Messiah are now applied to these reviled and persecuted followers of Jesus. And they are applied in the most universal way possible: the followers of Jesus are to be the salt and the light not just of Israel but of the world.[13]

Salt and light are images widely used in the ancient world and can mean many things.[14] They are open symbols; that is, they are images whose meaning is not fixed but is determined by the context in which they are used. But the context in Mt 5:13-16 does not make it clear what exactly these two images signify. It does not tell us what precise function of the Christian community is being indicated by them. Indeed it is likely that Matthew is not thinking of any very specific function, but is merely drawing our attention to the indispensable role the followers of Jesus are to play in the liberation of the world. How they are to play this role is made clear in the concluding verse of the pericope, which, as we have seen, is its "summarizing key."[15] Here we are told what it means in practice to be salt and light.

Because they are the salt of the earth and the light of the world, the followers of Jesus must let their light shine before others. That is, they are "to live in the world so that the world will see them and be moved to glorify God."[16] To do this they have not to practice ostentatious displays of piety (this is explicitly forbidden by Jesus in Mt 6:1-19), but must simply do the "good works" that will be spelled out for them in the Sermon on the Mount. Merely doing this, that is, merely living out their Christian Dharma, is an act of mission, because it will lead people to glorify God. The goal of mission, as spelled out in the mission command of the Sermon on the Mount, is therefore to lead people to give glory to God; the means to this goal is to live out one's Christian life; the way to live out one's Christian life is to follow the Sermon on the Mount. Because living out Christian life properly is already mission, the Sermon on the Mount, which marks out the contours of Christian living, becomes a strategy for mission!

3. THE SIGNIFICANCE OF MT 5:13-16

Several important truths about Church and mission emerge when we begin to reflect on what has been said about this mission command and its setting.

(a) The Sermon on the Mount is addressed not to any special group among the followers of Jesus, but to all his followers. Ulrich Luz has argued this well.[17] But what Luz and indeed most other commentators seem to have missed is that Matthew visualizes these followers of Jesus not as a collection of individuals but as a "Church" (16:18; 18:17). The individualism of our modern or postmodern culture blinds us to the essentially communitarian perspective of Matthew, for whom the followers of Jesus form a structured community and are usually thought of as such.[18] The mission command of 5:13-16, like the so-called Great Commission of 28:16-20, is therefore addressed not just to individual followers of Jesus, but to the Christian community as a whole. It is this community which is hailed as the salt of the earth and the light of the world, and which is summoned to let its light shine before people, so that they will be led to glorify God. The "good works" taught by the Sermon on the Mount as exemplifications of the selfless love which is the basic attitude of Christian life (22:34-40) are to be made visible in the praxis of the community as a whole, and not just of a Mother Teresa in it. Called for a mission to the world, the Church must fulfill this mission, first of all, by living visibly as Church. And a community becomes "Church" not simply by professing faith in Jesus (saying "Lord, Lord"), but by *doing* the will of the Father, as this is expressed in the Sermon on the Mount and the other teachings of Jesus (Mt 7:21-23).

(b) The ultimate basis of the Church's mission is therefore the witness of its community life and praxis. It is through its fidelity to the Christian Dharma, with its antigreed and its antipride,[19] that the Church remains "salt" that has not lost its saltiness and "light" that has not been hidden under a measure (5:14-15). Because mission is a communication of life (of "saltiness" or "light") and not merely enrollment in a club or conscription into an army, it must emerge spontaneously from the life of a witnessing community and spread, as it were, by infection. Any verbal proclamation, if it is to be authentic and not a form of what Matthew (and Jesus) would call "hypocrisy" (Mt 7:5; 15:7), must first be lived out in the Christian life of the community. A Church that does not live a conspicuously Christian life (a Church, for instance, that is ridden by caste, or devoured by consumerism, or caught up in struggles for status or power) can no more engage in authentic mission than can a bad tree produce healthy fruit (Mt 3:8-10; 7:16-20; 12:33). Its mission sours into "conquest," propaganda, or "Church growth"; and the communities it engenders are not spirit-filled Churches but infected reproductions of itself.

(c) So while verbal proclamation must be a part of Christian mission, it will always be a derivative part. This is especially so in India. For here a religious tradition that "*sees* the divine image" (*darshan*) [20] rather than "*hears* the word of God" has made people more sensitive to visual manifestations of religious experience in the life of individuals and communities than to mere words about it. It is the witness of individual and communitarian life, as the lives of our Indian saints have shown, that is crucial. We need to listen attentively to Mahatma Gandhi's words about "the gospel of the rose."[21]

(d) Genuine mission, flowing out of the living praxis of the Church, the mission command tells us, will lead people to give glory to God (5:16). The mission command of the Sermon on the Mount is thus strongly theocentric—not ecclesiocentric nor even Christocentric as is, for instance, the Great Commission. Because the ultimate manifestation of the glory of God is God's Reign (Mt 6:9-

10), one might argue that the ultimate aim of mission, implied in this text and spelled out elsewhere in the Bible, is the building up of the Reign of God. Mission does this whenever it contributes to the realization of God's plan for human and cosmic liberation (paradigmed in the confessional history of the Bible), whereby the "heavens and the earth" created in the beginning (Gen 1-2) are brought through a long process of struggle against the powers of sin and death, to their fullness in the new heavens and the new earth, which will appear at the end-time (Rev 21:1-4). The aim of mission is therefore not so much planting (or more accurately transplanting) the Church, nor conquering the world for Christ, nor fostering Church growth, as leading history to its fulfillment in the full realization of the Kingdom of God.

(e) This understanding of mission is, I believe, especially appropriate in India today. Because of its plurireligious horizon, an Indian missiology will tend, like all Indian theology, to be centered on God rather than on the Church or even on Christ. Such a theocentric focus, is nothing to be embarrassed about, for it is completely faithful to the Bible. The biblical story begins and ends not with the Church nor even with Jesus Christ but only with God, who is all in all (Rom 11:36; 1 Cor 8:6). It may be the task of an Indian theology to restore this theocentric focus to a Western Christianity, which, because it tends to stop short at Jesus (who is the way not the goal) or, worse, because it tends to sacralize the Church (which is a symbol and the servant of the Kingdom, but not the Kingdom itself),[22] may have lost its sense of the overwhelming reality of God.

(f) Reflection on the mission command of the Sermon on the Mount thus offers a double corrective to current understandings of Church and mission. (1) It extends the aim of mission from a narrowly ecclesiocentric (planting the Church) or Christocentric (making disciples of Jesus) goal to a fully theocentric one (building up the Kingdom). (2) It shifts the emphasis of missionary praxis from individual proclamation (often an alibi for genuine Christian life) to costly, prophetic community witness.

NOTES

1. For a near-exhaustive survey of the previous exegesis of this much-studied text, see Gerhard Friedrich, "Die formale Struktur von Mt 28:18-20," *Zeitschrift für Theologie und Kirche* 80 (1983): 137-83. The missiological significance of the text is discussed in David Bosch, *Transforming Mission: Paradigm Shifts in Theology of Mission* (Maryknoll, N.Y.: Orbis, 1991), 56-83; Lucien Legrand, *Unity and Plurality: Mission in the Bible* (Maryknoll, N.Y.: Orbis, 1990), 77-82; Donald Senior and Carroll Stuhlmueller, *The Biblical Foundations for Mission* (London: SCM Press, 1983), 251-52; G. M. Soares-Prabhu, "Following Jesus in Mission: Reflections on Mission in the Gospel of Matthew," in *Bible and Mission in India*, ed. J. Kavunkal and F. Hrangkhuma (Bombay: St Pauls, 1993), 65-73. See chapter 19 of this volume.

2. See Roger Hedlund, *Mission to Man in the Bible* (Madras: Evangelical Literature Service, 1983), 202-6; Alan Tippet, *An Introduction to Missiology* (Pasadena, Calif.:

William Carey Library, 1987), 14; Max Warren, *I Believe in the Great Commission* (London: Hodder & Stoughton, 1976), 54-55.

3. Soares-Prabhu, "Following Jesus in Mission," 65-73; Bosch, " Transforming Mission," 56-57; Legrand, *Unity and Plurality,* 82-83.

4. The variant "mission commands" of the risen Lord described by Matthew (28:16-20), Luke (24:44-49), and John (20:21-23)—the mission command in Mark (16:9-20) is not part of the original Gospel—are redactional formulations which express in terms of the theology of each evangelist an essential but unthematized dimension of the Easter experience. See Xavier Léon-Dufour, *Resurrection and the Easter Message* (New York: Holt, Rinehart & Winston, 1971), 80-88.

5. See the issue of *Concilium* 6 (1990) entitled *1492-1992: The Voices of the Victims,* ed. L. Boff and V. Elizondo; of *Missiology* 20, no. 2 (1992), on evangelization of the new world; of *Social Action* 42, no. 1 (1992) entitled *Christopher Columbus: Five Centuries of Colonialism* for some of the ambiguities of colonial mission in Latin America; see also Arun Shourie, *Missionaries in India: Continuities, Changes, Dilemmas* (Delhi: ASA Publications, 1994), along with the critical review of Kushwant Singh in *The Week* 12, no. 25 (June 12, 1994), 20-21, for an instructive glimpse into the continuing widespread Hindu prejudices about Christian missions in India.

6. See Aloysius Pieris, "Whither New Evangelism?," *East Asian Pastoral Review* 29 (1992): 270-82, for a splendid exposition of how "integral evangelization" is to be understood in Asia today.

7. Bernard Häring, "The Normative Value of the Sermon on the Mount," *Catholic Biblical Quarterly* 29 (1967): 375-85.

8. R. C. Tannehill, "The 'Focal Instance' as a Form of New Testament Speech: A Study of Mt 5:39b-42," *Journal of Religion* 50 (1970): 372-85.

9. G. M. Soares-Prabhu, "'The Dharma of Jesus': An Interpretation of the Sermon on the Mount," *Bible Bhashyam* 6 (1980): 358-81, and in *Theology of Liberation: An Indian Biblical Perspective*, Collected Writings of George M. Soares-Prabhu, S.J., vol. 4, ed. Francis X. D'Sa (Pune: Jnana-Deepa Vidyapeeth, 2001), 153-72. See chapter 12 of this volume.

10. Ulrich Luz, *Matthew 1-7: A Commentary* (Minneapolis: Augsburg, 1989), 252.

11. W. D. Davies and Dale C. Allison, *The Gospel According to Saint Matthew,* International Critical Commentary (Edinburgh: Clark, 1988), 1:470-71.

12. Ibid., 472.

13. W. A. Grundmann, *Das Evangelium nach Matthäus* (Berlin: Evangelische Verlagsanstalt, 1972), 136; Luz, *Matthew 1-7,* 249; Davies and Allison, *Gospel According to Saint Matthew,* 1:472.

14. See Davies and Allison, *Gospel According to Saint Matthew,* 1:472-73, for an excellent survey of the symbolic use of salt in the Old and New Testaments, in rabbinic texts, and in Greek literature. Three usages of salt stand out: (1) its use in daily life to flavor or preserve food (Job 6:6); (2) its use in cult as an element added to purify sacrifices (Ex 30:35; Ezek 43:24); and (3) its use in religious and social life to seal a relationship with God (Num 18:19—a covenant of salt) or with people (Ezra 4:14). Robert H. Gundry (*Matthew: A Commentary on His Literary and Theological Art* [Grand Rapids: Eerdmans, 1982], 75) speaks of the use of salt in small quantities as fertilizer for the soil, but this use is not attested to in contemporary writings and is questioned by Ernst Lohmeyer, *Das Evangelium des Matthäus,* 3rd ed. (Göttingen: Vandenhoeck & Ruprecht, 1962), 99. Davies and Allison (*Gospel According to Saint Matthew,* 1:473) rightly point out that no

particular usage of salt is singled out by Matthew, for whom salt was "probably equivocal and multivocal" and "not to be delimited to any particular referent."

15. Luz, *Matthew 1-7,* 252.

16. Davies and Allison, *Gospel According to Saint Matthew,* 1:478.

17. Luz, *Matthew 1-7,* 254-55.

18. We must not of course read our modern experience of a highly institutionalized and stratified "Church" into Matthew. A useful discussion of the "Church" in Matthew in terms of the Hellenistic institution of the household can be found in Michael H. Crosby, *House of Disciples: Church, Economics and Justice in Matthew* (Maryknoll, N.Y.: Orbis, 1988).

19. See G. M. Soares-Prabhu, "Antigreed and Antipride: Mark 10:17-27 & 10:35-45 in the Light of Tribal Values," *Jeevadhara* 24, no. 140 (1994): 149-50, and in *A Biblical Theology for India,* Collected Writings of George M. Soares-Prabhu, S.J., vol. 2, ed. Scaria Kuthirakkattel (Pune: Jnana-Deepa Vidyapeeth, 1999), 241-59, and compare this with the two axioms (1) the irreconcilable opposition between Yhwh and Mammon and (2) the irrevocable covenant between Yhwh and the poor, which Pieris ("Whither New Evangelism," 274-75) proposes as the basis of Christian life and mission.

20. Diana L. Eck, *Darsan: Seeing the Divine Image in India* (Chambersburg, Penn.: Anima Books, 1981).

21. M. K. Gandhi, *Christian Missions: Their Place in India,* ed. Bharatan Kumarappa (Ahmedabad: Navjivan, 1957), 162.

22. Michael Amaladoss, "Religious and Mission," *SEDOS Bulletin* 25 (1993): 208.

19

FOLLOWING JESUS IN MISSION

Reflections on Mission
in the Gospel of Matthew

There is no biblical text which is so articulate about mission as is the Gospel of Matthew. The Gospel ends with the so-called "Great Commission" (Mt 28:16-20), which is the most forthright call to mission to be found anywhere in the New Testament. It contains a Mission Discourse (Mt 10:1-42), which, for its length, its meticulous composition, and the wealth of the mission instruction it offers, is unparalleled in the Bible. And it reports other sayings of Jesus which explicitly (Mt 24:14) or implicitly (Mt 5:13-16) draw attention to the need for a worldwide mission. Together these texts of Matthew spell out an unusually clear and comprehensive theology of mission, which holds important lessons for us reflecting on mission in India today.

It will not, of course, be possible within the limits of a paper like this to attempt a detailed study of the texts in Matthew which speak about mission. An overall survey of their teaching would be possible, but not, I believe, particularly useful. Competent surveys of the mission theology of Matthew are available in recent works of missiology, notably in those of Donald Senior and Carroll Stuhlmueller[1] and David Bosch;[2] and there is little point in repeating what has been said so well there. Instead I shall attempt here a critical reading of only the two major mission texts of the Gospel: (1) the so-called Great Commission of Mt 28:16-20; and (2) the Mission Discourse of Mt 10:1-42. Taken together these two texts will, I believe, give a fairly good idea of what Matthew understood by mission. We may then (3) draw conclusions about how Matthew's understanding of mission is to be translated (not just linguistically but theologically) to provide appropriate lessons for doing mission in India today.

This article first appeared in *Bible and Mission in India Today*, ed. J. Kavunkal and F. Hrangkhuma (Bombay: St Pauls, 1993), 64-92.

1. THE GREAT COMMISSION (MT 28:16-20)

The so-called Great Commission of Mt 28:16-20 concludes the Gospel of Matthew, which is arguably the most meticulously constructed of the writings of the New Testament. The conclusion is a worthy finale to the Gospel. It offers a summary of the whole Gospel by weaving together its christological (Mt 28:18), ecclesiological (Mt 28:19-20a), and eschatological threads into a carefully crafted composition, whose theological density could rival that of the prologue of John. As Adolf Harnack said of it, "it is impossible to say anything greater and more than this in only forty words."[3] A study of the text will therefore provide a suitable starting point for investigating mission in Matthew.

1.1. The Structure and the Form of Mt 28:16-20

The text is most carefully structured. It falls into two clearly marked parts: (1) an introductory narrative featuring the eleven disciples (vv. 16-17) provides a setting for (2) a solemn pronouncement of Jesus (vv. 18-20).

SETTING

> v. 16 Now the eleven disciples went to Galilee, to the mountain to which Jesus had directed them.
>
> v. 17 And when they saw him they worshiped; but some doubted.

MESSAGE

> v. 18 And Jesus came and said to them,
> a) "All authority in heaven and on earth has been given to me.
>
> v. 19 b) Going therefore make disciples of all nations, baptizing them in the name of the Father and of the Son and of the Holy Spirit,
>
> v. 20 teaching them to observe all that I have commanded you.
> c) And surely, I am with you always, to the close of the age."

The narrative describes an encounter between Jesus and the disciples on an unnamed mountain in Galilee, to which they have been allegedly directed by him.[4] The place of the narrative in the Gospel and its reference to a pre-passion prediction of Jesus that he would meet his disciples in Galilee after his resurrection (Mt 26:32) identify the encounter as a post-Easter appearance of Jesus. But there is little else in the narrative to suggest this—except perhaps for the curious reaction of the disciples, who both worship Jesus and "doubt" (Mt 28:17).[5] Nothing else suggests that the Jesus who "comes to them" (*proselthōn*), as he had often "come" (*elthōn*) before (cf. Mt 8:14; 9:23; 13:54; 16:13; 26:43), is the risen Lord, who appears in a "risen body" that transcends the limitations of material existence, and can appear or disappear suddenly as in Lk 24:31, 36, or pass through closed doors at will as in Jn 20:19. All the elaborate process of the verification of the reality of the body of the risen Lord, which is so important in the appearance stories of Luke (Lk 24:36-49) and John (Jn 20:19-23; 26-29), is missing from Matthew. The focus of his story is not on the appearance of the risen Jesus but on the message he gives.

This message takes the form of a three-step proclamation. A revelatory statement (v. 18) is followed by a mission command (vv. 19-20a), which in turn leads to a concluding promise of supportive presence (v. 20b). Several attempts have been made to identify the literary form of this strongly patterned text, which, as it now stands is certainly an editorial composition of Matthew.[6] It has been variously compared (1) to a Near Eastern enthronement ritual, which supposedly contained three successive actions: the elevation of the new king to divine status, his presentation to the people, and his enthronement or investment with royal power;[7] (2) to a type of "divine pronouncement" (*Gottesrede*) comprising a revelatory statement, command, and a promise, such as is found (though never so compactly) in several Old Testament texts like Ex 20 or Deut 5;[8] (3) to the form used in Old Testament stories of the commissioning of charismatic leaders like Moses in Ex 3:4-12, Gideon in Judg 6:11-19, or Jeremias in Jer 1:4-10;[9] (4) to an "official decree" like that of Cyrus in 2 Chr 36:23 or that of Joseph, viceroy of Egypt, in Gen 45:9-11;[10] and (5) to the "covenant formula" derived from the Hittite suzerain treaties and widely used in the Old Testament covenant texts.[11]

All these attempts at identifying the form of Mt 28:16-20 have been shown to be untenable by Gerhard Friedrich in a wide-ranging and carefully argued survey of recent attempts to determine the "formal structure" of the text.[12] But Friedrich's own attempt to relate Mt 28:16-20 to the "I-am" sayings of John[13] seems to me as unconvincing as the positions he critiques. It is doubtful whether Mt 28:6-20 can be pigeonholed into any prefabricated Old or New Testament category at all. For while Matthew may have been influenced by some sort of "covenant logic" or biblical pattern of thinking in composing his text, it is not likely that he is following a precise literary model. The structure of his "mission command" in fact resembles most closely not any Old Testament text, but the mission instructions of the Buddha reported in the *Mahāvagga* I.11.1 of the *Vinaya Pitaka*.[14] The similarity of the two texts, as I have shown elsewhere, is quite remarkable.[15] Since Matthew is not at all likely to have known and copied this Buddhist text, this would indicate that the pattern he follows (revelation-command-promise) is simply the natural expression of a commissioning, the realization of a sort of transcultural functional "genre," which can generate similar texts in settings as widely different as Buddhist India of the third century B.C.E. and Hellenistic Palestine of the first century of our era. There is no need, I believe, to look for a specific Jewish or Hellenistic model for Matthew's text.

1.2. The Analysis of Mt 28:16-20

Of the three elements that shape this text, it is clearly the second, the mission command (vv. 19-20a), which is central. Both the revelatory statement (v. 18) which precedes and the promise (v. 20b) which follows it, reinforce the command. The first provides it with a legitimating basis (the authority of Jesus); the second offers a guarantee for the possibility of its future implementation (the continuing presence of Jesus). The focus of the passage is squarely on mission.

That is why the mission command is significantly much longer and more elaborate than the statement and promise that frame it. It has four verbs compared to the single verb of the others. But of these four verbs three ("going," "baptizing," "teaching") are qualifying participles. Only one, "making disciples of" or more accurately, "disciple" (*mathēteusate*), is a finite verb, and contains the main imperative of the command. This verb, which is characteristic of Matthew (Mt 13:52; 27:57; 28:19, and elsewhere in the New Testament only in Acts 14:21), tells us what mission means for him. To engage in mission is to strive to make "all nations" disciples of the risen Lord.

Whether one understands "all nations" (*panta ethnē*) exclusively, that is, as referring only to peoples other than the Jews, or inclusively as referring to the Jews as well,[16] the universality of the command is plain. It contrasts strikingly with the particularity of the mission instruction given by Jesus to his twelve disciples, which forbids them from going anywhere among the gentiles or entering the towns of the Samaritans (Mt 10:5), and restricts their mission to the "lost sheep of the house of Israel" (Mt 10:5-6; 15:24). This glaring contradiction is best resolved by supposing that Matthew is operating with a two-step scheme of salvation history implying two stages in the mission of Jesus.[17] The mission of the earthly Jesus is a centripetal mission directed to Israel in the hope that the conversion of his people will inaugurate the "eschatological pilgrimage of the nations to the mountain of God" announced in the Old Testament (Is 2:2; Mic 4:1; Ps 22:8), and so lead to the salvation of the world.[18] But the Jews, his own people, reject this mission. Their rejection, which builds up throughout the Gospel (cf. 21:28-32; 21:33-46; 22:1-14), reaches its climax in the Passion narrative, when (according to Matthew) the "whole people" (*pas ho laos*) formally rejects Jesus as the Messiah (Mt 27:25). This leads to the death of Jesus, which marks the end of his centripetal mission to Israel. But the vindication of that death by God through the resurrection invests Jesus with "all authority in heaven and on earth" (Mt 28:16) and inaugurates the centrifugal mission of the Church (Mt 28:16). The way is open for a universal post-Easter mission to all nations (Mt 28:18-20), which includes Jews, but no longer as a separate and privileged people, for the "true Israel" is now the "Church."

The universal mission to "disciple" all nations is to be achieved by baptizing (not circumcising) them, and by teaching them to observe what Jesus (not the Torah) had commanded. The polemic character of the command is evident. It draws attention to the newness of the community that is emerging over and against a "formative Judaism" distinguished by its circumcision and its Torah. The new community is to be formed through a new rite of initiation (baptism), which replaces circumcision, and through a new kind of teaching (the ethical instruction of Jesus), which, through its insistence on the core value of love (Mt 22:40), "fulfills," that is, offers a correct and corrective interpretation of the Torah.[19]

The unexpected order in which these two instructions appear (baptism precedes teaching!) has provoked comment. It has even been suggested that it may have been occasioned by the practice of infant baptism in Matthew's community, where infants would be baptized before they are taught.[20] But there is not the slightest evidence for this anywhere in the Gospel; and even if there were, it is unlikely that an inner community practice should influence the order (baptism-teaching) of a text referring to extra-community mission, where it is not infants who are to be baptized! Not too much importance, I suspect, is to be given to this "unusual" sequence. It is probably simply Matthew's way of giving more importance to "teaching" than to "baptizing," by making it the last and climactic directive of the command. It is not baptizing but teaching what Jesus has commanded that is the significant element in the mission of "discipling" all nations.

This is in complete agreement with the rest of Matthew's Gospel. Except when referring to the baptizing mission of John the Baptist (Mt 3:6-11), or to Jesus' own baptism by him (Mt 3:13, 14, 16) the verb "to baptize" (*baptizein*) is used by Matthew only here (Mt 28:19). There is certainly no suggestion in his Gospel that Jesus himself ever baptized or gave any great importance to this rite. To teach, on the other hand, is an utterly characteristic activity of Jesus in the Gospel. Jesus "teaches" (*didaskein*) in the Jewish synagogue (Mt 4:23; 9:35; 13:54) or in the Jerusalem Temple (Mt 21:23, 26, 55); on a mountain in the open country (Mt 5:2) or in the Galilean towns (Mt 11:1). He is normally (Mt 8:19; 12:38; 19:16; 22:24, 36) addressed as "teacher" (*didaskalos*) or described as such (Mt 9:11; 17:24) by people who approach him. His authoritative teachings, which are to be proclaimed to "all nations," are gathered into the five great discourses, found only in Matthew (Mt 5-7; 10; 13; 18; [23] 24-25). These form the structural backbone of the Gospel and look forward to its concluding mission command, in whose prescription to teach all nations ("teaching them to observe whatsoever I have commanded you") they find their *raison d'être*.

1.3. The Significance of Mt 28:16-20

Reading this carefully composed conclusion to Matthew's Gospel makes us aware of the following points:

(1) Though the weight of the text falls on its mission command, this command is not quite as "missionary" as might at first sight appear. It is not a command to "preach the Gospels," as in the longer ending of Mark (Mk 16:15), but to "make disciples of all nations," primarily by teaching them what Jesus has commanded. Although the command is introduced by the participle "going" (*poreuthentes*) and not by the imperative "go," as misleadingly translated in every English translation I know—it does not really signify a "sending forth." The participle is, as Lucien Legrand has argued well, probably a redundant auxiliary participle, of a kind frequent in Semitic writing, which has been added for emphasis or style and has no denotative value whatever. In its six other occurrences in Matthew (Mt 2:8; 9:13; 11:4; 21:6; 22:15; 27:66) "going" (*poreuthentes*) is always, I believe, used in this auxiliary sense with no distinct meaning

of its own. Legrand is therefore right in pointing out that while one cannot make disciples of all nations without going out to them, the accent of the command is not on the going out. Instead, "the image is rather one of a teacher seated and imparting instruction than that of a messenger coursing to the furthest corner of the earth."[21]

(2) I would go further and suggest that not only is the accent not on "going forth," but it is probably not even on "discipling." In view of the tension between universalism and particularism evidenced in the Gospel[22] one might argue that the stress of the command is not so much on "make disciples" as on "all nations." Once again, making disciples is presupposed, indeed is self-evident in Matthew's doubtless strongly missionary Hellenistic Jewish community. But what Matthew wants to do here is not so much to urge his community to mission (they needed no such urging), as to defend, against conservative Jewish particularism, the universal character of that mission.

(3) To read the text primarily as "the Great Commission" mandating Christians to a universal mission would therefore be something of a misunderstanding. Matthew's emphasis is not on the commissioning. Instead he uses the mission command, an integral part of the early Christian tradition about the "official" appearance of the risen Jesus to the Twelve,[23] to provide us with a summary of his Gospel. This gives, in a highly compact form, his understanding of Christian existence as disciples of the risen Lord, available now to Jew and gentile alike, provided they follow the teachings through which Jesus is present to the community until the end of the age.

(4) The christological thrust of the summary is evident. Jesus dominates all its three steps. It is *his* authority which is the basis of mission. Mission means to teach what *he* has commanded. It is sustained by *his* supportive presence. The characteristic Matthean "all" found in each of these steps ("all authority," "all nations," "all things," "all days") lends an awesome dimension to this portrayal of the risen Jesus, whose grandeur, like that of a towering Himalayan peak, grows inexorably on the traveler as he or she moves through the text. More than a mission command, Mt 28:16-20 is a profession of christological faith.

(5) Such a profession of faith does, however, have clear missionary implications. Wherever Matthew's emphases may lie, he has in fact formulated his summary with a mission command. Like the other elements in his concluding summary (its revelatory statement and its promise of supportive presence), this too sums up and brings to its appropriate conclusion a theme (mission) that runs all through the Gospel, from its infancy narrative (Mt 2:1-12) to its Eschatological Discourse (Mt 24:14). The story of the magi (Mt 2:1-12), stories of Jesus' encounter with believing gentiles (the officer in the Roman army in Mt 8:5-13, or the Canaanite woman in 15:21-28), and sayings of Jesus (Mt 5:13-16, or 24:14) not only anticipate and legitimize the universal mission command of Mt 28:18-20 but encapsulate Matthew's mission theology, according to which the essentially centripetal mission of Jesus becomes the centrifugal mission of the Church, because of the rejection of Jesus by the Jews. The so-called Great Com-

mission of Mt 28:18-20 does not fall like a thunderbolt from the skies. It comes as the climax of a complex, many-sided theme unfolding throughout the Gospel. This theme is most explicitly developed in the Mission Discourse of Mt 10, which provides, as it were, the real content of the formal "mission command" articulated in Mt 28:18-20. It is to this text that we now turn for light on the meaning of the so-called Great Commission, and for an insight into Matthew's understanding of mission.

2. THE MISSION DISCOURSE (MT 10:1-42)

The Mission Discourse is the second of Matthew's five great discourses. Like the others, it has been compiled by him from sayings on mission he found in his Markan, Q, and special Matthean (M) sources. Relatively short instructions on mission found in Mk 6:7-13 = Lk 9:1-6 (the sending of the Twelve) and in Lk 10:1-12 (the sending of seventy-two disciples) have been taken up by Matthew, put together, and greatly augmented with other sayings from Mark, Q, and M, to create a single elaborate Mission Discourse which forms the heart of his theology of mission. The skill and complexity of his composition can be seen from the breakdown of the discourse into its sources given in the chart below.

Call 1-5a	= 5b-6	Instruction - 7-15	Persecution 16-23	= 24-25	Exhortation - 26-39	Ending 40-42
Mk Mk 3:13-19 Mk 6:7	**M**	**Mk+Q** Mk 6:7-13 Lk 9:1-6 Lk 10:1-12	**Mk** Mk 13:9-13	**M**	**Q** Lk 12:2-9 Lk 12:51-52 Lk 14:26-27 Lk 17:33	**Q+Mk+M** Lk 10:16 Mk 9:37

2.1. The Composition of Mt 10

This remarkable arrangement of sources throws light on the nature and purpose of Matthew's Mission Discourse. It is significant that the instructions on mission are not followed, as they are in both Mark (Mk 6:12-13) and Luke (Lk 9:6), by a report of the actual going out of the Twelve. Though the discourse begins (Mt 10:5) with a sending of the Twelve ("these twelve Jesus sent out [*apesteilen*] with the following instructions"), it loses sight of this sending by the time it comes to its end. At the end of the discourse it is not the disciples but Jesus who "goes on from there (*metebē ekeithen*) to teach and to preach in the towns of Galilee" (Mt 11:1). Clearly Matthew does not intend the discourse to be read as an actual set of instructions given by Jesus to his twelve disciples at a particular point in his Galilean ministry. Rather he uses the story of the sending of the Twelve reported by his sources as an occasion to put together teachings on mission meant for his community. "All that Jesus says to the Twelve he says to the Church; and the mission of the Church is a continuation of the mission carried out in Jesus' life time."[24]

How much the Mission Discourse is oriented to his community is shown by the massive additions Matthew has made to it from the Eschatological Discourse in Mark (in vv. 16-19) and from Q sayings which speak about God's care experienced in persecution (in vv. 26-33) and about conflicts in the family brought about by following Jesus (in vv. 34-39). These clearly reflect the situation of Matthew's persecuted and divided community, not those of Jesus' own ministry. As Gerhard Barth puts it:

> Matthew bursts open the situation of a historical "then" during the earthly activity of Jesus; Mark 6:12 is omitted: that the disciples carry out the missionary commission of Jesus is not reported. On the other hand Mt 10:17ff from the apocalyptic discourse (Mark 13:9-13) is inserted and 10:23 has in mind the time between the resurrection of Jesus and the parousia. In that way the situation of the historical "then" is left behind and the missionary discourse now speaks simply of the sending forth of the disciples. Still more it is not a matter of sending out special missionaries but sending forth and persecution are essential for discipleship as such.[25]

These teachings on mission addressed by Matthew to his community are therefore more than a set of concrete instructions on missionary praxis. They are a lesson on Christian discipleship. His massive editing not only adapts the rules for mission given by Mark and Q for his community but works them up into an extensive theology, which defines not so much the nature of Christian mission, as the missionary dimension of Christian Life. Because the Twelve in Matthew typify the Matthean Church, the Mission Discourse of Mt 10, ostensibly addressed to the Twelve, is in fact, like the Sermon on the Mount, addressed to Matthew's community; and so, with an appropriate hermeneutical transposition, to the Church today. Mt 10 gives us a theology of mission which complements and gives substance to the bare imperative of the Great Commission. The thrust of this theology is indicated by the structure of the discourse.

2.2. The Structure and Significance of Mt 10

The discourse has been structured, I suggest, according to the following concentric pattern:

a The Call and Sending of the Twelve: Sent with the Authority of Jesus (10:1-4)
   b Instructions for Mission: Renunciation of Material Security (10:5-15)
      c Prediction of Persecution (10:6-32)
         d Basis of Persecution: Identity of Disciple with Jesus (10:24-25)
      c' Encouragement in Persecution (10:26-33)
   b' Exhortation for Mission: Renunciation of Family Ties (10:34-39)
a' The Reception of the Twelve: To Welcome Disciple Is to Welcome Jesus (10:40-42).

This structural pattern suggests that the discourse has been built along three thematic axes. The first (*a-d-a'*) defines the basis of mission, by identifying the missioner with Jesus; the second (*b-b'*) proposes a strategy for mission calling for freedom from dependence on material resources and from attachment to family ties; and the third (*c-c'*) describes the conditions of persecution and conflict in which the mission is to be carried out. What emerges from the combination of these is an extraordinarily vivid insight into what mission meant for Matthew's community and significant lessons about how mission is to be understood today. These can be best studied by reflecting on the three thematic axes that the structure of the discourse reveals.

2.2.1. THE BASIS OF THE MISSION

The center of the discourse (*d*, Mt 10:24-25) identifies the missioner with Jesus. This is also the burden of its opening and closing sections (*a*, Mt 10:1-5a and *a'*, Mt 10:40-42). The Twelve are sent out with the "authority" (*exousia*) of Jesus himself. Like him they are given the "authority" to cast out unclean spirits, to heal every disease and every infirmity (Mt 10:1 = 4:23; 9:35), and to proclaim the near arrival of the Kingdom of God (Mt 10:7 = 4:17). Because they continue his mission, they will experience the opposition which Jesus himself experienced (Mt 10:24-25 = 12:24-28); and the rejection of their mission will have the same eschatological consequence as the rejection of his (Mt 10:14-15 = 11:24). Indeed so close is the identity between them, that to welcome the missioner is to welcome Jesus who has sent him or her, and so ultimately to welcome God who has sent Jesus (Mt 10:40). This echoes the so-called *šālîaḥ* principle recognized all over the ancient Near East, whereby the one who is sent (*šālîaḥ*) enjoys the same status as the sender. And it implies an understanding of mission as a "sending" which originates not just from the community but from God. It is this God-grounded understanding of mission which later missiology elaborated into a theology of mission as a *Missio Dei*. Here mission is seen not so much as an activity of the Church as an attribute of God.[26] For the sending of the Church into the world by God is seen as an extension of the inner trinitarian sending of the Son by the Father and of the Spirit by the Father and the Son. Participation in mission then becomes a participation in "the movement of God toward people, since God is a fountain of sending love."[27]

2.2.2. A STRATEGY FOR MISSION

As part of this movement, the missioners sent by Jesus must pursue their mission with the same selflessness and trust in God that Jesus showed in his. This appears in the strategy for mission outlined in the second section of the discourse (*b*, Mt 10:5b-15), and its concentric parallel (*b'*, Mt 10:34-39). Four elements define this strategy:

(1) The *location* of the mission is clearly determined. The missioners are to go not to the gentiles nor to the Samaritans but only to "the lost sheep of the

house of Israel" (vv. 5-6). This restriction reflects the realities of early Christian history (the mission of Jesus was certainly restricted to Israel), and is, we have seen, theologically justified by Matthew by means of his two-step scheme of saving history. But its missiological significance goes beyond this. Whether the "lost sheep of the house of Israel" refers to the whole people of Israel led astray by its leaders as parallels in the Old Testament might suggest (Is 53:6; Jer 50:6; 34:5-6), or to the sinners and outcast among them, with whom Jesus regularly associated (Mk 2:15-17; Lk 15:1-2), it is clear that mission is always directed to the "lost." The locus of mission, then, is not to be determined by the predilections or ambitions of the missioner, but by the need of the people to whom he or she is sent.

(2) The *task* of those who are sent on mission is defined with precision. The missioners are to proclaim the near arrival of the Kingdom of God and to heal the sick and the disabled (vv. 7-8). Their mission thus comprises not verbal proclamation but healing action as well. It thus continues the holistic mission of Jesus, who proclaims the Kingdom not just in words but in works: in exorcisms which show that the rule of Satan has ended (Mt 12:28), in healings which announce the arrival of God's rule (Mt 11:2-5), in controversies with the religious and theological "establishment" which lay down the configuration of the new social order which God's rule brings (Mt 22:23-33; 22:34-40), and in table fellowship with tax collectors and sinners (Mt 9:9-12) which anticipates the realization of this order.[28]

That is why Matthew begins his narrative of the ministry of Jesus by juxtaposing the Sermon on the Mount (Mt 5-7) with the Miracle Cycle (Mt 8-9), a carefully organized collection of ten miracle stories which immediately follows the Sermon; and by framing the juxtaposed units with a pair of parallel summaries in which Jesus is shown going around the towns and villages of Galilee "teaching in their synagogues, preaching the good news of the kingdom and healing every disease and every infirmity" (Mt 4:23-25 = 9:35-37).

	preaching the good news		
summary =	Sermon on the Mount =	Miracle Cycle =	summary
4:23-25	5-7	8-9	9:35-38
	teaching	healing	

Jesus announces the good news of the Kingdom by teaching and healing. His teaching is exemplified in the Sermon on the Mount; his healing, a surprisingly significant element in his mission in Matthew,[29] is represented in the Miracle Cycle.[30] The disciples who share in the mission of their Master must, according to Matthew, engage in a similarly holistic mission in which verbal proclamation is joined to liberative action.

(3) This mission of preaching and healing is to be carried out in a spirit of quite extraordinary freedom from *material possessions*. The missioners are to

proceed on mission with no equipment whatever: "no gold, nor silver, nor copper in your belts, no bag for your journey, nor two tunics, nor sandals, nor a staff" (Mt 10:9).[31] They are to depend for sustenance on local support offered by sympathizers from whom they may claim sustenance ("the laborer deserves his *food*"[32]) but no monetary reward ("what you have received without charge give without charge"). Indeed it is precisely this total lack of equipment which both entitles the missioners to the support they receive and empowers them with the spiritual power, so that they can effectively impart "peace" (in the biblical sense of wholeness, health, healing) to the households which receive them (v. 12). Poverty is both the credential of the missioner as well as the source of his or her effectiveness.

The extreme radicality of these demands may reflect the missionary praxis of the wandering charismatic preachers who were responsible for the earliest Christian mission,[33] and who continued to flourish to Matthew's time.[34] But they seem to be too radical even for these, since the prohibition of sandals and staff would have made travel even within the rocky, snake-infested terrain of Palestine almost impossible. The demands are mitigated in Mark (Mk 6:8-9), and abrogated in the puzzling fragment of a mission instruction now found in the Passion narrative of Luke (Lk 22:35-37), where not only sandals and staff, but money and even a sword are allowed. All this suggests that instructions about equipment in Matthew are probably not to be taken literally. They are not practical directives, but, like the instructions of the Sermon on the Mount, are probably "focal instances"[35] or "goal directed norms,"[36] which are not so much prescriptions to be literally followed as illustrations of the spirit in which mission is to be undertaken. What is demanded is an attitude: freedom from acquisitiveness (mission must not become a source of gain) and a trust in divine providence so absolute that it can wholly dispense with even the minimum of material resources. Poverty and powerlessness are for Matthew an absolutely indispensable part of Christian mission.[37]

Such freedom from dependence on material possessions is to be paralleled by the missioner's *detachment from family ties*, the other source of security in Matthew's world. Following Jesus in mission will imply, the Mission Discourse suggests, inner family conflicts of great intensity (vv. 34-39). This is because the message that Jesus brings is a prophetic message. Like the message of the Old Testament prophets, it does not announce the "peace" of compromise with or of submission to injustice and evil, but brings the sword (*machaira*) of conflict (v. 34). To follow Jesus in a world given over to values which are the opposite of his inevitably leads to conflict—and not only to the inner spiritual conflict which each follower of Jesus undergoes as part of his or her conversion but to social conflicts with others, even with those in the close circle of one's extended family.

It is clear from Matthew's repeated insistence on the theme (Mt 10:21, 34-38) that such family conflicts were a significant problem in his community. By alluding to Mic 7:6 Matthew interprets them as part of the messianic woes which, according to prophetic tradition, would afflict the world at the end-time.

In this situation of eschatological tribulation, the followers of Jesus are called upon, not indeed to renounce family ties (cf. Mt 15:3-7) but to relativize them. All relationships, no matter how important they may be, must be subordinated to loyalty to Jesus.

Indeed such subordination must reach beyond material possessions or even family ties to one's own most personal being. The followers of Jesus in mission are expected to be affectively detached not only from their possessions and their families, but from their very "selves" (vv. 38-39). The Mission Discourse states this in the vivid and paradoxical idiom of Jesus. His followers, says Jesus, must be ready to take up their cross and follow him. That is, they must take on actively (and not merely patiently endure) the persecutions and conflicts which the Mission Discourse has mentioned as their lot;[38] and they must endure them, if need be at the cost of life itself (v. 39). They must do this because it is only by giving up this earthly life that the true life of the world to come can be found.[39]

The saying on losing one's life in order to find it is found four times in the Synoptics (Mt 16:25 = Mk 8:35 = Lk 9:24; Lk 17:33) and once in John (Jn 12:25). As uttered by Jesus, it meant far more than the promise of a "heavenly life" for those who had sacrificed their earthly life in his cause. This may seem to be the primary meaning of the saying in Matthew, but it is not its only meaning. Because for Matthew, as for Jesus, life to come was not discontinuous with this life. The saying of Jesus, so carefully treasured by his followers, was given by him as a compact formulation, a *sūtra* expressing his understanding of the goal and meaning of human life. One finds fulfillment (here and hereafter) to the extent that one gives one's life away in love. It is this understanding of existence that must determine the conduct of any genuinely Christian mission.

2.2.3. THE CONDITIONS FOR MISSION

Genuine mission, Matthew has told us, demands an attitude of detachment from possessions, from family ties, even from clinging to one's own life. This is necessary because the followers of Jesus will conduct their mission, as the Mission Discourse repeatedly insists, in a situation of extreme stress. The third axis of the discourse (*c*, Mt 10:16-23 and *c'*, Mt 10:26-33) describes the conditions of mission in terms of two complementary intertwined factors. The missioners (1) will be subject to extreme persecution by Jew (vv. 16-17) and gentile (v. 18) alike, abetted by members of their own family or clan (v. 21); but through all this they will (2) live under the protective care of God, who will not only inspire them with what they are to say in the judicial arraignments they will have to face (vv. 19-20), but will protect them in situations of danger, with a providential and supportive presence (vv. 26-31). The Mission Discourse thus gives concrete content to the formalized reassurance of the Great Commission (Mt 28:18).

According to the Mission Discourse, then, following Jesus in mission requires not only an attitude of total detachment from the "world" (possessions and family ties), but also a complementary attitude of absolute confidence in

God, even in situations of extreme peril. The missioner is not to be intimidated by fear of those who can kill the body, because they cannot harm the true self which transcends merely physical existence (Mt 10:28). God alone has control of the totality of human life, and God is not antagonistic to the missioner but deeply concerned about him or her. Underlying the missioner's confidence is the conviction that all creation is controlled by God. This conviction is the source of both the trust with which the wandering charismatics of the Sermon on the Mount are to rely on God (who feeds the birds of the air and clothes the lilies of the field) for their food and clothing (Mt 6:25-34), and for the confidence with which the missioners of the Mission Discourse must depend on God (who determines the life span even of worthless sparrows), for protection in times of persecution and the threat of death (Mt 10:26-31). The thrice repeated "do not be afraid" (*mē phobēthētē/phobeisthe*) of the Mission Discourse (Mt 10:26, 28, 31) echoes the thrice repeated "do not worry" (*mē merimnate/merimnēsēte*) of the Sermon on the Mount (Mt 6:25, 31, 34). If mission is to be conduced as an act of love for people, it is to be rooted in an act of trust in God's love for us.

3. CONCLUSION: LESSONS FOR MISSION IN INDIA TODAY

The two great "mission texts" of Matthew's Gospel which we have studied, the so-called Great Commission of Mt 28:16-20 and the Mission Discourse of Mt 10, are not primarily texts about mission but about Christian discipleship. They are addressed not to missionaries, but to the followers of Jesus as such. The Twelve (or eleven) disciples who are addressed are (as always in Matthew) prototypes of the community, which Matthew explicitly identifies as the disciples of the risen Lord (Mt 28:18). The words addressed to them do not offer a blueprint for mission, but spell out the missionary dimension of Christian life. They speak, that is, about *following Jesus in mission*.

This following Jesus in mission means far more than merely obeying a command to go out and recruit members for the Christian community. It is not just a commissioning to missionary activity, but a call to a life of missionary discipleship. Such a life calls for a radical detachment from possessions and family ties, for a radical trust in God, and a radical fidelity to Jesus in all the conflicts and persecutions which following him in mission will bring.

Mission, then, as Matthew understands it, is not experienced as a heteronomous "command" by means of which Christians are whipped into reluctant activity through guilt, but emerges as a spontaneous and joyful reaction to the experience of the risen Lord. It is not an enterprise that depends on human resources, intellectual or material, but it is carried out in a poverty and powerlessness that relies on God alone. It is realized not merely through verbal proclamation, but equally through liberative action, indeed most of all (as is explicitly affirmed in the third great mission text of Matthew, the "mission command" of the Sermon on the Mount in Mt 5:13-16) through the enduring witness of the Christian community.[40]

How different all this is from what one actually observes in the history of Christian mission, particularly on the last great period of mission history, the colonial mission, whose legacy we all carry, is obvious. An Asian looking at this mission, so closely associated with the centuries of colonial depredation that have created a crucified Third World, cannot but be aware of its profound ambiguities. Ambiguity has no doubt marked all missionary ventures, even mission in New Testament times, as the indications of power struggle that surface in the letters of Paul or of John clearly show. Mission has always had its human side. But looked at in the light of Matthew's Gospel there seems to be something particularly distorted in the colonial mission whose legacy has so deeply marked Christian life in India today, showing itself in the profound alienation of the Christian community from Indian life,[41] and in the panic reactions which words like "missionary or conversion" arouse among our people.

For the colonial mission was not a mission conducted in the powerlessness and poverty that Matthew recommends! It was an aggressive mission carried out under the patronage of avaricious and ruthless colonial powers, who in Latin America caused the greatest "demographic collapse" in history,[42] and in Africa and the Americas were responsible for the most massive and brutal slave trade that our planet has seen.[43] The colonial mission commanded immense material resources, which not infrequently were used as inducements to conversion. It seemed more concerned with the growth of the missionizing Churches (often disedifying competition with one another) than with the welfare of the people missionized. Too often "it treated people as objects to be converted, rather than as persons created in the image of God."[44] Whatever qualities of dedication and compassion individual missionaries may have shown, the colonial mission was part of a grim colonial scenario.[45]

It is against this background that we must read the mission texts in the Gospel of Matthew in India today. We shall then find in them not only a prophetic critique of our missionary praxis, but an invitation to a new paradigm for mission. This new paradigm invites us, I suggest, to shift our attention from Church growth to Church life. The Great Commission read in the light of the Mission Discourse of Mt 10 and the exhortation to mission in Mt 5:13-16 is to be understood not as a mandate to an aggressively militant mission, obsessed with "making disciples" ("Church growth"), but as an invitation to "follow Jesus" in mission (Church life). Such a following of Jesus can never be a "crusade," an act of violence against religions and cultures (options which Jesus explicitly refused), but always an act of loving service, carried out as Matthew has told us, in poverty and powerlessness, in dependence on God, in persecution and conflict. Mission, then, is not to be imaged as a "conquest" (winning the world for Christ), nor as a "sale" (selling the Gospel)—images of mission in the colonial and postcolonial worlds[46]—but, as Matthew images it, as light which illumines the darkness, when it is not hidden under a bushel, or as salt which gives savor, as long as it has not lost its saltiness (5:13-16). Mission, then, is not so much doing as being, not so much noisy proclamation as infectious witness. This is especially true for us in India, where a religious tradition which "sees the divine image" (*darshan*) rather than "hears the word of God"[47] has made people more sensitive to visual manifestations of religious experience in the life of individuals and communities than to mere words about it.

David Bosch has summed this up well in the concluding words of his magnificent book. Mission, he tell us there, "is the good news of God's love, incarnate in the witness of a community, for the sake of the world."[48] Mission is therefore concerned not with the power, security or growth of the missionizing Churches, but with the welfare of the missionized world. For all true Christian mission is ultimately the continuation of the mission of Jesus, who did not come primarily to build a Church or even found a religion, but to bring total liberation to humankind. It is only when mission is seen as part of the great arch of saving history reaching from the creation of "the heavens and the earth" in the "beginning" (Gen 1:1) to the inauguration of the "new heavens and the new earth" in which all reality finds its fulfillment at the end of time (Rev 21:1-4)—it is only then that its true dimension will be understood.

NOTES

1. Donald Senior and Carroll Stuhlmueller, *The Biblical Foundations for Mission* (London: SCM Press, 1983), 233-54.

2. David Bosch, *Transforming Mission: Paradigm Shifts in Theology of Mission* (Maryknoll, N.Y.: Orbis Books, 1991), 56-83.

3. Adolf Harnack, *Die Mission und Ausbreitung des Christentums in den ersten drei Jahrhunderten* (Leipzig: Heinrich'sche Buchhandlung, 1924), 45 n. 2, quoted in Bosch, *Transforming Mission,* 56.

4. In fact no mountain is mentioned when Jesus instructs his disciples to follow him into Galilee (Mt 26:32; 28:7-10). The mountain here, like the one in the Sermon on the Mount is a theological *topos* used by Matthew to indicate a plan of revelation (Joachim Lange, *Das Erscheinen des Auferstandenen im Evangelium nach Matthäus: Eine traditions- und redaktionsgeschichtliche Untersuchung zu Mt. 28:16-20,* Forschung zur Bibel 11 [Würzburg: Echter Verlag, 1973], 392-441). Jesus, who begins his ministry by teaching on a mountain (Mt 5:1), ends it by imparting a final "testament" also on a mountain (Mt 23:16).

5. Although the *hoi de edistasan* of Mt 28:17 is usually translated as "but some doubted" and interpreted to mean that disciples of Jesus other than the eleven who worshiped him continued to doubt (so Robert H. Gundry, *Matthew: A Commentary on His Literary and Theological Art* [Grand Rapids: Eerdmans, 1987], 594; Francis W. Beare, *The Gospel According to Matthew* [Peabody, Mass.: Hendrikson, 1987], 544), or that some of the eleven doubted (Lange, *Erscheinen des Auferstandenen,* 475), it is better translated "they, however, doubted" referring to the eleven, who are shown as both worshiping and doubting (so Ernst Lohmeyer, *Das Evangelium des Matthäus,* 3rd ed. [Göttingen: Van-

denhoeck & Ruprecht, 1962], 415; Walter Grundmann, *Das Evangelium nach Matthäus* [Berlin: Evangelische Verlagsanstalt, 1972], 576). The combination of "doubting" (*distazein*) and "worshiping" (*proskynein*), both characteristically Matthean words (the first found twice in Matthew only; the second thirteen times in Matthew as against twice each in Mk and Lk), occurs also in 14:31-33 and describes the characteristic attitude of the disciple as a representative of the Matthean community. This attitude is described here (14:31-33) and elsewhere in the Gospel, by another typically Matthean expression "little faith" (*oligopistos*) found in the New Testament four times in Mt (6:30; 8:26; 14:31; 16:8) and once in Lk (12:28). The faith of the community is a growing faith which continually overcomes doubt (Lange, *Erscheinen des Auferstandenen,* 435).

Matthew's "some however doubted" may also echo the traditional reactions of the disciples of Jesus to his post-Easter appearances, expressed in the other Gospels in stronger terms: "startled" (*ptoein*), "troubled" (*tarassein*), "disbelieving for joy" (*apistountes apo tēs charas*) in Lk 24:36-49; and "faithless" (*apistos*) in Jn 20:24-29, where the "doubt" of the disciples is personified in Thomas. The reaction of the disciples described by Matthew would thus provide an internal indication of the Easter character of his narrative.

6. This is evident from its strongly Matthean vocabulary and style (Joachim Gnilka, *Das Matthäusevangelium,* 2. Teil, Herders Theologischer Kommentar zum Neuen Testament [Freiburg: Herder, 1988], 505; Hubert Frankemölle, *Jahwebund und Kirche Christi,* Neutestamentliche Abhandlungen 10 [Münster: Aschendorf, 1973], 44-46) and from the way in which it gathers up the theological themes of the Gospel so admirably that it becomes "the key for the study of the whole book" (Wolfgang Trilling, *Das Wahre Israel: Studien zur Theologie des Matthäus-Evangeliums* [Munich: Kösel, 1964], 21). That Mt 28:16-20 is an editorial composition would not be questioned by critical scholars today. Whether and to what extent Matthew used earlier traditions in composing the passage is disputed. While Joachim Lange believes that Mt 28:16-20 is entirely a Matthean composition based on the Q saying in 11:17, most critics would hold that he had used sources. W. D. Davies and Dale C. Allison ("Matt. 28:16-20: Texts Behind the Texts," *Revue d'Histoire et de Philosophie Religieuses* 72 [1992]: 89-98) suggest, plausibly, three stages in the development of the text: (1) a primitive proto-commissioning narrative, (2) a pre-Matthean midrashic interpretation based on the Son of Man vision in Daniel 7 (the source of the *exousia* clause and the baptismal formula), and (3) the Matthean redactional reformulation of and assimilation to the traditions about Moses and the commissioning of Joshua (the source of the mountain), the order to go, the command to observe, and the promise of presence (see *New Testament Abstracts* 36 [1992]: no. 1285).

7. Otto Michel, 1950, "Der Abschluss des Matthäusevangeliums. Ein Beitrag zur Geschichte der Osterbotschaft," *Evangelische Theologie* 10 (1950): 22; Joachim Jeremias, *Jesus' Promise to the Nations* (London: SCM Press, 1958), 38-39.

8. Wolfgang Trilling, *Das Wahre Israel: Studien zur Theologie des Matthäus-Evangeliums* (Munich: Kösel, 1964), 45-49.

9. Benjamin J. Hubbard, *The Matthean Redaction of a Primitive Apostolic Commission: An Exegesis of Matthew 28:16-20,* Society of Biblical Literature Dissertation Series 19 (Missoula, Mont.: Scholars Press, 1974), 69-72.

10. Bruce Malina, "The Literary Structure and Form of Mt xxviii. 16-20," *New Testament Studies* 17 (1970): 96.

11. Frankemölle, *Jahwebund und Kirche Christi.* 46-61.

12. Gerhard Friedrich, "Die formale Struktur von Mt 28:18-20," *Zeitschrift für Theologie und Kirche* 80 (1983): 137-62.

13. Ibid., 164-170.

14. T. W. Rhys Davids and G. Oldenberg, *Vinaya Texts,* Part 1, The Sacred Books of the East 13 (1880; reprint, Varanasi: Motilal Banarsidass, 1968), 112-13.

15. G. M. Soares-Prabhu, "Two Mission Commands: An Interpretation of Matthew 28:16-20 in the Light of a Buddhist Text," *Biblical Interpretation* 2 (1994): 264-82.

16. Frankemölle, *Jahwebund und Kirche Christi,* 19-23; idem, "Zur Theologie der Mission im Matthäusevangelium," in *Mission im Neuen Testament,* ed. Karol Kertelge, Quaestiones Disputatae 93 (Freiburg: Herder, 1982), 114.

17. John P. Meier, *Law and History in Matthew's Gospel,* Analecta Biblica 71 (Rome: Biblical Institute Press, 1976), 35-40.

18. Joachim Jeremias, *Jesus' Promise to the Nations* (London: SCM Press, 1958), 55-73.

19. J. Andrew Overman, *Matthew's Gospel and Formative Judaism: The Social World of the Matthean Community* (Minneapolis: Fortress Press, 1990), 72-149.

20. Frankemölle, *Jahwebund und Kirche Christi,* 45 n. 171.

21. Lucien Legrand, *Unity and Plurality: Mission in the Bible* (Maryknoll, N.Y.: Orbis Books, 1990), 79.

22. Frankemölle, "Zur Theologie der Mission," 93-129.

23. Xavier Léon-Dufour, *Resurrection and the Easter Message* (New York: Holt, Rinehart & Winston, 1971), 80-88.

24. W. D. Davies and Dale C. Allison, *The Gospel According to Matthew,* vol. 2, *Commentary on Matthew VIII-XVIII,* International Critical Commentary (Edinburgh: T & T Clark, 1991).

25. Gerhard Barth, "Matthew's Understanding of the Law," in G. Bornkamm et al., *Tradition and Interpretation in Matthew* (London: SCM Press, 1963), 100-101.

26. Johannes Aagard, "Trends in Missiological Thinking During the Sixties," *International Review of Mission* 62 (1973): 11-15.

27. Bosch, *Transforming Mission,* 390.

28. G. M. Soares-Prabhu, "Signs Not Wonders: Understanding the Miracles of Jesus as Jesus Understood them," *The Way* 30 (1990): 314-16; idem, "The Table-Fellowship of Jesus: Its Significance for *Dalit* Christians Today," *Jeevadhara* 22 (1992): 143-54, and in *Biblical Themes for a Contextual Theology for Today,* Collected Writings of George M. Soares-Prabhu, S.J., vol. 1, ed. Isaac Padinjarekuttu (Pune: Jnana-Deepa Vidyapeeth, 1999), 223-40. See chapter 7 of this volume.

29. Helge Kjaer Nielsen, *Heilung und Verkündigung: Das Verständnis der Heilung und ihres Verhältnisses zur Verkündigung bei Jesus und in der ältesten Kirche* (Leiden: Brill, 1987), 124-25.

30. Nielsen notes that of the eleven summaries of Jesus' activity which Matthew gives, seven (Mt 8:16-17; 12:15-21; 14:13-14; 14:34-36; 15:29-31; 19:1-2; 21:4) mention only his healings. Note too the considerable space given to healings in the first of Matthew's summaries, 4:23-25.

31. The Greek verb *ktaomai* used here (v. 9) means literally "to procure," "to provide for," so that the instruction in Mt 10:9 is sometimes understood to mean "do not make provision before starting, but feel free to receive anything that is given to you on the journey" (Alan Hugh McNeile, *The Gospel According to St. Matthew* [London: Macmillan, 1928],

135). But this contradicts the strong injunction to gratuitous service ("freely you have received, freely give") that immediately precedes (v. 8). The word must be understood in the general sense of "to take" and interpreted to mean that the missioners must carry no equipment for their mission, nor accept anything except food for the services they render (Ulrich Luz, *Das Evangelium nach Matthäus,* Teilband 2, *Mt. 8-17,* Evangelisch-katholischer Kommentar zum Neuen Testament [Neukirchen-Vluyn: Neukirchener Verlag, 1990], 95-96).

32. Matthew has changed the traditional aphorism "the laborer deserves his hire (*misthos*)" (Lk 10:7; 1 Tim 5:18) to "the laborer deserves his food (*trophē*)" precisely to avoid contradicting his injunction that mission must be without charge.

33. Gerd Theissen, *The First Followers of Jesus* (London: SCM Press, 1978), 8-16.

34. Luz, *Das Evangelium nach Matthäus,* 2:95; and Jürgen Roloff, "Das Kirchenverständnis des Matthäus im Spiegel seiner Gleichnisse," *New Testament Studies* 38 (1992): 342.

35. R. C. Tannehill, "The 'Focal Instances' as a Form of New Testament Speech: A Study of Mt. 5:39b-42," *Journal of Religion* 50 (1970): 372-85.

36. Bernard Häring, "The Normative Value of the Sermon on the Mount," *Catholic Biblical Quarterly* 29 (1967): 375-85.

37. Luz, *Das Evangelium nach Matthäus,* 2:96.

38. Ibid., 148.

39. Ibid., 45; Beare, *Gospel According to Matthew,* 250; Davies and Allison, *Gospel According to Matthew,* 2:224.

40. Mt 5:13-16, with its focus on witness rather than on proclamation, balances 28:16-20, and must be taken into account for a proper understanding of Matthew's missiology. Lack of space has prevented me from studying this text in detail here. But I hope to do this in a future article.

41. Soares-Prabhu, "From Alienation to Inculturation: Some Reflections on Doing Theology in India Today," in *Bread and Breath: Essays in Honour of Samuel Rayan,* ed. T. K. John (Anand: Gujarat Sahithya Prakash, 1991), 59-78.

42. Wayne Elwood, "Hidden History: Columbus and the Colonial Legacy," *The New Internationalist* (December 1991), 6; see also *The Voices of the Victims: 1492-1992, Concilium* 6 (1990), ed. Leonardo Boff and Virgil Elizondo; Ignacio Ellacuría, "The Fifth Centenary of Latin America: Discovery or Cover Up?" *Social Action* 42 (1992): 40-50; Yacob Tesfai, "Invasion and Evangelization: Reflections on a Quincentenary," *International Review of Mission* 81 (1992): 525-41.

43. As Wayne Elwood notes, "Las Casas estimated that 50 million Indians perished in Latin America and the Caribbean within 50 years of Columbus' landing. Scholars now reckon that 90% of the indigenous population of the Americas was wiped out in a century and a half, the greatest demographic collapse in the history of the planet and the proportional equivalent of nearly half a billion people today. . . . The Atlantic slave trade lasted nearly 400 years during which time 15 (to 50) million Africans were shipped to the Americas. Conditions during the crossing were so horrific that between a half and a third of the African captives died *en route.* Of the rest most died within a decade of their arrival in the strange new land" (Elwood, "Hidden History," 6, quoted in David A. Kenith and John C. Boonstra, "Themes to Challenge the Mission of the Church," *International Review of Mission* 81 [1992]: 582).

44. Kenith and Boonstra, "Themes to Challenge the Mission of the Church," 599.

45. Bosch, *Transforming Mission,* 302-13.

46. Soares-Prabhu, "Missiology or Missiologies," *Mission Studies* 3 (1986): 86-87.

47. Diana L. Eck, *Darsan: Seeing the Divine Image in India* (Chambersburg, Penn.: Anima Books, 1981), 3-10.

48. Bosch, *Transforming Mission,* 519.

INDEX OF SELECTED PASSAGES

287

INDEX OF SUBJECTS

cross, and solidarity with the poor, 95
cult, prophetic protest of Jesus against, 44-45
culture clash in India, analogous to that in world of Jesus, 105

dalits, Christian: no place for discrimination against, in Christian community, 129-30; and table fellowship of Jesus, 127-30
Dharma, meaning of, 3, 175-77
Dharma of Jesus: and concern for the neighbor, 188-89; and freedom, 185-86; and the Lord's Prayer, 221; and the Sermon on the Mount, 184-90; and Soares-Prabhu, 3-4; and Sonship, 186-88
dhvani, and rhetorical criticism of the parables, 149
disciples: continuing the mission of Jesus, 276-77; and the experience of God, 88; as new Israel, 158; origin among the poor, 158; prejudices of, 156-57; as salt of the earth and light of the world, 262-63; supported by the Spirit, 22-23; as wandering charismatics, 110, 278

EATWOT (Ecumenical Association of Third World Theologians), 78
economics of affluence, 253
equality: affirmation of, as conflict provoking, 166; in the Jesus community, 111; of all humans, 166
exclusivism, in the early Christian community, 160
exorcism: as proof of the arrival of the Kingdom, 20; Spirit at work in, 20-21
experience of Christ, Raimundo Panikkar and, 84
experience of God: and the experience of fellow humans as brothers, 184-85, 197, 204. *See also Abba* experience.

faith, and miracles, 137
family, detachment from, for missioners, 278-79
fellowship: and commandment to love, 65-66; and Kingdom of God, 65-66
forgiveness: and being forgiven, 223-24; human, and divine pardon, 223; in the Lord's Prayer, 221-22; nonjudgmental attitude required for, 225; political dimension of, 226-28; psychological dimension of, 224-26; relationship of,

to repentance, 226-27; religious dimension of, 222-23; self-, 24; in teaching of Jesus, 220-28
freedom: of Jesus, 89; in the Jesus community, 108-9; and Kingdom of God, 64-65; as supreme goal of life in Buddhism, 170

Gandhi, Mahatma: and *ahiṃsā,* 171; forgiveness of, 170, 227-28; on Jesus, 85; nonviolent ethics of, 105-6; and the Sermon on the Mount, 105
God: experience of, 86-87; Jesus' experience of, as *"Abba,"* Father, 88-89; as king, 57
Great Commission, 269-74: damaging missiology derived from, 260; directed to all nations, 271, 273; foundational text for missiology, 259-60; and mission instructions of Buddha, 270; as a profession of christological faith, 273; structure and form of, 269-70; as a summary of Matthew's Gospel, 273
guruvada (of Hinduism), and liberative authority of Jesus, 34

Hinduism: encounter of, with Christianity, 105-6
holiness, relation of, to purity rules 123-24
hope, exhibited in Davidic messianism and apocalyptic, 60-61; expressed as Kingdom of God, 61-62

incarnation, as christological symbol of Jesus' solidarity with the poor, 94
Israel (nation), bonded labor in, 252
Israel (people): as object of Jesus' mission, 271, 276-77; as the people of God, 252

Jesus: appreciation of Samaritans, 158; approval and rejection of, in inaugural proclamation, 19; association of, with scribes and Pharisees, 157-58; attitude of, to the rich, 230-33; authority of, 31-35, 90-91; and the call to repentance, 43-44; compared to the Buddha, 169-70; compared to Mahatma Gandhi, 169; and conflict, 164-71; confrontation of, with the theological, religious, and political establishment, 95; grasped through praxis, 96; and a just society, 93; and liberation of the poor and oppressed, 19-20; and the

messianism: Davidic, among Old Testament prophets, 60; and the fall of Jerusalem, 60-61

metaphors: as *dhvani,* 149; parables as, 147-48

ministry of Jesus: connection with ministry of John, 54; among the despised and outcast, 54-55; exercised through proclamation, 55; prominence of teaching in, 27

miracles: and faith, 137; in Gospel of Mark, 135-36; in Gospel of Matthew, 136-37; Jesus' understanding of, 133-34; and liberation, 136; in New Testament church, 134-35; as proclamation of the Kingdom, 137; as signs of Jesus' power over the rule of Satan, 135-36; as signs of the Kingdom of God, 30, 134, 140-41; understanding of, in modern society, 138-41

mission: in the biblical story, 249-55; colonial, 281; and detachment from family, 278-79; and freedom from material possessions, 277-78; God-grounded understanding of, 276; in India today, 247, 255-56, 281-82; and the task of missioners, 277; universal, achieved by baptism and by teaching what Jesus commanded, 271

mission of the Church: based on community life and praxis, 264; ultimate aim of, the buildup of the Kingdom of God, 265

mission command (in Sermon on the Mount): interpretation of, 262-63; setting of, 261

Mission Discourse, 274-80; intended for Matthew's community, 274-75; structure of, 275-76; as a theology of mission for the Church, 275

mission of Jesus: directed to Israel, 271, 276-77; continued by his disciples, 276

name of God, revealed as Yahweh, 59; revealed as *Abba,* 59

neighbor: concern for, as central to Dharma of Jesus, 188-89; defined, 92; as the focus of love, 196; love of, the equivalent of love of enemy, 198-200; love of, paired with love of God, 197

New Testament, as constitution of the church, 78-79

Panikkar, Raimundo (on the experience of Christ), 84

parables: characteristic of Jesus' teaching, 35-37; and conscientization (Paulo Freire), 36; as critical teaching, 36-37; as dialogical teaching, 35-36; different settings of, 146; exegesis of, and *dhvani,* 145, 149; as metaphors, 147-48; rhetorical criticism of, 147-49; and subversion of the listener's world, 37; and subversion of myth, 36-37

politics of oppression, 253

poor: blessedness of, 238-39; disciples as originating from among, 158; good news preached to, 233-35; Harijans of India as, 238; identity of, 237-38; in India, 229; Jesus' option for, 157; and the Kingdom of God, 239; liberation of, 239; and love of Jesus, 93; Old Testament predilection for, 238-39; and Old Testament prophets, 43; as recipients of Jesus' teaching, 29-30, 54-55, 229-30; in the Sermon on the Plain, 235-37; solidarity of Jesus with, 94-95, 233; spiritualization of, in Matthew, 236

prayer(s): and *Abba* experience, 210; and action, 217-18; association with thanksgiving, 214-18; childlike attitude required for, 210-11, 215; as conversation, 210, 211; of Jesus, 209; Lord's Prayer, 211-12; of petition, 211-14; in teaching of Jesus, 208-18; unanswered, 214

prejudice: and anti-Semitism, 160; Christianity as protest against, 156-57; of the Church, 159-61; definition of, 155; of disciples, 156-57; religious, 156; and Western colonialism, 160-61

prophet(s): characteristics of Old Testament prophets, 42-43; concern of Old Testament prophets with the poor, 43; and the denunciation of idolatry, 253; Jesus as, 41-48; and social justice, 253

purity rules: analogous to caste system in India, 124; in postexilic Judaism, 123-24; radically redrawn by Jesus, 123-25

Rajneesh, Osho, 85

Reign of God. *See* Kingdom of God.

repentance, the theme of Jesus' proclamation of the Kingdom, 56, 63

resurrection: the goal of life, 95-97; as validation of the proclamation of Jesus, 254

riches: dangers of, 230-33; as obstacle to following Jesus, 230